Applications of Multi-Criteria Decision-Making Theories in Healthcare and Biomedical Engineering

Applications of Multi-Criteria Decision-Making Theories in Healthcare and Biomedical Engineering

Edited by

Ilker Ozsahin
DESAM Institute, Near East University, Turkish Republic of Northern Cyprus, Nicosia, Turkey; Department of Biomedical Engineering, Near East University, Turkish Republic of Northern Cyprus, Nicosia, Turkey; Brain Health Imaging Institute, Department of Radiology, Weill Cornell Medicine, New York, NY, United States

Dilber Uzun Ozsahin
DESAM Institute, Near East University, Turkish Republic of Northern Cyprus, Nicosia, Turkey; Department of Biomedical Engineering, Near East University, Turkish Republic of Northern Cyprus, Nicosia, Turkey; Medical Diagnostic Imaging Department, College of Health Sciences, University of Sharjah, Sharjah, United Arab Emirates

Berna Uzun
DESAM Institute, Near East University, Turkish Republic of Northern Cyprus, Nicosia, Turkey; Department of Mathematics, Near East University, Turkish Republic of Northern Cyprus, Nicosia, Turkey

ACADEMIC PRESS

An imprint of Elsevier

Academic Press is an imprint of Elsevier
125 London Wall, London EC2Y 5AS, United Kingdom
525 B Street, Suite 1650, San Diego, CA 92101, United States
50 Hampshire Street, 5th Floor, Cambridge, MA 02139, United States
The Boulevard, Langford Lane, Kidlington, Oxford OX5 1GB, United Kingdom

Library of Congress Cataloging-in-Publication Data
A catalog record for this book is available from the Library of Congress

British Library Cataloguing-in-Publication Data
A catalogue record for this book is available from the British Library

ISBN: 978-0-12-824086-1

For information on all Academic Press publications
visit our website at https://www.elsevier.com/books-and-journals

Publisher: Mara Conner
Acquisitions Editor: Sonnini Yura
Editorial Project Manager: Charlotte Rowley
Production Project Manager: Poulouse Joseph
Designer: Greg Harris

Typeset by Thomson Digital

Contents

7. Fuzzy PROMETHEE–based evaluation of prostate cancer treatment techniques

Ilker Ozsahin, Nuhu Abdulhaq Isa, Kevin Meck,
Sunsley Tanaka Halimani, Berna Uzun and Dilber Uzun Ozsahin

8. Comparative evaluation of point-of-care glucometer devices in the management of diabetes mellitus

Mubarak Taiwo Mustapha, Dilber Uzun Ozsahin
and Ilker Ozsahin

9.   Comparison of MRI devices in dentistry
Gürkan Ünsal and Dilber Uzun Ozsahin

10.   Application of fuzzy PROMETHEE on hearing aid
Dilber Uzun Ozsahin, Rukayat Salawu, Berna Uzun
and Ilker Ozsahin

14. Evaluation of the effectiveness of adult HIV antiretroviral treatment regimens using TOPSIS

Nazife Sultanoglu, Berna Uzun, Murat Sayan and Tamer Sanlidag

15. Evaluating the effectiveness of recommended HIV adult postexposure prophylaxis drug regimens by using fuzzy PROMETHEE

Berna Uzun, Nazife Sultanoglu, Tamer Sanlidag and Murat Sayan

16. The use of multicriteria decision-making method—fuzzy VIKOR in antiretroviral treatment decision in pediatric HIV-infected cases

Murat Sayan, Tamer Sanlidag, Nazife Sultanoglu and Berna Uzun

17. Evaluation of oral antiviral treatments for chronic Hepatitis B using fuzzy PROMETHEE

Figen Sarigül, Sadettin Hülagü and Dilber Uzun Ozsahin

18. Evaluation of migraine drugs using MCDM methods
Dilber Uzun Ozsahin, Lafi Hamidat, Funsho David Alimi, Berna Uzun and Ilker Ozsahin

19. Top cancer treatment destinations: a comparative analysis using fuzzy PROMETHEE
Nuhu Abdulhaq Isa, Dilber Uzun Ozsahin and Ilker Ozsahin

Contributors

Gürkan Ünsal, DESAM Institute, Near East University, Turkish Republic of Northern Cyprus, Nicosia, Turkey; Department of Dentomaxillofacial Radiology, Near East University, Turkish Republic of Northern Cyprus, Nicosia, Turkey

Valerie Oru Agbor, Department of Biomedical Engineering, Near East University, Turkish Republic of Northern Cyprus, Nicosia, Turkey

Funsho David Alimi, Department of Biomedical Engineering, Near East University, Turkish Republic of Northern Cyprus, Nicosia, Turkey

Ali Denker, Department of Mathematics, Near East University, Turkish Republic of Northern Cyprus, Nicosia, Turkey

Basil Bartholomew Duwa, Department of Biomedical Engineering, Near East University, Turkish Republic of Northern Cyprus, Nicosia, Turkey

Sunsley Tanaka Halimani, Department of Biomedical Engineering, Near East University, Turkish Republic of Northern Cyprus, Nicosia, Turkey

Lafi Hamidat, Department of Biomedical Engineering, Near East University, Turkish Republic of Northern Cyprus, Nicosia, Turkey

Sadettin Hülagü, Medical Faculty, Department of Gastroenterology, Kocaeli University, Izmit, Kocaeli, Turkey

Nuhu Abdulhaq Isa, Department of Biomedical Engineering, Near East University, Turkish Republic of Northern Cyprus, Nicosia, Turkey

Serife Kaba, Department of Biomedical Engineering, Near East University, Turkish Republic of Northern Cyprus, Nicosia, Turkey

Ayse Gunay Kibarer, Department of Biomedical Engineering, Near East University, Turkish Republic of Northern Cyprus, Nicosia, Turkey

Kevin Meck, Department of Biomedical Engineering, Near East University, Turkish Republic of Northern Cyprus, Nicosia, Turkey

Mubarak Taiwo Mustapha, DESAM Institute, Near East University, Turkish Republic of Northern Cyprus, Nicosia, Turkey; Department of Biomedical Engineering, Near East University, Turkish Republic of Northern Cyprus, Nicosia, Turkey

Kudakwashe Nyakuwanikwa, Department of Biomedical Engineering, Near East University, Turkish Republic of Northern Cyprus, Nicosia, Turkey

Dilber Uzun Ozsahin, DESAM Institute, Near East University, Turkish Republic of Northern Cyprus, Nicosia, Turkey; Department of Biomedical Engineering, Near East University, Turkish Republic of Northern Cyprus, Nicosia, Turkey; Medical Diagnostic Imaging Department, College of Health Sciences, University of Sharjah, Sharjah, United Arab Emirates

Ilker Ozsahin, DESAM Institute, Near East University, Turkish Republic of Northern Cyprus, Nicosia, Turkey; Department of Biomedical Engineering, Near East University, Turkish Republic of Northern Cyprus, Nicosia, Turkey; Brain Health Imaging Institute, Department of Radiology, Weill Cornell Medicine, New York, NY, United States

Rukayat Salawu, Department of Biomedical Engineering, Near East University, Turkish Republic of Northern Cyprus, Nicosia, Turkey

Tamer Sanlidag, DESAM Institute, Near East University, Turkish Republic of Northern Cyprus, Nicosia, Turkey

Figen Sarigül, Health Science University, Antalya Educational and Research Hospital, Clinical of Infectious Diseases, Antalya, Turkey

Murat Sayan, DESAM Institute, Near East University, Turkish Republic of Northern Cyprus, Nicosia, Turkey; Faculty of Medicine, Clinical Laboratory, PCR Unit Kocaeli University, Kocaeli, Turkey

Sameer Sheshakli, Department of Biomedical Engineering, Near East University, Turkish Republic of Northern Cyprus, Nicosia, Turkey

Tapiwa W. Simbanegavi, Department of Biomedical Engineering, Near East University, Turkish Republic of Northern Cyprus, Nicosia, Turkey

Nazife Sultanoglu, DESAM Institute, Near East University, Turkish Republic of Northern Cyprus, Nicosia, Turkey; Faculty of Medicine, Department of Medical Microbiology and Clinical Microbiology, Near East University, Turkish Republic of Northern Cyprus, Nicosia, Turkey

Berna Uzun, DESAM Institute, Near East University, Turkish Republic of Northern Cyprus, Nicosia, Turkey; Department of Mathematics, Near East University, Turkish Republic of Northern Cyprus, Nicosia, Turkey

Chapter 1

Introduction

Ilker Ozsahin[a,b,c], Dilber Uzun Ozsahin[a,b,d], Berna Uzun[a,e] and
Mubarak Taiwo Mustapha[a,b]

[a]DESAM Institute, Near East University, Turkish Republic of Northern Cyprus, Nicosia, Turkey;
[b]Department of Biomedical Engineering, Near East University, Turkish Republic of Northern
Cyprus, Nicosia, Turkey; [c]Brain Health Imaging Institute, Department of Radiology, Weill
Cornell Medicine, New York, NY, United States; [d]Medical Diagnostic Imaging Department,
College of Health Sciences, University of Sharjah, Sharjah, United Arab Emirates; [e]Department
of Mathematics, Near East University, Turkish Republic of Northern Cyprus, Nicosia, Turkey

1.1 Introduction

Application of multi-criteria decision-making (MCDM) theory is the use of computational methods that incorporate several criteria and order of preference in evaluating and selecting the best option among many alternatives based on the desired outcome. It is applied to different fields to obtain an optimum solution to a problem where there are many parameters to consider that cannot be decided by the users' experiences. The application gives a ranking result based on the selected criteria, their corresponding values, and assigned weights. The application of MCDM theory in biomedical engineering and healthcare is a new approach that can be enormously helpful for patients, doctors, hospital managers, engineers, etc. Whether it is improving healthcare delivery or making a sound and safe decision for the benefit of the patient, healthcare professionals and other decision makers are always entangled with decision-making dilemmas. In real-life problems, there are many critical parameters (criteria) that can directly or indirectly affect the consequences of different decisions. Stakes are always high whenever human life is in danger, so it is always important to make the right decisions. When deciding whether to use a particular medication, treatment, or medical equipment, not only are the problems with multiple criteria very complex, but multiple parties are also deeply affected by the effects.

There are many methods available for solving MCDM problems. However, the MCDM methods discussed in this textbook are the Analytic Hierarchy Process (AHP), Technique for Order of Preference by Similarities to Ideal Solution (TOPSIS), Elimination Et Choix Traduisant la Realité (ELECTRE), Preference Ranking Organization Method for Enrichment of Evaluations (PROMETHEE), ViseKriterijumska Optimizcija i Kaompromisno Resenje (VIKOR), and Data

Applications of Multi-Criteria Decision-Making Theories in Healthcare and Biomedical Engineering.
http://dx.doi.org/10.1016/B978-0-12-824086-1.00001-3

Envelopment Analysis (DEA). AHP is based on mathematics and psychology. Rather than recommending the best alternative, AHP encourages decision makers to find a solution that better suits their goal and perception of the problem. It offers a comprehensive and rationally oriented context in which the decision problem can be organized, quantified, and evaluated. TOPSIS is a very useful MCDM method. This is an alternative approach that measures weights for each parameter, normalizes scores for each criterion, and determines the numerical difference for each alternative and the optimal alternative, which is the best score for every criteria. ELECTRE is another popular MCDM method used to eliminate any unacceptable alternatives. PROMETHEE is suitable when groups of people are working on complex issues, particularly those with various parameters that require several views and viewpoints that have long-term consequences in their decisions. This provides unique advantages when it is difficult to quantify or compare important elements in the decision, or when cooperation between departments or team members is limited by their different requirements or expectations. Other multicriteria decision-making MCDM methods that will be discussed include VIKOR, fuzzy logic–based MCDM methods, and DEA.

1.2   The components of the MCDM problem

EXPERT/DECISION MAKER	ALTERNATIVES	CRITERIA

There are three key components to every MCDA problem: expert/decision maker, alternatives, and criteria.

1. Expert/decision-maker: Responsible person for identifying the problems and subsequently finding a way to solve them. In some problems, one decision maker can decide by just using his or her expertise, but when problems are complicated and have multiple criteria, it becomes difficult to base a decision purely on intuition. When a problem with multiple criteria occurs, a compromise is made by the decision makers on which alternative should be prioritized or weighted heavily.
2. Alternatives: These are the choices you have to make. It is possible to identify or develop an alternative solution. A decision space refers to the set of all possible alternatives.
3. Criteria: These are the component features of each alternative. Every alternative is compared using the same criteria. For instance, in comparing treatment techniques for cancer, alternatives such as radiation therapy, chemotherapy, etc., will be compared based on cost, efficacy, and dosage.

The knowledge of the alternatives of the real-life problems, properties of their parameters, and the priority given to the parameters have a great effect on the consequences of the decisions. In this book, the application of MCDM has been provided for the real-life problems that occur in healthcare and biomedical engineering issues.

Chapter 2

Theoretical aspects of multi-criteria decision-making (MCDM) methods

Berna Uzun[a,b], **Ilker Ozsahin**[a,c,d], **Valerie Oru Agbor**[c] and **Dilber Uzun Ozsahin**[a,c,e]

[a]*DESAM Institute, Near East University, Turkish Republic of Northern Cyprus, Nicosia, Turkey;* [b]*Department of Mathematics, Near East University, Turkish Republic of Northern Cyprus, Nicosia, Turkey;* [c]*Department of Biomedical Engineering, Near East University, Turkish Republic of Northern Cyprus, Nicosia, Turkey;* [d]*Brain Health Imaging Institute, Department of Radiology, Weill Cornell Medicine, New York, NY, United States;* [e]*Medical Diagnostic Imaging Department, College of Health Sciences, University of Sharjah, Sharjah, United Arab Emirates*

2.1 Introduction

Decision-making involving multiple criteria analysis is one of the fastest-growing disciplines in terms of deriving or resolving conflicting issues or ideas [1] based on your area of interest. We all have to make decisions in life, whether it be in our day-to-day activities—such as what we will wear, eat, the time and duration of sleep—or what we will buy—even at the time of purchase, we still develop the attitude to choose from a list of alternatives—or the career we want to follow, as well as many other things that require us to make a decision regarding whether we will do them or not. Considering all of this, this study particularly focuses on making a decision, but this time the decision is no longer about deciding to do something or not, it involves alternatives in a particular domain with specific characteristics. For example, if I want to buy a mobile phone or computer, I would rather ask myself a series of questions that would become my criteria (characteristics). Therefore, decision-making or analysis is no longer one-sided but qualitative, quantitative, or a combination of both. With the above-mentioned factors or properties, one could say that decision-making is no longer a one-sided process that simply involves choosing between two things. Rather, it has become a complex problem involving making a decision that has to satisfy the preferences of a population or society of people. Decision-making is now an issue left for expert consultation. In order to solve this issue, many researchers and authors have started to develop theories, but each time one theory emerges to solve a particular problem, some questions still remain unanswered.

Applications of Multi-Criteria Decision-Making Theories in Healthcare and Biomedical Engineering.
http://dx.doi.org/10.1016/B978-0-12-824086-1.00002-5

For one reason or another, we choose or decide to do something in particular, leaving other things behind at a given time. However, the reason for taking that course of actions is best known to the decision maker, who is influenced by a number of different factors. For example, reading this book right now shows that you have chosen to do so over other things, perhaps because you just want to increase your vocabulary in this field or you want to increase your understanding of the field of multi-criteria decision-making analysis while leaving other things aside; only you know the criteria you have chosen, but you should know that you are already a decision maker. Multi-criteria decision analysis is a subdiscipline of operational research; considering the work that has been done in this domain, it would be fitting to review the evolution of this discipline.

2.2 History of multi-criteria decision-making analysis (MCDA)

The concept of multi-criteria decision analysis has been used since life began on surface of the earth. It might interest you to know that even animals use instinctive reasoning or judgement to make their own decisions. If animals can make good use of this concept, what can humans, who are far more intelligent than animals, achieve? Although this concept has existed since the origins of life, it was not documented or recorded to assist in making decisions when the need arose. This situation was resolved by the American scientist, polymath, inventor, and businessman Benjamin Franklin (1706–90). At the time, he was known as someone who would not take a side on an important issue without first documenting and demonstrating the argument. Using logical reasoning, he wrote down all the available opinions on both sides and then argued both for and against the hypothesis, using the same criteria to form his arguments. When he compared the arguments, the side with the greater weight of evidence was considered. This logic is evident in some of his accomplishments, which included being one of the Founding Fathers, drafting of the Declaration of Independence and the U.S. Constitution, and his contributions to the negotiation of the Treaty of Paris. As time passed, others continued in the path that Franklin had shown. Records show that it was in 1951 that problems with multiple objectives were expressed, and this occurred in the conditions of nonlinear programming by Kuhn and Tucker [2]. In 1955, 4 years after Kuhn and Tucker's work, an article was published by Charnes, Cooper, and Ferguson that discussed the real nature of "goal programming," [3] although this name was in fact first used 6 years later, in their 1961 book.

The concept of goal programming, which was first used and documented by Charnes and Cooper, has now became the backbone of operational research and the science of management from which many researchers have obtained their inspiration. This work in particular inspired many researchers and writers who have made significant contributions to the development of this field of study, such as Bruno Contini and Stanly Zionts, who both worked with Cooper. In 1968, 7 years after the previous publication, they published a multi-criteria negotiating model. This was far from being the end of the process, as many researchers continued their hard work, who at all costs and by all means wanted to propose a solution to complicated multi-criteria problems, including Zionts and Jyrki Wallenius who started working together at the European Institute for Advanced Studies in Management in Brussels in 1983. Drawing inspiration from Zionts's past work and goal programming, they developed the Zionts-Wallenius interactive method that would help in resolving problems in multiple objective linear programming. However, that was not all they achieved together: at the end of the 1970s, Pekka Korhonen, a friend and workmate of Wallenius, joined them to work collaboratively on methods and support systems for decision-making. Their work greatly influenced students and colleagues and continues to contribute to the domain.

Apart from the work of Zionts, Cooper, Wallenius, and others in their team, other researchers and authors focused on this subject in seemingly the same period of time. This is seen in the work of Ron Howard and G.E. Kimball in 1959. Howard first used the term "decision analysis" around the mid-1960s. From the past to the present, significant collaboration has taken place between researchers and Howard was not an exception as he worked together with James E. Matheson to publish a book in 1968. Some years later in the 1970s, Thomas Saaty along with fellow authors Ernest Forman and Luis Vargas introduced the analytic hierarchy process (AHP). In 1976, Ralph Keeney and Howard Raiffa published a book that was very important in the field of multiattribute value theory. This work became the source of several studies in decision analysis and multi-criteria decision-making.

Also, in the mid-1960s, the ELimination Et Choix Traduisant la REalité (ELECTRE) theory was introduced by Bernard Roy and colleagues. With the evolution and fast development of different theories and ideas, this domain needed to establish an identity and, in 1975, a new group was created in Europe known as the Multiple Criteria Decision Aiding.

2.2.1 Birth of the special group on MCDM

The newly created group continued to have an effect for a period of approximately 4 years, until 1979 when researchers in Konigswinter, Germany, established the group known as the Special Interest Group on MCDM. As is normal for any group or association, there must be a leader to ensure the smooth running of its activities, and the group's first leader was Zionts. The first and second annual meeting was held in France and New York, respectively. The fourth was held just a year after the third meeting in 1980. These annual meetings were then held every 2 years in different countries until 1994 when the 11th conference was held and the following year (1995), the 12th international conference, followed by an interval of 2 years, after which the 13th international conference was held in South Africa and the 14th was held the following year in 1998 in Charlottesville (USA). The next meeting was held in the year 2000 in Ankara,

Turkey, which was the 15th conference. From that time onward, no conference was missed, but instead there were some changes in years, as we can see with the 19th and 20th conferences organized with just a year's difference in 2008 and 2009, respectively. These conferences continued in 2019 with the 25th conference, which was held in Istanbul, Turkey, and the 26th, which is scheduled to be held in June 2021 in Portsmouth, United Kingdom.

2.3 Definition of concepts

It should be noted that this book will present an in-depth discussion of MCDA, but before we continue with MCDA, it is important to understand each term as well as that it involves other concepts like multi-criteria decision-making (MCDM) and decision analysis (DA).

Multiple (multi): The word multiple is similar to words such as numerous, many, and several, which means that there are diverse criteria.

Criteria: This is the standard or principle by which something is judge or assessed. For example, decision-making on pharmaceuticals could involve criteria such as product, manufacturer, service, and value.

Decision: The Latin origin of the word "decision" literally means "to cut off." Making a decision is about "cutting off" choices, essentially cutting you off from another course of action. In fact, making a decision frees you from the shackles of endless choices so that individuals or groups can get to where they want to go. In summary, a decision is a conclusion or resolution reached after consideration.

Analysis: Analysis is the process of breaking a complex topic or matter into smaller parts in order to gain a better understanding of it. According to the dictionary definition, it can be described as a detailed examination of the elements or structure of something.

Multi-criteria decision-making (MCDM): It is a discipline in its own right that deals with decisions involving the choice of a best alternative from several potential candidates subject to several criteria or attributes that may be concrete or vague.

Decision analysis (DA): It is a systematic, quantitative, and visual approach for addressing and evaluating important choices confronted by decision maker/s (it is the mobilization of resources or inputs being processed in view of acquiring desired objectives, goals, or outputs geared toward profit maximization or solving societal problems). It can be used by individuals or groups attempting to make decisions related to risk management, capital investments, and strategic business decisions.

2.4 Multi-criteria Decision Analysis (MCDA)

This is a stepwise formula for solving decision problems. It can also be considered a theory on its own that is concerned with making decisions in problems based on different choices. The making of decisions can be considered a discipline in itself or can involve other disciplines. In order to achieve our aim or goal as individuals, groups, or as a society we need to remember two very important facts in decision-making, which are:

1. We can use decision models or theories to help people as individuals, groups, or as a society to know the reasons why they make decisions or to understand the motivating force that is behind any decision.
2. We also use decision models to be able to design how to make a decision and, of course, we would never want to make decisions that would affect us negatively. Therefore, the same models would help us know which decisions are good and positive and how they can be achieved.

Multi-criteria decision analysis is one of many different types of analyses that exist, but using this concept of decision analysis is more advantageous because it is not limited to only one aspect, such as monitory or nonmonetary units, before it is performed, but can be carried out in either area. As humans, we get to choose between several options in everything we do in our lives, and we usually carry out our activities without major problems, but problems can be encountered when it comes to making decisions that involve others or making decisions on behalf of other people, whether you are in a position of authority or an expert who is paid for providing assistance in decision-making. In all of these situations, we have to remember that each decision is made to satisfy needs and that it is important avoid making errors that can have significant consequences. The idea of evaluating the risks when choosing among different alternatives now becomes a problem because no one will ever want to do something or engage in an activity that is not ultimately beneficial. This requires decision makers to engage in more thinking when selecting what is most likely to be the ideal solution and not look for a perfect match that might never be found, since each option has both positive and negative aspects. This is where MCDA is used as an appropriate tool in the hands of an expert who can inform, analyze, justify, and clarify those making decisions in order to be successful.

This was demonstrated to be true in 1979 with the publication of Stanley Zionts's work entitled "If Not a Roman Numeral, Then What?" [4]. In this article, he attempted to persuade all readers to adopt his ideas. Only a year later, his objectives were met as significant progress was observed in this discipline with the creation of different groups and associations. One of them was the international society of MCDM, which involved many fields.

2.4.1 Important steps to follow

Before we get to do anything, planned or unplanned, several steps must be taken, whether we like it or not. Multi-criteria decision analysis is no exception to this rule. There are a number of steps to be considered, as described in the following sections.

2.4.1.1 Step 1: Identify the problem

One of the greatest concerns of people who want to make decisions is to first identify what the problem is. It is important to remember that part of the solution to a problem is understanding the exact nature of the problem. At all levels, be it in public or private enterprise, situations generally arise where people want to make decisions but do not fundamentally understand why they are doing so (as they are not even aware of the problem), and in such situations, the issue may not even be solved but rather became more complex, as part of the MCDA requires the identification of the problem.

2.4.1.2 Step 2: Make objectives

After the problem is identified, the objectives must be defined. In each decision-making process or experiment, the objective is a guide to the result. This fact might be surprising, but should not be because it is your objective that determines whether you have achieved your goal or not. For example, each time someone intends to buy an object, the person would often want to buy what is most inexpensive and yet has good quality, so be it small or big, the cost and quality is our objective.

2.4.1.3 Step 3: Define criteria

Selecting the right criteria is important in MCDA. The criteria are in some way linked to the objectives in that they are our measure of success. With respect to the objectives, it is important to set meaningful criteria. Here, we would need to identify the criteria to be able to compare the options we have. After fixing the objectives, we need criteria that make sense. For example, if two scenarios, one in which a person wishes to buy a mobile phone and another person wishes to buy fruit, are compared, are the objectives the same? The answer is yes because both people want to buy something that is inexpensive and of good quality. However, the question now is what would be the criteria in each case or are the criteria the same as the objectives! Their criteria are not the same since they are two different subjects. In the case of buying fruit, the price might be low but other factors related to quality come to mind, such as shelf life of the fruit, that is, how long it might be suitable for consumption. When buying a mobile phone, we also look for a brand with a low price, but in terms of the quality, we would not consider taste nor how long it would take to be ready, but the focus will be on other factors such as the storage capacity, the camera quality, and even the version. Therefore, from these examples, it can be seen that criteria are particularly important.

2.4.1.4 Step 4. Develop a list of options

Having the right criteria is not enough, nor does it mean that our problem is completely solved, but the process is underway. The criteria that we adopt will make sense and be complete only when we have a list of alternatives on which we can carry out our analysis. This issue arises because today we have many things that might have the same function and, at times, quantity, but the cost and quality may not be the same. For example, when applying to universities, you may be concerned with factors such as ranking, accommodations, and how they transmit knowledge in order to be able to choose the best option. Since they are different, you will have to choose one according to your criteria.

2.4.1.5   Step 5: Evaluate options

Evaluating options here simply means that we would have to rank them. We could also be required to consider the consequences associated with each option or alternative. From the results that we would obtain, we can be confident that we are minimizing most of the attached risk. Each time we consider an option, we need to always remember the objective of the experiment and determine if the risks exceed what we could potentially gain, as well as how easy or difficult it is to achieve the objective. In production systems, it is important to evaluate the cost of inputs, the process, and the outputs.

2.4.1.6   Step 6: Calculation

In this step, it is important to know that we are using all the data mentioned above to calculate and then select the highest score, which will be the option closest to the ideal. Also, in this step, we obtain the result by taking the product of the score of each criterion and its weight, then summing the scores of each criterion. To obtain the final score, we then add all the other scores. From the calculation, we would then have to choose the option with the highest scores.

2.4.1.7   Step 7. Documentation

After obtaining the desired results, all that remains is to monitor the implementation and also preserve it for future use, just as models and theories are recorded in books for use in decision-making and learning.

Using MCDA presents various advantages when compared with other decision-making tools that are not based on specific criteria:

- It is simple and clear.
- We can easily adjust criteria.
- It is reliable.
- It is applicable in many fields of study.
- It helps decision makers express themselves.
- Different types of ata can be combined.

2.4.2   MCDA Methods

There are several theories that we will consider in detail, but first we will summarize them by reviewing their areas of application, advantages, and inconveniences:

The AHP is also as easy to use as PROMETHEE, and its ranking structure can easily be adjusted to conform to different sizes of problems and it is not data demanding [5]. It is applicable for public policy, resource management, political strategy, and planning. Like the other methods, it has its limitations, such as the interdependence that exists between the criteria and options—it might not be consistent between the conclusion and ranking criteria and there is rank reversal.

The technique for order of preference by similarity to ideal solution (TOPSIS) method has a simple process that is not difficult to use and program. The positive aspect of this method is that the stages do not change regardless of the number of attributes [6]. The TOPSIS method is applicable in areas such as transport, technology, and economics to name a few. However, some of the disadvantages are that it keeps the consistency of judgment and it is difficult to weight.

The ELECTRE method is a useful approach because it takes utility and vagueness (unclear) into account [7] and it is applicable in fields like transport and managing water environment. However, its disadvantage is that its processes as well as its end products are not easy to explain in simple language, its processes and outcomes can be difficult to explain in simple terms, and here outranking causes the strengths and weaknesses of the alternatives not to be directly identified.

The preference ranking organization method for enrichment evaluation (PROMETHEE) technique is quite easy and does not need a proportionate criteria assumption [8]. This can be applied in areas such as energy, the environment, water management, healthcare, education, business, finance, transport, agriculture, and production, but the PROMETHEE method does not provide a clear method for assigning weight.

The VlseKriterijumska Optimizcija I Kaompromisno Resenje (VIKOR) method is a type of MCDA that can be used to resolve decision-making problems that are contradictory and differ in terms of identities, considering that some options may need to be overlooked in order to settle conflict [9]. Here, the person making the decision will be seeking the best possible solution that is closest to the ideal, and the possibilities are measured with regard to the defined criteria. It is applicable in engineering. Since it deals with contradicting identities, it may be inconvenient to work with it, especially when selecting among significantly different candidates.

Data envelopment analysis (DEA) can handle more than one input and output and the efficiency can also be carefully considered and measured [10]. This method is applicable in areas such as economics, medicine, software engineering, utilities, road safety, computer technology, business problems, and agriculture. Although DEA is a popular method used in resolving issues, it also has shortcomings in that it cannot be used with data that is not precise. Here, what is put in and what comes out must be known.

Fuzzy logic, or fuzzy set theory, makes use of imprecise inputs, takes into account insufficient data, and is applicable in fields like engineering, economics, the environment, and social and business problems [11]. It is disadvantageous in that it is not easy to develop and it must be tried several times before using.

2.4.2.1 AHP

AHP is a quantitative and qualitative method developed by Saaty, which allows the decision maker to include their experience, knowledge, and intuition in the analysis of uncertain MCDA problems [12].

AHP simplifies complex problems. The decision maker can develop an understanding of the definition of the problems and its elements. AHP allows both objective and subjective thoughts to be included in the decision process. In addition, it is more suitable for group decisions than other methods [13]. AHP is a mathematical technique that can evaluate qualitative or quantitative variables together, taking into account the priorities of the group or individual in the decision-making process [14–16].

2.4.2.1.1 Stages of the AHP

AHP consist of three main steps [17]. Creating a hierarchical structure for the solution of the problem is the first step of AHP [18]. After the hierarchical structure is created, the binary comparison matrix (superiorities are determined) showing the relative importance of the criteria is calculated [19]. Saaty's eigenvector method is used to calculate relative importance [20].

Then, whether the values in the matrix are consistent or not are checked by determining the consistency rate [21]. If the consistency rate is acceptable, the priority order of the alternatives can be obtained [22].

- **Establishing the model (hierarchical structure) and formulating the problem:** Preferring a hierarchical structure in solving problems in AHP means dividing the problem into several levels. The process of creating a hierarchical structure is called modeling [23]. Modeling allows decision-makers to effectively compare criteria, subcriteria and alternatives [24]. The ultimate goal of the problem (objective) is located at the top of the hierarchy and is created first [25]. The criteria to achieve this goal are located at the second level of the hierarchy, while alternatives are located at the lowest level of the hierarchy [26]. The hierarchical structure is shown in Fig. 2.1 below [27].

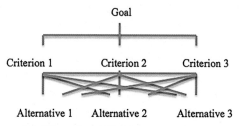

FIGURE 2.1   An example of hierarchy in AHP [27].

TABLE 2.1 Creating a binary comparison matrix for the criteria [23,30].

	Criterion 1	Criterion 2	...	Criterion i
Criterion 1	W_1/W_1	W_1/W_2	...	W_1/W_i
Criterion 2	W_2/W_1	W_2/W_2	...	W_2/W_i
...			...	
Criterion i	W_i/W_1	W_i/W_2	...	W_i/W_i

- **Creation of binary comparison matrix and determination of weights:**
  The second step of AHP is calculating the binary comparisons matrix. After creating a hierarchical structure, the relative importance of each criterion is calculated [23]. The relative importance of the criteria can be found only by obtaining a pairwise comparison, namely by comparing the two criteria with each other [28]. Pairwise comparison is based on the experience and knowledge of the decision maker [23]. The pairwise comparison method used by AHP was first introduced by Fechner in 1860 [29]. The pairwise comparison matrix for the criteria is shown in Table 2.1.

  After creating the hierarchy, it is necessary to calculate how many times the criteria (relative significance) are more important to each other. The decision maker determines the degree of importance between the criteria based on a scale of 1–9. However, decision maker should create the binary comparison matrix for each criterion separately. If there is m-alternative and n-criteria in a decision matrix A, then n-binary comparison matrix with $m \times m$ in size should be created in this process. Table 2.2 shows the 1–9 scale used in binary comparison [31].

  Then, the relative significance between the criteria and the alternatives based on each criterion should be calculated, after creating a comparison matrix and giving the numerical values to the criteria with the help of the ruler in Table 2.2. The best way of calculating the relative importance in the binary comparison matrix is Saaty's eigenvector method [34].

- **Determining the relative weights of the criteria (W) and calculating the consistency ratio:**

  The eigenvector is calculated by the following formula [35].

$$W_i = \frac{1}{n}\sum_{j=1}^{n} \frac{a_{ij}}{\sum_{j=1}^{n} a_{ij}} \tag{2.1}$$

After calculating the relative significance of the criteria by determining the eigenvector, it is necessary to calculate the consistency ratio (CR) of the comparison matrix [36]. The aim is to determine whether the decision maker behaves consistently when comparing criteria. If CR exceeds 0.10, the decision

TABLE 2.2 1–9 Saaty Scale used for pairwise comparison [32,33].

Importance	Definition	Explanation
1	Similar importance	Both of the components have the same effect, within the objective.
3	Moderate importance	One component has a normal advantage compared to the other element.
5	Strong importance	One component is favored over another.
7	Very solid and demonstrated importance	One element is favored and is emphasized in practice, compared to the othercomponents that are present.
9	Extreme importance	One component is advocated in comparison with the other; this is based on the weight of the demonstrated evidence and facts.
2,4,6,8	Inter - values	

maker should review the values entered into the matrix due to its inconsistency [37]. The closer the CR is to zero, the higher the consistency of the decision matrix [38]. The following formulas were preferred by Saaty for the determination of the inconsistency of the comparison matrix [39].

$$CR = \frac{CI \; (Consistency \; Index)}{RI \; (The \; average \; random \; index)}$$

$$CI = \frac{\lambda_{max-n}}{n-1}$$

where:

$$\lambda_{max} = \frac{\sum_{i=1}^{n} \frac{d_i}{w_i}}{n} \quad (i = 1, 2, \ldots, n)$$

and

$$d_i = AXw = \begin{pmatrix} a_{11} & \cdots & a_{1n} \\ \vdots & \ddots & \vdots \\ a_{1n} & \cdots & a_{nn} \end{pmatrix} \begin{pmatrix} w_1 \\ \vdots \\ w_n \end{pmatrix} \quad (2.2)$$

As seen in formula 2, after multiplying the relative priorities by the columns of the comparison matrix, we add up the weighted total vector. After the elements of the weighted total vector are divided into the relative priority corresponding

TABLE 2.3 The average random consistency index (*RI*) [41].

n	1	2	3	4	5	6	7	8	9	10	11	12
RI	0	0	0.58	0.90	1.12	1.24	1.32	1.41	1.45	1.49	1.51	1.54

to it, the arithmetic means of the result gives λ_{max} [40]. The values of the *RI* ratios according to matrix dimension (*n*) are shown in Table 2.3 [41].

The problem is solved in the last stage of the AHP. In this part, a mixed priority vector is used, which will be used as a ranking of decision alternatives. In the creation of this mixed priority vector, the weighted average of the priority vectors determined for each variable is taken. The final priorities achieved are also called alternative decision scores. The decision maker chooses one of the alternatives according to this result [42].

2.4.2.2 TOPSIS

TOPSIS is a multi-criteria decision analysis method that was initially developed by Ching-Lai Hwang and Yoon in 1981 [43] with further advancements by Yoon in 1987 [44], and Hwang, Lai, and Liu in 1993 [45]. TOPSIS is based on the concept that the best option should have the minimum distance to the positive ideal solution (PIS) and maximum distance to the negative ideal solution (NIS) [46].

The TOPSIS technique has been regularly used to deal with dynamic issues. This method depends on an examination of all the choices available for the problem; an example of application on nuclear power plants is provided in [47]. This proposed procedure can be significantly helpful in several domains and different problems such as the airline and automotive industries [48].

In the TOPSIS method, the weights and opinions (alternatives) considered have to be represented by numbers. Through this method, decision-making by a single individual may be more effective than over decision-making by a group of people since a single individual has an objective to achieve, whereas in the group, different individuals must accept the proposed solution before it is implemented. The TOPSIS method, like any other method, contains steps that must be followed to make a multi-criteria decision. To make it more understandable, the various steps are discussed using both the individual and group approach when necessary. There are seven steps, as listed below.

1. Construct the decision matrix and determine the weight of the criteria.
2. Calculate the normalized decision matrix.
3. Calculate the weighted normalized decision matrix.
4. Determine the positive ideal solution and the negative ideal solution.
5. Calculate the separation measures from the positive ideal solution.
6. Calculate the relative closeness to the positive ideal solution.
7. Rank the preference order or select the alternatives closest to 1.

To fully understand this method and how it should be applied, it is necessary to develop each step consecutively.

Step 1. Construct the decision matrix and determine the weight of the criteria [49]

The initial step in the TOPSIS method is to construct the decision matrix, where the alternatives are defined in the rows and the criteria in the columns. Then, the second part involves the determination of the weights of the criteria. We will use the scale that helps us understand that the sum of the weights must be equal to one (2.1). To represent the above mathematically, we have

a. For an individual or one-person decision-making process, we consider $X = \left(x_{ij}\right)$ to be a decision matrix and $W = \{w_1, w_2, ..., w_n\}$ is the weight vector, where $x_{ij} \in R$, $w_j \in R$, and all $w_1 + w_2 + ... + w_n = 1$

b. For group decision-makers, we consider $X^k = \left(x_{ij}^k\right)$ to be the decision matrix, $W^k = \left\{w_1^k, w_2^k, ..., w_n^k\right\}$ is the weight vector for k decision-makers, k is a set of real numbers from $k = \{1, 2, 3 ....k\}$, where $x_{ij}^k \in R$, $w_j^k \in R$, $w_1^k + w_2^k + ... + w_n^k = 1$. Additionally, on our decision matrix, the criteria can be considered to be beneficial or nonbeneficial criteria. For example, the cost is a nonbeneficial criterion, while the performance is a beneficial criterion. After we have determined our decision matrix and the weights, we proceed with the next step for the normalized decision matrix.

Step 2. Calculate the normalized decision matrix [49]

To calculate the normalized decision matrix, we need to first prepare our criteria to be able to compare by transforming the dimensional attributes into nondimensional attributes. We also need to ensure that all our criteria are uniform since they are normally expressed in different units. Therefore, we use a normalized scale. For the normalization of a decision matrix, there are formulas that can be used to calculate the normalized value x_{ij} as follows:

$$X_{ij} = \frac{x_{ij}}{\sqrt{\sum_{i=1}^{m} x_{ij}^2}} \tag{2.3}$$

$$X_{ij} = \frac{x_{ij}}{\max\left(x_{ij}\right)} \tag{2.4}$$

$$X_{ij} = \begin{cases} \dfrac{x_{ij} - \min\left(x_{ij}\right)}{\max\left(x_{ij}\right) - \min\left(x_{ij}\right)}, & \textit{for beneficial criterion} \\[4mm] \dfrac{\max\left(x_{ij}\right) - x_{ij}}{\max\left(x_{ij}\right) - \min\left(x_{ij}\right)}, & \textit{for non-beneficial criterion} \end{cases} \tag{2.5}$$

these formulas are valid for $i = 1,\ldots, m$ and $j = 1,\ldots, m$. i and j are the values on a table of alternatives and criteria, i is the alternative, and j is the criterion. After calculating the normalized decision matrix, we now calculate the weighted normalized matrix.

Step 3. Calculating the weighted normalized matrix (V_{ij}) [49]
To calculate the V_{ij}, we use the formula:

$$V_{ij} = X_{ij} \cdot w_j \tag{2.6}$$

Where X_{ij} is the normalized decision matrix and wj is the weight of the criteria. Therefore, the weighted normalized decision matrix is a product of the normalized decision matrix (X_{ij}) and the weight of the criteria (w_j). This exercise is done for each criterion. This step is applicable when we have only one decision maker.

Step 4. Determining the positive ideal solution and the negative ideal solution [49]

The ideal solutions mentioned in this step are the combination of the extreme points of the parameters, either in the positive direction or the negative direction. Here, these two ideal solutions are treated separately.

The positive ideal solution denoted as A^+ has the following formula:

$$A^+ = \left(V_1^+, V_2^+, \ldots, V_n^+\right) = \left[\left[\max_i v_{ij} \mid j \in I\right], \left[\min_i v_{ij} \mid j \in J\right]\right] \tag{2.7}$$

and the negative ideal solution denoted as A^- has the formula

$$A^- = \left(V_1^-, V_2^-, \ldots, V_n^-\right) = \left[\left[\min_i v_{ij} \mid j \in I\right], \left[\max_i v_{ij} \mid j \in J\right]\right] \tag{2.8}$$

From these two formulae, I and J are related to the criteria, I is associated with the beneficial criteria that needed to be maximum and J is associated with the nonbeneficial criteria, which needed to be minimum, where $i = 1,\ldots, m$ and $j = 1,\ldots, n$. After calculating the positive and negative ideal solution, we should then calculate the separation measures between them.

Step 5. Calculating the separation measure from the positive and negative ideal solution [49]

When using the TOPSIS method, distant matrices can be applied. To calculate the separation of alternatives from the positive or negative ideal solution, certain formulae are used.

The separation of the individual alternatives from the positive ideal solution is given as

$$d_i^+ = \left[\sum_{j=1}^{n} \left(V_{ij} - V_j^+\right)^p\right]^{1/p}, \quad i = 1, 2, \ldots m \tag{2.9}$$

For the separation of the individual alternative from the negative ideal solution, we have

$$d_i^- = \left[\sum_{j=1}^{n} \left(V_{ij} - V_j^-\right)^p\right]^{1/p}, \quad p \geq 1 \tag{2.10}$$

If $p = 2$:

$$d_i^+ = \sqrt{\sum_{j=1}^{n} \left(V_{ij} - V_j^+\right)^2} \tag{2.11}$$

And using them to calculate when $p = 2$ means that we are calculating the Euclidean distances of each alternative from the positive ideal solution and negative ideal solution (d_i^+ and d_i^-), respectively.

Step 6. Calculating the relative closeness to the positive ideal solution [49]

The relative closeness to the positive ideal solution can be denoted by (R_i) and calculated using the formula (2.12):

$$R_i = \frac{d_i^-}{d_i^- + d_i^+} \text{ with } i = 1, \ldots, m \text{ where } 0 \leq R_i \leq 1 \tag{2.12}$$

Step 7. Rank the alternatives [49]

The alternative with the higher R_i value is the better alternative. The ranking results can be obtained based on the R_i values of each alternative.

2.4.2.3 ELECTRE

The ELECTRE method is a multi-criteria decision-making method first introduced by Beneyoun in the mid-1960s [50]. It is based on dual superiority comparisons between decision points for each criterion. The method proceeds to the solution in eight steps as shown below [51]:

Step 1. Creating the decision matrix (A)

Decision points (alternatives), whose superiorities are supposed to be compared, should be provided in the lines of the decision matrix, and the evaluation factors (the criteria or the parameters of the alternatives) to be used in decision-making should be provided in the column of the decision matrix. Matrix A is the initial matrix created by the decision maker and can be shown as seen below:

$$A_{ij} = \begin{bmatrix} a_{11} & \cdots & a_{1n} \\ \vdots & \ddots & \vdots \\ a_{m1} & \cdots & a_{mn} \end{bmatrix}$$

Step 2. Creating the standard decision matrix (X)

The standard decision matrix uses the elements of matrix A and is calculated using the following formula:

$$x_{ij} = \frac{a_{ij}}{\sqrt{\sum_{k=1}^{m} a_{kj}^2}} \tag{2.13}$$

After the calculations, the X matrix is obtained as follows:

$$X_{ij} = \begin{bmatrix} x_{11} & \cdots & x_{1n} \\ \vdots & \ddots & \vdots \\ x_{m1} & \cdots & x_{mn} \end{bmatrix}$$

Step 3. Creating the weighted standard decision matrix (Y)

The importance of evaluation factors (criteria) for the decision maker may differ. In order to reflect these significance differences in the ELECTRE solution, the Y matrix should be calculated. In order to do this, the decision maker must first determine the weight of the evaluation factors (w_i), where:

$$\sum_{i=1}^{n} w_i = 1 \tag{2.14}$$

Then, the Y matrix is created by multiplying the elements in each column of the X matrix with the corresponding w_i value as shown below:

$$Y_{ij} = \begin{bmatrix} w_1 x_{11} & w_2 x_{12} & \cdots & w_n x_{1n} \\ \vdots & \vdots & \ddots & \vdots \\ w_1 x_{m1} & w_2 x_{m2} & \cdots & w_n x_{mn} \end{bmatrix}$$

Step 4. Determination of concordance sets (C_{kl}) and discordance sets (D_{kl})

For the determination of the concordance sets of the alternatives, the Y matrix should be used and the decision points should be compared with each other in terms of each evaluation factor. The concordance sets can be defined by the relationship shown in the formula below:

$$C_{kl} = \left\{ j, \, y_{kj} \geq y_{lj} \right\} \tag{2.15}$$

This formula basically depends on a comparison between the values of the decision matrix row elements. In a multiple decision problem with m alternatives, the number of concordance sets is $(m.m - m)$. The number of concordance set elements maximum can be equal to the number of evaluation elements (n).

For example, where $k = 2$ and $l = 3$, C_{23} concordance set can be obtained by comparing the 2nd and 3rd rows and there are five evaluation factors, C_{23} should contain a maximum of five elements.

In this example, if the comparison results are as follows:

$$y_{21} > y_{31}$$
$$y_{22} > y_{32}$$
$$y_{23} < y_{33}$$
$$y_{24} = y_{34}$$
$$y_{25} < y_{35}$$

$C_{23} = \{1, 2, 4\}$.

In the ELECTRE technique, for each concordance set, a discordance set exists, which is the complement set of the concordance set. The discordance sets contain the elements j, which are not contained in the corresponding concordance set.

In the example, since $C_{23} = \{1, 2, 4\}$, then $D_{23} = \{3, 5\}$.

When creating the concordance sets in the ELECTRE method, the meaning and the aim of the evaluation factors should be carefully observed. For example, if the relevant evaluation factor aim is maximization, then formula (2.15) will be used for the concordance set. However, if the aim of the evaluation is minimization, then the condition of being in the concordance sets will be opposite as $y_{kj} < y_{lj}$.

Step 5. Creation of concordance (C) and discordance matrices (D)

Concordance sets are used for creating the concordance matrix (C). Matrix C is mxm in size and does not take a value where $k = l$. Elements of the matrix C are calculated with the relationship shown in the formula below.

For example, if $C_{23} = \{1, 2, 4\}$ the c_{12} element of the matrix C will be calculated as $c_{23} = w_1 + w_2 + w_4$. The matrix C is shown as below:

$$C = \begin{bmatrix} - & c_{12} & c_{13} \ldots c_{1m} \\ c_{21} & - & c_{23} \ldots c_{2m} \\ & & \cdot \\ & & \cdot \\ & & \cdot \\ c_{m1} & c_{m2} & c_{m3} \ldots & - \end{bmatrix}$$

The elements of the discordance matrix (D) are calculated by the formula below:

$$d_{kl} = \frac{max\left|y_{kj} - y_{lj}\right|_{j \in D_{kl}}}{max\left|y_{kj} - y_{lj}\right|_{\forall j}} \tag{2.16}$$

For example, from the comparison of the elements of the 1st and 2nd lines of the Y matrix, for calculation of the d_{23} (where $k = 2$ and $l = 3$), where the values $j = 3$ and $j = 5$ should be considered from the elements of the discordance set $D_{23} = \{3, 5 \}$ and the maximum absolute value of $\left|y_{23} - y_{33}\right|$ and $\left|y_{25} - y_{35}\right|$ should be chosen for the nominator and for the denominator of the formula, the maximum absolute difference of the 2nd and 3rd line of the matrix Y is chosen.

Like the C matrix, the D matrix is mxm in size and does not take values where $k = l$. Matrix D is shown below:

$$D = \begin{bmatrix} - & d_{12} & d_{13} \ldots d_{1m} \\ d_{21} & - & d_{23} \ldots d_{2m} \\ & & \cdot \\ & & \cdot \\ & & \cdot \\ d_{m1} & d_{m2} & d_{m3} \ldots & - \end{bmatrix}$$

Step 6. Creation of the concordance superiority (F) and discordance superiority (G) matrices

The concordance superiority matrix (F) is $m \times m$ in size and the elements of this matrix are obtained by comparing the concordance threshold ($\underline{c}$) with the elements of the concordance matrix (c_{kl}), where the concordance threshold ($\underline{c}$) is calculated with the formula below:

$$\underline{c} = \frac{1}{m(m-1)} \sum_{k=1}^{m} \sum_{l=1}^{m} c_{kl} \tag{2.17}$$

In the formula, m shows the number of decision points. In other words, the ($\underline{c}$) value is calculated by multiplying the sum of the elements of the C matrix with $1/m(m-1)$. The elements (f_{kl}) of the matrix F take a value of either 1 or 0 as seen in formula (2.18) and there is no value in its diagonal as it shows the same decision points.

$$f_{kl} = \begin{cases} 1, & \text{if } c_{kl} \geq \underline{c} \\ 0, & \text{if } c_{kl} < \underline{c} \end{cases} \tag{2.18}$$

The discordance superiority matrix (G) is also $m \times m$ in size and is created similarly. The value of the discordance threshold value ($\underline{d}$) can be calculated with the formula (2.19):

$$\underline{d} = \frac{1}{m(m-1)} \sum_{k=1}^{m} \sum_{l=1}^{m} d_{kl} \tag{2.19}$$

In other words, the ($\underline{d}$) value is calculated by multiplying the sum of the elements of the D matrix with $1/m(m-1)$.

The elements of the matrix G (g_{kl}) also take the value 1 or 0 as seen in formula (2.20), and there is no value on its diagonal as it shows the same decision points. If:

$$g_{kl} = \begin{cases} 1, & \text{if } d_{kl} \geq \underline{d} \\ 0, & \text{if } d_{kl} < \underline{d} \end{cases} \tag{2.20}$$

Step 7. Creation of total dominance matrix (E)

Elements of the total dominance matrix (E) are equal to the cross product of f_{kl} and g_{kl} elements as shown in the formula below. Here, the matrix E is $m \times m$-sized, depending on the matrices C and D, and it consists of 1 or 0 values.

Step 8. Determining the importance order of decision points

The rows and columns of matrix E show decision points. For example, E matrix is calculated as follows,

$$E = \begin{bmatrix} - & 1 & 0 \\ 1 & - & 1 \\ 0 & 0 & - \end{bmatrix}$$

$e_{12} = 1$, $e_{23} = 1$ and $e_{23} = 1$. This shows the absolute superiority of the 1st decision over the 2nd decision, and absolute superiority of the 2nd decision over the 1st and 3rd decisions. In this case, if A_i $(i = 1, 2, 3)$ denotes the decision points, the importance order will be determined as A_2, A_1, and A_3.

2.4.2.4 PROMETHEE

PROMETHEE is a method for multi-criteria decision analysis. This method can be used in many fields such as government, transportation, business, healthcare, and education [52]. Its application is appropriate in these areas because it gives decision makers a direct approach that would help them find alternatives to attain their aim. Like most multi-criteria decision-making methods, the PROMETHEE method is also based on mathematics and has subtypes such as PROMETHEE I and PROMETHEE II. This method was developed in the 1980s and many others have contributed to its development until today.

The fundamental components of the PROMETHEE strategy was first presented by Prof Jean-Pierre Wheats (CSOO, VUB Vrije Universiteit Brussel) in 1982 [53]. It was later developed and executed by Professor Jean-Pierre Grains and Professor Bertrand Mareschal (Solvay Brussels School of Financial Matters and the Board, ULB Université Libre de Bruxelles), including expansions such as GAIA [54]. The clear methodology called GAIA permits the leader to picture the main features of a decision problem: with significant effort, he/she can recognize clashes or cooperative energies between measures, to identify clusters of actions and to highlight remarkable performances. The prescriptive methodology called PROMETHEE gives the leader both complete and incomplete rankings of the activities. PROMETHEE has effectively been utilized in numerous dynamic settings around the world. A long list of scientific publications about extensions, applications, and discussions related to the PROMETHEE method was published in 2010 [55].

Numerous MCDM strategies are available in the literature and PROMETHEE is one of the MCDM techniques. PROMETHEE is the shortened form of the inclination positioning association technique for enhancement assessment. It is a positioning strategy that is considered as basic in origination and calculation in contrast with numerous other MCDM techniques. The biggest difference between PROMETHEE and other MCDM strategies is the inward relationship of PROMETHEE during the dynamic procedure [56]. It is well adapted to the decision problems where a finite set of alternatives is to be outranked and subjected to multiple conflicting criteria [57]. The PROMETHEE technique depends on the pairwise correlations of options with respect to each criterion. The PROMETHEE has at least three advantages. The principal advantage is that the outranking strategy is easy to use. The second advantage is the success of PROMETHEE in applications to real-life planning problems. And the third advantage of PROMETHEE lies in completeness of ranking [58].

PROMETHEE I and PROMETHEE II permit partial and complete positioning of options, respectively [59]. The PROMETHEE I is used to acquire partial ranking, while PROMETHEE II is utilized for complete ranking. These two strategies were created by Brans et al. The PROMETHEE technique has been broadly utilized in numerous applications with respect to its plausibility in the outranking of choices as well as its availability in multiple versions. Murat et al. used PROMETHEE I and PROMETHEE II to evaluate performance in the academic sector [60]. The PROMETHEE method was applied to assess five potential pipeline courses. The PROMETHEE II technique was utilized to evaluate five kinds of tires for mining machinery. Seven rules were utilized during the assessment [61]. Smet and Liduoh brought forth a special emphasis on the PROMETHEE and GAIA strategies used to assess 10 colleges [62].

PROMETHEE I: This is a partial ranking of the actions, that is based on the positive and negative flows. It includes preferences, indifferences, and incomparabilities (partial preorder).

PROMETHEE II: This is a complete ranking of the actions, which is based on the multi-criteria net flow [63–66]. It includes preferences and indifferences (preorder).

The PROMETHEE method starts with an assessment of the options regarding the rules. These assessments basically require numerical information where their usage needs data on the overall significance of the standards and further data on the decision maker's preference function. The data is obtained when the decision makers compare the contribution of the alternatives with respect to each criterion. The computational techniques in PROMETHEE incorporate the following steps:

1. Determine the criteria.
2. Determine the weight of the criteria.
3. Normalize the decision matrix (preferable).
4. Determination of deviation by pair wise comparison.
5. Define the preference function.
6. Calculate the aggregate preference function.
7. Determine the leaving and the entry outranking flow.
8. Calculate the net outranking flow for each alternative.
9. Determine the ranking of all the considered alternatives depending on the value of $\phi(a)$.

These different steps are discussed in detail below:

Step 1. Determine the criteria and the set of possible alternatives in a decision problem

To develop a model, we would need to focus on whatever we want to do; in other words, we need to have a goal that we want to achieve or attain. In order to attain this goal, it requires criteria and these criteria have to be well defined because they would help us to use good judgement. The number of criteria to be used is not stated anywhere as it depends on the individual preferences or the complexities of the problem.

Step 2. Determine the weight of the criteria

Therefore, to develop the weight in the AHP, we need to use the fundamental scale that was developed by Saaty in 1980 in which a table with three columns is drawn, w where column is used for the scale, another to define the weight and the third for the explanation of the weight. This scale has numerical values. Whenever the scale is at one (2.1), it simply means that the criteria are of the same or equal importance. However, there are times that we need to apply compromise, which is when we choose intermediate values between two judgements. We use this scale to be able to assign numerical values to the criteria since numbers are not always assigned to the criteria as they are often in words.

When using the PROMETHEE method the weight is mostly calculated by using the either the AHP or the linguistic fuzzy scale and

$$\sum_{j=1}^{k} w_j = 1 \qquad (2.21)$$

Step 3. Normalize the decision matrix

We normalize a decision matrix using the formulas (2.22), (2.23).
For beneficial criteria:

$$R_{ij} = \frac{\left\lfloor x_{ij} - max\left(x_{ij}\right)\right\rfloor}{\left[max\left(x_{ij}\right) - min\left(x_{ij}\right)\right]} (i = 1, 2 ..., n \ and \ j = 1, 2, ..., m) \qquad (2.22)$$

For nonbeneficial criteria:

$$R_{ij} = \frac{\left\lfloor x_{ij} - min\left(x_{ij}\right)\right\rfloor}{\left[max\left(x_{ij}\right) - min\left(x_{ij}\right)\right]} (i = 1, 2 ..., n \ and \ j = 1, 2, ..., m) \qquad (2.23)$$

Before we can normalize the matrix, we have to classify the criteria as beneficial and nonbeneficial. The criteria with lowest value desired is considered as nonbeneficial criteria, and the criteria with highest value required is known as the beneficial criteria. From the formulas, we are required to calculate the maximum and minimum values for each criterion. To calculate the beneficial criteria, we simply do the difference of a particular value and the minimum value divided by the difference between the maximum value and the minimum value.

The same is done for the nonbeneficial criteria, where we calculate the difference of the maximum and particular value, then divide by the difference between the maximum and minimum value.

Step 4. Determination of deviation via pairwise comparison

In this step we have to represent the deviation between alternatives on a table separately with respect to each criterion:

$$d_j(a,b) = g_j(a) - g_j(b) \qquad (2.24)$$

$d_j(a,b)$ is the difference of the alternative a and alternative b on each criterion.

Step 5. Calculate the preference function

$$P_j(a, b) = F_j\left[d_j(a,b)\right] \tag{2.25}$$

Where $P_j(a, b)$ is the function of the difference between the evaluations of alternative a and alternative b on each criterion.

Preference functions

The execution of the PROMETHEE strategy requires preference functions. The preference function of PROMETHEE is a capacity used to characterize difference between the alternative decision units.

We can determine this preference function based on the decision maker priority. From the equation (2.25), we see that when the difference is smaller than or equal to zero, then we substitute the preference function value with zero. However, when the difference of one criterion is greater than zero, then we consider the difference as the preference function value. There are several types of preference functions, as shown in Fig. 2.2.

Step 6. Calculate the preference index $\pi(a, b)$

To calculate the preference index, we need to take into account the criteria weight. The formula is as follows:

$$\pi(a, b) = \frac{\sum_{j=1}^{n} P_j(a, b) w_j}{\sum_{j=1}^{n} w_j} \tag{2.26}$$

We notice that each time an alternative is compared with itself, there is no value assigned.

Step 7. Determine the positive and negative outranking flows

Here, two different formulas are used for calculating the positive flow of an alternative a $(\Phi^+(a))$ and the negative outranking flow alternative of an alternative a $(\Phi^-(a))$.

For the positive outranking flow value:

$$\Phi^+(a) = \frac{1}{n-1} \sum_{x \in A} \pi(a, x) \text{ where } (x \neq a) \tag{2.27}$$

This value can be obtained by averaging all the values in the row.

For the negative outranking flow alternative

$$\Phi^-(a) = \frac{1}{n-1} \sum_{x \in A} \pi(x, a) \text{ where } (x \neq a) \tag{2.28}$$

This is calculated by averaging all the values in the column.

The aforementioned step (2.7) is for PROMETHEE II and PROMETHEE I, we sum the values in the rows to obtain the positive flow Φ^+ and sum all the values in the column to obtain the negative flow value Φ^-.

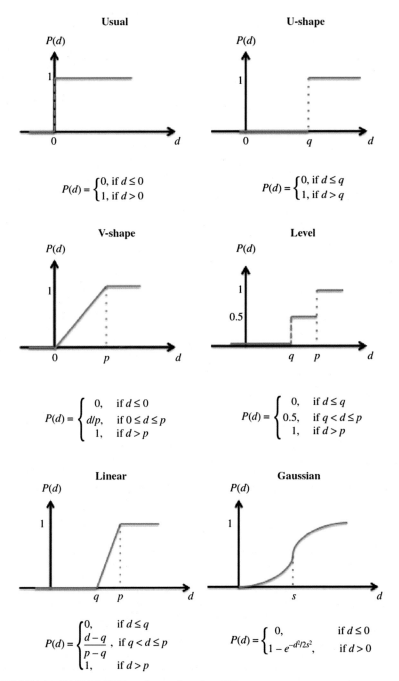

FIGURE 2.2 PROMETHEE preference functions [59].

Step 8. Calculate the net flow for each alternative
The formula to calculate the net outranking flow is

$$\Phi^{net}(a) = \Phi^{+}(a) - \Phi^{-}(a) \qquad (2.29)$$

which is the difference between the positive outranking flow and the negative outranking flow values.

Step 9. Determine the ranking of all the considered alternatives depending on the value of Φ^{net}

The alternatives are ranked according to the net outranking flow value, where we see that the bigger the value, the better the alternative.

In PROMETHEE I, instead of calculating the rank, two things are calculated. We need to remember that the lower the entry flow value, the better the alternative. The higher the positive outranking flow value, the better the alternative. We have to consider the equations below,
a is preferred to b (aPb) if:

$$\Phi^{net}(a) > \Phi^{net}(b) \qquad (2.30)$$

a is indifferent to b (aIb) if:

$$\Phi^{net}(a) = \Phi^{net}(b) \qquad (2.31)$$

2.4.2.5 VIKOR

VIKOR is an acronym that stands for Visekritenjumska Optimizacija I Kompromisno Resenje, which means "multi-criteria optimization and compromises solution." This idea of compromise was first used by Po-Lung Yu and Milan Zeleng in 1973 [67], and in 1979 the Serbian S. Opricovic worked on the theory and the applications were published a year later in 1980 [68]. And the name VIKOR appeared in 1990. The definite applications were carried out in 1998.

The VIKOR method is a multi-criteria decision-making analysis, and like any other method of analysis, there are some steps to follow to solve problems. This method can be considered linear normalization.

The basic concept here is defining the positive and negative ideal points in the solution space. The TOPSIS method that will also be discussed in this issue determines a solution with the shortest distance from the ideal solution and the farthest distance from the negative ideal solution, but the VIKOR method does not consider the relative importance of the distances. The VIKOR theory has the following steps [69]:

Step 1. Establish the decision matrix as seen in Table 2.4.

Step 2. Calculate the best (f_j^{*}) and the worst (f_j^{-}) values of each criteria

In this step the best (f_j^{*}) and the worst (f_j^{-}) values should be collected for each evaluation factor. If the aim of the criterion-j is defined as maximum (for ex. if it shows the quality of a product) the best value will be calculated with the formula (2.32):

TABLE 2.4 General form of a decision matrix for the use of VIKOR technique.

Alternative/criteria	Criterion 1	Criterion 2	...	Criterion N
Alternative 1	f_{11}	f_{12}	...	f_{1N}
Alternative 2	f_{21}	f_{22}	...	f_{2N}
...	...	...	...	...
Alternative M	f_{M1}	f_{M2}	...	f_{MN}

$$f_j^* = \max_i f_{ij} \tag{2.32}$$

If the aim of the criterion-j is defined as minimum (for ex. if it shows the cost of a product) the best value will be calculated with the formula (2.33):

$$f_j^* = \min_i f_{ij} \tag{2.33}$$

Step 3. Calculate the Utility (S_i) and Regret (R_i) measures as in formula (2.34) and (2.35), where w_j denotes the weights of the criteria, which represents the relative importance degrees:

$$S_i = \sum_{j=1}^{n} w_j \left[\frac{f_j^* - f(ij)}{f_j^* - f_j^-} \right] \tag{2.34}$$

$$R_i = \max_i \left(w_j \left[\frac{f_j^* - f(ij)}{f_j^* - f_j^-} \right] \right) \tag{2.35}$$

Step 4. Calculating the value of Q_i:
Q_i values can be calculated with the relation shown in formula (2.36):

$$Q_i = v \left[\frac{S_i - min(S_i)}{max(S_i) - min(S_i)} \right] + (1-v) \left[\frac{R_i - min(R_i)}{max(R_i) - min(R_i)} \right] \tag{2.36}$$

Here v can take any value from 0 to 1 and shows the weights of the strategy that provides the maximum group utility, while $(1-v)$ shows the weight of the individual regret. The value of the v can be considered as 0.5.

Step 5. Rank the alternatives based the Q_i, R_i and S_i values in decreasing order. This will provide three lists to the decision maker. And an alternative with the minimum Q_i provides the best solution (A') if it satisfies the following conditions:

Condition 1: (Acceptable advantage)

This condition states that there is a difference between the best and the closest to the best option.

$$Q(A'') - Q(A') \geq DQ \tag{2.37}$$

where $Q(A'')$ has the second minimum values of Q_i and $DQ = 1/(m-1)$, where m denotes the number of the alternatives, then A'.

Condition 2: (Acceptable stability)

A' must have the best value/s of the R_i and/or S_i among the other alternatives.

In this method, if one of the conditions is not d-satisfied, then the compromise solutions set can be proposed as below:

- If only the second condition is not satisfied: A' and A''.
- If the first condition is not satisfied, A', A'', . A^M, where M determined as the maximum decision point satisfies the condition $Q(A^M) - Q(A') < DQ$.

2.4.2.6   DEA

DEA, which is an activity/performance evaluation method, uses the engineering approach as the ratio of the weighted sum of the outputs to the weighted sum of the inputs:

$$The\ effectiveness\ of\ the\ unit-i = \frac{summation\ of\ the\ weighted\ outputs}{summation\ of\ the\ weighted\ inputs}$$

$$= \frac{u_1 y_{1j} + u_2 y_{1j} + \ldots + u_s y_{sj}}{v_1 x_{1j} + v_2 x_{1j} + \ldots + v_m x_{mj}}$$

where

u_s: the weight of the $s-th$ output
v_m: the weight of the $m-th$ input
y_{sj}: The quantity of the $s-th$ output of the $j-th$ unit
x_{mj}: The quantity of the $m-th$ input of the $j-th$ unit.

It is not always easy for decision makers to determine all u and v values in calculating this ratio. DEA, by using the linear programming technique for the data set, provides the determination of a different set of weights for each decision unit. Each decision unit is evaluated with a set of weights that will maximize its effectiveness against other decision units. Therefore, assessments made with DEA are relative evaluations. There are many different models used in DEA. CCR, the most basic model, used in the study conducted by [70]. The effectiveness of any target unit is the fractional programming model as shown below:

max FP_0;

$$\frac{u_1 y_{10} + u_2 y_{20} + \ldots + u_s y_{s0}}{v_1 x_{10} + v_2 x_{20} + \ldots + v_m x_{m0}} \tag{2.38}$$

Constraints:

$$\frac{u_1 y_{1j} + u_2 y_{2j} + \ldots + u_s y_{sj}}{v_1 x_{1j} + v_2 x_{2j} + \ldots + v_m x_{mj}}, \left(j = 1, 2, \ldots, n\right) \tag{2.39}$$

$$\begin{aligned} v_1, v_2, \ldots, v_m &\geq 0 \\ u_1, u_2, \ldots, u_s &\geq 0 \end{aligned} \tag{2.40}$$

where 0 indices denote the interested decision unit.

The aim function in (2.1) aims to determine the u and v sets of weights, which will maximize the effectiveness of decision unit 0. The constraint conditions ensure that the weighted output/input ratio does not exceed 1 for each decision unit. In this case, the efficiency will be a value between [0,1]. Since, the fractional programming set is more difficult to solve, expressing it as a linear programming problem can solve this problem.

max FP_0 ;

$$\begin{aligned} u_1 y_{10} + u_2 y_{20} + \ldots + u_s y_{s0} \\ v_1 x_{10} + v_2 x_{20} + \ldots + u_m x_{m0} = 1 \end{aligned} \tag{2.41}$$

Constraints

$$\begin{aligned} u_1 y_{1j} + u_2 y_{2j} + \ldots + u_s y_{sj} - v_1 x_{1j} + v_2 x_{2j} + \ldots + v_m x_{mj} &\leq 0 \\ v_1, v_2, \ldots, v_m &\geq 0 \\ u_1, u_2, \ldots, u_s &\geq 0 \end{aligned} \tag{2.42}$$

This proposed linear programming model has the equivalent solution with the given fractional programming model [10]. One of the current issues in DEA is the restriction of weights determined by the model. The weights determined by the model contain flexibility, which could lead to irrational effectiveness estimation [71]. In some applications, a solution may arise where the weight of important inputs and outputs for some decision units is low, so that some other decision units appear to be more effective due to their superiority in inputs and outputs that are not so important. In order to solve these types of issues, weight restrictions are applied. The value judgments are used in determining the weight restrictions.

The first study on weight restrictions in DEA was proposed in 1986 by Thomson et al. to support the selection of a location for the construction of a nuclear physics laboratory to be established in Texas [72]. Dyson and Thanassoulis restricted their input and output weights from the management's perspective [73]. Beasley restricted inputs and outputs based on their importance levels while evaluating the chemistry departments of 52 universities [74]. Wong and Beasley (1990) proposed proportional weight restrictions [75].

Various methods have been developed for weight restrictions in DEA, such as the assurance region method, cone-ratio method, and absolute weight constraints methods. Furthermore, weight restrictions change the solution of the model. There is no single method that is universally accepted for determining constraints (or relative relationships of weights). In some applications only expert opinion (ex: [74]) or concrete information (ex: [76]) like price and cost are included in the judgments. In recent years, AHP and Delphi techniques [75,77,78] have been recommended for use in the determination of weight restrictions.

2.4.2.7 Fuzzy logic–based MCDM

Fuzzy logic is a method that studies system reasoning, which takes a view of the notions of truth and falsehood. Fuzzy logic analyzes natural language vagueness and several other fields. Fuzzy logic is a technique of soft computing that embraces suboptimality and vagueness, producing excellent solutions [79]. It was initially launched by Lofti A. Zadeh, a computer science professor [80–82]. Fuzzy logic basically allows for the characterization of transitional values between evaluations like high, low, yes, no, real, false etc. The implementation of a human-like perspective can handle ideas like "very quick" or "relatively tall" [83].

Customary concept of the established membership, which originated in ancient Greek conflicts with fuzzy logic. A descriptive logic theory was put forth by Aristotle and other philosophers who came before him as the "laws of thought" [84]. The "law of excluded middle" states that every proposal should be true or false. This law was initially interpreted by Parmenide (400 BC), while philosophers like Heraclitus and Plato objected to it. Heraclitus also stated whether or not anything may be real, but philosophers such as Hegel, Marx, and Engels objected to this reasoning. Fuzzy logic is an extension of Boolean logic. The theory of mathematics in fuzzy sets is based on this.

Advantages of fuzzy logic systems
- Simple and easy to understand.
- Is widely used in business and practical applications.
- Provides the only reasoning that is acceptable.
- Solves problems of uncertainty in different study areas.
- It requires no special input.
- Changes and adaptations are possible.
- It gives a complex problem the best answer.

Disadvantages
- This cannot be universally accepted because of the system's inaccuracies, which are important for the final results to be made.
- In comparison to machine learning, it lacks capacity.
- For the validation and verification of the device, comprehensive testing and hardware is needed.
- Such tasks can be difficult.

2.4.2.7.1   Fuzzy sets

A fuzzy set is an extension of classical sets and can be interpreted as a part of a group. It allows for differential adhesion in the set [80]. It can be done by containing a component with different levels of membership. Classical sets have 0 or 1, compared to the fuzzy sets with [1] value.

2.4.2.7.1.1   The mathematical definition of fuzzy sets A fuzzy set $\tilde{A}$ in *IR* is a set of ordered as below:

$$\tilde{A} = \left\{ \left(x, \mu_{\tilde{A}}(x) \right) \mid x \in IR \right\} \tag{2.43}$$

In here $\mu_{\tilde{A}} : IR \rightarrow [0,1]$ and $\mu_{\tilde{A}}(x)$ represents the membership function of the fuzzy set [85–87].

2.4.2.7.1.2   Representation of fuzzy sets In discreet and continuous cases, the fuzzy set may be described:

- Where "*U*" is discrete and finite:

$$\tilde{A} = \left\{ \frac{\mu_{\tilde{A}}(x_1)}{x_1} + \frac{\mu_{\tilde{A}}(x_2)}{x_2} + \frac{\mu_{\tilde{A}}(x_3)}{x_3} + \dots \right\} = \sum_{i=1}^{n} \frac{\mu_{\tilde{A}}(x_i)}{x_i} \tag{2.44}$$

- Where "*U*" is continuous and infinite:

$$\tilde{A} = \left\{ \int \frac{\mu_{\tilde{A}}(x)}{x} \right\} \tag{2.45}$$

As shown above, each element's set is defined by the symbol summation, in which *U* is the universe of information.

2.4.2.7.1.3   Fuzzy sets operations The following relationships describe the union, intersection, and the complement operation on fuzzy sets.

- Union:

$$\mu_{\tilde{A} \cup \tilde{B}}(x) = \mu_{\tilde{A}} \vee \mu_{\tilde{B}}, \quad \forall x \in U \tag{2.46}$$

V denotes the "max" operation.

- Intersection:

$$\mu_{\tilde{A} \cap \tilde{B}}(x) = \mu_{\tilde{A}} \wedge \mu_{\tilde{B}}, \quad \forall x \in U \tag{2.47}$$

$\wedge$ denotes the "min" operation.

- Complement:

$$\mu'_{(A)}(x) = 1 - \mu_{\tilde{A}}(x) \tag{2.48}$$

There may be some cases there:

$$\tilde{A} \cap \tilde{A}' \neq 0 \tag{2.49}$$

2.4.2.7.1.4 Properties of fuzzy sets The key properties of the fuzzy sets can be described as follows;

1. Commutative property: This involves fuzzy set $\tilde{A}$ and $\tilde{B}$, and states that:

$$\tilde{A} \cup \tilde{B} = \tilde{B} \cup \tilde{A} \tag{2.50}$$

$$\tilde{A} \cap \tilde{B} = \tilde{B} \cap \tilde{A} \tag{2.51}$$

2. Associative property: This involves fuzzy sets $\tilde{A}$, $\tilde{B}$, and $\tilde{C}$, and states that:

$$\tilde{A} \cup (\tilde{B} \cup \tilde{C}) = (\tilde{A} \cup \tilde{B}) \cup \tilde{C} \tag{2.52}$$

$$\tilde{A} \cap (\tilde{B} \cap \tilde{C}) = (\tilde{A} \cap \tilde{B}) \cap \tilde{C} \tag{2.53}$$

3. Distributive property: this involves fuzzy sets $\tilde{A}$, $\tilde{B}$, and $\tilde{C}$, and states that:

$$\tilde{A} \cup (\tilde{B} \cap \tilde{C}) = (\tilde{A} \cup \tilde{B}) \cap (\tilde{A} \cup \tilde{C}) \tag{2.54}$$

$$\tilde{A} \cap (\tilde{B} \cup \tilde{C}) = (\tilde{A} \cap \tilde{B}) \cup (\tilde{A} \cap \tilde{C}) \tag{2.55}$$

4. Idempotency property: Provided there is a given fuzzy set $\tilde{A}$, it can be stated that:

$$\tilde{A} \cup \tilde{A} = \tilde{A} \tag{2.56}$$

$$\tilde{A} = \tilde{A} \cap \tilde{A} \tag{2.57}$$

5. Identity property: For a given fuzzy set $\tilde{A}$ and a universal set U, it can be stated that:

$$\tilde{A} = \tilde{A} \cup \varnothing \tag{2.58}$$

$$\varnothing = \tilde{A} \cap \varnothing \tag{2.59}$$

$$A = \tilde{A} \cap U \tag{2.60}$$

$$U = \tilde{A} \cup U \tag{2.61}$$

Transitive property: Provided there are fuzzy sets $\tilde{A}$, $\tilde{B}$, and $\tilde{C}$, the property states:

If $\tilde{A} \subseteq \tilde{B}$ and $\tilde{B} \subseteq \tilde{C}$, then $\tilde{A} \subseteq \tilde{C}$ \hfill (2.62)

a) Involution property: Provided there is a fuzzy set $\tilde{A}$, it can be stated that:

$$\bar{\bar{\tilde{A}}} = \tilde{A} \tag{2.63}$$

b) De Morgan's Law: This law plays a significant role in demonstrating redundancies and logical inconsistency. It states:

$$\overline{\tilde{A} \cup \tilde{B}} = \bar{\tilde{A}} \cap \bar{\tilde{B}} \tag{2.64}$$

$$\overline{\tilde{A} \cap \tilde{B}} = \bar{\tilde{A}} \cup \bar{\tilde{B}} \tag{2.65}$$

2.4.2.7.1.5 Membership function It has been proven that fuzzy logic is not logic that is fuzzy, but rather logic (rational) that is utilized to express fuzziness. The best way of defining the fuzziness is generating a suitable membership function.

In his first research paper, Lofti A. Zadeh[11] described membership features as "fuzzy sets" (Fig. 2.3). The main features of membership (Fig. 2.4) include:

- They distinguish fuzziness.
- They used occurrences as opposed to knowledge to solve real-life problems.
- They mostly can be shown in a graph.

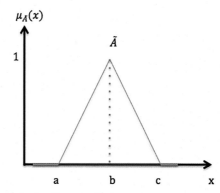

FIGURE 2.3 **An example of a triangular fuzzy set.**

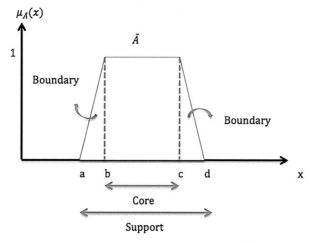

FIGURE 2.4 Membership function features.

The main membership functions properties are;

a) Core: The core of the fuzzy set $\tilde{A} \in IR$ can be obtained by the equation below:

$$\mu_{\tilde{A}}(x) = 1 \qquad (2.66)$$

b) Support: The support of the fuzzy set $\tilde{A} \in IR$ can be defined by the equation below:

$$\mu_{\tilde{A}}(x) > 0 \qquad (2.67)$$

c) Boundary: The boundary of the fuzzy set $\tilde{A} \in IR$ can be defined by the range below:

$$1 > \mu_{\tilde{A}}(x) > 0 \qquad (2.68)$$

A fuzzy number is a fuzzy set on the real line that satisfies the conditions of normality and convexity.

2.4.2.7.2 Fuzzification

Fuzzification can be described as transforming a fuzzy set into a fuzzier set or a fuzzy set of crisp sets. There are two different fuzzification technique available, as defined below:

1. Support fuzzification (s-fuzzification) method:

The fuzzified set can be obtained with the relation of the following function:

$$\tilde{A} = \mu_1 Q(x_1) + \mu_2 Q(x_2) + \ldots + \mu_n Q(x_n) \tag{2.69}$$

where $Q(x_i)$ denotes the kernel of fuzzification. This technique can be applied by keeping μ_i constant and x_i being converted to a fuzzy set $Q(x_i)$.

2. Grade fuzzification (g-fuzzification) method:

This technique is almost similar with the above method with the difference of the meaning of two parameters. In this technique x_i denotes a constant and μ_i denotes a fuzzy set.

2.4.2.7.3 Defuzzification

This is a process that transforms the fuzzy value into crisp value. This process is very important for obtaining meaningful results, especially in engineering applications. Defuzzification can be represented as "rounding it off." The following operations are available for the defuzzification:

1. Max-membership method: This technique is restricted to maximum output functions. It is also called the height method. Mathematically, it can be defined as formula (2.70).

$$\mu_{\tilde{A}}(x^*) > \mu_{\tilde{A}}(x), \quad \forall x \acute{o} X \tag{2.70}$$

where x^* is the defuzzified output.

2. Centroid Method: This method is also recognized as the center of area method. The output x^* can be calculated with the formula (2.71).

$$x^* = \frac{\int \mu_{\tilde{A}}(x).x dx}{\int \mu_{\tilde{A}}(x).dx} \tag{2.71}$$

3. Weighted average method: With this technique, the membership function has been weighted with its maximum membership value. The output x^* can be calculated with the formula (2.72).

$$x^* = \frac{\Sigma \mu_{\tilde{A}}(\overline{x_i}).(\overline{x_i})}{\Sigma \mu_{\tilde{A}}(\overline{x_i})} \tag{2.72}$$

4. Mean-max membership: This method can be recognized as the middle of the maxima. The output x* can be calculated by the formula (2.73).

$$x^* = \frac{\sum_{i=1}^{n} \overline{x_i}}{n} \tag{2.73}$$

2.4.2.7.4 Fuzzy sets algebraic operations

In here, the mainly used algebraic operations of the fuzzy sets are summarized as below:

1. Algebraic product:

$$\tilde{A}.\tilde{B} \Leftrightarrow \mu_{\tilde{A}.\tilde{B}} = \mu_{\tilde{A}}.\mu_{\tilde{B}} \tag{2.74}$$

2. Algebraic sum:

$$\tilde{A} + \tilde{B} \Leftrightarrow \mu_{\tilde{A}+\tilde{B}} = \mu_{\tilde{A}} + \mu_{\tilde{B}} - \mu_{\tilde{A}}.\mu_{\tilde{B}} \tag{2.75}$$

3. Bounded-sum:

$$\tilde{A} \oplus \tilde{B} \Leftrightarrow \mu_{\tilde{A}\oplus\tilde{B}} = 1 \wedge (\mu_{\tilde{A}} + \mu_{\tilde{B}}) \tag{2.76}$$

4. Bounded-difference:

$$\tilde{A} \ominus \tilde{B} \Leftrightarrow \mu_{\tilde{A}\ominus\tilde{B}} = 0 \vee (\mu_{\tilde{A}} - \mu_{\tilde{B}}) \tag{2.77}$$

5. Bounded-product:

$$\tilde{A} \odot \tilde{B} \Leftrightarrow \mu_{\tilde{A}\odot\tilde{B}} = 0 \vee (\mu_{\tilde{A}} + \mu_{\tilde{B}} - 1) \tag{2.78}$$

where $\vee, \wedge, +, -$ denote the max, min, arithmetic sum, and arithmetic difference, respectively.

References

[1] What is a multiple criteria decision analysis (MCDA)? Definition from toolshero (2020), https://www.toolshero.com/decision-making/multiple-criteria-decision-analysis-mcda/.

[2] Multiple criteria decision making. https://www.mcdmsociety.org.

[3] A. Charnes, W.W. Cooper, Management Models and Industrial Applications of Linear Programming, Wiley, New York, (1961).

[4] S. Zionts, MCDM—if not a roman numeral, then what?, Interfaces 9 (4) (1979) 94–101.

[5] S. Lai, Preference-based interpretation of AHP, Int. J. Man. Sci. 23 (4) (1995) 453–462.

[6] Y. Ic, An experimental design approach using TOPSIS method for the selection of computer-integrated manufacturing technologies, Robot. Com.-Int. Manuf. 28 (2) (2012) 245–256.

[7] P. Konidari, D. Mavrakis, A multi-criteria evaluation method for climate change mitigation policy instruments, Energ. Policy 35 (12) (2007) 6235–6257.

[8] M. Behzadian, S. Otaghsara, M. Yazdani, J. Ignatius, A state-of-the-art survey of TOPSIS applications, Expert Syst. Appl. 39 (17) (2012) 13051–13069.

[9] P.L. Yu, A class of solutions for group decision problems, Manag. Sci. 19 (8) (1973) 936–946.

[10] A. Charnes, W.W. Cooper, E. Rhodes, Measuring the efficiency of decision-making units, EJOR 2 (1978) 429–444.

[11] L. Zadeh, Fuzzy sets, Inform. Control 8 (3) (1965) 338–353.

[12] M. Chena, S.-C. ve Wang, The critical factors of success for information market: using analytic hierarchy process (AHP) approach, Exp. Sys. Appl. 37 (1) (2010) 694–704.

[13] A. Tüzemen, A. ve Özdağˇogˇlu, Doktora Ögˇrencilerinin Es¸ Seçiminde Önem Verdikleri Kriterlerin Analitik Hiyerars¸i Süreci Yöntemi İle Belirlenmesi, Atatürk Üniversitesi İİBF Dergisi 21 (1) (2007) 215–232.

[14] M. Dağdeviren, D. Akay, M. ve Kurt, İs¸ Degˇerlendirme Sürecinde Analitik Hiyerars¸i Süreci ve Uygulaması, Gazi Üniversitesi Mühendislik ve Mimarlık Fakültesi Dergisi 19 (2) (2004) 131–138.

[15] N. Bolloju, Aggregation of analytic hierarchy process models based on similarities in decision makers' preferences, Eur. J. Oper. Res. 128 (3) (2003) 499–508.

[16] R. Lin, J. Lin, J. Chang, H. Chao, P. ve Julian, Note on group consistency in analytic hierarchy process, Eur. J. Oper. Res. 190 (3) (2008) 672–678.

[17] Y. Wind, T.L. ve Saaty, Marketing applications of the analytic hierarchy process, Manage. Sci. 26 (7) (1980) 641–658.

[18] S.-H. An, G.-H. Kimb, K.-I. ve Kang, A case-based reasoning cost estimating model using experience by analytic hierarchy process, Build. Environ. 42 (7) (2007) 2573–2579.

[19] D. Cao, L. Leung, J. ve Law, Modifying inconsistent comparison matrix in analytic hierarchy process: a heuristic approach, Decis. Support. Syst. 44 (4) (2008) 944–953.

[20] M.S. Garcia-Cascales, M. ve Lamata, Selection of a cleaning system for engine maintenance based on the analytic hierarchy process, Comput. Indust. Eng. 56 (4) (2009) 1442–1451.

[21] Y. Chou, Y.-Y. ve Hsu, Human resources for science and technology: analyzing competitiveness using the analytic hierarchy process, Technol. Soc. 30 (2) (2008) 141–153.

[22] M. Yılmaz, Analitik Hiyerars¸i Süreci (AHS) ve Bir Uygulama: Lider Bir Kütüphane Müdürü Seçimi, Türk Kütüphaneciligˇi 24 (2) (2010) 206–234.

[23] B. Chandran, B. Golden, E. ve Wasil, Linear programming models for estimating weights in the analytic hierarchy process, Comput. Oper. Res. 32 (9) (2005) 2235–2254.

[24] D. Lee, J. Hwang, Decision support for selecting exportable nuclear technology using the analytic hierarchy process: a Korean case, Energ. Policy 38 (1) (2010) 161–167.

[25] R. Pineda-Henson, A.B. Culaba, G.A. ve Mendoza, Evaluating environmental performance of pulp and paper manufacturing using the analytic hierarchy process and life-cycle assessment, J. Ind. Ecol. 6 (1) (2008) 15–28.

[26] T. Braunschweig, B. ve Becker, Choosing research priorities by using the analytic hierarchy process: an application to international agriculture, R&D Manag. 34 (1) (2004) 77–86.

[27] Y. Wang, J. Liu, T. ve Elhag, An integrated AHP-DEA methodology for bridge risk assessment, Comput. Ind. Engineer. 54 (3) (2008) 513–525.

[28] M.J. Sharma, I. Moon, H. ve Bae, Analytic hierarchy process to assess and optimize distribution network, Appl. Math. Comput. 202 (1) (2008) 256–265.

[29] M. Lamata, An alternative solution to the analytic hierarchy process, Int. J. Intell. Syst. 21 (4) (2006) 425–441.

[30] T.L. Saaty, An exposition of the AHP in reply to the paper "Remarks on the analytic hierarchy process", Manag. Sci. 36 (3) (1990) 259–268.

[31] T.L. Saaty, Axiomatic foundation of the analytic hierarchy process, Manag. Sci. 32 (7) (1986) 842–843.

[32] M.J. Sharma, I. Moon, H. ve Bae, Analytic hierarchy process to assess and optimize distribution network, Appl. Math. Comput. 202 (1) (2008) 256–265.

[33] T.L. Saaty, How to make a decision: the analytic hierarchy process, Interfaces 24 (6) (1994) 19–43.

[34] J.W. Hurley, The analytic hierarchy process: a note on an approach to sensitivity which preserves rank order, Comput. Oper. Res. 28 (2) (2001) 185–188.

[35] R. Ramadhan, V.H. Al-Abdul, S. ve Duffuaa, The use of an analytical hierarchy process in pavement maintenance priority ranking, J. Qual. Mainten. Eng. 5 (1) (1999) 25–39.

[36] K. Hafeez, N. Malak, Y. ve Zhang, Outsourcing non-core assets and competences of a firm using analytic hierarchy process, Comput. Oper. Res. 34 (12) (2007) 3592–3608.

[37] W.E. Stain, P.J. ve Mizzi, The Harmonic Consistency Index for the analytic hierarchy process, Eur. J. Oper. Res. 177 (1) (2007) 488–497.

[38] X. Jian-Zhong, W. Li-Jing, L. ve Jun, A study of AHP-fuzzy comprehensive evaluation on the development of eco-enterprise, Int. Conf. Manag. Sci. Eng. (2008).

[39] Y.-D. Zhou, M.-L. ve Shi, Rail transit project risk evaluation based on AHP model, Sec. Int. Conf. Inform. Comput. Sci. 3 (2009) 236–238.

[40] İ. Güngör, D.B. ve İş‚ler, Analitik Hiyerars‚i Yaklas‚ımı İle Otomobil Seçimi, Zonguldak Karaelmas Üniversitesi Sosyal Bilimler Dergisi 1 (2) (2005) 21–33.

[41] H.S. Wang, Z.H. Che, C. ve Wu, Using analytic hierarchy process and particle swarm optimization algorithm for evaluating product plans, Expert Syst. Appl. 37 (2) (2010) 1023–1034.

[42] F. Zahedi, The analytic hierarchy process: a survey of the method and its applications, Interfaces 16 (4) (1986) 99–100.

[43] C.L. Hwang, K. Yoon, Multiple Attribute Decision Making: Methods and Applications, Springer-Verlag, New York, (1981).

[44] K. Yoon, A reconciliation among discrete compromise situations, J. Oper. Res. Soc. 38 (3) (1987) 277–286, doi: 10.1057/jors.1987.44.

[45] C.L. Hwang, Y.J. Lai, T.Y. Liu, A new approach for multiple objective decision making, Comput. Oper. Res. 20 (8) (1993) 889–899, doi: 10.1016/0305-0548(93)90109-v.

[46] A. Assari, T. Mahesh, E. Assari, Role of public participation in sustainability of historical city: usage of TOPSIS method, Ind. J. Sci. Technol. 5 (3) (2012) 2289–2294.

[47] Giorgio Locatelli, Mauro Mancini, A framework for the selection of the right nuclear power plant (PDF), Int. J. Prod. Res. 50 (17) (2012) 4753–4766, doi: 10.1080/00207543.2012.657965.0020-7543.

[48] R. Greene, R. Devillers, J.E. Luther, B.G. Eddy, GIS-based multi-criteria analysis, Geogr. Comp. 5/6 (6) (2011) 412–432, doi: 10.1111/j.1749-8198.2011.00431.x.

[49] M. Yahya, H. Gökçekus‚, D. Ozsahin, B. Uzun, Evaluation of wastewater treatment technologies using TOPSIS, Desalin. Water Treat. 177 (2020) 416–422, doi: 10.5004/dwt.2020.25172.

[50] B. Roy, Classement et choix en présence de points de vue multiples, Revue Française D'informatique Et De Recherche Opérationnelle 2 (8) (1968) 57–75, doi: 10.1051/ro/196802v100571.

[51] D. Alper, C. Bas‚dar, A comparison of TOPSIS and ELECTRE methods: an application on the factoring industry, Bus. Econ. Res. J. 8 (3) (2017) 627–646.

[52] J.P. Brans (1982). "L'ingénierie de la décision: élaboration d'instruments d'aide à la décision. La méthode PROMETHEE". Presses de l'Université Laval.

[53] B. Mareschal, J.P. Brans, Geometrical representations for MCDA. the GAIA module, Eur. J. Oper. Res. (1988).

[54] P. Vincke, J.-P. Brans, A preference ranking organization method: The PROMETHEE method for multiple criteria decision-making, Manag. Sci. 31 (1985) 647–656.

[55] M. Behzadian, R.B. Kazemzadeh, A. Albadvi, M. Aghdasi, PROMETHEE: A comprehensive literature review on methodologies and applications, Eur. J. Oper. Res. (2010).

[56] R.U. Bilsel, G. Buyukozkan, D. Ruan, A fuzzy preference ranking model for a quality evaluation of hospital web sites, Int. J. Intel. Syst 21 (11) (2006) 1181–1197.

[57] F. Ulengin, Y. Topçu, S.O. Sahin (2001). An integrated decision aid system for Bosporous water crossing problem. Euro. J. Oper. Res. 134: 179–192.

[58] S. Murat, H. Kazan, S.S. Coskun (2015). An application for measuring performance quality of schools by using the PROMETHEE multicriteria decision making method. Proc. Soc. Behav. Sci. 195 (1): 729–738.

[59] J. Brans and B. Mareschal, "PROMETHEE METHODS", *Cin.ufpe.br*, 2019. https://www.cin. ufpe.br/~if703/aulas/promethee.pdf.

[60] S. Murat, H. Kazan, Coskun SS, An application for measuring performance quality of schools by using the PROMETHEE multicriteria decision making method, Proc. Soc. Behav. Sci. 195 (1) (2015) 729–738.

[61] M. Tavana, M. Behzadian, M. Pirdashti, H Pirdashti, A PROMETHEE-GDSS for oil and gas pipeline planning in the Caspian Sea basin, J. Energy Econ. 36 (1) (2013) 716–728.

[62] Y.D. Smet, K Liduoh, An introduction to multi-criteria decision aid: the PROMETHEE and GAIA methods, J. Bus. Intell. 138 (1) (2013) 150–176.

[63] I. Ozsahin, B. Uzun, N.A. Isa, G.S.P. Mok, D.U. Ozsahin, Comparative analysis of the common scintillation crystals used in nuclear medicine imaging devices, in 2018 IEEE Nuclear Science Symposium and Medical Imaging Conference Proceedings (NSS/MIC), Sydney, Australia, 2018, pp. 1–4. doi:10.1109/NSSMIC. 2018.8824485.

[64] I. Ozsahin, S. Abebe, G. Mok, A multi-criteria decision-making approach for schizophrenia treatment techniques, Arch. Psych. Psychother. 22 (2) (2020) 52–61, doi: 10.12740/ app/111624.

[65] T. Gichamo, H. Gökçekus,, D. Ozsahin, G. Gelete, B. Uzun, Evaluation of different natural wastewater treatment alternatives by fuzzy PROMETHEE method, Desalin. Water Treat. 177 (2020) 400–407, doi: 10.5004/dwt.2020.25049.

[66] M. Sayan, T. Sanlidag, N. Sultanoglu, B. Uzun, F.S. Yildirim, D.U. Ozsahin (2020). Evaluating the efficacy of adult HIV post exposure prophylaxis regimens in relation to transmission risk factors by multi criteria decision method, in: R, Aliev, J. Kacprzyk, W. Pedrycz, M. Jamshidi, M. Babanli, F. Sadikoglu (Eds.), 10th International Conference on Theory and Application of Soft Computing, Computing with Words and Perceptions—ICSCCW-2019. ICSCCW 2019. Advances in Intelligent Systems and Computing, vol. 1095. Springer, Cham.

[67] Yu Po Lung, A class of solutions for group decision problems, Manag. Sci. 19 (8) (1973) 936–946.

[68] Milan Zelrny, Compromise programming, in: J.L.M. CochraneZeleny (Ed.), Multiple Criteria Decision Making, University of South Carolina Press, Columbia, 1973, pp. 262–301.

[69] Duckstein Lucien, Opricovic Serafim, Multiobjective optimization in river basin development, Water Resources Res. 16 (1) (1980) 14–20.

[70] B. Uzun, E. Kıral, Evaluating US dollar index movements using Markov chains—fuzzy states approach, in: R. Aliev, J. Kacprzyk, W. Pedrycz, M. Jamshidi, F. Sadikoglu (Eds.), 13th International Conference on Theory and Application of Fuzzy Systems and Soft Computing—ICAFS-2018. ICAFS 2018. Advances in Intelligent Systems and Computing, vol. 896. Springer, Cham.

[71] W.W. Cooper, L.M. Seiford, K. Tone, Data Envelopment Analysis, Kluwer Academic Publishers, (2000).

[72] R.G. Thompson, F.D. Singleton, R.M. Thrall, B.A. Smith, Comparative site evaluations for locating a high-energy physics lab in Texas, Interfaces 16 (6) (1986) 35–49.

[73] R.G. Dyson, E. Thanassoulis, Reducing weight flexibility in data envelopment analysis, J. Oper. Res. Soc. 39 (6) (1988) 563–576.

[74] J.E. Beasley, Comparing university departments, OMEGA 18 (2) (1990) 171–183.

[75] Y.H. Wong, J.E. Beasley, Restricting weight flexibility in data envelopment analysis, J. Oper. Res. Soc. 41 (9) (1990) 829–835.

[76] E. Thanassoulis, R. Allen, Simulating weights restrictions in data envelopment analysis by means of unobserved DMUs, Manag. Sci. 44 (2) (1998) 586–594.

[77] L.M. Seiford, J. Zhu, Identifying excesses and deficits in Chinese industrial productivity (1953–1990): a weighted data envelopment analysis approach, OMEGA 26 (2) (1988) 279–296.

[78] J. Shang, T.A. Sueyoshi, A unified framework for the selection of a flexible manufacturing system, Eur. J. Oper. Res. 2 (1995) 429–444.

[79] M. Sayadi, M. Heydari, K. Shahanaghi, Extension of VIKOR method for decision making problem with interval numbers, Appl. Math. Model. 33 (5) (2009) 2257–2262, doi: 10.1016/j.apm.2008.06.002.

[80] H. Nguyen, E. Walker, 3rd edn., A First Course in Fuzzy Logic, Chapman and Hall/CRC Press, Boca Raton, (2006).

[81] L. Zadeh, Fuzzy sets, *Inform. Control* 8 (3) (1965) 338–353, doi:10.1016/s0019-9958(65)90241-x.

[82] L. Zadeh, Outline of a new approach to the analysis of complex systems and decision processes, IEEE Transactions on Systems, Man, and Cybernetics 3 (1) (1973) 28–44, doi:10.1109/tsmc.1973.5408575.

[83] L. Zadeh, Fuzzy algorithms, Inform. Control 12 (2) (1968) 94–102, doi:10.1016/s0019-9958(68)90211-8.

[84] L. Zadeh, Making computers think like people [fuzzy set theory], IEEE Spectrum 21 (8) (1984) 26–32, doi:10.1109/mspec.1984.6370431.

[85] B. Uzun, E. Kıral, 'Application of Markov chains—fuzzy states to gold price', Procedia Comp. Sci. 120 (2017) 365–71, doi:10.1016/j.procs.2017.11.251.

[86] E. Kiral, Modeling Brent oil price with Markov chain process of the fuzzy states, Pressacademia 5 (1) (2018) 79–83, doi: 10.17261/pressacademia.2018.785.

[87] E. Kiral, B. Uzun, Forecasting closing returns of Borsa Istanbul Index with Markov chain process of fuzzy states, Pressacademia 4 (1) (2017) 15–24, doi: 10.17261/pressacademia.2017.362.

Chapter 3

Fuzzy PROMETHEE-based evaluation of brain cancer treatment techniques

Dilber Uzun Ozsahin[a,b,c], Kevin Meck[b], Sunsley Tanaka Halimani[b], Berna Uzun[a,d] and Ilker Ozsahin[a,b,e]

[a]DESAM Institute, Near East University, Turkish Republic of Northern Cyprus, Nicosia, Turkey; [b]Department of Biomedical Engineering, Near East University, Turkish Republic of Northern Cyprus, Nicosia, Turkey; [c]Medical Diagnostic Imaging Department, College of Health Sciences, University of Sharjah, Sharjah, United Arab Emirates; [d]Department of Mathematics, Near East University, Turkish Republic of Northern Cyprus, Nicosia, Turkey; [e]Brain Health Imaging Institute, Department of Radiology, Weill Cornell Medicine, New York, NY, United States

3.1 Introduction

Brain cancer results from abnormal growth of cells within the brain tissue. It starts as a primary tumor arising from structures in the brain like the blood vessels and membranes. The common primary brain cancers include gliomas, meningiomas, medulloblastomas, pituitary tumors, and acoustic neuromas (schwannomas) and astrocytomas [1], which are classified according to the origin of the cells that are involved in the formation of the tumor. Sometimes, brain cancer occurs as a secondary tumor resulting from metastasis from cancers in different parts of the body. Brain cancer has no direct causes but there are possible risk factors that may lead to the development of cancer. These include radiation, cigarette smoking, genetic risks and HIV infection [2]. According to [3], an estimated 700,000 people live with a primary brain tumor in the US. The five-year survival rate for people who have been diagnosed with brain cancer stands at 34% for men and 36% for women according to a survey conducted in the USA in 2018 [4]. Treatment of brain cancer is vital in order to minimize the mortality rates of the disease. Various treatment techniques exist and are explained in Section 3.2. It is very important to select the best treatment option among the several options considering the type, location, and size of the tumor and the patient's health status.

The fuzzy preference ranking organization method for enrichment evaluations (PROMETHEE) algorithm compares these treatment alternatives

Applications of Multi-Criteria Decision-Making Theories in Healthcare and Biomedical Engineering.
http://dx.doi.org/10.1016/B978-0-12-824086-1.00003-7

considering selected criteria and gives them grades between [0, 1] interval using a preference function [5]. This method has successfully been used in real-life situations and some examples can be given as follows: In the health sector for breast cancer treatment techniques [6], nuclear medicine imaging devices evaluation [7], ranking equipment failure modes [8], and organization evaluation. Fuzzy PROMETHEE is a simple, efficient, and flexible method allowing it to adapt to many different problems and provide solutions.

This study employs a fuzzy-based decision-making method, which helps the patient and the physician choose the best form of treatment for the patient. This research applies the fuzzy PROMETHEE in order to rank the treatment techniques we selected in this study, based on certain criteria including the costs, treatment times, dosages, success rates, advantages, disadvantages, and side effects of the procedure, as well as recovery periods.

3.2 Treatment techniques

3.2.1 Surgery

Surgery is the primary method used for the treatment of low-grade brain tumors [9] such as pineal astrocytic, pilocytic astromas, anaplastic glioblastomas, oligodendroglial, and mixed gliomas. This treatment technique is approached in a number of ways. Brain cancer surgery costs can range between $6,000 and $12,000 in India, while it can cost as much as $50,000–$150,000 in other parts of the world. On average, a session can last 4–6 h [10] The type of surgical approach to be performed is selected depending on the type, location, and grade of the tumor. The most common types of brain surgery procedures include craniotomy, endonasal endoscopy, neuro-endoscopy, and shunt.

A craniotomy is the process by which part of the skull bone is removed to expose the part of the brain with a tumor so that it can be surgically removed [11]. Scans are performed before and during the procedure to obtain the specific details of the location of the tumor. The procedure is done while the patient is under general anesthesia. The procedure involves the use of a scalpel or special scissors for incision while the surgeon uses blue fluorescent light and a microscope to be able to precisely target the tumor and its peripherals while avoiding healthy tissue. Other methods that can be used to visualize the location of the tumor include intraoperative cortical stimulation and magnetic resonance imaging (MRI). Intraoperative cortical stimulation involves the surgeon electrifying the area around the tumor in order to determine its functionality so as to avoid areas of functional importance. Functional MRI is also used to determine the brain's functional properties and can be done before the surgery [12]. The process of ultrasonic aspiration is used in order to break up the tumor using vibrations while suctioning the broken-off pieces. The removed bone will then be replaced and secured using metal brackets or sutures. However, craniotomy can be performed while the patient is conscious if the tumor's location is near or in areas that control important functions such as locomotion and sense of touch. A general anesthetic is administered and gradually reduced so that the patient becomes conscious and is asked to perform tasks like movements or speech while attached to a machine that monitors his or her neurophysiological activities. The brain itself will not feel pain because it does not have pain receptors [13]. It can take 4–6 days for the patient to recover in the hospital after the surgery.

Neuroendoscopy is a method in which an endoscope is inserted through a small hole drilled into the skull and is also called keyhole surgery. This method allows the neurosurgeon to access areas of the brain that are harder to reach with traditional surgery [14]. Neuroendoscopy is performed while the patient is under anesthesia. The endoscope has a camera that allows the surgeon to monitor its movements and the procedure via a monitor. Forceps and scissors are also attached to the endoscope, which the surgeon uses to remove parts of the tumor.

Endonasal endoscopic surgery involves the use of an endoscope to access the brain via the nose [14]. Endonasal endoscopy allows for the removal of tumors such as pituitary tumors but it also depends on the size of the tumor as this approach is more suitable for smaller tumors. The surgeon can make a cut on the thin wall of the bone and cartilage that separates the nostrils. The endoscope is then inserted to the tumor via this incision, which is then removed using the forceps attached to the endoscope.

The advantages of this form of neuroendescopy and endonasal endoscopic surgery are that they are minimally invasive and therefore minimal scarring occurs after the surgery. However, the risks of endonasal endoscopic surgery are loss of vision due to damage caused to the optic nerves or a reduction in hormonal activities that originate from the pituitary gland. [13]

Another type of surgery involves the use of a shunt [15]. This method is effective for patients who develop increased intracranial pressure due to their brain tumor, which can cause headaches and drowsiness [12]. A shunt is placed into a brain ventricle through a hole in the skull, while the other end is positioned in the abdominal area to drain the excess fluid caused by the tumor into the abdomen where it is absorbed. The catheter is placed under the skin and goes from the brain to the abdomen via the neck. The procedure can take up to 1 hour with a hospital recovery time of 1–2 days after the surgery [16]. However, the surgical removal of brain cancer cannot completely remove all cancer cells in the brain, thus leaving room for reoccurrence of the cancer. To ensure the cancer is completely removed, other treatments like chemotherapy and radiation therapy are used in addition to surgery.

The average success rate of brain cancer surgery is 70% [17]. The advantages of performing surgery are that it poses no risks of radiation exposure nor toxicity to the patient. Comparing surgery with other treatment options, it has less long-term side effects after the procedure. These side effects include depression, headaches, and dizziness.

The risks of performing surgery are that the patient may experience seizures, weakness, meningitis, brain swelling, infections, and spinal fluid leakages. Tissue damage and bleeding may also occur, which can be life threatening. The other disadvantages of surgery compared to other treatment techniques are that it offers limited reachability and requires more expertise because it is a difficult procedure that requires human precision and such services are costly. It can take a patient 6 weeks to recover from the surgery [18].

3.2.2 Chemotherapy

Chemotherapy is the use of pharmaceutical drugs as a treatment technique for cancer. The drugs can either stop the cancer cells from dividing further or completely destroy and kill the cancer cells [19]. Chemotherapy is usually applied in conjunction with surgery or radiotherapy for high-grade tumors or for recurring tumors. This is because chemotherapy for brain cancer is rendered less effective because the brain has a blood barrier that makes it more difficult for the drugs to reach their targeted tumors in the brain. Chemotherapy is a noninvasive process and the types of chemotherapy can be classified as follows:

Systemic chemotherapy, whereby the drugs are injected into a muscle or vein or taken by mouth; they reach the cancer cell through the bloodstream. In this method, a cannula can be placed into a vein to deliver the drug into the bloodstream or through a central line that is placed in a major blood vessel near the heart or the neck if it is for short-term purposes. In order to do this, the patient undergoes minimally invasive surgery where imaging is used to accurately connect the central line to the vein. This connection can stay in place throughout the patient's treatment and this avoids the need to continuously puncture a patient each time they need treatment. Unfortunately, problems may arise from administering the drugs intravenously. A patient may contract an infection from the punctures or blood clots may develop. The lines may also become obstructed themselves and this can be painful for the patient. The central line may also cause some discomfort because it is placed for a longer period. The drugs can also be taken orally as tablets or capsules. This poses less complications as no perforations are required and it is a more traditional way of taking drugs that can be done while the patient is mobile or performing other duties.

The second type of chemotherapy can be classified as regional chemotherapy. In this type of chemotherapy, the drugs are placed directly into either the brain or the cerebrospinal fluid and they take effect on cancer cells around that area. Intrathecal chemotherapy is a type of regional chemotherapy where the anticancer drug can be injected directly into the fluid-filled space to take effect on the cancer cells there. The drug can be delivered in the form of wafers. The wafer is made of gel and dissolves slowly over 2–3 weeks and is released into the brain tissue [20]. The advantage of regional chemotherapy is that, unlike systematic chemotherapy, it bypasses the brain-blood barrier, making the drugs more effective. It also has reduced side effects on the body because it is more concentrated on the tumor in the brain.

Another type of chemotherapy is called combination chemotherapy in which more than one drug is used to fight the cancer [13,19]. Procarbazine, Lomustine,

Vincristine, and Carmustine [21] are some of the drugs used for brain tumor treatment, but the most commonly prescribed drug for high-grade brain cancers such as glioblastomas, mixed gliomas, and anaplastic astrocytoma is called Temozolomide [22]. Procarbazine, Lomustine, and Vincristine can be taken in combination. Procarbazine, Lomustine, and Temozolomide can be taken orally while Carmustine can be used as an implant in regional chemotherapy. However, Vincristine is taken intravenously [23]. Dosages are given in cycles and each cycle dosage may differ depending on the tumor location, size, and the extent to which it has spread in the body. A patient's health, age, how the patient responds to the medication, and side effects are factors in determining the chemotherapy treatment plan. Temozolomide, which was used as a benchmark for the purposes of the research, has a dosage of 150–200 mg/m 2PO/IV or 75 mg/m 2PO/IV [24]. On the downside, resistance is a major failure of chemotherapy in treating brain cancer and this is caused by many factors, the primary one being small pumps called p-glycoproteins found on the surface of cancer cells that actively take the chemotherapy drugs from inside the cell to outside. Another major problem with chemotherapy for brain cancer treatment is finding the correct drug formula that is effective in crossing the blood-brain barrier, which contributes to the low success rate of 46% [25]. This means the process is often expensive, depending on the location of the tumor in the brain. It can cost between $10,000 and $200,000 for a full chemotherapy treatment [26]. Chemotherapy relieves symptoms caused by the brain tumor but the drugs themselves have their own side effects. These include vomiting, loss of appetite, diarrhea, hair loss, fatigue, breathlessness, and fetal injury. Combined with radiotherapy and surgery, the side effects on the patient are increased. With chemotherapy, the patient risks infertility, bleeding, seizures, stroke, brain swelling, and memory loss. Other chemotherapy drugs can also cause kidney damage. Chemotherapy drugs reduce white blood cell count, which increases risks of getting other infections, some of which can be serious.

3.2.3 Targeted therapy

Targeted therapy is a type of nuclear medicine technique that identifies and attacks the tumor cells. Unlike chemotherapy, this procedure is precise and affects only tumor cells while sparing normal tissue because it targets the molecules and cellular processes that cause tumors to grow more rapidly than the normal cells. Another difference between targeted therapy and chemotherapy is that chemotherapy focuses more on destroying tumor cells, whereas targeted therapy focuses more on inhibiting tumor cell proliferation. Targeted therapy looks at the difference in growth proteins between normal and cancerous cells or mutant proteins that may be synthesized as a result of the tumor. These proteins are then used as targets for the drugs. Monoclonal antibody therapy and the use of nano-engineered enzymes are the two main approaches to targeted therapy. Monoclonal antibody therapy uses antibodies from a specific single type of immune system cell. The antibodies will identify and disable the different agents on either the cancer cells or even normal substances that cause the growth of the tumor [27]. Bevacizumab is a drug used in targeted therapy, especially for high-grade tumors such as recurrent glioblastoma. This drug is a monoclonal antibody that stops the formation of new blood vessels, which supply nutrients required for growth of the tumor [28]. These blood vessels also supply oxygen to the tumor and other chemical substances required by the tumor cells to function. Cancer cells can make a protein called vascular endothelial growth factor (VEGF), which promotes synthesis of blood vessels, i.e. angiogenesis. Normal cells can also produce VEGF, but in cancer cells, the protein is produced in larger quantities to promote rapid growth of the tumor. To prevent angiogenesis, the targeted therapy drug Bevacizumab blocks this VEGF by attaching itself to the markers on the tumor cells, thereby interfering with blood vessel formation and growth and slowing down or halting tumor growth. Bevacizumab is administered at dosages of 10mg/kg/IV every 2 weeks. The first treatment session can last 90 mins but other sessions can last between 30 mins and 60 mins [29]. The common side effects associated with the drug are hypertension, diarrhea, kidney failure, blood clots, hemorrhage, anemia, weak immune system due to reduced white blood cells and increased risk of heart failure and stroke. Patients may also experience chest pain, headaches, and dry or inflamed skin. Another drug used for targeted therapy is Everolimus (Afinitor), which disables a protein called mTOR that helps the tumor to grow and divide [28]. mTOR is involved in signal transduction, which is when a cell receives signals from its environment that are transferred into the cell for a response. It promotes cell growth and division, so the drug acts to inhibit its activities to prevent such action. Everolimus (Afinitor) is used for subendymal giant cell astrocytomas (SEGAs), which cannot be removed by surgery alone [30]. The drug is taken orally on a daily basis. Side effects are nausea, loss of appetite, increased blood sugar and cholesterol levels, rash on the skin, and fluid build-up. Other risks associated with Everolimus (Afinitor) are lung damage, which can cause breathlessness. The use of nano-engineered enzymes is another type of targeted therapy. This type of treatment facilitates the attachment of the enzymes to the tumor cells and allows the body's natural cell degradation process to occur [27]. This will naturally remove the tumor from the body. According to a study conducted by [31], cannabis oil is used to reduce and eliminate the brain tumors. Generally, targeted therapy is more effective in treating brain cancer than other methods as it can be specialized to the patient's treatment requirements [27]. A drug called Larotrectinib is also being developed as a targeted therapy drug against brain cancer, although the drug is not specifically for brain cancer targeted therapy. The drug targets TRK (tropomyosin receptor kinase) fusion proteins found in 90% of rare cancers [32], such as glioblastoma. TRK is involved in cell growth, communication, and signaling, and mutation of this protein results in it causing uncontrolled growth for tumors. Larotrectinib has shown promising results, although the drug is still under development. Overall, targeted therapy offers a major advantage because of its ability to specifically target tumors without damaging normal tissue. It is also noninvasive. However, this treatment technique comes with its own disadvantages. The tumors can develop resistance to the drugs. This happens when the target proteins on the tumors mutate, thereby rendering the drug ineffective because it has no receptors to attach to and attack. Tumors can also develop other growth pathways that do not necessarily require the growth proteins targeted by the drugs. Targeted therapy drugs are also more difficult to develop because they are made to be specific to a marker on the tumor.

3.2.4 Radiotherapy

Radiotherapy involves the exposure of controlled doses of gamma rays or X-rays to the brain with the intent of destroying or slowing down the growth of cancerous tumors with minimal damage to normal tissue. This technique is often the standard of brain cancer treatment, especially for patients with meningeal tumors, glioblastoma, and astrocytic tumors. It can be used to relieve symptoms caused by the tumor, including headaches caused by the tumor exerting pressure on the skill or pushing against tissue. Radiotherapy can be divided into external beam radiation therapy (EBRT) and internal radiation therapy called brachytherapy [33,34].

In EBRT, radiation beams originate from an external machine to the brain tumor. A linear accelerator (LINAC) machine is used as the source of radiation delivering X-rays (photons) to the tumor. Before the treatment session, a patient has to go through a simulation, which involves planning for the treatment course. During the simulation process, the patient may be required to wear a gown and asked to lie on a table. A mask will then be made by placing a wet sheet of plastic mesh onto the patient's face, then molding it around the face. The mask is intended to immobilize the patient so that they maintain the same position during treatment sessions. Sometimes, straps are used to hold the face in place. Markings are then made on the skin or mask using permanent ink to guide the radiation therapist on the patient's position during the treatment session. Computed tomography (CT) or MRI scans are used to determine the beam target area [35]. After mapping the treatment area, the oncologists complete the planning stage of the treatment. In this stage, they determine the dosage to be used, the shapes and angle of the beams based on the tumor shape and size. After completing the treatment simulation and planning, the patient's treatment schedule is made and sessions are booked. During the treatment session, the patient lies on the LINAC machine table with their personalized mask holding them in the position determined in the simulation stage. The LINAC machine delivers radiation beams to the patient as it rotates around the patient to aim the beams from different angles. The radiation oncologists control the machine and monitor the patient from an adjacent room. The dosage depends on the tumor location, tumor size, patient response, and the treatment plan, but is usually approximately 45–60 Gy [36]. A treatment session is about 15 mins [37] and can last between 2 and 7 weeks [37]. EBRT can be further divided into three-dimensional conformal radiation therapy (3-D CRT), image-guided radiation therapy (IGRT), and intensity-modulated radiation therapy (IMRT) [38].

3-D CRT allows for a 3-D view of the tumor, thus enabling the oncologist to program the LINAC machine to deliver the radiation beams according to the exact shape and size of the tumor. This method is effective for tumors that are irregularly shaped and causes minimum damage to healthy tissue.

IGRT is similar to 3-D CRT and uses imaging techniques to precisely track the tumor location prior to each treatment, as the tumor may have moved, which ensures that the radiation beams are still targeted toward the tumor and avoid healthy tissue.

IMRT is a more advanced form of 3-D CRT. It delivers small radiation beams at different angles with different intensities. It uses advanced computer algorithms to match the complex tumor shapes. The fact that radiation can be delivered at different intensities means that some areas can be targeted using higher dosages, while minimizing damage to healthy tissue.

Radiation may also be given during surgery (intraoperative radiation therapy) for tumors that cannot be removed completely via a surgical approach [38]. External radiation therapy is an advantageous treatment technique with a high success rate of 69% [39]. It is painless and can reach areas that surgery is unable to access. Radiation does not remain in the body during and after the treatment. EBRT is fairly priced compared with other treatment techniques with costs of about $10,000–$25,000 in India [40] and $10,000–$50,000 for other parts of the world [26].

Brachytherapy, on the other hand, is the insertion of radioactive material near or into the tumors of the brain. The radiation material emits radiation that kills the tumor. Higher radiation doses can be used for brachytherapy with minimal damage to normal tissue due to the placement of the radioactive isotopes. These isotopes come in the form of a seed, pellet, ribbon, wire, needle, capsule, balloon, or tube. [41]. To insert these implants into the brain area, surgery is required or they may be inserted via tubes. The catheters are placed near the tumor, using imaging such as X-rays or CT to determine the exact tumor location and destination of the implants. The implants can be temporary, only remaining in the brain for minutes or days, or they can stay in the brain permanently. The oncologist will determine how long the implant should stay in the brain depending on the tumor size, location, and overall health. It is also dependent on whether the patient is undergoing other treatments. Brachytherapy can be divided into two categories: high-dose radiation (HDR) and low-dose radiation (LDR). The radiology oncologist will decide which one is better suited for the patient, but LDR is mainly used for low-grade cancers while HDR is for high-grade cancers.

LDR brachytherapy involves the radioactive isotope emitting lower dosages of radiation but over a longer period of time. This can take between several hours to a few days on an inpatient basis. If it is permanent, the radioactive material gives off radiation, but ultimately stops after a few weeks or months. They can stay in the brain as they no longer emit harmful radiation. The disadvantage is that during this radioactive period, the patient emits radiation and is therefore encouraged to exercise social distancing.

Intracavity balloon-catheter brain brachytherapy is a new treatment using a gliasite radiation Therapy system (RTS) that has been approved by the Food and Drug Administration. It uses an inflatable balloon catheter to deliver a dose of radiation to the tumor during surgery. A low dosage of radiation is administered through a catheter and into a balloon, which then exposes the tumor to radiation. Iotrex solution, which is an aqueous saline solution of molecularly bound radioactive iodine [42], is used as the radiation source. Prescribed radiation doses are approximately 40–60 Gy, measured at 0.5–1 cm from the balloon surface [42]. Intracavity balloon-catheter brain brachytherapy is used for malignant brain tumors, such as high-grade gliomas, brain metastases, and recurrent tumors.

High-dose radiation therapy makes use of radioactive material that emits higher dosages of radiation. This is allowed for about 30 min [43]. This process can be repeated for 1–2 weeks with the catheter being kept in place or removed after each treatment [44]. Iodine-125 is the most commonly used radioactive isotope, but recently Cesium began to be used as an alternative. Due to the localization of the radioactive material with the brain tumors, there is minimal damage to healthy brain tissue [45]. The process is minimally invasive but there may be a risk of bleeding and infection. The catheters may also be uncomfortable for the patient.

The disadvantage of using radiation to treat patients is that hair loss may occur, as well as fatigue, hearing problems, loss of appetite, confusion, and irritation on the skin. Mild to severe brain damage may occur due to some normal tissue damage. Immediately after treatment, swelling, vision problems, nausea, and headaches may occur as side effects. Dead tissue may also accumulate in the brain because the brain does not have an efficient lymph system to remove dead cells. This build-up of dead cells causes inflammation and possible brain damage, which may require surgery to remove the cells.

3.2.5   Radiosurgery

Radiosurgery is the use of precise, high-energy beams concentrated on the brain tumors without interacting with healthy tissues. No incisions are needed for this technique and it is an advanced form of radiation therapy that differs with standard radiotherapy in terms of the level of accuracy and precision of the beams as well as the high dosages used in a single session. For brain cancer treatment, the radiosurgery procedures employed are gamma knife, LINAC, and proton beam therapy. The procedures are largely the same as those utilized when undergoing external beam radiation therapy. First, the patient attends a pretreatment session that involves positioning the patient using a frame for the head and restraints to prevent movement. Markings or tattoos are also used to guide the oncologist on the correct head position. CT or MRI scans will be used to map the brain so as to determine the tumor location, size, and shape to regulate the beam pathway and dosage required [46]. Once the treatment plan is finalized and all the criteria have been set, the patient will start the treatment. The treatment sessions are also similar in the way the patient lies on the radiation machine table in the position determined by the simulation stage. Contrast material is then injected via an IV line as well as a sedative to help the patient relax. CT scans or X-rays are used to ensure the patient is in the exact position for treatment. The machine will then deliver doses of radiation to the patient. The radiation used is the major difference between the use of gamma knife and proton beam therapy.

Gamma knife uses beams of highly focused gamma-ray radiation. The machine has about 192 radiation sources, which emit tiny beams that converge on the tumor without harming healthy tissue. These can be given in short daily treatments over several weeks or in one session using high dosages. This procedure is conducted on an outpatient basis with one session lasting from 15 min to 4 h [47]. Gamma knife is mainly used for malignant brain cancers such as meningiomas, glial tumors, and pituitary adenomas [48]. It can cost between $45,000 and $60,000 [49].

Proton-beam radiation therapy delivers radiation in the form of proton beams. Proton beams are specific because they release most of their energy at a specific depth after being emitted by a machine called a cyclotron. This depth can be controlled by the oncologist and keeps the radiation from affecting normal tissue, whereas with X-rays, the radiation can be absorbed by the body before reaching the tumor and as it leaves the body, which damages healthy tissue. The session lasts about 20 min over a period of 5–7 weeks [50,51]. The downside of proton beam therapy is that it is a very expensive procedure costing about $100,000–$250,000 [52]. This is mainly due to the fact that the machine used for proton beam therapy is very expensive, costing in the range of $35,000,000–$125,000,000 [53], meaning only a limited number of health institutions can even afford such a treatment. The procedure also requires highly skilled oncologists to determine the depth and dosages.

Overall, radiosurgery is also advantageous because it requires one session or a few sessions at the most, whereas traditional radiotherapy requires more treatment sessions spread over a number of weeks because of the high dosages used. It also has less severe side effects than traditional radiotherapy because of its precision and accuracy, which ensures that healthy tissue is not damaged. However, common side effects of radiosurgery are nausea, vomiting, swelling of the brain, seizures, headaches, hair loss, vision problems, and skin redness. Radiosurgery is also more expensive than traditional radiotherapy.

3.2.6 Hyperthermia

Hyperthermia is the use of heat to damage brain cancer tumors by using microwaves, laser, radio waves, or ultrasound. The heat from hyperthermia treatment causes tumor cells to be more sensitive to radiation or chemotherapy as it prevents cellular repair of the tumor and increases blood flow to the tumor, thus making it easier for drug delivery. The heat can also destroy the tumor cells completely. It is used for malignant astrocytoma and glioblastoma, which are very sensitive to heat. The type of hyperthermia approach used for brain cancer is interstitial local hyperthermia, in which the heat is delivered to the tumor area via a probe [54]. The patient first undergoes a pretreatment stage where the brain is mapped using imaging such as MRI in order to determine the anatomy of the tumor. An incision is made on the scalp and the skull is drilled in order to expose the brain to the probe or catheter. Imaging devices such as CT or MRI provide navigation through real-time images for the physicians to ensure the probe is placed in proximity to the tumor. Different devices have been employed for thermal ablation and hyperthermia of the brain, depending on the type of energy they emit. Such devices include thermal probes, radiowave/microwave emitters, lasers, and ultrasound.

Thermal probes are the most basic type of heat delivery devices used, which are simply heat conductors inserted into the brain. Radiowave or microwave hyperthermia uses electromagnetic waves to give off heat onto the tumor. High-intensity focused ultrasound uses transducer arrays to give off focused ultrasound, which induces heating with great accuracy. The most commonly used is laser interstitial thermal therapy, which uses laser light to damage the tumor cells. The photons of the laser are absorbed by the tumor cells, where they release heat energy [55].

An optimal temperature of about 43°C is applied for hyperthermia or temperatures and >50°C for thermal ablation. Higher temperatures may cause damage to other tissues of the brain [54,56]. A treatment session can last 60 mins [57] with the whole treatment duration standing between 3–5 weeks [58]. Advantages of hyperthermia treatment are that it is the least costly treatment with prices of $2,500–5,000 [59] and can be used for high-grade tumors, tumors that are inoperable by surgery, or tumors that are in proximity to sensitive brain structures. Hyperthermia can also boost the immune response to the cancer. The procedure is minimally invasive, painless, and nontoxic, as no drugs or radiation are used. It is also precise but keeping temperatures constant is often difficult, especially because the brain is very sensitive to heat. Hyperthermia also increases the effectiveness of other treatments such as chemotherapy and radiation therapy. Side effects of hyperthermia include swelling, burns, blisters, blood clots, and necrosis.

3.3 Materials and methodology

Fuzzt PROMETHEE is a multi-criteria decision-making method used across many disciplines of research. In fuzzy PROMETHEE, the input data are treated as fuzzy numbers, with the purpose of considering the uncertainty contained in the data [8]. This decision-making tool aids the decision maker in identifying the best alternative from a group of options according to his/her goals and their own understanding of the problem.

This method is particularly important to give clarity on decisions that are difficult to quantify or compare, especially if two or more individuals have different perspectives as in this study. A patient, physician, researcher, or a medical device company has different perspectives on the elements that make a treatment technique the most or the least favorable.

In order to evaluate the brain cancer treatment alternatives, we collected the main criteria of the alternatives, including the radiation dose, side effects, success rate, recovery time, session duration, cost of the treatments, and cost of the machine (Table 3.1). Because of the treatment alternatives' vague criteria, we defined the criteria with a triangular fuzzy linguistic scale, as seen in Table 3.2. In addition, we used the same fuzzy linguistic scale to calculate the importance degree of the criteria. Then, we applied the Yager index to defuzzify the fuzzy data of the criteria and, lastly, we applied the visual PROMETHEE decision lab software to obtain the results.

The linguistic scale of importance shows the sets of triangular fuzzy numbers. Each fuzzy set is given a scale for evaluation (graded), depending on how the set will define the criteria investigated. The seven criteria investigated in this study have been assigned an importance rating from VH to VL in relation to a corresponding fuzzy set. The specific criteria for each fuzzy set are selected based on how criteria make a specific therapy technique superior to others, e.g. success rate is of paramount importance since it is the goal of any treatment

TABLE 3.1 Treatment alternatives, common criteria, and their corresponsing values.

Criteria	Cost of treatment ($)	Cost of machine ($)	Radiation dose (Gy)	Session duration (min)	Recovery time (week)	Side effects	Success rate
Surgery	H	0	0	VH	L	M	H
Radiation therapy	H	H	M	VL	H	VH	H
Chemo-therapy	H	L	VH	L	L	VH	M
Targeted therapy	M	0	0	M	M	H	M
Radiosur-gery	VH	VH	M	M	VL	H	H
Hyper-thermia	VL	VH	0	L	VL	H	M

VH: Very high; H: High; M: Medium; L: Low; VL: Very low

TABLE 3.2 Linguistic scale of importance.

Linguistic scale for evaluation	Triangular fuzzy scale	Evaluation criteria
Very high (VH)	(0.75, 1, 1)	Radiation dose, side effects, success rate
High (H)	(0.50, 0.75, 1)	Recovery time, session duration
Medium (M)	(0.25, 0.50, 0.75)	Cost of treatment, cost of machine
Low (L)	(0, 0.25, 0.50)	
Very low (VL)	(0, 0, 0.25)	

technique, so it is given a fuzzy set with the highest grading, which in this case is VH. Other criteria are also assigned to their fuzzy sets in a similar way. Furthermore, a Gaussian preference function was used for the comparison of the alternatives corresponding to their parameter. Visual PROMETHEE decision lab program was then applied and the results are presented in the next section.

3.4   Results and discussion

According to the selected criteria and assigned weights, by using the linguistic scale of importance and the Gaussian preference function, surgery is the most preferred alternative of the six brain cancer therapy techniques investigated in this study. Targeted therapy is also among the best alternatives after surgery, while hyperthermia, radiation therapy, chemotherapy, and radiosurgery are the least effective methods respectively, as demonstrated by their increasing negative net flow (Table 3.3).

The results obtained in this study are subject to change according to the weighting perspective and the inclusion of more criteria. The linguistic scale of importance is crucial for the results and this scale changes according to the interests of different individuals. For instance, a patient would give more weighting to success rate, recovery time, and cost of treatment, while a company would give more weighting to the cost of the machine. Due to the flexibility in weighting, our decision-making process in this study takes a balanced perspective across the healthcare spectrum, incorporating patients, medical personnel, and companies.

In addition to this research, future research can be expanded by taking into account a combination of therapy techniques. This is because brain cancer treatment usually involves a combination of treatments; for example, some patients undergo surgery followed by radiation therapy or chemotherapy. Some patients also use a combination of drugs for their treatments, which is not included in this study. This combination of treatments may improve success rates and change other criteria such as dosages and recovery times (Fig. 3.1).

TABLE 3.3 Complete ranking of brain cancer treatment alternatives.

Ranking	Alternative	Positive outranking flow	Negative outranking flow	Net flow
1	Surgery	0.0084	0.0015	0.0069
2	Targeted therapy	0.0067	0.0013	0.0054
3	Hyperthermia	0.0052	0.0050	0.0002
4	Radiation therapy	0.0028	0.0047	-0.0019
5	Chemotherapy	0.0033	0.0058	-0.0025
6	Radiosurgery	0.0006	0.0086	-0.0080

The main features of the PROMETHEE method are simplicity, clarity, and stability. A significant advantage of the PROMETHEE method over other multiple decision-making methods is that it allows the decision-maker to make a particular choice in terms of an evaluation factor or to limit the evaluation factor to the values it determines. It performs this function by using preference functions. The PROMETHEE method takes into account the preference function determined by the decision makers for each criteria. Thus, each criteria can be evaluated in a different way. This allows a better decision. In daily life, some criteria are expressed linguistically and it is very difficult to model them numerically. The disadvantage of the PROMETHEE method is that it is not appropriate for these criteria, which are expressed in a nonprecise linguistic manner. The use of the fuzzy PROMETHEE method, which is an improved version of the PROMETHEE method, in cases where input values are generally based on the thoughts and experiences of decision makers and are determined qualitatively, makes the data suitable for analysis.

3.5 Conclusions

This study utilizes fuzzy PROMETHEE as a decision-making tool for brain cancer treatment techniques using a compilation of fuzzy input data. This approach is seen to be effective as concluded in previous studies and will provide a convenient and calculated decision for patients and their respective healthcare providers when selecting the appropriate treatment procedure. The use of fuzzy PROMETHEE also provides increased accuracy and practicality as it uses criteria from individual treatment methods as input data. The results from this research will go toward improving healthcare services for both patients as well as physicians.

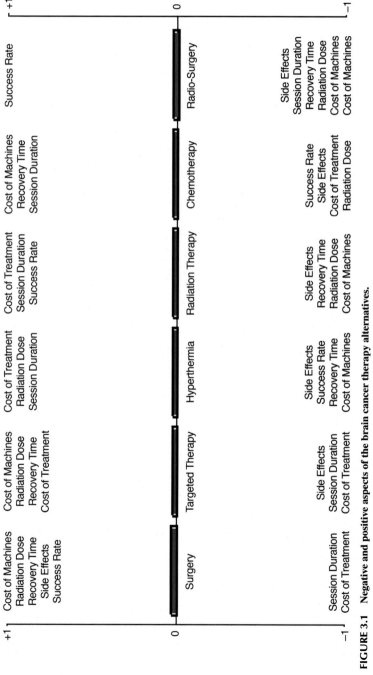

FIGURE 3.1 Negative and positive aspects of the brain cancer therapy alternatives.

References

[1] Tumor types. National Brain Tumor Society (2019), http://braintumor.org/brain-tumor-information/understanding-brain-tumors/tumor-types/. Accessed 31.1.19.

[2] Charles Patrick Davis, Brain cancer types, symptoms, causes, types, stages, and treatment. eMedicineHealth (2019), https://www.emedicinehealth.com/brain_cancer/article_em.htm. Accessed 31.1.19.

[3] Quick brain tumor facts. National Brain Tumor Society (2019), http://braintumor.org/brain-tumor-information/brain-tumor-facts/. Accessed 31.1.19.

[4] Brain tumor. Cancer.Net (2019), https://www.cancer.net/cancer-types/brain-tumor. Accessed 31.1.19.

[5] A. Digalwar, P. Date, Development of fuzzy PROMETHEE algorithm for the evaluation of Indian world-class manufacturing organisations, Int. J. Serv. Oper. Manage. 24 (3) (2016) 308.

[6] D. Uzun Ozsahin, I. Ozsahin, A fuzzy PROMETHEE approach for breast cancer treatment techniques, Int. J. Med. Res. Health Sci. 7 (5) (2018) 29–32.

[7] D. Uzun Ozsahin, B. Uzun, M. Musa, A. Helwan, C. Wilson, F. Nurçin, N. Şentürk, I. Ozsahin, Evaluating cancer treatment alternatives using fuzzy PROMETHEE method, Int. J. Adv. Comp. Sci. Appl. 8 (10) (2017) 177–182.

[8] M. Moreira, C. Dupont, M. Vellasco, PROMETHEE and fuzzy PROMETHEE multicriteria methods for ranking equipment failure modes. 15th International Conference on Intelligent System Applications to Power Systems, 2009.

[9] Brain tumor—treatment options. Cancer.Net (2019), https://www.cancer.net/cancer-types/brain-tumor/treatment-options. Accessed 31.1.19.

[10] Neurosurgery for brain tumours. The Brain Tumour Charity (2020), https://www.thebraintumourcharity.org/understanding-brain-tumours/treating-brain-tumours/adult-treatments/neurosurgery-adults. Accessed 30.4.20.

[11] Craniotomy. Mayfield Clinic (2019), https://mayfieldclinic.com/pe-craniotomy.htm. Accessed 31.1.19.

[12] Surgery for brain tumors and spinal cord tumors. Amp.cancer.org (2020), https://amp.cancer.org/cancer/brain-spinal-cord-tumors-adults/treating/surgery.html. Accessed 30.4.20.

[13] Surgery for brain tumours—Brain and spinal cord tumours. Cancer Research UK (2020), https://www.cancerresearchuk.org/about-cancer/brain-tumours/treatment/surgery/remove-brain-tumour. Accessed 30.4.20.

[14] Neurosurgery for brain tumours. The Brain Tumour Charity (2019), https://www.thebraintumourcharity.org/understanding-brain-tumours/treating-brain-tumours/adult-treatments/neurosurgery-adults/. Accessed 31.1.19.

[15] Surgery for adult brain and spinal cord tumors. Cancer.org (2019), https://www.cancer.org/cancer/brain-spinal-cord-tumors-adults/treating/surgery.html. Accessed 31.1.19.

[16] About your ventriculoperitoneal (VP) shunt surgery. Memorial Sloan Kettering Cancer Center (2020), https://www.google.com/amp/s/www.mskcc.org/cancer-care/patient-education/about-your-ventriculoperitoneal-vp-shunt-surgery%3Famp. Accessed 30.4.20.

[17] Survival rates for selected adult brain and spinal cord tumors. Cancer.org (2020), https://www.cancer.org/cancer/brain-spinal-cord-tumors-adults/detection-diagnosis-staging/survival-rates.html. Accessed 3.5.20.

[18] D. Mangiardi, My meningioma story and me. Brain-Surgery.com (2020), https://brain-surgery.com/discharged-after-brain-surgery-what-happens/. Accessed 30.4.20.

[19] Childhood brain and spinal cord tumors treatment overview. National Cancer Institute (2019), https://www.cancer.gov/types/brain/patient/child-brain-treatment-pdq. Accessed 31.1.19.

[20] Chemotherapy treatment—Brain tumour (primary). Cancer Research UK (2020), https://www.cancerresearchuk.org/about-cancer/brain-tumours/treatment/chemotherapy/treatment. Accessed 30.4.20.

[21] Chemotherapy for adult brain and spinal cord tumors. Cancer.org (2019), https://www.cancer.org/cancer/brain-spinal-cord-tumors-adults/treating/chemotherapy.html. Accessed 31.1.19.

[22] Temozolomide. The Brain Tumour Charity (2019), https://www.thebraintumourcharity.org/understanding-brain-tumours/treating-brain-tumours/adult-treatments/temozolomide. Accessed 31.1.19.

[23] Chemotherapy for a brain tumour. Macmillan.org.uk (2020), https://www.macmillan.org.uk/cancer-information-and-support/treatments-and-drugs/chemotherapy-for-a-brain-tumour. Accessed 30.4.20.

[24] Glioblastoma—we need better treatments, but can we afford them? Medicynic (2020), https://www.google.com.cy/amp/s/medicynic.com/2010/04/19/glioblastoma-we-need-better-treatments-but-can-we-afford-them/amp/. Accessed 30.4.20.

[25] What is the cost of brain surgery in India? Quora.com (2020), https://www.quora.com/What-is-the-cost-of-brain-tumor-surgery-in-india. Accessed 30.4.20.

[26] How much does brain cancer treatment cost? CostHelper (2020), http://health.costhelper.com/brain-cancer.html. Accessed 30.4.20.

[27] M. Gil-Gil, C. Mesia, M. Rey, Bevacizumab for the treatment of glioblastoma, Clin. Med. Ins.: Oncol. (2013) 7.

[28] Targeted therapy for adult brain and spinal cord tumors. Cancer.org (2019), https://www.cancer.org/cancer/brain-spinal-cord-tumors-adults/treating/targeted-therapy.html. Accessed 31.1.19.

[29] Avastin (Bevacizumab): side effects, how it works, and more. Breastcancer.org (2020), https://www.breastcancer.org/treatment/targeted_therapies/avastin. Accessed 30.4.20.

[30] Targeted therapy for adult brain and spinal cord tumors . Cancer.org (2020), https://www.cancer.org/cancer/brain-spinal-cord-tumors-adults/treating/targeted-therapy.html. Accessed 30.4.20.

[31] Cannabis oil use: growing phenom appears safe, helpful in brain cancer. Cure Today (2019), https://www.curetoday.com/articles/cannabis-oil-use-growing-phenom-appears-safe-helpful-in-brain-cancer. Accessed 31.1.19.

[32] Larotrectinib exhibits antitumour effects in some rare cancer patients. Curebraincancer.org.au (2020), https://www.curebraincancer.org.au/news/1586/larotrectinib-exhibits-anti-tumour-effects-in-some-rare-cancer-patients. Accessed 30.4.20.

[33] A guide to modern radiotherapy. Society of Radiographers (2019), https://www.sor.org/learning/document-library/guide-modern-radiotherapy. Accessed 31.1.19.

[34] Radiation therapy for brain tumors. Texas Oncology (2019), https://www.texasoncology.com/types-of-cancer/brain-cancer/radiation-therapy-for-brain-tumors#Hyperthermia. Accessed 31.1.19.

[35] Linear accelerator. Ele.uri.edu (2019), http://www.ele.uri.edu/Courses/bme181/S13/2_ShaneR_2.pdf. Accessed 31.1.19.

[36] Brain cancer treatment protocols: treatment. Emedicine.medscape.com (2020), https://emedicine.medscape.com/article/2005182-overview#a1. Accessed 30.4.20.

[37] American Brain Tumor Association (2020), http://www.abta.org/secure/conventional-radiation.pdf. Accessed 30.4.20.

[38] Getting external beam radiation therapy. Google.com (2020), https://www.google.com/amp/s/amp.cancer.org/treatment/treatments-and-side-effects/treatment-types/radiation/external-beam-radiation-therapy.html. Accessed 30.4.20.

[39] Access NCBI through the World Wide Web (WWW). Mole. Biotech. (1995) 3 (1) 75.

[40] What is the cost of radiotherapy in India? (2020), https://www.quora.com/What-is-the-cost-of-radiotherapy-in-India. Accessed 30.4.20.

[41] Brachytherapy? Kansas University Cancer Center (2020), https://www.kucancercenter.org/cancer/cancertreatments/brachytherapy?reloadts=158777280020010. Accessed 30.4.20.

[42] Brachytherapy intracavitary balloon catheter for brain cancer. Bluecrossnc.com (2020), https://www.bluecrossnc.com/sites/default/files/document/attachment/services/public/pdfs/medicalpolicy/brachytherapy_intracavitary_balloon_catheter_for_brain_cancer.pdf. Accessed 3.5.20.

[43] Brain tumor treatment. Radiologyinfo.org (2020), https://www.radiologyinfo.org/en/info.cfm?pg=thera-brain. Accessed 3.5.20.

[44] https://www.ncbi.nlm.nih.gov/pmc/articles/PMC3354996/#!po=4.58333.

[45] S. Schwarz, N. Thon, K. Nikolajek, M. Niyazi, J. Tonn, C. Belka, et al. Iodine-125 brachytherapy for brain tumours - a review, Rad. Oncol. 7 (1.) (2012).

[46] M. Kocher, A. Wittig, M. Piroth, H. Treuer, H. Seegenschmiedt, M. Ruge, et al. Stereotactic radiosurgery for treatment of brain metastases, Strahlentherapie und Onkologie 190 (6) (2014) 521–532.

[47] Radiotherapy for a brain tumour. Macmillan.org.uk (2020), https://www.macmillan.org.uk/cancer-information-and-support/treatments-and-drugs/radiotherapy-for-a-brain-tumour. Accessed 30.4.20.

[48] M. Anderson, Q&A: Gamma knife® radiosurgery for brain tumors. MD Anderson Cancer Center (2020), https://www.mdanderson.org/publications/cancerwise/qa-gamma-knife-radiosurgery-for-brain-tumors.h00-158517990.html. Accessed 30.4.20.

[49] How much does stereotactic radiosurgery cost? CostHelper (2020), http://health.costhelper.com/stereotactic-radiosurger.html. Accessed 30.4.20.

[50] The Brain Tumor Charity (2020), https://www.thebraintumourcharity.org/brain-tumour-diagnosis-treatment/treating-brain-tumours/child-treatments/proton-beam-therapy/. Accessed 30.4.20.

[51] Tcr.amegroups.com (2020), http://tcr.amegroups.com/article/viewFile/1120/html/6182http://tcr.amegroups.com/article/viewFile/1120/html/6182. Accessed 30.4.20.

[52] Proton therapy is coming to the UK but what does it mean for patients? (2020), https://amp/scienceblog.cancerresearchuk.org/2013/09/16/proton-therapy-is-coming-to-the-uk-but-what-does-it-mean-for-patients/amp/. Accessed 30.4.20.

[53] Peter Shadbolt, Is proton therapy the 'magic bullet' for cancer? CNN (2020), https://edition-m.cnn.com/2015/01/22/tech/mci-proton-therapy/index.html. Accessed 30.4.20.

[54] Y. Jiahang Sun, Treatment of malignant glioma using hyperthermia. PubMed Central (PMC) (2019), https://www.ncbi.nlm.nih.gov/pmc/articles/PMC4145998/. Accessed 31.1.19.

[55] Thermal therapy approaches for treatment of brain tumors in animals and humans. Researchgate (2020), https://www.researchgate.net/publication/318889667_Thermal_Therapy_Approaches_for_Treatment_of_Brain_Tumors_in_Animals_and_Humans. Accessed 30.4.20.

[56] J. Raizer, K. Fitzner, D. Jacobs, C. Bennett, D. Liebling, T. Luu, et al. Economics of malignant gliomas: a critical review, J. Oncol. Pract. 11 (1) (2015) e59-e65.

[57] J. Sun, M. Guo, H. Pang, J. Qi, J. Zhang, Y. Ge, Treatment of malignant glioma using hyperthermia, Neural. Regen. Res. 8 (29) (2013 Oct 15) 2775.

[58] Hyperthermia treatment for brain tumors. Barnes-Jewish Hospital(2020), https://www.barnes-jewish.org/Medical-Services/Neurology-Neurosurgery/Brain-and-Spine-Tumors/Hyperthermia-Treatment-for-Brain-Tumors. Accessed 30.4.20.

[59] Hyperthermia or heat treatment brain tumour patients. Peoplepledge.com.au (2020), http://peoplepledge.com.au/blog/the-cost-of-hyperthermia-or-heat-treatment-like-oncothermia-in-australia-for-individuals-with-brain-tumours/. Accessed 30.4.20.

Chapter 4

Evaluation of stage IV brain cancer treatment techniques

Dilber Uzun Ozsahin[a,b,c], Ali Denker[d], Ayse Gunay Kibarer[b] and Serife Kaba[b]

[a]DESAM Institute, Near East University, Turkish Republic of Northern Cyprus, Nicosia Turkey; [b]Department of Biomedical Engineering, Near East University, Turkish Republic of Northern Cyprus, Nicosia, Turkey; [c]Medical Diagnostic Imaging Department, College of Health Sciences, University of Sharjah, Sharjah, United Arab Emirates; [d]Department of Mathematics, Near East University, Turkish Republic of Northern Cyprus, Nicosia, Turkey

4.1 Introduction

Brain cancer is a cancerous (malignant) or noncancerous (benign) growth of abnormal cells in the brain. Brain cancer can appear either as a primary brain tumor that begins in the brain and is very unlikely to advance to other areas of the body, or as a secondary tumor, which is caused by cancer that starts in a different part of the body and advances to the brain.

During a brain cancer diagnosis, the doctor checks various parts of the brain by examining muscle strength, reflexes, and capacity to distinguish between hot and cold (i.e., response to stimulus by the brain). Other tests can also be carried out using magnetic resonance spectroscopy, PET scan, SPECT scan, etc. The results of these tests will determine the extent of growth of the cancerous cells; this stage of the cancer gives information regarding the state of the cancer and the extent to which it has advanced beyond the brain. Brain tumors have four stages [1]. These stages are based on how fast the tumor grows and its capacity to penetrate neighboring tissues. Grade I and II are called low-grade tumors because they grow slowly, while grade III and IV are usually the fastest developing tumors, called high-grade tumors. Low-grade tumors are classified as noncancerous, while high-grade tumors are classified as cancerous. However, it is important to note that both low-grade and high-grade tumors are associated with health risks, so regular checkups are important.

According to the Brain Tumor Treatment Conditions and Treatments of UCSF Medical Center (2019), the treatment of brain cancer is dependent on the following factors:

- Type of tumor

Applications of Multi-Criteria Decision-Making Theories in Healthcare and Biomedical Engineering.
http://dx.doi.org/10.1016/B978-0-12-824086-1.00004-9

- Location of the tumor in the brain
- Size of the tumor and how far it has advanced
- How abnormal the cells appear
- Overall health and fitness condition of patient

This report focuses on treatment techniques of stage IV brain cancer, which is a high-grade tumor. Glioblastoma is the most frequent high-grade tumor [2]; it either directly appears as a stage IV glioblastoma or is developed from a low-grade astrocytoma (Stage II or III) [3]. The Central Brain Tumor Registry of the United States stated that glioblastoma accounts for 14.9% and 55.4% of all primary brain tumors and of all gliomas, respectively [4]. It represents the highest number of cases of all malignant tumors with an estimated 12,390 new cases predicted in 2017. Glioblastoma can be treated with the following techniques [4–6]:

- Surgery: Surgery is performed to extract as much tumor as feasible
- Radiotherapy: Use of radiation to target cells that cannot be removed by surgery
- Chemotherapy: Use of drugs to kill the tumor cells
- Targeted drug therapy: Swallowed orally or administered intravenously into the vein
- Tumor treating fields (TTF)

4.2   Stage IV brain cancer treatment techniques

4.2.1   Surgery

Surgery is the basic treatment for removing brain tumors without causing severe damage. Stage IV cancer requires chemotherapy or radiotherapy, even after surgery. The following are the reasons why surgery is carried out for stage IV cancer:

- To obtain tissue that will be examined with a microscope in order to confirm diagnosis.
- To remove all or as much tumor as possible.
- To relieve intracranial pressure caused by the cancer (intracranial pressure is the measurement of the pressure of brain tissue and the cerebrospinal fluid surrounding the brain and spinal cord). [7]

There are three categories of surgery for brain tumors:

- Biopsy
- Craniotomy
- Shunt

Biopsy: In a biopsy, a small section (representative part) is cut out of the tumor in order to verify the diagnosis [4]. A pathologist examines the specimen of the tumor and determines the type of the tumor. It can be performed as either a surgical procedure to extract the tumor or it can be applied just to obtain a specimen of the tumor for further experimentation.

Two approaches are followed when carrying out a biopsy. One is an open biopsy, which involves uncovering the tumor and extracting a small part of it, while the other is a needle biopsy, in which a laceration is made into the skin, and then an opening is made into the skull [8]. Then, the doctor inserts a slender curved needle into the skull and guides the needle into the area of interest. A small amount of the tumor is extracted and, finally, the needle is withdrawn.

For precision of the needle biopsy procedure, scanning equipment like MRI and CT is used. This is called Stereotactic (accurate positioning of probes inside the brain to obtain 3-dimensional images) needle biopsy and is used for patients with profound or numerous tumors.

Craniotomy: A craniotomy is the surgical removal of part of the bone from the skull to expose the brain. Specialized tools are used to remove the section of bone called the bone flap. The bone flap is temporarily removed, then replaced after the brain surgery is done.

This simply involves cutting into the skull: crani- (skull), -otomy (cutting into). In this procedure, a part of the scalp is trimmed and a laceration is made through the skin. Specially designed apparatuses are used by the operating surgeon(s) to remove a part of the skull to reveal the region of brain where the tumor is located. After this procedure, the bone is replaced and the scalp gets stitched.

During the procedure, the operating surgeons guide themselves with their anatomical knowledge and their perception of the preoperational scans.

Shunt: A shunt is a hollow tube placed in the brain to remove excess fluid within the brain and reduce intracranial pressure within the skull.

A catheter is inserted through a ventricle in the brain; the other end of the catheter tube is run beneath the scalp, toward the neck. From there, it runs to one more body cavity where the fluid is depleted. The right atrium of the heart and the abdominal cavity are the cavities used for the fluid drainage. Some shunts are provisional and are removed after the procedure is finished, although others are left in place.

4.2.2 Radiation therapy

Radiation therapy is a cancer treatment that uses high energy X-ray beams to destroy the cancer tumor. Radiation therapy for stage IV brain cancer is used as the only treatment for cancer or in combination with other treatments such as surgery or chemotherapy. Three treatment techniques for stage IV brain cancer involving radiotherapy are listed below:

1. External beam radiation therapy (EBRT): This involves an apparatus that controls a radiation beam from the outer part of the body.
2. Stereotactic radiation therapy (gamma knife therapy): This directs a radiation dose directly at the tumor with the aid and guidance of a computer and

image. It offers the potential to provide a sort of radiation boost to a portion of the radiation field in newly diagnosed patients or to treat a small recurrence while being an alternative to open surgery [4,9,10].
3. Brachytherapy: A radioactive implant is implanted near or in the tumor.

External beam radiation therapy (EBRT): With this technique, radiation beams are delivered from outside the body to a tumor. A radiation machine called a linear accelerator (Linac) is used in this therapy. The Linac produces high radiation beams that infiltrate the tissues, and it delivers the radiation to the region of the patient's tumor. Radiation oncologists control the machine to make sure radiation beams are delivered straight to the tumor and kill the cancer cells while saving neighboring tissues.

Proton radiation therapy: This is an advanced form of EBRT that uses protons rather than x-rays or Gamma rays to treat cancer. It is also a type of external-beam therapy which delivers radiation from a machine outside the body.

Stereotactic radiation therapy (gamma knife therapy): This is a noninvasive technique for the treatment of stage IV brain cancer. It is most often used for small tumors and uses high doses of focused pencil-thin radiation beams targeting only the tumor with the assistance of imaging techniques such as MRI and CT.

SRT can be used as a follow up to EBRT or surgery. Gamma knife therapy and Linac are machines used to deliver SRT.

Internal radiation therapy (brachytherapy): This involves the implantation of radioactive material near or into the tumor. This attacks the tumor from the inside. In this technique, it is delivered into the tumor bed through a catheter with the guidance of CT and MRI. A tumor bed is the tissue that surrounds the cancerous tumor and provides it with oxygen, nutrients, and growth factors.

Depending on the type of isotope used, the implant is left in place permanently or temporarily, according to the type of cancer.

4.2.3 Chemotherapy

Chemotherapy is a type of treatment used for stage IV brain cancer that uses drugs to eradicate tumor cells. It works by stopping or slowing the growth of the tumor, which grows and divides quickly. This technique involves orally swallowing a pill or making use of Intravenous (IV) or injection.

Systematic chemotherapy: In this technique, antidrugs are administered orally in pill form or injected into the vein. For some types of brain cancers, chemo drugs are given straight through the cerebrospinal fluid (CSF: a luminous, colorless fluid) into the brain or spinal column. To help with this, doctors surgically install a unique container beneath the scalp and this container is connected to a tube that passes through a ventricle of the brain where the CSF circulates.

Local chemotherapy: In this technique, a dissolvable Gliadel wafer containing carmustine (an anticancer chemotherapy drug) is used to treat certain types of brain tumors. It is placed and left in the cavity after removing a part of tumor during the surgery. The wafers slowly discharge the chemotherapy for a considerable number of days. Since local chemotherapy is carried out very close to the brain tumor at the resection area, it helps the drug absorption at the tumor site in addition to minimizing the side effects.

After making use of one of these techniques, patients are scanned every 2–3 months with an MRI of the brain during effective treatment.

4.2.4 Targeted drug therapy

This technique identifies the tumor's particular genes, proteins, or surrounding tissues that add to a tumor's advancement or continuity. Drugs that are designed to target cancer cells are used in this therapy [11]. They do not affect the normal cells and prevent the cancer tumor from growing and increasing. A recent survey has shown that tumors have various objectives. In order to choose the most efficient treatment, doctors usually run different tests to analyze the genes, proteins, and alternative components in the tumors. This makes it possible for the doctors to determine the most effective treatment.

Small-molecule drugs: This type of drugs blocks the process that helps cancer cells grow, spread, and multiply. This type of therapy is concentrated on terminating the angiogenesis. Angiogenesis is the development of new blood vessels and the tumor needs nutrients from blood vessels to grow and spread. Antiangiogenesis therapy starves the tumor and stops its development. An angiogenesis inhibitor that is in drug form is usually swallowed by the patient.

Monoclonal antibodies: This drug blocks a particular target usually located outside of cancer cells or in the region surrounding the cancer. In this technique, the functioning of the drug is comparable to when a plastic plug is connected to an electric socket. The plug will stop the electricity from streaming out of the socket. It can also dispatch harmful materials straight to cancer cells. These drugs are usually given intravenously (IV).

4.2.5 Alternating electric field therapy or tumor treating fields (TTF)

According to research, exposing some types of tumor cells to alternating electric fields, which are also known as tumor-treating fields, can interfere with the cell's ability to grow and spread. Tumor-treating fields provide mitotic capture and apoptosis of promptly dividing cells. A portable and wearable device known as an Optune is used in this therapy. This device, which generates electric fields, is still being researched but has undergone various stages of approval by the FDA already. The device delivers therapy over transducer arrays, which are usually fixed on the patient's scalp. To be able to use the Optune, the patient's head must be shaved. The arrays give low-intensity, varying electric fields called TTFields.

The Optune system is a wearable device that was approved by the FDA in 2011 for glioblastoma multiforme (GBM). The Optune is used in consolidation with chemotherapy called temozolomide (TMZ) on patients who have a diagnosed GBM on the condition that they have had surgery to remove the tumor.

In this technique, the head is first shaved and four sets of electrodes are planted on the scalp. The electrodes are linked to a battery pack kept in a backpack and are worn for most of the day. They set up mild electric currents called tumor-treating fields (TT fields) and the TT fields are delivered to the location of the tumor cells.

A new study has also proven that patients who were treated with a combination of electric field therapy and chemotherapy have a higher life expectancy than patients who were treated only with chemotherapy.

4.3 Materials and methods

4.3.1 Fuzzy logic

Obtaining crisp data that accurately defines real life situations is a very challenging endeavor. Additional to this challenge is the description of imprecise data or information that is not completely true or false. Boolean logic has a system of extremities, a situation is either true (1) or false (0), and no room for in-between states or uncertainties is allowed. In fuzzy logic, however, a machine can treat situations with a degree of uncertainty attached. For instance, Boolean logic in treating the temperature of a room will either state that the room is hot or cold, but at what point does the temperature cross over from being cold to being hot? On the other hand, Fuzzy logic provides the alternatives of very cold, cold, warm, hot, very hot, and so on in order to solve the problem associated with uncertainty.

Fuzzy logic is preferred and has an advantage over other methods, such as predictable logic, Bayesian control, probability theory, classical theory, and many other such systems because fuzzy logic provides a system of computing with words, meaning that words are used to represent numbers in computing and reasoning.

4.3.2 Multi-criteria decision making

Multi-criteria decision making (MCDM) also referred to as multiple criteria decision analysis (MCDA), is a research area that involves the analysis of various available choices in a situation or research area which spans daily life, social sciences, engineering, medicine, and many other areas. MCDM is one of the most popular decision-making tools utilized in various fields [12–22].

MCDM analyses the criteria to determine whether each criterion is a favorable or unfavorable choice for a particular application. It also attempts to compare this criterion, based on the selected criteria, against every other available option in an attempt to assist the decision maker in selecting an option with the minimal compromise and maximum advantages. The criteria used in the analyses of these criteria can be either qualitative or quantitative criteria.

Division of MCDM can be made into two categories based on the method used to determine the weight of each alternative.

1. **Compensatory decision making:** Involves the evaluation of the criteria, of the criteria including the weak points and strong points of the criteria and allows the strong points of each criteria to compensate for the weak points, thereby putting all the criteria of the criteria into consideration. An example of a compensatory decision-making tool is the analytical hierarchy process (AHP)—a technique used mostly when the environment for the analysis is complex. It is used in the comparison of criteria that are difficult to quantify.
2. **Outranking decision making:** This method compares the criteria of the criteria in couples in order to determine which criteria ranks higher than the others based on the comparisons. A popular example of an outranking decision-making method is elimination and choice expressing reality (ELECTRE), a method that is used to choose, rank, and sort alternatives to solve a problem.

4.3.3 Preference ranking organization method for enrichment evaluations (PROMETHEE)

PROMETHEE is a multi-criteria decision making tool that allows a user to analyze and rank available alternatives based on the criteria of each alternative. PROMETHEE compares the available alternatives based on the selected criteria.

PROMETHEE is preferred over other multi-criteria decision methods for reasons such as:

- PROMETHEE can be used to handle qualitative and quantitative criteria simultaneously.
- PROMETHEE deals with fuzzy relations, vagueness, and uncertainties.
- PROMETHEE is easy to handle and provides the user maximum control over the weights of the criteria.

Using PROMETHEE requires only two pieces of information from the decision maker: information regarding the weights of the selected criteria, and the preference function to be used in comparing the alternatives' contribution with regard to each criteria.

Different preference functions (Pj) are available on PROMETHEE for the definition of different criteria. The preference function defines the difference between the evaluations with two alternatives (a and at) in relation to a specific criteria and a preference degree ranging between 0 and 1. The preference functions for practical purposes that can be used at the discretion of the decision maker include: usual function, V-shape function, level function, U-shape function, linear function, and Gaussian function. A detailed description of the preference functions that are used, their ranking, and how to make a decision on which function best suits a scenario was presented by J.P. Brans et al [23]. A quick summary of the preference functions is shown in Table 4.1 [23]. Generally,

TABLE 4.1 Complete ranking of brain cancer treatment alternatives.

Complete ranking	Alternative	Positive outranking flow	Negative outranking flow	Net flow
1	Tumor-treatment fields (TTF)	0.3448	0.0500	0.2948
2	Targeted drug therapy	0.2010	0.2154	–0.0144
3	Radiation Therapy	0.2643	0.3004	–0.0361
4	Surgery	0.1373	0.2163	–0.0790
5	Chemotherapy	0.1194	0.2848	–0.1654

type III (V-shape) and type V (linear) preference functions are mostly used for data with quantitative measures, while type I (usual shape) and type IV (level) preference functions are mostly used for qualitative data.

4.4 Results

The results obtained are shown in Fig. 4.1.

Table 4.1 shows a complete ranking of brain cancer treatment techniques based on the criteria used.

4.5 Discussion

The treatment of brain tumors is important for patients who are affected by this abnormal growth of cells, so that they can live for a few more months. The treatment method applied to stop the growth of cancer cells is also very important. Furthermore, the patients obtain the maximum results from the treatment and they feel comfortable while the treatment is being administered.

Fuzzy PROMETHEE affords the decision maker the opportunity to analyze the different criteria, including criteria that do not consist of crisp data, as well as the opportunity to perform this analysis with the available criteria.

PROMETHEE is a multi-criteria decision aid system that can be applied in a variety of contexts. However, PROMETHEE, as well as other similar techniques, must currently never be used in place of an actual expert opinion. The purpose of using such a system should be only to provide extra supporting data. Moreover, results gained from such a system should not be followed blindly if they disagree with the expert opinion. This is especially true for the healthcare sector. The fuzzy logic and fuzzy-PROMETHEE techniques were applied by [13–22].

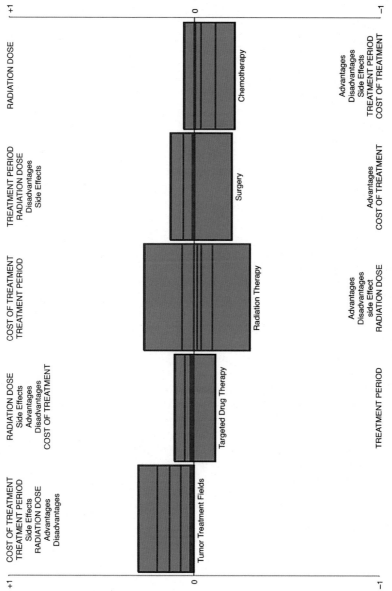

FIGURE 4.1 **Ranking results of treatment methods for stage IV brain cancer.**

4.6 Conclusions

With the application of fuzzy PROMETHEE in the analysis of the different treatment techniques for brain cancer, we were able to achieve reliable results that could aid both physicians and patients in terms of starting a favorable treatment option. The results of this analysis showed that radiation therapy is the most preferable treatment with a favorable cost of treatment, treatment time, time per session, survival rate, and cost per session.

The findings of this study provide the decision maker the opportunity to view the available treatment techniques available along with the features that make them favorable or not.

Using fuzzy PROMETHEE gives the user a wide range of control over the criteria, taking into account the condition and preferences of the patient. Fuzzy PROMETHEE can determine the optimum combination of criteria. Based on the criteria preferences of the decision maker, PROMETHEE is best able to compare devices. Depending on the information fed into PROMETHEE, the decision maker can gain invaluable insights and acquire information to aid in the decision-making process. As a result, late-stage brain tumor patients can receive the best available treatment and techniques available to them. They can have confidence that they are receiving the best scientifically proven treatment, treatment that is both tailored to their individual needs and also constantly being reviewed and adjusted. Therefore, hospital doctors and administrators can use it as an alternative information source for malignant brain tumor patients.

References

[1] https://www.nhs.uk/conditions/brain-tumours/.

[2] F. Lieberman, Glioblastoma update: molecular biology, diagnosis, treatment, response assessment, and translational clinical trials, F1000Res 6 (2017) 1892.

[3] Y. Rajesh, I. Pal, P. Banik, S. Chakraborty, S.A. Borkar, G. Dey, et al. Insights into molecular therapy of glioma: current challenges and next generation blueprint, Acta. Pharmacol. Sin. 38 (5) (2017) 591–613.

[4] L.G. Tataranu, V. Ciubotaru, T.L. Cazac, O. Alexandru, O.S. Purcaru, D.E. Tache et al. (2018). Current trends in glioblastoma treatment. IntechOpen. DOI: 10.5772/intechopen.75049.

[5] https://www.cancer.org.au/about-cancer/types-of-cancer/brain-cancer.html.

[6] https://www.cancer.net/cancer-types/brain-tumor/treatment-options.

[7] https://www.cancer.net/cancer-types/brain-tumor/treatment-options.

[8] https://mayfieldclinic.com/pe-brainbiopsy.htm.

[9] Brain tumor treatment. Radiologyinfo.org. (2019). https://www.radiologyinfo.org/en/info.cfm?pg=thera-brain.

[10] R. Crowley, N. Pouratian, J. Sheehan, Gamma knife surgery for glioblastoma multiforme, Neurosurg. Focus 20 (4) (2006) E17.

[11] https://www.cancer.net/navigating-cancer-care/how-cancer-treated/personalized-and-targeted-therapies/understanding-targeted-therapy.

[12] A. Mardani, A.M.D. Jusoh, K. Nor, Z. Khalifah, N. Zakwan, A. Valipour, Multiple criteria decision-making techniques and their applications – a review of the literature from 2000 to 2014, Economic Research-Ekonomska Istraživanja. 28 (1) (2015) 516–571.

[13] D. Uzun Ozsahin, B. Uzun, M. Sani, A. Helwan, C.N. Wilson, F.V. Nurcin, N. Şentürk, I. Ozsahin, Evaluating cancer treatment techniques using fuzzy PROMETHEE method, Int. J. Adv. Comput. Sci. Appl. 8 (2017) 177–185.

[14] D. Uzun Ozsahin, I. Ozsahin, A fuzzy PROMETHEE approach for breast cancer treatment techniques, Int. J. Med. Res. Health Sci. 7 (5) (2018) 29–32.

[15] D. Uzun Ozsahin, N. Isa, B. Uzun, I. Ozsahin, Effective analysis of image reconstruction algorithms in nuclear medicine using fuzzy PROMETHEE, 2018 Advances in Science and Engineering Technology International Conferences (ASET), 2018.

[16] D. Uzun Ozsahin, B. Uzun, M. Musa, N. Şentürk, F. Nurçin, I. Ozsahin, Evaluating nuclear medicine imaging devices using fuzzy PROMETHEE method, Procedia Comput. Sci. 120 (2017) 699–705.

[17] D. Uzun Ozsahin, B. Uzun, M. Sani, I. Ozsahin, Evaluating X-ray-based medical imaging devices with fuzzy preference ranking organization method for enrichment evaluations, Int. J. Adv. Comput. Sci. Appl. 9 (3) (2018).

[18] D. Uzun, B. Uzun, M. Sani, A. Helwan, C. Nwekwo, F. Veysel, et al. Evaluating cancer treatment alternatives using fuzzy PROMETHEE method, Int. J. Adv. Comput. Sci. Appl. 8 (10.) (2017) 10.14569/ijacsa.2017.081024.

[19] I. Ozsahin, T. Sharif, D. Ozsahin, B. Uzun, Evaluation of solid-state detectors in medical imaging with fuzzy PROMETHEE, J. Instrum. 14 (1) (2019) C01019–C11019, doi: 10.1088/1748-0221/14/01/c01019.

[20] E. Kiral, B. Uzun, Forecasting closing returns of Borsa Istanbul Index with Markov Chain Process of fuzzy states, PressAcademia 4 (1) (2017) 15–24, doi: 10.17261/pressacademia.2017.362.

[21] B. Uzun, E. Kıral, Application of Markov chains: fuzzy states to gold price, Procedia Comput. Sci. 120 (2017) 365–371, doi: 10.1016/j.procs.2017.11.251.

[22] M. Maisaini, B.I. Uzun, D. OzsahinUzun, Evaluating lung cancer treatment techniques using fuzzy PROMETHEE approach, Advances in Intelligent Systems and Computing 896, Springer, 2019, pp. 209–215.

[23] J. Brans, P. Vincke, B. Mareschal, How to select and how to rank projects: The Promethee method, Eur. J. Oper. Res. 24 (2) (1986) 228–238.

Chapter 5

Analysis of early stage breast cancer treatment techniques

Dilber Uzun Ozsahin[a,b,c], Sameer Sheshakli[b], Ayse Gunay Kibarer[b], Ali Denker[d] and Basil Bartholomew Duwa[b]
[a]DESAM Institute, Near East University, Turkish Republic of Northern Cyprus, Nicosia, Turkey; [b]Department of Biomedical Engineering, Near East University, Turkish Republic of Northern Cyprus, Nicosia, Turkey; [c]Medical Diagnostic Imaging Department, College of Health Sciences, University of Sharjah, Sharjah, United Arab Emirates; [d]Department of Mathematics, Near East University, Turkish Republic of Northern Cyprus, Nicosia, Turkey

5.1 Introduction

Gene alteration is one among many factors that is responsible for many abnormal cell problems in the human body system. This may result to cell growth (tumor) that may bring about changes in the body cells. The gene in the center of the cell is known as the center of operations because of its ability to be positioned in the center of each cell inside the nucleus. The cells in the body tend to interchange themselves in a prearranged manner, which enables new, healthy cells to replace old, dying cells. This however, may cause other genes to "step up" or "step down" due to the transformation in the cell. After these changes in the gene the cell obtains the ability to duplicate itself in an uncontrolled manner, creating more complicated and ineffective series of cells that tend to generate a tumor [1]. Breast cancer (BC) is a disease that affects the cells in the breast and is caused by defective genes, which lead to rapid uncontrolled growth of the cells. The BC can be divided into various forms, depending on the type of the cells altered and converted to cancer. Stage II BC can be treated using any of the multimodality treatment techniques available, such as chemotherapy, surgery, targeted therapy, radiation therapy, and hormonal therapy. However, BC therapy depends hugely on the stage of the cancer, age of the patient, and other medical conditions of the patient [2].

In this study, average patient's age and weights are considered. We also describe different techniques involved in the evaluation, which are explained in the next section.

Applications of Multi-Criteria Decision-Making Theories in Healthcare and Biomedical Engineering.
http://dx.doi.org/10.1016/B978-0-12-824086-1.00005-0

5.1.1 Surgery

Stage II BC is recorded to be treated using lumpectomy or mastectomy. In a mastectomy, both breasts are partially or completely removed, while lumpectomy involves the removal of the cancerous infected part and the surrounding tissue. However, reappearance of the disease occurs when the breast undergoes lumpectomy than the mastectomy. It is also advisable that those who undergo lumpectomy also be treated with radiation therapy.

"Breasts-conserving therapy" is a process by which lumpectomy is combined with radiation therapy. This method is shown to give a positive outcome in treating BC compared to the lumpectomy treatment.

The Roxxane Nelson study shows that the surgery cost for stage II BC (includin breast-conserving surgery and mastectomy) has been reduced from $10,552 to $3,592 [3]. Surgery involving the stage II BC is of two types: the lumpectomy gives patients the liberty of leaving the hospital after surgery is carried out. It is also advisable for the patient to rest after this procedure, which will enable the patient to have a fast healing process. It is also preferable for the patient to abstain from exertion, such as exercise, driving, household chores, or stressful situations.

The other type of surgery is the mastectomy, which is the total removal of the breast tissue due to cancerous cells. In this method of surgery a strict supervision is given to the patient at the hospital for 5–7 days (sometimes as long as 3 weeks). This process speed the healing processes. The process includes a strict follow-up appointment with the surgeon and any observable complications are referred for proper assessment by the surgeon. In addition, it is important for the patient to be aware of the healing time which may take a long time for a proper healing, especially when the lymph nodes are removed during the surgery [4]. Sometimes, the mastectomy is performed to rebuild the breast through a process that preserves a breast skin to grow naturally, this process is referred as skin-sparing mastectomy. The healing process after stage II BC surgery depends on the type of surgery done, the size of the tumor, and other noticeable features. The duration for curing the disease and the patient's recovery time can vary; it may take 3–12 weeks for complete healing to occur.

The side effects of the various types of surgery have similar characteristics; it is however possible to have different side effects, which may depend on the patient's type of body and body system. In other words, the more time is needed for a surgery, the more discomfort a patient will experience. A patient may take longer to recover from surgery, which may cause infection when it is not well managed. Fluid may gather in the patient's breast or armpit, which may cause the place to swell, a condition known a seroma may occur. In other conditions the patient may develop a prolonged swelling of the arm, breast, hand, and chest, known as lymphoedema. The whole process can be uncomfortable and may reduce locomotion in the patient and may increase risks of skin contamination. Surgery is considered beneficial and the best alternative to treat and completely remove cancerous cells from the system. Thus, the surgeon removes the tumor and some of the cells in the margins, which are used to check for the spread of the disease. If the cancer cells are not spread to the margin, the tissue is now called the "clear margins" [5].

Preoperative chemotherapy, is one of the treatment methods that is administered to patients with BC stage II or sometimes stage III; this therapy aims to minimize the cells infected and increase the possibility of performing "breast-conserving surgery or the lumpectomy" instead of the mastectomy process. Studies have shown that breast-conserving surgery and mastectomy are difficult surgeries yet a significant number of patients recover successfully. These surgeries are said to be effective and reduce risk of reappearance of the cancer between 1% and 3%, respectively.

Survival rate (SR) is also the percentage of people who live for a minimum of 5 years after diagnosed with the BC. This is compared with previous results obtained from a large number of people with BC. Women with stage II BC have approximately a 5-year SR, which is up to 93% [6].

5.1.2 Radiation therapy

BC radiation therapy is done using X-rays at high energy, or using protons or any other atoms at high intensity in order to kill cells, especially rapidly reproducing tumor cells. Cancerous cells have a greater tendency to be affected by radiation therapy than normal cells. Radiation therapy can be applied in two different ways: External radiation, in which the machine delivers radiation from outside the body to the cells that are affected by cancer; external type of radiation is considered to be the most used type. Internal radiation (brachytherapy) is a radiation that is done using wire or implanted device, placed close to the cancerous cells. A radiation delivery device can be implanted for short periods of time inside the breast close to the cells affected by cancer, these radiation materials start emitting radiation to kill any cancerous cell that has produced inside the breast [7]. The cost of radiation therapy cannot be determined precisely, depending on the location. A study in February 2016 in the United States on 4425 women with BC stage I/II proved that the average costs permitted by the medical insurance company for the patient in that year after diagnosis of BC was $82, 121 [8]. Even though radiation therapy lowers the risk of recurrence of the tumor, it does not completely get rid of the risk. The risks of radiation therapy differ depending on two factors: the first one is the type of treatment and the second factor is which breast tissue is infected. The patient should be informed that side effects may be noticeable toward the end of radiation treatment. And should be informed that it may take weeks after completing the sessions for side effects to clear up [9]. Hence, the side effects are different from one patient to another. Each patient may be affected with one or more of the side effects, such as tiredness. This symptom is more common among patients who undergo radiation therapy; fatigue will become worse as the treatment continues. And the patient should keep in mind that this symptom may persist for some weeks after finalizing the treatment. Reddening or darkening of skin may occur; radiation will affect the skin in different ways. Since it is a type of energy it may cause redness on the skin located over the treated area, and it may cause darkness or discoloration on the skin where the rays from the radiation leave the body. Furthermore, radiation causes the loss of hair from different parts of the body, and may cause problems in moving the arm and shoulder if the surgery is done at the armpit area, and may cause breathing, heart, and bone problems which might last for many years (in rare cases) and may increase the risk of bone breaks [10].

Radiation time will be determined by the radiation treatments used. Many modern procedures are needed to lower the number of sessions to less than 33. Usually the radiation causes continue for several weeks after the surgery. According to the American Cancer Society, the 5-year SR for stage II BC is around 85%–90% for women who have completed radiation treatment [11]. Individual trial assessing the radiation use after breast surgery "NSABP B-06 trial (I)" exposed a BC return rate of 35% in the lumpectomy-alone group compared to 10% in the lumpectomy plus radiation group [12].

5.1.3   Chemotherapy

The chemotherapy method is applied in stage II cancer. It can also be applied before and after surgery. It is applicable before surgery if the defected cells are observed to blowout of the lymph nodes located in the armpit or to adjacent bones. In this case, the process of chemotherapy is termed as "neoadjuvant therapy."

Recorded studies have shown chemotherapy administered after surgery to minimize the possible reappearance and occurrence of the disease (BC). It is an established fact to note that the early detection of BC by X-ray or Eco may lead to reduce the possible healing. Chemotherapy is also ranked highest compared to other treatments in terms of cost. Also, a similar study done in the United States (February 2016) found chemotherapy, which costs about $13, 373 for one patient with stage II BC for a one-day treatment, to be the most expensive treatment when compared with other methods [13].

Furthermore, the risks and benefits involved in using chemotherapy can be categorized as two major treatments before surgery. This process may involve total removal and termination of cells and tumors without removing the breast. This will reduce the reccurrence of the BC cells. On a general perspective, the chemotherapy process is done sequentially four times, every 15 days or every 7 days for every 8 weeks. However, it takes from 16 to 21 weeks for a complete cycle to finish chemotherapy process.

In many cases, an oncologist supervises the patient's bloodwork before a session. This is recorded with numerous side effects of chemotherapy in patients. However, this side effect depends on the patient. These side effects include anemia (low red blood cell), alopecia (loss of hair), hemorrhage (bleeding), and also low white blood cell count.

Chemotherapy is beneficial depending on the patient's prognosis. Patients with the worst prognosis benefit from the greatest SR, while the individuals with the best prognosis acquire the least gain in SR. A clear study case conducted in the United States (2008) shows 182, 460 patients diagnosed with BC, in which 156, 991 had stage II BC among women younger than 48 years old [7].

5.1.4 Targeted therapy

Targeted therapy involves the use of drugs that target cancer cells that work effectively to change the cell matrix and assist the body to control and develop cancer [14]. This method of therapy is applicable when the cancerous injuries contain HER2 receptors (human growth factor 2), which can make cells, grow and divide. It is recorded that 15 out of 100 BCs are HER2 positive cancer. Major drugs used for the treatment are trastuzumab (Herceptin), otherwise known as Herzuma, which is a monoclonal counteracting agent. The monoclonal antibodies are tied to proteins in the cancer cell. The Herceptin drug is used every 3 weeks for a whole year. Meanwhile the trastuzumab is not administered to patients who are diagnosed with heart problems but can be administered before surgery. It is also administered to patients diagnosed with secondary BC or sometimes for patients with recurrent BC. It is recorded that two thirds of patients with cancer in the US take intravenous (IV) or oral medications, which have an SR of at least 5 years after the diagnosis. Another study published on May 18, 2015, in the *Journal of Clinical Oncology* recorded that from 2001 to 2011, BC patients had an increased insurance cost of more than $14, 000. Subsequently, patients' expenses and self-spending for cancer drugs has also risen to about $200 per patient per month for oral drugs and $900 per month for injectable antigens in cancer treatment. Meanwhile, total insurance payments each year in 2010 were approximately $65, 000 per patient. However, side effects of this medication can be mild but severe for some patients. Among the severe side effects of trastuzumab or pertuzumab is heart failure experienced by a considerable number of women. This effect is not observed after the medicine is discontinued. Another effect of pertuzumab is diarrhea, experienced by patients. Pregnant women are not advised to use these drugs, which may tend to cause miscarriage [8].

The advancement in science and research in oncology has made target therapy to become the first technological approach in treating cancer. Similar studies have also shown the effectiveness of the target treatment, having the highest percentage in terms of tumor elimination and mitigation of cancer in advanced cases, which tends to target cancer cells and eliminate them without affecting the normal cells. Thus, other side effects when compared to other technologies are considered moderate. The targeted treatment is considered to be superior when we compare it with chemotherapy drugs. A study by scientists and researchers recorded that a 5-year SR of BC patients is observed after the tumor is discovered. In other words, the average 5-year SR in people with BC is 90% and the SR of 10 years among patients is 83%. Hence, if the disease is found only in the breast, it is observed that the percentage for a 5-year SR in women with cancer is 99%, while the SR decreases to 85% for patients that the cancer spreads to the lymphatic lymphoma. Furthermore, the duration of the targeted treatment depends on the response of the tumor to the treatment, the size of the tumor, and also the location of the tumor in the body. Some tumors are very responsive to drugs, such as trastuzumab, while others are not. This generally depends on the developed mechanism and approach used for the proper treatment [9].

5.1.5 Hormone therapy

Hormone therapy (HT) is one therapy that is considered to be systematic. In other words, it influences many numbers of cancerous cells in the human body, which also include the breast. Some types of BC are hidden by some of the body hormones. A clear example is estrogen, which is affiliated with body receptors that exist in ER+ and PR+ cancerous cells. These hormones assist in growth development. Hormone therapy is applied in patients who have positive hormonal receptors (ER+, PR+). This process is not recommended for patients with negative hormonal receptors (ER−, PR−). Tamoxifen is a drug that is resisted by estrogen.

Toremifene (Fareston) is a selective estrogen receptor modulator that operates in a similar manner to tamoxifen, and is used to cure metatastic BC when tamoxifen is not active in treatment. Both tamoxifen and toremifene are administered orally. Another drug used to prevent and damage estrogen receptors is fulvestrant. Furthermore, drugs manufactured by nonprofit organizations, such as letrozole (Femara), anastrozole (Arimidex), and exemestane (Aromasin) work well in treating BC; these drugs are pills taken on a daily basis for 5 years to reduce the possible reccurrence of BC. Sometimes, adjuvant therapy is applied after the surgery and after taking taxomifen, and is recorded as a successful and better alternative [10].

For premenopausal women, ovary closure or removal eliminates the central source of estrogen that makes the ovaries active in postmenopause. This allows the application of other hormonal treatments such as aromatase inhibitors. Recent randomized clinical trials (RCTs) compared the effects of anastrozole (Femara) to tamoxifen in postmenopausal women having BC and showed advanced hormonal sensitivity attached to both factors. Another study on RCT experiments revealed the substantial advantage of letrozole when compared to tamoxifen in terms of the response rate and the incidence of breast-conserving surgery based on utility and toxicity data; therefore tamoxifen can be replaced by anastrozole or letrozole. Meanwhile, the cost analysis was carried out to give estimates on the costs attached to the use of tamoxifen. The cost per patient for litrosol and anastrozole is $2883 and $2847, respectively, compared to tamoxifen is $2258, respectively. When we analyze the costs and benefits of the drugs, the additional cost for the year was free of progression, which is $12, 500 and $19, 600 for letrozole and anastrozole when compared with tamoxifen; moreover, both letrozole and anastrozole are perfect replacements for tamoxifen in preparation of the therapy. The side effect of tamoxifen and toremifene may be that the woman becomes temperamental and has mood swings. Another symptom experienced by ladies who have BC is the presence of a tumor that causes pain and swells the muscles and bones.

In the case of fulvestrant (Faslodex) the common side effects of treatment are hot flashes, night sweats, headache, nausea, pain in the areas of injection, and pain in bones. Despite having these side effects, fluvestrant is known to prevent estrogen, which can theoretically cause bone weakness for an extended period of time. Fulvestrant is applicable in postmenopausal patients. In other words, suppression of the ovaries can cause sign of menopause. Hormonal therapy (HT) for BC is applied in treating hormone-sensitive cancers where estrogen and hormones such as progesterone encourage the growth of certain types of BC. These cancers are referred by physicians as BC+ because of the estrogen receptors. However, the physician determines if the cancer is positive for estrogen receptors through analyzing the cancer cells. Hence, hormonal therapy for BC can assist in preventing the re-emergence of cancer, thus reducing the risk involved in cancer transmission to other breast tissues. Meanwhile, when the progress of cancer is either reduced or stopped, the tumor size is minimized before surgery is performed. The American Cancer Society gives the following percentages for the 5-year SR: stage 0: 100%; stage 1: 100%; stage 2: 93%; stage 3: 72%; stage 4 (the scattered stage): 22%.

This measurement included females with the foremost positive and negative HER2 cancers. This means a female with positive BC that causes rheumatoid arthritis may likely have a greater chance of survival. The duration of treatment largely depends on whether it is administered before or after surgery and also depends on the condition of the tumor. Postmenopausal patients receive hormone therapy after surgery for positive BC for a period of 5 year; this is called hormone therapy. In many cases, the physician recommends different medications to be applied after 5 years. However, if the patient applied tamoxifen for 5 years, the physician may recommend aromatase inhibitor for a specific period of time. It is recorded that postmenopausal patients undergo hormone therapy prior to surgery for early-stage BC with a hormone therapy duration of 12–37 weeks prior to the surgery. This process may largely depend on the patient's condition; this makes the treatment plan differ from another patient's [11].

5.2 Fuzzy logic and PROMETHEE

Fuzzy logic method involves having a corresponding value that provides mechanism in applying information and knowledge. This process focuses on the conclusion by using unspecified expressions such as the linguistic variables solely determined by words. Another technique is the preference ranking organization method for enrichment evaluations (PROMETHEE), known as the multicriteria decision-making method that allows finite values (numbers) to be ranked. This approach is known to be simple and effective. Proposed by Brans, the

TABLE 5.1 Visual PROMETHEE application for breast cancer treatment alternatives.

Criteria *Therapies*	Cost ($)	Healing time	Survival rate	Side effect	Benefits	Risks
Surgery	L	W	H	L	M	M
Radiation Therapy	M	W	L	M	M	L
Chemotherapy	H	M	H	H	M	H
Targeted therapy	H	M	H	L	M	M
Hormone therapy	H	Y	VH	M	L	L

H = high, M = medium, L = low; W = weeks, M = months, VH = very high, Y = years

PROMETHEE method is a type of strategy that relates with great substitution of sets. This enables an effective comparison among an outlined set. Fuzzy and the PROMETHEE methods combined is referred to as an analytical technique with a better structure to compare linguist or fuzzy input [12]. This study represents a collective data with numbers represented on the table below. The data is applied to the PROMETHEE lab program; V-shape function represents the healing time; cost, SR, side effects, benefits, and risks are outlined in a linear function [15–23] (Table 5.1).

5.3 Results

The table below shows the visual PROMETHEE decision lab program applied and the results obtained.

Table 5.2 shows the complete ranking of the stage II BC treatments, respectively, to the chosen criteria, which is necessary for the performance of the therapy.

TABLE 5.2 Visual PROMETHEE results for colon cancer treatment.

Complete ranking	Alternatives	Positive outranking flow	Negative outranking flow	Net flow
1	Surgery	0.0656	0.0068	0.0588
2	Targeted therapy	0.0279	0.0218	0.0061
3	Hormone therapy	0.0382	0.0452	–0.0070
4	Radiation therapy	0,0369	0,0481	–0.0112
5	Chemotherapy	0,0128	0,0595	–0,0467

5.4 Conclusion

The BC stage II was analyzed using fuzzy PROMETHEE method for the alternatives such as surgery, chemotherapy, hormone therapy, radiation therapy and targeted therapy. This study shows the strengths and the weaknesses of the breast cancer stage II treatment techniques. And surgery was considered as the most promising and effective technique amongst the other alternatives based on the selected importance weights for the criteria. Surgery was also recorded as the safest and the most reliable method. The targeted therapy was considered as the second most promising method. Hormone therapy was also recorded as the third most effective method. In addition, another recorded effective therapy was radiation therapy. The least measured effective method recorded was the chemotherapy method. The fuzzy PROMETHEE method assisted us in achieving good decision results on BC treatment stage II patients. This decision was based on results and ranking, which helped the decision makers, such as patients, physicians, and even organizations, in selecting a better clinical approach as the perfect treatment.

References

[1] S.J. Pettitt, D.B. Krastev, I. Brandsma, A. Dréan, F. Song, R. Aleksandrov, C.J. Lord, Genome-wide and high-density CRISPR-Cas9 screens identify point mutations in PARP1 causing PARP inhibitor resistance, Nat. Communicat. (2018, May 10) 9.

[2] P. Goss, J. Ingle, S. Martino, et al., Updated analysis of the NCIC CTC MA.17 randomized placebo (P) controlled trial of letrozole (L) after five years of tamoxifen in postmenopausal women with early stage breast cancer. Proceedings from the 40th Annual Meeting of the American Society of Clinical Oncology Best of Oncology Symposium, New Orleans, LA, 2004 (Abstract #847).

[3] A. Feinstein, J. Long, P. Soulos, X. Ma, J. Herrin, K. Frick, et al. Older women with localized breast cancer: costs and survival rates increased across two time periods, Health Affairs 34 (4) (2015) 592–600.

[4] A. De Groef, M. Van Kampen, E. Dieltjens, et al. Effectiveness of postoperative physical therapy for upper-limb impairments after breast cancer treatment: a systematic review, Arch. Phys. Med. Rehab. 96 (6) (2015) 1140–1153.

[5] S. Muneer, J. O'Shaughnessy, 2006 highlights from the 42nd Annual Meeting of the American Society of Clinical Oncology; Atlanta, GA, June 2006, Clin. Breast Canc. 7 (3) (2006) 215–220.

[6] N. Davidson, Diseases of the Breast: Jay R. Harris, Marc E. Lippman, Monica Morrow, Samuel Hellman, eds. Philadelphia: Lippincott-Raven, 1996. 1047 pp., illus. $169. ISBN 0-397-51470-0, J. Nat. Canc. Inst. 89 (1) (1997) 85–185.

[7] Early Breast Cancer Trialists' Collaborative GroupEffects of chemotherapy and hormonal therapy for early breast cancer on recurrence and 15-year survival: an overview of the randomised trials, Lancet 365 (9472) (2005) 1687–1717.

[8] C.X. Ma, M. Dickler, Treatment approach to metastatic hormone receptor-positive, HER2-negative breast cancer: Endocrine therapy. https://www.uptodate.com/contents/treatment-approach-to-metastatic-hormone-receptor-positive-her2-negative-breast-cancer-endocrine-therapy?source=search_result&search=everolimus&selectedTitle=5~150. Accessed 10.11.2020.

[9] R. Nahta, D. Yu, M. Hung, G. Hortobagyi, F. Esteva, Mechanisms of disease: understanding resistance to HER2-targeted therapy in human breast cancer, Nat. Clin. Pract. Oncol. 3 (5) (2006) 269–280.

[10] Cancer.org, Hormone therapy for breast cancer. American Cancer Society (2019), https://www.cancer.org/cancer/breast-cancer/treatment/hormone-therapy-for-breast-cancer.html. Accessed 20.02.19.

[11] Breastcancer.org, Hormonal therapy: what to expect. Breastcancer.org (2019), https://www.breastcancer.org/treatment/hormonal/expect. Accessed 10.12.18.

[12] J.P. Brans, P. Vincke, B. Mareschal, How to select and how to rank projects: the PROMETHEE method, Eur. J. Operat. Res. 24 (1986) 228–238.

[13] H. Van Remoortel, M. Hornikx, H. Demeyer, D. Langer, C. Burtin, M. Decramer, et al. Daily physical activity in subjects with newly diagnosed COPD, Thorax 68 (10) (2013) 962–963.

[14] Christ Longhurst. Targeted radiotherapy for breast cancer reduces side effects. (2017). Nursing Standard, Retrieved from https://rcni.com/nursing-standard/newsroom/journal-scan/targeted-breast-cancer-radiotherapy-reduces-side-effects-92901

[15] D. Uzun Ozsahin, B. Uzun, M. Sani, A. Helwan, C.N. Wilson, F.V. Nurcin, N. Şentürk, I. Ozsahin, Evaluating cancer treatment techniques using fuzzy PROMETHEE method, Int. J. Adv. Comput. Sci. Appl. 8 (2017) 177–185.

[16] D. UzunOzsahin, I. Ozsahin, A fuzzy PROMETHEE approach for breast cancer treatment techniques, Int. J. Med. Res. Health Sci. 7 (5) (2018) 29–32.

[17] D. Uzun Ozsahin, N. Isa, B. Uzun, I. Ozsahin, Effective analysis of image reconstruction algorithms in nuclear medicine using fuzzy PROMETHEE. 2018 Advances in Science and Engineering Technology International Conferences (ASET).

[18] D. Uzun Ozsahin, B. Uzun, M. Musa, N. Şentürk, F. Nurçin, I. Ozsahin, Evaluating nuclear medicine imaging devices using fuzzy PROMETHEE method, Proc. Comput. Sci. 120 (2017) 699–705.

[19] D. Uzun Ozsahin, B. Uzun, M. Sani, I. Ozsahin, Evaluating X-ray-based medical imaging devices with fuzzy preference ranking organization method for enrichment evaluations, Int. J. Adv. Comput. Sci. Appl. 9 (3) (2018).

[20] D. Uzun, B. Uzun, M. Sani, A. Helwan, C. Nwekwo, F. Veysel, et al. Evaluating cancer treatment alternatives using fuzzy PROMETHEE method, Int. J. Adv. Comput. Sci. Appl. 8 (10) (2017)doi: 10.14569/ijacsa.2017.081024.

[21] I. Ozsahin, T. Sharif, D. Ozsahin, B. Uzun, Evaluation of solid-state detectors in medical imaging with fuzzy PROMETHEE, J. Instrumen. 14 (01) (2019) C01019–C11019, doi: 10.1088/1748-0221/14/01/c01019.

[22] E. Kiral, B. Uzun, Forecasting closing returns of Borsa Istanbul Index with Markov chain process of fuzzy states, Pressacademia 4 (1) (2017) 15–24, doi: 10.17261/pressacademia.2017.362.

[23] B. Uzun, E. Kıral, Application of Markov chains-fuzzy states to gold price, Proc. Comput. Sci. 120 (2017) 365–371, doi: 10.1016/j.procs.2017.11.251.

Chapter 6

Fuzzy PROMETHEE–based evaluation of skin cancer treatment techniques

Ilker Ozsahin[a,b,c], Dilber Uzun Ozsahin[a,b,d], Kevin Meck[b], Sunsley Tanaka Halimani[b] and Berna Uzun[a,e]

[a]*DESAM Institute, Near East University, Turkish Republic of Northern Cyprus, Nicosia, Turkey;* [b]*Department of Biomedical Engineering, Near East University, Turkish Republic of Northern Cyprus, Nicosia, Turkey;* [c]*Brain Health Imaging Institute, Department of Radiology, Weill Cornell Medicine, New York, NY, United States;* [d]*Medical Diagnostic Imaging Department, College of Health Sciences, University of Sharjah, Sharjah, United Arab Emirates;* [e]*Department of Mathematics, Near East University, Turkish Republic of Northern Cyprus, Nicosia, Turkey*

6.1 Introduction

Skin cancer occurs when cells in the outermost layer of the skin called the epidermis start to grow at an uncontrolled rate to form abnormal tissue due to unrepaired deoxyribonucleic acid (DNA) damage, which is usually caused by ultraviolet radiation. Skin cancer is further classified according to the area from which the cancer originates and its ability to spread. This separates skin cancer into basal cell carcinoma (BCC), squamous cell carcinoma (SCC), and melanoma skin cancer [1]. BCC and SCC are identified as nonmelanoma skin cancers because they barely spread to other parts of the body, unlike melanoma skin cancer, which can spread to other tissues in the body. It is highly unusual for basal-cell skin cancers to metastasize, which may have a fatal impact on the body. Red, pink, or brown shiny patches or bumps, or pink growths with blood vessels running across them, characterize these cancers [2]. The blood vessels appear in the basal cells within the layers of the skin.

More than a third of all new cancers are skin cancers with BCC, accounting for most skin cancer cases reported and making it the most common type of skin cancer type, while SCC is the second most common type of skin cancer after BCC (Basal Cell Carcinoma (BCC)—SkinCancer.org) Symptoms include open sores, wart-like sores or elevated growths, and scaly red patches, and they have scaly crusts that bleed. These symptoms originate in the squamous cells, which is the inner lining of the skin just under the outer surface.

Applications of Multi-Criteria Decision-Making Theories in Healthcare and Biomedical Engineering.
http://dx.doi.org/10.1016/B978-0-12-824086-1.00006-2

Melanoma is the third type of skin cancer and although the rarest one among the three, it is the most aggressive because it has the ability to easily metastasize [3]. When it spreads to other parts of the body, it becomes difficult to treat but it can be detected early and cured. The term "to cure" here in this research is used "to treat" patients since there is no cure for cancer but there are treatments that can help to cure some patients. Sometimes, the term "cure" is used when the cancer does not come back in the following 5 years. People with melanoma usually have sores or moles that do not heal and may itch or bleed, growths with many pigments, or asymmetrical moles with diameters of about 6 mm and with irregular borders [4].

When one experiences these signs, a doctor may need to be consulted in order to do a confirmation diagnosis test. After being diagnosed with skin cancer, one is expected to go through the treatment, which will be further discussed. In this chapter, we investigate the application of a multicriteria decision-making method—fuzzy preference ranking organization method for enrichment evaluations (PROMETHEE)—to come up with the best therapy technique for the patient, which we will also apply on the data collected from various sources. While the therapy techniques for skin cancer are highly effective in improving survival rates, it is important to prevent reoccurrence of the cancer.

6.1.1   Problem statement

Doctors as well as patients have difficulties when selecting the most appropriate skin cancer treatment technique to suit the patient's specific needs and available provisions. Different medical professionals (doctors, nurses, biomedical engineers, etc.) have differing views on which skin cancer treatment technique is the best. There are many skin cancer treatment techniques and this research aims to rank the 12 most common techniques to decide which one is the best, using fuzzy PROMETHEE decision-making algorithms.

6.2   Surgical treatment techniques

6.2.1   Surgery

Surgery is the most commonly used treatment technique for skin cancer. There are many surgical options for the treatment of skin cancer but this study focuses on the seven most prominent procedures which are Mohs surgery, cryosurgery, curettage and electrodesication, dermabrasion, excision, shave excision, and laser surgery. These surgical procedures are used to treat actinic keratosis, squamous cell carcinoma, or cell carcinoma and, depending on the type of tumor, its location and grade, a physician will choose the most suitable one from the different options. Data was collected from several sources and case studies, and then analyzed and compared using fuzzy PROMETHEE to determine the best surgical alternative for the treatment of skin cancer.

6.2.2 Mohs surgery

Mohs surgery aims to remove minimum health tissue and to leave the smallest possible scar while removing a tumor. This type of surgery is particularly helpful in the treatment of skin cancers that are large and have no distinct borders, in areas such as the genitals, the face, toes, fingers, and ears. Mohs surgery is very effective in treating BCC and SCC, although it can sometimes be used in some melanomas. The average cost for Mohs surgery is between $1000 and $3000 [5]. Mohs surgery is often used as the preferred skin cancer treatment option because of its high cure rate and low recurrence rate [6].

The patient is injected with local anesthetic before the beginning of the procedure. The surgeon then uses a scalpel to cut through a visible layer of skin cancer from the skin surface. This layer of the tumor is removed and labeled by the surgeon before being sent to the lab where it is frozen before being cut out into pieces for further examination under the microscope to check for the presence of cancer cells. During this time, the patient will be bandaged as they wait for the results, in which case, if the lab tests conclude the presence of more skin cancer cells beyond the examined layer, the surgeon has to remove another layer of the skin. This is done continuously until no more cancer cells are present in a slice of cut-out tissue.

Mohs surgery has many advantages, which make it the preferred choice of most doctors and patients. These include the fact that it maximizes the functional and cosmetic outcome of the procedure. It also offers a permanent cure for skin cancers, with 99% cure rates [5,7] and complete removal of the tumor. Less healthy tissue is lost during the procedure and it boasts high success rates and low recurrence rates of 1% [6]. Some drawbacks to this procedure are that it is still invasive and costly. It may also leave some scars on the patient. Side effects and risks are bleeding, pain or tenderness around the surgical site, infection, and nerve damage.

6.2.3 Cryosurgery

This procedure is also known as cryotherapy. Extremely cold temperatures are used to destroy the abnormal cells. This cold environment is created by spraying or rubbing argon, carbon dioxide, and liquid nitrogen gases onto the cancerous area on the skin. The effect of this might be painful and the patient may feel burning feeling. A thermometer may be inserted into the treatment area in the form of a needle to monitor the temperatures to make sure that the right temperatures are reached. As the temperature drops, ice crystals start to form within the tumor cells. This will cause the cells to rupture hence killing the cancerous cells itself. This will result into the development of a wound which is accompanied by redness and blistering and may last for a few days after the procedure. Recovery period may range between 7 and 18 days. Magnetic resonance imaging or ultrasound techniques are also used to monitor the freezing of the cells to prevent damage to healthy tissue. However, damage to nerve tissue is a major risk factor for this procedure. The procedure may need to be repeated in some cases for up to three sessions. A session can cost approximately between $150 and $200. Cryotherapy is used for BCC and SCC. Cryotherapy is an effective procedure with cure rates of 97% [8] and recurrence rates of 3% [8].

Cryosurgery poses great advantages as it is minimally invasive with minimized pain and bleeding. There is minimum damage to healthy tissue. It can be performed on patients of all ages. Its low cost and low risk of scarring also make it a great choice for most patients. On the downside, it can result in nerve damage and blistering after surgery. Some patients complain that the procedure is rather uncomfortable and painful. Cryosurgery is not effective on large flat moles. Patients may also experience some swelling, scarring, and loss of sensation in the treatment area for 12–18 mo. In addition, they may also observe some loss of pigmentation, loss of hair in treatment area, bleeding, and blisters.

6.2.4 Curettage and electrodesication

Curettage and electrodesication are a skin cancer therapy technique used to treat nonmelanoma skin cancers, namely BCC and SCC. A specialized electrode with a spoonlike end called a curette is used in this procedure. It costs approximately $200–$300. The patient is first injected with a local anesthetic. The physician scraps away the cancerous tissue using the curette. After scrapping, an electric current is used to burn the wound to stop bleeding and kill off any remaining cancerous cells with minimal damage to surrounding tissue. The scraped layer of tissue is sent to the lab for examinations to determine if a second session is necessary. The scrapping and burning procedure are done on average three times until the firm dermis layer is reached.

A major limitation of this procedure is that it cannot be used in areas of the body where hair grows, such as armpits, beard, or genital areas because of complications that arise when the tumor grows on a hair follicle, which may hinder effectiveness of the procedure. The procedure also has high facial recurrence rates, which are unfavorable for patients who have the cancer in the facial areas. Other effects of the procedure are pain and swelling in addition to bleeding, scarring, and crusting. The procedure, however, has high cure rates ranging from 91% to 97% for low-risk basal cell carcinoma and 96% for low-risk squamous cell carcinoma [9]. It is also easy to perform according to some doctors and has good cosmetic results on small tumors. No sutures are used and it provides rapid diagnosis.

6.2.5 Dermabrasion

Dermabrasion is an exfoliation technique, which aims to rub away the tumor using a small-motorized device called a dermabrader, which consists of a rapidly rotating wheel. This method is used for early stage skin cancers, namely actinic keratosis. The patient will be injected with local anesthetic or numbing spray, but for more complicated procedures, general anesthesia may be used. The doctor will then use the dermabrader, which uses its rapidly rotating wheel that removes layers of skin. As the doctor moves the dermabrader across the treatment area with constant and gentle pressure, new layers of smoother skin will be left exposed.

Major advantages of dermabrasion are that it has short recovery time and is nearly painless. However, patients exhibit increased sensitivity to sunlight and the procedure is not suitable for patients with open wounds. Patients who undergo dermabrasion are also prone to change in skin color, which usually darkens due to exposure to sunlight in the months following surgery. Swelling and scarring may also occur in patients who undergo dermabrasion.

6.2.6 Excision

Excision is the cutting out of skin cancer using simple or shave excision. This procedure can be used for both nonmelanoma skin cancer and melanoma skin cancer under local anesthesia. Excision may average between $900 and $2000. Recurrence rates for this procedure are about 10% [6] along with cure rates of 92%–95% [10].

6.2.6.1 Simple excision

The tumor is cut out using surgical apparatus. The tumor together with surrounding tissue is cut out. The surrounding tissue is called the margin and is removed to ensure that any cancerous cells that have spread are removed together with the main mass of the tumor. The approach used for this type of excision is called elliptical excision. In this procedure the doctor will draw an elliptical border around the treatment area and cut around the edges of this marked area to remove cells that are more cancerous. The procedure may take between 30 and 60 min.

6.2.6.2 Shave excision

A sharp razor or blade is used to shave off the abnormal area. Small horizontal cuts are made while cutting out the abnormal area. This procedure does not require any sutures or stitches and it leaves a significantly smaller scar than other excisions. However, in some instances an electrode is used along the edges of the excision site to further reduce the visibility of any scar.

Excision offers complete cancer removal and procedures that are easy to perform, although it may leave a large defect. Excision also leaves the patient with significant damage to healthy tissue, and the patient risks nerve damage and infection. Blood vessels may also be left damaged and the skin may be left scarred. Some patients show skin discoloration after excision.

6.2.7 Laser surgery

Laser surgery is a surgical approach that uses laser beams to treat skin cancers, usually actinic keratosis, but can sometimes be applied to squamous cell carcinoma in the epidermal layer of the skin or in thin basal-cell carcinomas although the patient may risk recurrence when this is done. A laser beam is used in place of a surgical scalpel to cut out the tumor without cutting through deeper layers. The cells are vaporized when they are burnt by the laser beam, so bloodless cuts are made. This provides significantly more precision than the use of a scalpel, which has success rates of about 95% [11]. CO_2 and argon lasers are the laser types that are used for skin cancer laser surgery. The procedure is expensive with prices of a session sitting at around $1000–$2330. On the contrary, laser surgery puts the patient at risk of scarring, crusting, or skin discoloration. Some patients say the postprocedure is painful and they show evidence of swelling.

6.3 Nonsurgical treatment techniques

These treatment techniques do not involve any surgical procedures and come in the form of radiation or drugs.

6.3.1 Radiation therapy

Radiation therapy is simply the use of ionizing radiation in order to destroy cancer cells at a cellular level by preventing them from growing. It achieves this by attacking the DNA within the cells, which is responsible for protein synthesis and therefore growth of the cancerous cells. This may be a primary or secondary line of skin cancer treatment after surgery. Radiation therapy is administered if the skin cancer has spread to other parts of the body or areas that are not accessible by surgery. It may also be used in conjunction with surgery or for symptom relief purposes. Radiation therapy may be administered in mainly two different ways: external beam and internal beam.

6.3.1.1 External beam radiation therapy (EBRT)

External beam radiation therapy is a form of radiotherapy that aims at delivering radiation from a machine called a linear accelerator in the form of X-rays to the cancerous cells. It has recurrence rates of about 7.5%–15.8% and 5-year cure rates of 90% [12]. The cost of EBRT is about $2500–$3500 [13].

Procedure: Simulation and planning

The first step in radiotherapy treatment is the planning procedure, which involves location of tumor determining its size using imaging devices such as CT. Still an immobilizing device will also hold the patient, which is custom made to keep the patient in the correct and most comfortable position in preparation for treatment. Marker seeds will also be implanted into the patient to help locate the tumor. Following these steps, the radiation team can determine the specific dose needed and the approach to use for delivery.

Treatment session

The patient lies down in the position determined during planning session, using the customized immobilization device. The radiation team will move to the next room and monitor the patient while operating the machinery. The radiation team and the patient will still be able to communicate. The machine will deliver radiation beams of doses of approximately 52 Gy [13] (although these may vary), while rotating. The process takes place over an average of 3.5 weeks for about 17 factions [13], with sessions lasting between 30 min. and 60 min.

External beam radiation therapy can be further divided into more delivery mechanisms. The main three ones are explained further.

Intensity modulated radiation therapy (IMRT)

IMRT delivers radiation doses from different directions matching the tumor shape but the doses are then customized to allow the machine to deliver varied radiation doses to the different areas receiving radiation to minimize harmful dosages to normal tissue.

Image-guided radiation therapy (IGRT)

IGRT allows the use of imaging while the machine delivers radiation doses. This means the machine can readjust when a patient moves or any other changes to the tumor shape or location occur. IGRT can be used in conjunction with IMRT.

Advantages of radiation therapy are that it is mostly precise to tumor location and painless, as compared to conventional methods of treatment. It is also noninvasive. The radiation dose may cause fatigue and some skin irritation. The side effects are its major downfall, with some patients risking having secondary cancers after the procedure. Erection problems were reported in some men and may lead to infertility.

Internal radiation therapy (brachytherapy)

The goal of skin cancer brachytherapy is to place the radiation source directly on or near the skin cells affected by the cancer. This radiation therapy costs between $2000 and $4500 [13]. The radiation kills the cancer cells with limited damage to the nearby healthy tissue, which is near the skin and thereby shows an overall recurrence rate of 5% and cure rates of between 96% and 98% [14]. These cure rates are dependent upon radiation dosages, the number of fractions of doses, and the size and depth of the lesion as well as its histological features. It is mainly used on melanoma of the eye. There are two brachytherapy approaches used in skin cancer: high-dose rate (HDR) brachytherapy and electronic brachytherapy (Ebx).

HDR brachytherapy uses precise radioactive seeds that are delivered onto the treatment area using catheters. Before the radiation exposure, the physician marks the skin area affected by the cancers. The area marked also includes a small region of healthy tissue surrounding the cancer, which is a major disadvantage as normal tissue is also destroyed. Next, a custom mold or catheter flaps or surface applicators can be used, for example, Leipzig or Valencia, depending on the surface of the body requiring treatment. Surface applicators are for flat surfaces while catheter flaps are used for areas too large to use an applicator.

Custom molds are used for irregular surfaces such as ears and nose.

Molds are made using specialized polymers or alginate. The catheters are embedded into the mold. Radioactive Ir 192 is used as a radiation source, delivered from a machine.

The dose of 42 Gy is delivered in six factions over a 2-week period [13]. A session can last between 5 and 10 min [15]. The doses are fractioned according to the amount of radiation given each time and can be either hypofractionation or hyperfractionation. Hypofractionation involves using large doses each session and it may have side effects that are more serious. Hyperfractionation, however, is the use of smaller doses with fewer side effects, although the sessions are performed twice or more per day.

Electronic brachytherapy (Ebx) is a newer technique, which uses a miniaturized X-ray source in the form of a mini accelerator to generate low energy X-rays to deliver a precise radiation dosage onto the cancer cells without any incision. Currently the machines that are used for electronic brachytherapy for skin cancer are Intrabeam (Zeiss), Xoft (iCAD), Papillon (Ariane), Photoelectric Therapy (Xstrahl), Esteya (Elekta), and SRT 100 (Sensus Healthcare). An applicator through which the radiation travels is applied onto the skin surface. Electronic brachytherapy delivers low doses to organs at risk as well as low doses of radiation leakages, hence little shielding is needed and no radioactive waste is produced.

Advantages of brachytherapy are that it is minimally invasive, has short treatment times, and is highly precise. However, it is known to leave some scars on some patients. Patients may also risk exposure to infections. Other side effects are mild redness, dry or peeling skin, and slight discoloration, as well as minimal hair loss at the site of radiation.

6.3.2   Chemotherapy

This treatment approach focuses on drugs that aim to kill cancer cells. Chemotherapy would be an option as it spreads throughout the whole body and attacks the rapidly dividing cancer cells. The drugs have special chemicals that prevent further division of cancer cells by damaging DNA or ribonucleic acid (RNA) with genes coding for cell growth, thereby preventing growth of the cancer. Chemotherapy in skin cancer can be divided into the following types.

6.3.2.1   Systematic chemotherapy

These drugs are administered via injection into the veins or taken orally as a pill. This method is mainly used for squamous cell carcinoma because it is more likely to spread, and not basal cell carcinoma, which does not easily spread. Systematic chemotherapy is usually administered when the cancer has spread in areas of the body that cannot be accessed by conventional methods of therapy, such as surgery. It is also an option for those patients who have melanoma skin cancer in which the cancer has spread throughout the body. In addition to this, chemotherapy is often used in combination with other treatment techniques, such as surgery, to further avoid recurrence of the cancer and completely remove the cancer. Common systematic chemotherapy drugs are doxorubicin, topotecan, 5-fluorouracil (5-FU), cisplatin, capecitabine, and etoposide. These are used to treat nonmelanoma skin cancers. Melanoma can also be treated using another group of drugs such as temozolomide, paclitaxel, carboplatin, nab-paclitaxel, vinblastine and dacarbazine [16]. A systematic chemotherapy approach that can be used for patients with localized melanoma in the legs or arms is called isolated limb perfusion. A band or a device called a tourniquet is used to block blood circulation to and from the isolated area. The major arteries and veins are clamped and tubes are inserted inside them so that blood may flow to the machine, which mixes the blood with the chemotherapy drugs. This procedure allows high doses of medication to be used, thereby increasing the effectiveness of the drugs to kill cancer. This is because the medication is flushed out after each chemotherapy session, which lasts about 90 min. [16].

6.3.2.2   Topical chemotherapy

This chemotherapy option is when the medicine is administered, usually in cream form, by applying it onto the skin. The most common drug for this form of treatment is 5-fluorouracil (5-FU), which, when applied, attacks the cancer cells that directly come into interaction. It is applied twice a day at dosages of 0.5 mL and 2 mL for about 2–12 weeks [17]. Its cure rates are high at about 90% [18]. However, cancers that have spread to other tissues, which cannot be reached by the medication, remain unharmed, which limits its effects. Another limitation of topical chemotherapy is that the medication can also be affected by sunlight, so protection is also needed.

Advantages of chemotherapy are that no surgery needed and the patient is not exposed to radiation. It is noninvasive, simple, and takes a very short time to perform. Application of medication can be done at home, so the patient's daily lifestyle is not greatly affected. The drawbacks of chemotherapy are that it has a limited effect on cancer, it attacks normal healthy tissue, and it might trigger allergic reactions. Chemotherapy also cannot be used on pregnant women or women who are breastfeeding. It can also cause infertility, hair loss, mouth sores, fatigue, loss of appetite, nausea and vomiting, and diarrhea, if taken systematically. Topical chemotherapy may cause crusting, itchiness, weeping, burning, and some pain at the site of application [19].

6.3.3 Photodynamic therapy

Photodynamic therapy is the use of light-sensitive drugs to target skin cancer. The physician can inject the drugs into the patient or they can be applied onto the skin. The two most commonly used photosensitive drugs for skin cancer are aminolevulinic acid (ALA) and methylaminolevulinate (MAL). MAL has better penetration than ALA as well as a shorter absorption time. Skin cancer areas absorb the drugs more in an absorption process that may take from an hour to up to 72 h. The drug can be active only when it is exposed to light from a laser. The patient will be exposed to light from a laser within the absorption spectra of the photosensitive agent, focused on the treatment area in a process that takes about 15 min. LEDs or lasers can be used as a source of light. The photosensitive drug kills the cancer cells by producing an active form of oxygen, which destroys cancer cells or blood vessels around the cancer, thereby depriving it of nutrients leading to cell death. The drugs can also activate the immune system to attack the cancer cells. MAL drug is in the form of a cream. When applied, it is covered with a bandage. After a few hours of absorption, the doctor will remove the bandage before using the light source to activate the drug. This causes burning or stinging sensations and skin may become red or blister for a few days before recovery.

This method minimizes damage to normal tissue, as the drugs are selective to skin cancer areas. Photodynamic therapy has no long-term side effects, is minimally invasive, and can be administered in a doctor's office. This treatment method also allows the doctor to administer the same drugs multiple times to the same treatment area. There is little or no scarring and results have shown improved skin appearance, tone, color, and texture.

Contrary to this, photodynamic therapy leaves the patient with photosensitive drugs after treatment, which may be activated by UV light. The patient should therefore protect himself or herself from sunlight after the procedure. Another disadvantage of the procedure is that its effectiveness is dependent on tissue oxygenation, light penetration, and wavelength. It also cannot be used to treat melanoma because it is more of a localized treatment approach. Its effectiveness is also limited to smaller cancers and cancers near the skin surface, because larger tumors and cancers that are deep within the skin are difficult to penetrate with light. Other side effects and risks of the procedure are severe ascites, cancer cachexia, chronic liver disease, cirrhosis, renal failure, constipation, fever, chest discomfort, and nausea.

6.3.4 Immunotherapy

Immunotherapy harnesses the power of the body's own immune system to use it against the skin cancer by boosting or restoring it. Immune response usually involves B-cells and T-cells, which are adaptive because they can detect specific antigens on foreign cells/pathogens. B-cells and T-cells detect these foreign antigens, leading to an immune response. This involves B-cells making antibodies and T-cells destroying the infected cells. The aim of medication is to stimulate the T-cells for immune response [20]. Common immunotherapy approaches include the following:

Cemiplimab-rwlc is an immune checkpoint inhibitor or checkpoint blockade immunotherapy. Cancer cells engage receptors called PD-1, which is a receptor that prevents T cells from attacking the body's own cells and acts as a stop signal for immune response. When cancer cells bind to PD-1, they deactivate these receptors making the T-cells "blind" to the cancer cells. The drugs used in this immunotherapy method block the binding of T-cells and cancer cells by blocking PD-1 so that they do not deactivate T-cells and this keeps the immune response active [20]. Other drugs used are pembrolizumab (Keytruda) and nivolumab (Opdivo) which are used in melanoma skin cancer. These drugs are taken intravenously for a period of between 2 and 3 weeks [21].

CTLA-4 inhibitors: Ipilimumab (Yervoy) inhibits CTLA-4 receptors, which act the same as PD-1 receptors to keep the immune system in check. The drug will block CTLA-4 from interacting with the cancer cells, thereby allowing T-cells to attack the cancer.

Other approaches are called intralesional immunotherapy, which are BCG vaccine and oncolytic virus therapy.

Bacille Calmette-Guerin (BCG) vaccine: This vaccine is used to stimulate the immune system. The vaccine is made up of bacteria, which is injected into the body and triggers an immune response, which attacks both the bacteria and the cancerous cells. BCG vaccine is used to treat stage III melanomas [21].

Oncolytic virus therapy: This is the use of genetically altered viruses to attack cancer cells. An example is talimogene laherparepvec (Imlygic), also known as T-VEC. These viruses work by directly attacking the cancer cells or by triggering an immune response, which results in production of more white blood cells.

Imiquimod cream is the most commonly used immunotherapy approach, which uses a cream that triggers immune response.

Cytokines (interferon- alfa and interleukin-2) are immune boosters. They boost the immune system by promoting formation of more T-cells. They also aid in cell death and activation of white blood cells (macrophages) [21].

Immunotherapy has some advantages, one of which is that it is specific to cancer cells and thereby does not attack healthy tissue. Besides the slight sting of the injection, it is painless and reduces overall toxicity. On the contrary, the body may adapt to the medication, thereby weakening the medication. Some patients exhibit partial response to the treatment and may take longer to expel the cancer from the body. In other patients, it may cause autoimmunity whereby the medication may start attacking body organs, such as lungs, kidneys, intestines, etc. Other side effects of the drugs are weight gain, nausea, cough, itchiness, appetite loss, diarrhea, and heart palpitations.

6.3.5 Targeted therapy

Targeted therapy is a treatment technique that targets specific cancers using their chemical or genetic characteristics. For nonmelanoma skin cancers, SMO inhibitor drugs are used—mainly vismodegib (Erivedge®) and sonidegib (Odomzo®)—which attack the cancer along the hedgehog cell-signaling pathway. The hedgehog cell-signaling pathway is pivotal in fetal development during pregnancy and is crucial for some adult cells.

However, patients with basal cell carcinoma exhibit increased activity in this pathway; hence these drugs attack this stronghold of cancer growth. This poses a risk for pregnant women as this can interfere with pregnancy and can distort a woman's period.

Vemurafenib (Zelboraf®) and dabrafenib (Tafinlar®) are targeted therapy drugs used to treat advanced skin cancers and melanoma and are referred to as BRAF inhibitors. BRAF is a protein that helps cells to grow. When this protein mutates, it causes uncontrollable growth of the melanoma cancer cells. This mutation accounts for up to 50% of melanoma cases [22]. These drugs help inhibit BRAF with V600E mutation, which is the one most commonly found in melanoma skin cancer. Trametinib (Mekinist®), binimetinib (Mektovi), and cobimetinib (Cotellic) are MEK inhibitor drugs, which are used in conjunction with BRAF inhibitors. MEK proteins and BRAF proteins work the same so the drugs are often used together, although MEK inhibitors show very low patient response unless used with BRAF inhibitors [22].

Another group of targeted therapy drug are used as C-KIT inhibitors, for example, imatinib mesylate (Gleevec), which inhibit a protein that helps the cancer to grow. This class of drugs is mainly used for acral or mucosal melanoma.

Advantages of targeted therapy are that it causes less damage to normal tissue because it is specific to certain chemical targets in the body. It is also noninvasive and painless. Disadvantages are that it is not suitable for pregnant women. Men who are under this form of therapy cannot donate blood or semen, as this may affect the fetus. Couples ae encouraged to practice contraception during the time when one of the partners is undertaking targeted therapy. It is also not suitable with breastfeeding and causes premature epiphyseal fusion. Side effects and risks of administering these drugs also include muscle spasms, dyspepsia, weight loss, fatigue, nausea, diarrhea, loss of appetite, vomiting, and alopecia.

6.4 Methodology

6.4.1 Preference ranking organization method for enrichment of evaluations (PROMETHEE)

PROMETHEE is a multicriteria decision-making analysis method used across many disciplines of research [1,5–7]. In fuzzy PROMETHEE the input data are treated as fuzzy numbers, with the purpose of considering the uncertainty contained in the data. This decision-making tool aids the decision maker to identify the best alternative from a group of options according to his/her goals and their own understanding of the problem.

This method is particularly important to give clarity on decisions that are difficult to quantify or compare, especially if two or more individuals have different perspectives as in this study. A patient, physician, researcher, and a medical device company, all offering different perspectives on the elements that make a treatment technique the most or the least favorable.

In order to establish our results from the fuzzy PROMETHEE algorithm, we collect the criteria that we would want to use to define each skin cancer treatment alternative. For surgical approaches as well as other techniques, our criteria include the types of cancer treatable, average cost of treatment, session duration, treatment duration, cure rate, recurrence rate, recovery period, pros and cons as well as risks, and side effects as illustrated in Table 6.1. Having inputted our criteria from different sources, we use define the criteria using a fuzzy linguistic scale to standardize the vague criteria using Table 6.1. This fuzzy linguistic scale was then used to calculate the degree of importance of each parameter and applied. The data was then defuzzified using the Yager index, and then the PROMETHEE-GAIA decision lab software was used to come up with the results of our decision-making algorithm.

6.5   Results and discussion

The results obtained in this study are subject to change according to the weighting perspective. The linguistic scale of importance is particularly important for the results, and this scale changes according to the interests of different individuals. For instance, a patient will give more weighting to success rate and recovery time while a company will give more weighting to cost of the machine. Due to the flexibility in weighting, our decision-making process in this study takes a balanced perspective across the healthcare spectrum from the patients, medical personnel and companies thus coming up with the results in Tables 6.2 and 6.3.

6.5.1   Surgical techniques

Results in this section rank only the surgery techniques used for skin cancer treatment. It is necessary to compare the methods in this group of techniques (surgical techniques) on their own since surgery is the most used method to treat for skin cancer. This result therefore suggests the overall performance of the surgery techniques investigated in this study. Dermabrasion, although not necessarily a surgery technique, has been added in this group of results since it is often used as a before or after procedure to the surgery techniques. According to the obtained results (Table 6.2), by using the linguistic scale of importance

TABLE 6.1 Visual PROMETHEE application.

Criteria	Cost of treatment	Session duration	Treatment duration	Cure rate	Recovery period	Advantages	Disadvantages	Side effects
Unit	($)	(Min)	(Sessions)	(%)	(Days)			
Preferences								
Min/Max	Min	Min	Min	Max	Min	Max	Min	Min
Weight	0.50	0.50	0.50	0.92	0.75	0.75	0.75	0.50
Alternatives								
Mohs surgery	2000	120.0	1.0	99.0	17.5	Very high	Low	Mid
Cryosurgery	175	5.0	1.5	97.0	12.5	High	High	Very high
Curettage and electrodesication	250	60.0	1.0	94.0	17.5	Mid	High	High
Dermabrasion	1450	45.0	1.5	96.5	28.0	Low	Mid	High
Excision	1400	45.0	1.0	93.0	10.0	High	Mid	High
Laser surgery	1650	15.0	1.0	95.0	21.0	Low	Low	High
EBRT	3000	45.0	3.5	90.0	42.0	Mid	High	High
Brachytherapy	3250	7.5	2.0	92.5	30.0	Mid	High	Very high
Chemotherapy	800	1.0	5.0	90.0	31.0	Mid	Very high	Very high
Photodynamic therapy	2050	15.0	1.0	75.0	3.0	Very high	Low	Mid
Immunotherapy	5800	1.0	6.0	73.0	17.5	High	Mid	Low
Targeted therapy	75,000	1.0	43.0	45.0	45.0	Low	High	Low

TABLE 6.2 Ranking of surgery alternatives for skin cancer treatment techniques.

Complete ranking	Therapy techniques	Positive outranking flow	Negative outranking flow	Net flow
1	Cryosurgery	0.3501	0.0438	0.3063
2	Excision	0.2365	0.1625	0.0741
3	Mohs surgery	0.2126	0.2236	−0.0110
4	Curettage and electrodesication	0.1466	0.2250	−0.0784
5	Laser surgery	0.1357	0.2589	−0.1232
6	Dermabrasion	0.1137	0.2815	−0.1678

TABLE 6.3 Ranking of other techniques for skin cancer treatment.

Complete ranking	Therapy techniques	Positive outranking flow	Negative outranking flow	Net flow
1	Photodynamic therapy	0.4016	0.2047	0.1969
2	Chemotherapy	0.3396	0.1449	0.1947
3	Brachytherapy	0.3149	0.1986	0.1162
4	Immunotherapy	0.2860	0.2560	0.0300
5	EBRT	0.2087	0.2948	−0.0861
6	Targeted therapy	0.0779	0.5297	−0.4518

(Table 6.1) and the Gaussian preference, cryosurgery is the best alternative of the five skin cancer surgery techniques investigated in this study. Excision, Mohs surgery, and curettage and electrodesication are second, third, and fourth, respectively. Laser surgery and dermabrasion are the least effective methods, respectively, as evidenced by their increasing negative net flow (Table 6.2).

6.5.2 Nonsurgical techniques

Results in this section rank the other popular treatment alternatives to skin cancer that cannot be classified under surgery. This result gives an overview on how the nonsurgical techniques investigated in this study rank among themselves. According to the obtained results (Table 6.3), by using the linguistic scale of importance (Table 6.1) and the Gaussian preference, the best alternative of the other six skin cancer treatment techniques investigated in this study is photodynamic therapy. The second-best alternative is chemotherapy while HDR brachytherapy and immunotherapy are third and fourth, respectively. EBRT and Targeted therapy are the least effective methods respectively as evidenced by their increasingly negative net flow (Table 6.3).

6.5.3 Surgery techniques and nonsurgical techniques combined

This section provides the complete ranking of all the skin cancer treatment alternatives investigated in this study regardless of their classification (surgical or nonsurgical techniques). When combined, all the six surgery techniques and the other six techniques rank from the best to the least effective method as follows: cryosurgery, excision, Mohs surgery, laser surgery, curettage and electrodesication, photodynamic therapy, dermabrasion, chemotherapy, brachytherapy, immunotherapy, and lastly EBRT. These results as per Table 6.4 were obtained by using the linguistic scale of importance (Table 6.1) and the Gaussian preference function.

TABLE 6.4 Complete ranking of skin cancer treatment alternatives.

Complete ranking	Therapy techniques	Positive outranking flow	Negative outranking flow	Net flow
1	Cryosurgery	0.4108	0.0626	0.3482
2	Excision	0.3117	0.1443	0.1674
3	Mohs surgery	0.3417	0.1773	0.1644
4	Laser surgery	0.2840	0.1918	0.0922
5	Curettage and electrodesication	0.2676	0.1796	0.0880
6	Photodynamic therapy	0.3204	0.2516	0.0688
7	Dermabrasion	0.2431	0.2218	0.0213
8	Chemotherapy	0.2401	0.2837	−0.0436
9	Brachytherapy	0.1895	0.2685	−0.0790
10	Immunotherapy	0.2159	0.3291	−0.1132
11	EBRT	0.1144	0.3828	−0.2684
12	Targeted therapy	0.0942	0.5403	−0.4461

6.6   Conclusions

The study utilizes fuzzy PROMETHEE as a decision-making tool for skin cancer treatment techniques. The effectiveness of this method has been showed in previous studies by [23] and [24]. The study wishes to aid patients and their respective healthcare providers with an easy decision-making tool for skin cancer treatment The use of fuzzy PROMETHEE in skin cancer treatment is practical as it incorporates individual criteria from each treatment alternative as input. Results from this research are expected to improve healthcare services for both the patient as well as physicians in order to come up with the most appropriate cancer treatment alternative.

References

[1]   Skin cancer (2019), https://en.wikipedia.org/wiki/Skin_cancer.

[2]   Basal cell carcinoma. WebMD, https://www.webmd.com/melanoma-skin-cancer/basal-cell-carcinoma.

[3]   Skin cancer (melanoma) (2019), https://www.nhs.uk/conditions/melanoma-skin-cancer/.

[4]   Melanoma symptoms. Cancer Treatment Centers of America, https://www.cancercenter.com/melanoma/symptoms/.

[5]   G.W. Cole, Mohs surgery for skin cancer. MedicineNet (2019), https://www.medicinenet.com/mohs_surgery/article.htm.

[6]   Decision: Just scrape it off ("ED&C"). e=Patient Dave (2019), https://www.epatientdave.com/2012/05/10/decision-just-scrape-it-off-edc/.

[7]   Reasons why skin cancer surgery isn't so scary. Everyday Health (2019), https://www.everydayhealth.com/news/reasons-why-skin-cancer-surgery-isnt-scaryJEMEC,

[8]   G. Jemec, The symptomatology of hidradenitis suppurativa in women, NEJM 366 (2012) (2019) 158–164, doi: 10.1056/NEJMcp1014163.

[9]   P.J. Holt, Cryotherapy for skin cancer: results over a 5-year period using liquid nitrogen spray cryosurgery. NIH (2019), https://www.ncbi.nlm.nih.gov/pubmed/3166941.

[10]   Curettage and electrodesiccation (2019), https://skincancer.net/treatment/curettage-electro-desiccation-surgery.

[11]   T. DiChiara, Common treatments for basal and squamous cell cancers you should know. VeryWellHealth (2019), https://www.verywellhealth.com/basal-cell-and-squamous-cell-carcinomas-3010842.

[12]   D.S. Lim, Laser surgery for skin cancer (2019), http://www.myskincancercentre.com.au/laser-for-skin-cancer/.

[13]   M. Ludgate, Radiotherapy for malignant skin diseases. DermNet NZ. (2019), https://www.dermnetnz.org/topics/radiotherapy-for-malignant-skin-diseases/.

[14]   Radiological Society of North America, Brachytherapy proves effective in treating skin cancer, ScienceDaily (2019).

[15]   HDR brachytherapy eases skin cancer treatment. CHI Health (2019), https://www.chihealth.com/en/about-us/press-room/publications/microscope/oncology/skin-cancer-treatment.html.

[16]   High dose rate (HDR) brachytherapy for skin cancer. New York Oncology/Hematology (2019), https://newyorkoncology.com/treatments-programs/cancer-treatments/high-dose-rate-hdr-brachytherapy/brachytherapy/.

[17]   Chemotherapy (2019), https://skincancer.net/treatment/chemotherapy/.

[18] Fluorouracil topical (5-FU, Carac®, Efudex®, Fluoroplex). | OncoLink (2019), https://www.oncolink.org/cancer-treatment/oncolink-rx/fluorouracil-topical-5-fu-carac-r-efudex-r-fluoroplex.

[19] Fluorouracil (5-FU) for nonmelanoma skin cancer (2019), https://www.cardiosmart.org/healthwise/uh13/53/uh1353.

[20] Fluorouracil (2019), https://en.wikipedia.org/wiki/Fluorouracil.

[21] Immunotherapy (2019), https://skincancer.net/treatment/immunotherapy/.

[22] Immunotherapy for melanoma skin cancer (2019), https://www.cancer.org/cancer/melanoma-skin-cancer/treating/immunotherapy.html.

[23] Targeted therapies (2019), https://skincancer.net/treatment/targeted-therapy.

[24] D. Uzun Ozsahin, B. Uzun, M. Sani, A. Helwan, C. Nwekwo, F. Veysel, et al. Evaluating cancer treatment alternatives using fuzzy PROMETHEE method, Int. J. Adv. Comp. Sci. Appl. 8 (10) (2017).

Further reading

[1] D. Uzun Ozsahin, B. Uzun, M. Sani, I. Ozsahin, Evaluating X-ray–based medical imaging devices with fuzzy preference ranking organization method for enrichment evaluations, Int. J. Adv. Comp. Sci. Appl. 9 (3) (2018).

[2] D. Ozsahin, I. Ozsahin, A fuzzy PROMETHEE approach for breast cancer treatment techniques, Int. J. Med. Res. Health Sci. 7 (5) (2018) 29–32.

[3] D. Uzun, B. Uzun, M. Sani, A. Helwan, C. Nwekwo, F. Veysel, et al. Evaluating cancer treatment alternatives using fuzzy PROMETHEE method, Int. J. Adv. Comp. Sci. Appl. 8 (10) (2017)doi: 10.14569/ijacsa.2017.081024.

[4] D. Uzun Ozsahin, B. Uzun, M. Musa, N. Şentürk, F. Nurçin, I. Ozsahin, Evaluating nuclear medicine imaging devices using fuzzy PROMETHEE method, Proc. Comp. Sci. 120 (2017) 699–705, doi: 10.1016/j.procs.2017.11.298.

Chapter 7

Fuzzy PROMETHEE–based evaluation of prostate cancer treatment techniques

Ilker Ozsahin[a,b,c], Nuhu Abdulhaq Isa[b], Kevin Meck[b], Sunsley Tanaka Halimani[b], Berna Uzun[a,d] and Dilber Uzun Ozsahin[a,b,e]

[a]*DESAM Institute, Near East University, Turkish Republic of Northern Cyprus, Nicosia, Turkey;* [b]*Department of Biomedical Engineering, Near East University, Turkish Republic of Northern Cyprus, Nicosia, Turkey;* [c]*Brain Health Imaging Institute, Department of Radiology, Weill Cornell Medicine, New York, NY, United States;* [d]*Department of Mathematics, Near East University, Turkish Republic of Northern Cyprus, Nicosia, Turkey;* [e]*Medical Diagnostic Imaging Department, College of Health Sciences, University of Sharjah, Sharjah, United Arab Emirates*

7.1 Introduction

Prostate cancer is the second and most common cancer in men after lung cancer [1]. Approximately, more than 80% of men above the age of 70 have a high chance of getting cancer [2]. It is largely curable when diagnosed and treated early; however, patients with advanced prostate cancer have a less favorable prognosis. The early symptoms of the cancer are quite difficult to detect which is a major reason why most men live with prostate cancer for several years without noticeable indications. Moreover, most of the symptoms associated with prostate cancer are usually common symptoms associated with urinary tract infections and other diseases in and around the bladder and urethra area. Part of this reason is that prostate cancer is slow growing and mostly symptom-free. The main function of the prostate is to produce a secretion, which forms a part of the seminal fluid that is essential for the survival, mobility, and performance of the sperm from the testicles, which is subsequently ejaculated. The prostate is built like a capsule in which prostate-specific antigen (PSA) are produced. PSA is a secreted alkaline that is rich in enzymes and prostate glands. The prostate is situated just under the bladder in front of the rectum. It is built like a capsule or a walnut shape [3]. It encircles the upper part of the urethra. The prostate, bladder, urethra, seminal vessels, and many other organs work together under the arithmetic contraction during the processes of urination and ejaculation, etc., by closing and opening one side to block the flow of a specific fluid (e.g., urine) in order to allow the flow and passage of the other (e.g., semen), and vice versa. As

Applications of Multi-Criteria Decision-Making Theories in Healthcare and Biomedical Engineering.
http://dx.doi.org/10.1016/B978-0-12-824086-1.00007-4

the man grows older, the prostate grows bigger in volume, a process commonly known as benign prostate hyperplasia (BPH). That means new cells are growing faster than they are killed and begin to affect the normal functions of the urethra and the bladder. The worst case of a prostate problem is carcinoma. Carcinoma involves uncontrollable division and multiplication of malignant cells where they spread to nearby organs such as the seminal vessels and other parts of the body (when they breach the capsule). Prostate cancer in both the benign and malignant states can cause damages to the glandular tissues in and around the prostate area, which will result in leakage of PSA into the bloodstream. Early detection of prostate cancer has always been a challenge but currently, the presence of high-value PSA in the blood is one of the most common indications of the possibility of cancer. In most cases, cancer develops for several years without any noticeable symptom; some tumors develop to a volume that obstructs urination or that exposes them to palpation via the rectum. In the worst cases, the prostate cancer aggressively grows and breaches the capsule and infiltrates nearby organs, or the cancer cells will separate and enter the bloodstream and be transported to other parts of the body to eventually grow and cause organ failure. Risk factors include smoking, age, and family history. Studies suggest black men are more likely to get prostate cancer than men of other races [4].

In this study, we hypothesize that the fuzzy preference ranking organization method for enrichment evaluations (PROMETHEE) can be used to rank the prostate cancer therapy techniques. Based on the provided criteria and weighing of the criteria, we believe we can achieve a reasonable result. The provided criteria are converted into fuzzy input data, after which it will be defuzzified for application in visual PROMETHEE program. The result of our analysis will solely depend on the provided criteria and our weighing of the criteria. At the end of this study, we hope to provide a ranking of alternative solutions to the problems of decision making in therapy techniques for the treatment of prostate cancer using fuzzy PROMETHEE.

7.2 Prostate cancer therapy techniques

There are several therapy techniques that are used in controlling and killing prostate cancer. There are several therapy techniques that are used in controlling and killing prostate cancer including chemotherapy, brachytherapy, hadron therapy, hormonal therapy, and surgery, to mention a few. The length of treatments regardless of treatment option varies from patient to patient and the stage of cancer, etc.

7.2.1 Chemotherapy

Chemotherapy is the use of chemicals to fight against cancer. These chemicals are referred to as anticancer drugs that kill or shrink the cancer cells or slow down the growth of cancer cells (e.g., docetaxel (Taxotere), cabazitaxel

(JEVTANA), mitoxantrone (Novantrone), estramustine (e)) [5]. The anticancer drugs are administered intravenously or orally into the cancer patient where they travel through the bloodstream in the body to attack cancers that have spread out from the capsule of the prostate gland to distant organs. Therefore, chemotherapy is a good treatment option for metastasized prostate cancer. Chemotherapy, just like other cancer treatment techniques can be coupled together with other treatment techniques such as hormone therapy or surgery for optimum performance. However, chemotherapy is usually not advised for a patient with a slow-growing tumor within the prostate gland (early stage of prostate cancer). Although the chemotherapy drugs are administered one at a time, chemotherapy can take a long period of time due to the cycles involved (the period from one drug to another and the time it takes the body to recover). The chemotherapy drugs are manufactured in such a way to attack rapidly dividing cells.

Chemotherapy also comes with several side effects that depend on the drug type, dosage, and length of the treatment. However, these side effects can be minimized or controlled before, during, or after the treatment procedures. Some of the major disadvantages of chemotherapy are drug toxicity to normal cells. Chemotherapy is not a cure for cancer; rather it slows down the growth of cancer cells and increases survival rate and quality of life. It kills and shrinks cancer but results in bone loss, radioactive dose exposure, long period of treatment, fatigue, nausea, and hair loss [6].

7.2.2 Radiotherapy

Radiotherapy is a treatment option that delivers a radiation beam on cancer cells to terminally destroy their genetic function and structure, and prevent their division and growth. [7]. This technique is divided into external and internal beam radiotherapy. External beam radiography delivers high energy X-rays from outside the patient to the target cancerous cell while internal beam radiography delivers high energy X-rays from inside the patient to the cancerous cells. This treatment option is effective in treating cancer cells within the prostate; however, it is sometimes used to treat cancer that has just spread outside the prostate capsule (lymph nodes, bladder, rectum, etc.). Unlike surgery, the treatment option is painless but it can cause serious side effects. There are several types of radiotherapy treatments such as palliative radiation therapy, adjuvant radiation therapy, and targeted radiation therapy. Unfortunately, radiotherapy is not usually effective when cancer has spread to other parts of the body, but it can be used to relieve patients from the symptoms [8]. Radiotherapy treatment can also be combined with other techniques for more effective treatment. Some of the advantages of radiotherapy include going on with normal activities after treatment, painless procedure, sessions take only 10–20 minutes, and no overnight hospital stay. The disadvantages include the need for visitation to radiotherapy specialist (within your city, or outside the country) for your treatment plan 5 days a week for several weeks. Several side effects are involved, in the case where radiotherapy fails, cancer cells come back more aggressively [9]. Radiation dose could lead to other problems. Other side risks include bladder problems, rectal leakage or bleeding, and difficulty with erections. It takes about 20 minutes a session, 5 days a week for 4–8 weeks. Radiation therapy machines can be found costing below or above $3 million [10,11].

7.2.2.1 Intensity-modulated radiation therapy (IMRT)

IMRT is a popular type of radiotherapy that belongs to the category of external beam radiotherapy [12]. It is an advanced form of 3-D therapy that employs simulation, which makes effective calculations on the area, shape, and position of cancer, and the exact dose needed for that cancer. It moves around the patient in several projections, targeting the prostate with intensity adjustment so that different areas get different dose [13]. This is better than traditional radiotherapy because less healthy cells surrounding the prostate would be affected and radiation dose is reduced. It causes increased urinary incontinence and urinary tract bleeding, radiation proctitis, radiation cystitis, and lymphedema. Treatment usually takes 5 days a week for 4–8 weeks.

7.2.2.2 Proton beam radiation therapy

This treatment is a type of radiotherapy that uses protons instead of X-rays and is quite similar to the techniques used in IMRT. Unlike X-ray which has uncontrolled radiation energy before and after it hits the target cancer cells, protons actually are more controllable and release very little radiation energy when they pass through healthy tissues after a certain distance, thereby causing little damage, that is, the specialist can control the path to which the proton releases most of the energy needed to fight cancer [14]. This means that proton beam radiation can, in theory, deliver more radiation to the prostate while doing less damage to nearby normal tissues [15]. Right now, proton beam therapy is not widely available because the machines needed to generate protons are very expensive.

7.2.3 Hormone therapy

Hormone therapy is one of the suggested treatments for the early stage of prostate cancer. It is also referred to as androgen deprivation therapy or androgen suppression therapy. Androgen is an important hormone in men and is responsible for triggering growth and maintenance of both primary and secondary characteristics (including prostate, broad shoulders, deep voice, physique, etc.) in men. The androgens such as testosterone and dihydrotestosterone actually fuel the growth of prostate cancer cells [4]. Therefore, suppressing them to inhibit the stimulation and growth of cancer cells as well as shrink them to a controllable size is the goal of this treatment option. However, this treatment option is not a cure for prostate cancer and comes with several severe risks and side effects, like bone weakness, when used for a long period of time. It is often combined with other treatments so that the cancer size can be shrunk for effective treatment. Patients feel upset at different times during their hormone therapy, which leads to chronic bone loss, sexual dysfunction, shrinkage of testicles and penis, and loss of muscle mass. Treatment is usually given for 6 months to 3 years.

7.2.4 Surgery

Surgery is also an option for treating prostate cancer in its early stage to remove the prostate gland and cancer within it. It is a treatment option that does not involve any kind of radiation risk. There are several types of surgery for prostate cancer treatment where radical prostatectomy is the most popular and widely used one. It involves complete removal of the prostate gland and some surrounding tissues like the seminal vessels and the prostatic urethra. [4]. Furthermore, anastomosis may be subsequently performed between the junction of the bladder and urethra [16]. Other surgeries include open access, robot-assisted laparoscopy, and transurethral resection of the prostate. Urinary incontinence and erectile dysfunction are the two major side effects that are associated with radical prostatectomy. Patients sometimes can suffer from general surgical risks such as blood loss/clot, infection, and damage to nearby organs, etc. [4]. This treatment option removes cancer, reduce mortality rates, but it is greatly limited at the early stage of cancer. It also leads to dry orgasms, inability to ejaculate, and restricted activities. It also leads to problems of urinary incontinence and sexual dysfunction. Surgery usually takes 3 hours and some patients may return to normal activities in 1–2 weeks. The average cost of surgery is around $23,000 (MediGence, 2018) [4].

7.2.5 Therapeutic vaccine treatment

This treatment option trains the immune system to identify the tricky nature of cancer cells and subsequently fight them. The vaccines used are made from harvested immune cells from the patient's body and exposed to or cultured with prostatic acid phosphatase that is also harvested directly from prostate cancer cells [17]. The process of harvesting white blood cells (immune cells) and exposing them to harvested prostatic acid phosphatase is repeated. This process is repeated two more times, 2 weeks apart, so that three doses of cells are administered. Vaccine treatment has been proven to improve survival rate by several months, however, it does not cure cancer. Unlike other treatment options, vaccine treatment has milder side effects such as fever, chills, pain, fatigue, and sometimes breathing and blood pressure problems. These side effects last for only a couple of days after treatment [4]. Therapeutic vaccine treatment is generally more expensive compared to chemotherapy, radiotherapy, and hormone therapy. It leads to back and joint pain, nausea, and headache. Treatment is given three times, 2 weeks apart. The survival rate is high. The price of therapeutic vaccine treatment is around $93,000 [18].

7.2.6 Bone-directed treatment

This treatment is an option or, in fact, a goal for palliative treatment of late-stage prostate cancer when cancer has spread to other parts of the body and is affecting the bones (softening the bone). This situation of bone softening is referred to as bone metastasis and is usually associated with severe pain leading to bone fractures and life-threatening increase in calcium levels in the blood [4]. Bone-directed treatment can be achieved through special drugs as well as hormone therapy, chemotherapy, and vaccine treatment. Popular drugs include Bisphosphonates, Denosumab (Xgeva, Prolia), Corticosteroids, pain medicine, and some radiopharmaceuticals [19]. This treatment prevents and controls the development of bone metastases, reduces high calcium levels caused by cancer, and prevents fractures.

7.3 Methodology

A few but popular therapy techniques used in the treatment of prostate cancer are selected. Along with these therapy techniques, some criteria vital to the success of the therapy treatment options are also selected. The data from each technique is analysed and weighted according to a scale of importance. The input data goes through the fuzzy PROMETHEE decision-making algorithm that calculates the best outcome and then ranks our output data from best to worst.

7.3.1 Criteria selection and preference

As mentioned earlier, there are criteria that are important and needed for the success of each therapy techniques. The criteria selected include cost and survival rates that are very important, and session duration, risks ,and side effects such as fever and nausea may be less important. Side effects, risks, and cons were categorized into a single criteria preference in order to get a rough estimate in percentage. This was achieved by creating a table that grouped similar side effect/risks/cons into rows that correspond to therapy techniques arranged in columns (Table 7.1). The criteria were graded from very high (VH) to very low (VL) importance. The preference scale value in percentage is as follows; Very High (VH, 100), High (H, 80), Medium (M, 60), Low (L, 40), and Very Low (VL, 20). The therapy techniques that had more than one side effect/risk/con were summed and divided by their total to obtain the mean by percentage. The grading considered the duration, severity, availability of treatment. of the side effect/risk/con. Table 7.2 uses the same method used in Table 7.1 to grade the advantages of the therapy techniques in percentage. The treatment of prostate

TABLE 7.1 Side effects and the degree of concern.

Side effects/risks/cons	Grade (severity)	Therapy techniques
Impotence, loss of sexual infertility, dry orgasm	VH	Surgery, Hormone therapy, Radiotherapy, Chemotherapy
Shrinkage of testicles and penis length	L	Hormone therapy
Loss of muscle mass and bone	VH	Hormone therapy
Urinary incontinence, rectal leakage	H	IMRT, chemotherapy, radiotherapy
Erection problem	H	Proton beam radiation therapy, Surgery, radiotherapy, hormone therapy
Skin redness, numbness, stress, headache, weakness, back and joint pain	VL	Proton beam radiation therapy, radiotherapy, IMRT, bone-related
Fever (low white blood cells) and anemia	H	Chemotherapy, vaccine
Fatigue, nausea, hair loss,	M	Proton beam radiation therapy, chemotherapy, vaccine, bone-directed treatment, hormone therapy
Radiation proctitis	H	Radiotherapy
Lymphedema	M	Surgery, radiotherapy
Gastrointestinal	H	Proton beam radiation therapy, radiotherapy, IMRT
Breathing and blood pressure	H	Hormone therapy,
Radiation dose	H	Radiotherapy, chemo, IMRT,
Expensive	H	proton beam radiation therapy, vaccine
Stage limitation	H	Surgery, bone-directed treatment

cancer using radiotherapy is limited by the stage of the prostate cancer. What this means is that there are stages in which radiotherapy is recommended and can perform effectively and efficiently to shrink and kill the prostate cancer cells in the region of interest; however, there are stages in which radiotherapy is not necessary due to the high level of radiation risk, side effects, cost, and underperformance.

Staging is also another important criterion to be considered. It shows the extent of the spread of prostate cancer as well as the effectiveness of the therapy

TABLE 7.2 Characteristics advantages related to the therapy techniques and their graded scale of importance.

Advantages	Grade (importance)	Therapy techniques
Removes cancer	H	Surgery
Painless, short time, precise and safe delivery	M	Proton beam radiation therapy, IMRT
No radiation dose	H	Surgery, vaccine, bone-directed treatment
Bone metastasis and blood calcium control	VH	Bone-directed treatment
Kills cancer	H	Chemotherapy, Proton beam radiation therapy, IMRT, Radiotherapy
Cheap	M	Chemotherapy, Bone-directed treatment
Shrinks cancer	M	Hormone therapy, chemotherapy

techniques [4]. Prostate cancer is divided or staged into four stages as follows: stage I (early stage and slowly dividing and spreading cancer cells, i.e. nonaggressive), stage II (early stage but cancer cells tend to divide and grow quickly within the prostate capsule), stage III (cancer has spread outside the capsule), and stage IV (cancer has spread to other parts of the body), according to the AJCC (American Joint Committee on Cancer) TNM staging system [20]. The stages were assigned values as I (25), II (50), III (75), and IV (100). For example, chemotherapy is effective for stage III and IV i.e. 75 + 100 = 175. The total of the calculated stage limit value for the techniques is 1375. Therefore, 175/1375x100 = 12.7%. The stage limit values in % for all the therapy techniques are presented in Table 7.3. Table 7.3 also shows the overall values for side effects/risks/cons, pros and stage limits (in %) for all the selected therapy techniques.

Finally, the selected therapy techniques alongside their criteria and corresponding values are shown in Table 7.4.

7.3.2 Fuzzy PROMETHEE

The idea of fuzzy PROMETHEE is achieved from the fusion of fuzzy logic and PROMETHEE. Fuzzy logic can be defined as a class of multivalued logic that permits intermediate values in form of multivalued logic, in which the truth values of variables may be any number between 0 and 1, that is, the truth

TABLE 7.3 Graded side effects, pros and stage limits in percentages (%).

Therapy	Side effects/ risks/cons	%	Pros	%	Stage limit	%
Surgery	VI, H, H, M	11.1	H, H	14.0	I, II	5.5
Hormone	VI, L, VH, H, M, H, M	17.4	M	5.3	II, III, IV	16.4
Chemo	VI, H, H, H, M	13.9	H, M, M	17.5	III, IV	12.7
Proton	H, VL, M, H, H	11.1	M, H	12.3	I, II, III, IV	18.9
Radio	VI, H, H, H, H, H, M, VL	20.1	H	7.0	I, II, III	10.9
Vaccine	H, M, H, M	9.7	H	7.0	III, IV	12.7
Bone	VL, M, H, M	7.6	VH, M, H	21.1	IV	7.3
IMRT	H, VL, H, H	9.0	M, H	12.3	II, III, IV	16.4
Total	2880		1140		1375	

values are obtained in degrees ranging from completely true to completely false. Fuzzy logic systems are applied to the design process to enhance efficiency and simplicity. PROMETHEE was developed by Brans et al. (1984, 1986) [21]. It is a multi-criteria decision-making (MCDM) technique that mutually compares related alternatives with regards to their related and selected criteria. PROMETHEE is quite more advantageous compared to other MCDM techniques due to its efficiency and easiness in concepts and applications. The PROMETHEE method requires only two types of information: the information on the weights of the criteria considered and the decision-makers preference function when comparing the contribution of the alternatives in terms of each separate criteria [22].

There have been a few types of research based on the approach of fuzzy PROMETHEE. They include Goumas and Lygerou [23], Bilsel et al. [24], Geldermann et al. [25], Chou et al. [26], Tuzkaya et al. [27], Ozgen et al., (2011) [28,29], and Uzun Ozsahin and Ozsahin [30]. In the real-life conditions, most of the time it is not feasible to collect crisp data to define a problem properly and make an optimal decision. Using fuzzy sets allows the decision maker to define the problem under a vague condition.

The main aim of the fuzzy PROMETHEE model was comparison between two fuzzy sets. For this aim, Yager (1981) found an index, which was determined with the centre of weight of the surface of the membership function to compare the fuzzy numbers. Yager (1981) defined the magnitude of a triangular fuzzy number corresponding to the center of a triangle with the YI= (3n−a + b)/3

TABLE 7.4 Selected therapy techniques with their criteria and corresponding values.

Therapy	Session time (min)	Treatment duration	Cost ($)	Comfort	Side effect (%)	Survival rate (%)	Stage limit (%)	Pros (%)
Surgery	180	1 session	23,716.7	M	11.1	83	05.5	80
Hormone	45	6 months to 3 years	26,896	VH	17.4	41	16.4	60
Chemotherapy	60	10 cycles	12,833.3	L	13.9	53.1	12.7	66.7
Proton therapy	30	1 session	32,428.0	H	11.1	91.3	18.9	70
Radiotherapy	20	5 days a week for 4–8 weeks	42,772	VL	20.1	75	10.9	80
Vaccine treatment	60	3 times, 2 weeks apart	93,000	VH	9.7	85	12.7	80
Bone treatment		Once every 3–4 weeks	7,553	H	7.6	87	7.3	80
IMRT	20	6–8 weeks	29,616	M	9.0	83.0	16.4	70

TABLE 7.5 A linguistic scale of importance.

Linguistic scale for evaluation	Triangular fuzzy scale
Very high (VH)	(0.75, 1, 1)
Important (H)	(0.50, 0.75, 1)
Medium (M)	(0.25, 0.50, 0.75)
Low (L)	(0, 0.25, 0.50)
Very low (VL)	(0, 0, 0.25)

formula. For alternative treatment techniques of prostate cancer to be evaluated in terms of relevant criteria and their importance weight, the linguistic fuzzy scale used in this study is given in Table 7.5.

7.3.3 Application of fuzzy PROMETHEE

After the necessary criteria of the prostate cancer treatment techniques were collected, the Gaussian preference function was used for each criteria. Then, the Yager index for defuzzification of the linguistic data was applied. Lastly, PROMETHEE GAIA decision lab software was used to evaluate the prostate cancer therapy techniques (Table 7.6).

7.4 Results and discussion

The positive outranking flow signifies that bone-directed treatment shows the highest positive outranking flow as well as the lowest negative outranking flow (Table 7.7). On the other hand, hormone therapy is shown to have the lowest positive outranking flow. Fig. 7.1 below visually demonstrates the magnitudes (positive and negative) of each treatment technique on a scale from −1 to 1. Positive outranking flow values shows the strength of the therapy techniques while negative outranking flow values shows the weakness of the therapy techniques. Furthermore, the net flow is the distance between positive flow and negative flow, it provides the full ranking.

The positive and negative side of each criteria was determined and shown in Fig. 7.1. As it can be seen from the figure, bone-directed treatment is ranked the highest because it has high survival rate, low session time, low side effects, reasonable cost, and high comfort; however, it is highly limited to the last stage of cancer (metastasis stage). Proton therapy, on the other hand, has most of the criteria in the positive outranking flow and just pros in the negative outranking flow. Unlike bone-directed treatment, treatment, proton therapy is not limited by stage of cancer and thus, proton therapy can be thought of as the best therapy option among the selected criteria, since it has no stage limit. Hormone therapy

TABLE 7.6 Visual PROMETHEE application for prostate cancer treatment alternatives.

Criteria	Session time	Treatment cost	Comfort	Recovery time	Side effects	Survival rate	Stage limit	Pros
Unit	minutes	$		weeks	%	%	%	%
Preferences (min/max)	min	min	max	min	min	max	max	max
Weight	0.50	0.50	0.50	0.75	0.75	0.92	0.50	0.50
Evaluations								
Surgery	180	M	M	L	11.1	83	5.5	80
Hormone therapy	45	M	VH	H	17.4	41	16.4	60
Chemotherapy	60	L	L	L	13.9	53.1	12.7	66.7
Proton therapy	30	M	H	M	11.1	91.3	18.9	70
Radiotherapy	20	H	VL	VH	20.1	75	10.9	80
Vaccine treatment	60	VH	VH	VH	9.7	85	12.7	80
Bone-directed treatment	15	VL	H	M	7.6	87	7.3	80
IMRT	20	M	M	M	9	83	16.4	70

TABLE 7.7 Complete ranking of prostate cancer treatment alternatives.

Complete ranking	Alternative	Positive outranking flow	Negative outranking flow	Net flow
1	Bone-directed treatment	0.3656	0.0913	0.2743
2	Proton therapy	0.3796	0.1194	0.2642
3	IMRT	0.1232	0.1232	0.1760
4	Vaccine treatment	0.2529	0.1385	0.1144
5	Surgery	0.1879	0.2521	–0.0642
6	Radiotherapy	0.2030	0.3248	–0.1217
7	Chemotherapy	0.1146	0.3980	–0.2834
8	Hormone therapy	0.1085	0.4641	–0.3557

is ranked the lowest due to high and significant side effects such as bone metastasis, muscle loss, and loss of fertility and sexual performance. Furthermore, hormone therapy can be given continuously for a long period of time (very high recovery time) resulting in more side effects. In general, the criteria for bone-directed treatment, proton therapy, and IMRT are more on the positive side, as compared to hormone, chemo, and radiotherapy, and lastly the criteria for vaccine treatment and surgery are roughly shared between the negative and positive outranking flow.

The result of our analysis solely depends on the provided criteria and our weighing of the criteria. This study can be improved if more criteria are added, and more precise weighing of the criteria can be employed. In this study, the Decision Lab visual PROMETHEE program was used to obtain the ranking. This program is user-friendly and decision maker can change the criteria easily and compare the therapy techniques according to selected criteria.

7.5 Conclusions

An optimum decision in the therapy technique evaluation by employing fuzzy PROMETHEE, a multi-criteria decision-making technique is achieved. The study shows that the proposed method is very effective at giving solutions to decision-making problems in closely related therapy techniques. This study simply and clearly shows that fuzzy PROMETHEE provides a ranking of alternative solutions to the problems of decision-making in therapy techniques for the treatment of prostate cancer.

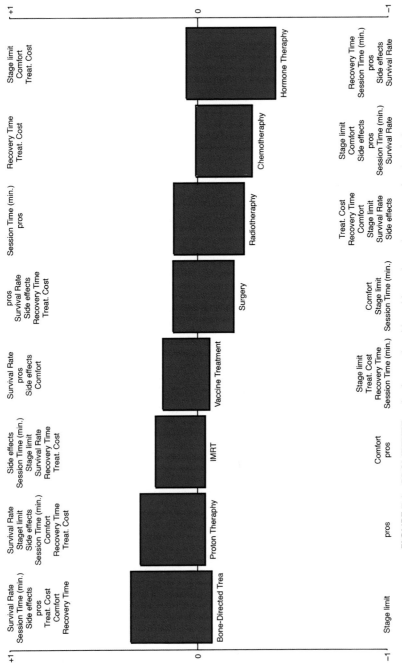

FIGURE 7.1 PROMETHEE evaluation results with positive and negative aspects of each technique.

References

[1] WCRF. https://www.wcrf.org/dietandcancer/cancer-trends/prostate-cancer-statistics. Accessed 4.08.20.

[2] WBMD. Prostate cancer risk factors. (2019). https://www.webmd.com/prostate-cancer/guide/prostate-cancer-risk-factors#1. Accessed 24.08/20.

[3] Live Science. Prostate cancer symptoms and treatment. (2010). https://www.livescience.com/9934-prostate-cancer-symptoms-treatment.html.

[4] American Cancer Society. Chemotherapy for prostate cancer. (2016). https://www.cancer.org/cancer/prostate-cancer/treating/chemotherapy.html.

[5] American Cancer Society. Prostate cancer treating by stage. (2016). https://www.cancer.org/cancer/prostate-cancer/treating/by-stage.html.

[6] American Cancer Society. Prostate cancer-treating surgery. (2016). https://www.cancer.org/cancer/prostate-cancer/treating/surgery.html#written_by.

[7] American Cancer Society. Prostate-cancer treating radiation-therapy. (2016). https://www.cancer.org/cancer/prostate-cancer/treating/radiation-therapy.html.

[8] Prostate Cancer UK. Chemotherapy. (2016). https://prostatecanceruk.org/prostate-information/treatments/chemotherapy.

[9] Prostate Cancer UK. External beam radiotherapy. (2016). https://prostatecanceruk.org/prostate-information/treatments/external-beam-radiotherapy.

[10] D.R. Langreth. Whelan, The $150 million zapper: Does every cancer patient really need proton-beam therapy?, Forbes Magazine (2009). https://www.forbes.com/forbes/2009/0316/062_150mil_zapper.html#98632312068f.

[11] J.V. Dyk, E. Zubizarreta, Y. Lievens, Cost evaluation to optimize radiation therapy implementation in different income settings: a time-driven activity-based analysis, Radioth. Oncol. 125 (2017) 178–185.

[12] Prostate Cancer UK. External beam radiotherapy. (2016). https://prostatecanceruk.org/prostate-information/treatments/external-beam-radiotherapy.

[13] American Cancer Society. Vaccine treatment for prostate cancer. (2016). https://www.cancer.org/cancer/prostate-cancer/treating/vaccine-treatment.html.

[14] MD Anderson Cancer Center. What is proton therapy? (2018). https://www.mdanderson.org/patients-family/diagnosis-treatment/care-centers-clinics/proton-therapy-center/what-is-proton-therapy.html.

[15] What is hadron therapy? The European Network for Light Ion Hadron Therapy. (2018). http://enlight.web.cern.ch/what-is-hadron-therapy.

[16] B. Bjørn, Surgery of prostate cancer, J Oncol. Encyclo.Oslo University Hospital, Norway, Oslo, 2016.

[17] D. Samadi. Prostate cancer treatment options for vaccine treatment. (2018). http://prostatecancer911.com/prostate-cancer-treatment-options-vaccine-treatment/.

[18] C. Hutchison, A. Unit. Cancer vaccine: 4 months of life worth $100K? (2010). https://abcnews.go.com/Health/ProstateCancerNews/provenge-cancer-vaccine-months-life-worth-100k/story?id=11269159.

[19] D.L. Suzman, S.A. Boikos, M.A. Carducci, Bone-targeting agents in prostate cancer, Cancer Metast. Rev. 33 (2-3) (2014) 619–628 https://doi.org/10.1007/s10555-013-9480-2.

[20] J.M. Slater. Prostate cancer stages and survival rates. (2018). https://protons.com/proton-treatments/prostate-cancer/diagnosis-prostate-cancer.

[21] J.P. Brans, P. Vincle, A preference ranking organization method, Manage. Sci. 31 (6) (1985) 647–656.

[22] C. Macharis, J. Springael, K. de Brucker, A. Verbeke, PROMETHEE and AHP: the design of operational synergies in the multicriteria analysis. Strengthening PROMETHEE with ideas of AHP, Eur. J. Oper. Res. 153 (2) (2004) 307–317.

[23] M. Goumas, V. Lygerou, An extension of the PROMETHEE method for decision making in a fuzzy environment: ranking of alternative energy exploitation projects, Eur. J. Oper. Res. 123 (2000) 606–613.

[24] R.U. Bilsel, G. Buyukozkan, D. Ruan, A fuzzy preference ranking model for quality evaluation of hospital web sites, In. J. Intell. Syst. 21 (11) (2006) 1181–1197.

[25] J. Geldermann, T. Spengler, O. Rentz, Fuzzy outranking for environmental assessment: case study, iron and steel making industry, Fuzzy Sets Syst. 115 (1) (2000) 45–65.

[26] W.-C. Chou, W.-T. Lin, C.-Y. Lin, Application of fuzzy theory and PROMETHEE technique to evaluate suitable ecotechnology method: a case study in Shismen reservoir watershed, Taiwan, Ecol. Eng. 31 (2007) 269–280.

[27] G. Tuzkaya, B. Gülsün, C. Kahraman, D. Özgen, An integrated fuzzy multi-criteria decision-making methodology for material handling equipment selection problem and an application, Expert Syst. Appl. 37 (4) (2010) 2853–2863.

[28] D. Uzun Ozsahin, B. Uzun, M. Musa, N. Şentürk, F. Nurçin, I. Ozsahin, Evaluating nuclear medicine imaging devices using fuzzy PROMETHEE method, Proc. Comput. Sci. 120 (2017) 699–705.

[29] D. Uzun Ozsahin, N.A. Isa, I.I. Ozsahin, B. Uzun, Effective analysis of image reconstruction algorithms in nuclear medicine using fuzzy PROMETHEE. 2018, Advances in Science and Engineering Technology International Conferences (ASET) (2018).

[30] D. Uzun Ozsahin, I. Ozsahin, A Fuzzy PROMETHEE approach for breast cancer treatment techniques, Int. J. Med. Res. Health Sci. 7 (5) (2018) 29–32.

Further reading

[1] H. Zincke, J.E. Oesterling, M.L. Blute, E.J. Bergstralh, R.P. Myers, D.M. Barrett, Long-term (15 years) results after radical prostatectomy for clinically localized (stage T2c or lower) prostate cancer, J. Urol. Nov 152 (5 Pt2) (1994) 1850–7. https://www.ncbi.nlm.nih.gov/pubmed/7523733.

[2] A. Barrell. Prostate cancer surgery: staging, surgery, types, outlook (2017). https://www.medicalnewstoday.com/articles/317591.php.

[3] J.P. Brans, P. Vincke, B. Mareschal, How to select and how to rank projects: the PROMETHEE method, Eur. J. Oper. Res. 24 (1985) 228–238.

[4] Cost Helper. How much does prostate cancer treatment Cost? CostHelper.com. (2018). http://health.costhelper.com/prostate-cancer-treatment.html.

[5] B. Brennhovd, J. Iversen, Prostate cancer. In: Oncology Encyclopedia, Oncology Encyclopedia, Norway, (2016).

[6] L. Chang. Treatment options for prostate cancer. (2018). https://www.webmd.com/prostate-cancer/prostate-cancer-treatment-options#2.

[7] D. Gharote. Prostate cancer: what is bone directed therapy? (2018). https://www.lybrate.com/topic/prostate-cancer-what-is-bone-directed-therapy/38ec5be61442b2d92fb126743bce06c0.

[8] B. Guess. Chemotherapy for prostate cancer: why bother? (2006). https://pcri.org/chemotherapy-for-prostate-cancer-why-bother/.

[9] H. Ballentine Carter. Pros and cons of prostate cancer treatment options: prostate cancer. HealthCommunities.com. (2014). http://www.healthcommunities.com/prostate-cancer/treatment-advantages-disadvantages_jhmwp.shtml.

[10] Health Line. Prostate cancer: prognosis and life expectancy for bone metastases. (2018). https://www.healthline.com/health/prostate-cancer-prognosis-life-expectancy-bone-metastases#outlook.

[11] G. Hess, A. Barlev, K. Chung, J.W. Hill, E. Fonseca. Cost of palliative radiation to the bone for patients with bone metastases secondary to breast or prostate cancer. (2012). https://www.ncbi.nlm.nih.gov/pmc/articles/PMC3561237/.

[12] M. Krishna, K. Bremner, J. Luo, G. Tomlinson, S. Alibhai. Long-term health care costs for prostate cancer patients on androgen deprivation therapy. (2016). https://www.ncbi.nlm.nih.gov/pmc/articles/PMC5081016/.

[13] T. Lumby. Cancer patient buys his own chemo machine off eBay for an incredible price. (2018). https://www.mirror.co.uk/news/uk-news/cancer-patient-buys-chemotherapy-machine-11995716.

[14] R. Nelson. Insurers nix payment for prostate cancer proton therapy. (2013). https://www.medscape.com/viewarticle/810257#vp_1.

[15] C. Nordqvist. Longer survival rates after surgery for prostate cancer patients. Medical News Today (2007, October 9). https://www.medicalnewstoday.com/articles/84936.php.

[16] A. Ozgen, G. Tuzkaya, U.R. Tuzkaya, D. Ozgen, A multi-criteria decision making approach for machine tool selection problem in a fuzzy environment, Int. J. Comput. Intell. Syst. 4 (4) (2000) 431–445.

[17] Prostate Cancer Foundation. What are the side effects of prostate cancer treatment? (2018). https://www.pcf.org/c/side-effects/.

[18] Prostate cancer free. Prostate cancer treatment side effects treatment vs. side effects. (2018). https://prostatecancerfree.org/prostate-cancer-treatment-side-effects/.

[19] Medigence. Prostate cancer treatment and surgery cost guide: expected costs breakdown, best hospitals. (2018). https://medigence.com/blog/prostate-cancer-treatment-surgery-cost-guide/.

[20] Provision CARES for Proton Therapy. The survival rate for prostate cancer. Archives: Provision CARES Proton Therapy. (2018). https://www.provisionproton.com/tag/survival-rate-for-prostate-cancer/.

[21] Y. Ranchod, A. Pietrangelo. Proton therapy for prostate cancer: benefits, risks, and more. (2017). https://www.healthline.com/health/prostate-cancer/proton-therapy-for-prostate-cancer#preparation.

[22] J. Reacher. How long do prostate cancer treatment side effects last? (2012). https://prostate.net/articles/how-long-do-prostate-cancer-treatment-side-effects-last.

[23] D. Samadi. Prostate cancer treatment pros and cons. (2018). https://prostatecancer911.com/prostate-cancer-treatment-pros-cons/.

[24] B. Seal, S.D. Sullivan, S. Ramsey, C.V. Asche, K.M. Shermock, S. Sarma, et al. Treatments and corresponding costs of prostate cancer. (2015). https://www.medscape.com/viewarticle/840143.

[25] The University of Iowa. Prostate-cancer surgery prices are elusive. ScienceDaily (2014, June 9). www.sciencedaily.com/releases/2014/06/140609113351.htm.

[26] The University of Missouri-Columbia. Surgery improves survival rates for men with prostate cancer if radiation treatments fail. ScienceDaily (2016, March 10). www.sciencedaily.com/releases/2016/03/160310141234.htm.

[27] UCLA Prostate Cancer Program. IMRT and you. Prostate Cancer Program, UCLA Urology, Los Angeles. (2018). http://urology.ucla.edu/prostate-cancer/imrt-and-you.s

[28] UCLA Prostate Cancer Program. Radiation therapy prostate cancer. Prostate Cancer Program, UCLA Urology, Los Angeles. (2018). http://urology.ucla.edu/prostate-cancer/radiation-therapy-prostate-cancer.

[29] University of Florida Health Proton Therapy Institute. Frequently asked questions about proton therapy. (2015). https://www.floridaproton.org/what-is-proton-therapy/faq#q13 in press.

[30] D. Uzun Ozsahin, B. Uzun, M. Sani, A. Helwan, C. Nwekwo, F. Veysel, et al. Evaluating cancer treatment alternatives using fuzzy PROMETHEE method, Int. J. Adv. Comput. Sci. Appl. 8 (10) (2017).

[31] V. Verma, V. Mishra, P. Mehta. A systematic review of the cost and cost-effectiveness studies of proton radiotherapy. (2016). https://onlinelibrary.wiley.com/doi/full/10.1002/cncr.29882.

[32] Zero cancer. Prostate cancer side effects. (2018). https://zerocancer.org/learn/current-patients/side-effects/.

Chapter 8

Comparative evaluation of point-of-care glucometer devices in the management of diabetes mellitus

Mubarak Taiwo Mustapha[a,b], Dilber Uzun Ozsahin[a,b,c] and Ilker Ozsahin[a,b,d]
*[a]DESAM Institute, Near East University, Turkish Republic of Northern Cyprus, Nicosia, Turkey;
[b]Department of Biomedical Engineering, Near East University, Turkish Republic of Northern
Cyprus, Nicosia, Turkey; [c]Medical Diagnostic Imaging Department, College of Health Sciences,
University of Sharjah, Sharjah, United Arab Emirates; [d]Brain Health Imaging Institute,
Department of Radiology, Weill Cornell Medicine, New York, NY, United States*

8.1 Introduction

Diabetes mellitus (DM) is a metabolic disorder characterized by increased blood glucose level. It represents a major public health issue, not only due to its high prevalence and incidence but also because it is associated with high morbidity and mortality rates in nearly all countries of the world [1]. It continues to increase in numbers and significance as changing lifestyles lead to reduced physical activity, and increased obesity. Insulin is a hormone that monitors blood sugar level [2]. Hyperglycemia is a common effect based on uncontrolled diabetes over time, which leads to serious damage to many body systems. Diabetes is one of the leading causes of death, resulting in 4 million deaths worldwide [3,4]. In 2017, 425 million people were estimated to have diabetes worldwide [3,4]. More than 80% of deaths from diabetes occur in low- and middle-income nations. Over time, diabetes can harm the heart, blood vessels, eyes, kidneys, and nerves [4]. Early diagnosis may be accomplished through relatively inexpensive blood testing. Management of diabetes involves lowering blood glucose level along with other known risk factors. To prevent and manage diabetes, the patient must maintain a healthy meal regimen, exercise regularly, maintain normal body weight, and avoid smoking cigarette [5]. While type 1 DM can be managed by insulin injection, type 2 DM is managed with or without insulin injection [6]. Insulin reduces blood glucose level [7]. Bariatric surgery is used

Applications of Multi-Criteria Decision-Making Theories in Healthcare and Biomedical Engineering.
http://dx.doi.org/10.1016/B978-0-12-824086-1.00008-6

in type 2 DM, especially when the individual is obese [8]. Gestational diabetes usually goes away after the baby is delivered.

The essential hormone responsible for the regulations of glucose uptake from the blood to the cells of the body, muscle, tissues and liver is insulin. So, a defect in insulin-producing cells plays a major role in all forms of DM [9]. Glucose is supplied to the body from three sources:

1. Intestinal absorption of food.
2. Glycogenolysis (catabolism of stored glucose in the liver).
3. Gluconeogenesis (generation of glucose from noncarbohydrate substrates).

Insulin plays a major role in adjusting glucose levels in the body. It can inhibit catabolism of glycogen, transport of glucose into muscular and adipose tissue, and can initiate the storage of glucose in the form of glycogen. When there is a rising level of glucose in the bloodstream, the beta cells present in the islets of Langerhans in the pancreas are released. This typically brings the blood glucose level back to normal. Conversely, when there is fasting or starvation, the beta cells present in the islets of Langerhans in the pancreas stimulate the release of glucagon, thereby raising the glucose level to normal.

This process is usually controlled by glucagon which acts in a reversed manner to insulin [10]. In an event that the measure of insulin is inefficient or if cells react inefficiently to insulin, then absorption of glucose by the body will not occur and it is not properly stored in the liver and muscle. Glycosuria occurs when the concentration of glucose in the body persists over a certain period. This is as a result of the kidney reaching its reabsorption threshold [11]. This further leads to inhibition of the reabsorption of water by the kidney resulting in polyuria. Dehydration also occurs, leading to increased thirst (polyphagia).

A glucometer is used to determine the concentration of glucose in the blood. It is a key element of home-blood-glucose-monitoring (HBGM) by people with DM. A small drop of blood obtained by pricking the thumb with a lancet is placed on a disposable test strip that the meter reads and uses to calculate the blood glucose level. Results are displayed in mg/dl or mmol/l. Many glucometers employ the oxidation of glucose to gluconolactone catalyzed by glucose oxidase. Others use a similar reaction catalyzed instead by another enzyme, glucose-dehydrogenase. This has the advantage of sensitivity over glucose oxidase but is more susceptible to interfering reactions with other substances. In the blood glucose monitoring industry, it is well accepted that three 'C' terms drive people's willingness to test: cost, comfort, and convenience. The comfort advantage of noninvasive technology is easily understood.

Point-of-care (POC) testing typically refers to the performance of a diagnostic laboratory test outside of a traditional laboratory and near the site of patient care, in either in-patient settings or out-patient clinics [12–14]. The driving thought behind POC testing is to pass on the results of the test beneficially and speedily to the patient. The use of mobile devices in the healthcare setting also enables the healthcare provider to quickly access patient test results sent from a POC testing device [14]. A reduction in morbidity and mortality has been associated with such rapid turnaround times.

Three main types of diabetes occur; type 1 diabetes occurs when the pancreas fails to produce the necessary amounts of the insulin hormone needed by the body [6]. It is sometimes referred to as juvenile diabetes or insulin-dependent diabetes mellitus (IDDM) and the cause is unknown [6]. Type 2 diabetes results when the body cells are unable to utilize the insulin secreted by the pancreas. Type 2 diabetes is sometimes referred to as non-insulin-dependent diabetes mellitus (NDDM) or adult-onset diabetes (Nandimath et al., 2016). Gestational DM result when an expectant mom without a prior history of diabetes suddenly develops hyperglycemia [15].

Type 1 diabetes arises when there is a destruction of the beta cells of the islet of Langerhans in the pancreas resulting in insulin insufficiency [16]. Type 1 diabetes occurs in two circumstances:

1. Immune-mediated cause
2. Idiopathic cause

Type 1 diabetes related to immune-mediated cause arises when the immune system is flawed, dysfunctional, or deteriorated. Idiopathic causes occur from an unknown cause [16]. Most type 1 diabetes is of immune-mediated cause thereby resulting in 10% of DM cases in Canada, the United States, and Europe [16]. In this case, sensitivity and receptivity to insulin are usually normal. Type 1 diabetes can also be passed down from generations (inherited) [16], with several genes prompting the risk of diabetes [16]. Type 1 diabetes can also result in environmental factors, which include diet and viruses [16]. Dietary causes include gliadin while no specific factor associated with viruses has been supported [17]. Type 1 diabetes is mostly diagnosed during childhood.

Type 2 DM is associated with insulin resistance, which sometimes comes with comparatively inadequate insulin secretion (Diagnosis and Classification of Diabetes Mellitus, 2008). This occurs because the insulin receptor designated to respond to insulin action is defective; nonetheless, the specific defects are not known. Type 2 diabetes constitutes the major occurrence of metabolic disorder [18]. Patients with type 2 diabetes usually show prior evidence of prediabetes in the course of their life before being confirmed to have type 2 DM. Type 2 diabetes can also be a result of the lifestyle of an individual [19]; however, genetic implication also persists [19–21]. The lifestyle in question here includes lack of exercise or any other physical activity, and obesity as a result of unhealthy consumption of diet and stress [22]. Consuming sugar-sweetened drinks in excess also results in increased risk [21].

Gestational diabetes manifests like type 1 and type 2 DM. It usually comprises insufficient insulin production and receptivity. Unlike type 1 and type 2 diabetes, gestational diabetes is fully treatable with the patient having a full recovery. Although medical supervision is required throughout pregnancy. If left untreated, gestational diabetes could become harmful to both the health of the fetus and mother. The affected fetus could manifest diseases such as congenital heart failure, central nervous system abnormalities, skeletal muscle malfunction, and macrosomia.

The predominant symptoms of chronic diabetes include: polyuria (increased urination), polydipsia (increased thirst), and polyphagia (increased hunger) [23]. Usually, symptoms manifest within weeks or months in type 1 diabetes and take longer to appear in type 2 DM. There are recorded cases where symptoms do not show in type 2 DM [24]. Other symptoms include weight loss, tiredness, diabetes ketoacidosis, diabetic retinopathy, diabetic dermatomes, itchy skin, blurred vision, headache, fatigue, slow healing of cuts, vision changes, and skin rashes [24,25]. When the three types of diabetes are left untreated, a long-term complication is inevitable [26]. The symptoms may manifest in weeks, months, and even years. Complications range from coronary artery disease [26] to macrovascular diseases such as stroke and peripheral artery disease. Diabetes could also increase the risk of having cataracts, glaucoma, and other retina problems.

Since there are many available glucometers in the market, it is necessary to evaluate them individually to ascertain their strengths and weaknesses and be able to suggest which is the most preferred for usage by people living with diabetes. Evaluation can be performed in many ways. Some researchers employed a direct comparative evidence-based review of glucometers based on turnaround time, patient sample volume, preanalytical and postanalytical factors, and cross infection [27]. Others used methods such as comparative performance methods and clinical and experimental studies to know which glucometer is best. Here, samples were taken from volunteers (diabetics) and the accuracy of the glucometer is analyzed with other glucometer and laboratory chemistry analyzers.

In our study, multicriteria decision-making (MCDM) will be utilized for the evaluation of selected glucometer. This method will be applied to evaluate multiple conflicting criteria such as the cost of glucometer, sample volume, blood source, turnaround time, the enzyme used and result range. The MCDM method allows for input of both quantitative and qualitative data. The cost of glucometer, sample volume, and turn-around time are quantitatively analyzed while the blood source, the enzyme used, and result-range are qualitatively analyzed. Several studies have been conducted using the MCDM method. Some of these studies include: Capacity Evaluation of Diagnostic Tests for COVID-19 Using Multi-Criteria Decision-Making Techniques [28], A Multi-Criteria Decision-Making Approach for Schizophrenia Treatment Techniques [29], Fuzzy PROMETHEE Analysis of Leukaemia Treatment Techniques [30], Evaluation of Sterilization Methods for Medical Devices [31], Evaluating Lung Cancer Treatment Techniques Using Fuzzy PROMETHEE Approach [32], Evaluating Cancer Treatment Alternatives using Fuzzy PROMETHEE Method [33], and Evaluating Nuclear Medicine Imaging Devices using Fuzzy PROMETHEE Method [34]. Having seen its use and effectiveness in the field of medicine,

MDCM utilization will be applied to this study to evaluate the selected glucometer in the management of diabetes mellitus.

8.2 Selected glucometers

8.2.1 Freestyle Lite

Patients living with DM can utilize Abbott Freestyle Lite glucometer to manage their metabolic condition. Apart from being simple and smaller than the usual types of glucometer, it requires no coding. This simplicity makes it possible to hold it comfortably on the palm. The display screen is very organized and can easily be understood without stress. There are two distinct features of this type of glucometer: one is its quick turnaround time of just 5 seconds and the other is its ability to use 0.3 microliters of a fresh capillary blood sample taken from the tip of the thumb with a lancing device. With no coding required, diabetics can utilize the FreeStyle Lite test strip to get a quick, precise blood glucose result. The Abbott FreeStyle Lite incorporates bigger numbers, making the display straightforward to interpret and elastic grasps make it less demanding to hold.

8.2.2 Accu-Chek Aviva

This slim and fragile glucometer is designed to be user-friendly and a comfortable choice for diabetes patients who will like to constantly know their sugar level. With an easy to handle elastic gasp, the Accu-Chek Aviva can easily be used. It needs only a little volume of a blood sample to accurately run a blood glucose test. The test strips are utilized to restore a quick and solid blood sugar level. Four different updates can be configured for various occasions to help in recalling when to test blood sugar level. This device has embedded in it an extra battery that can hold time and memory for as long as 72 hours in case the main battery is removed or come short of control.

8.2.3 OneTouch Verio IQ

This glucometer identifies high and low results, thereby helping individuals who self-alter their insulin measurements to settle on informed choices. It also demonstrates how frequently the user had high and low results. The meter surpasses the 2013 ISO blood glucose meter precision guidelines with more than 99% of results falling inside the accuracy boundaries. Testing in a dark room is made substantially less demanding because when a test strip is inserted, the Verio IQ illuminates its screen and the test strip and also features a 750-result memory. The Verio IQ gives extremely precise outcomes because each blood test is broken down 500 times ahead of when the result is delivered and the meter makes up for meddling variables, for example, vitamin C and pain relievers. The test strips require a little blood test of only 0.4 microliters and blood can be connected to either the left or right half of the test-strip, which makes it simpler to apply blood from fingers on either hand.

8.2.4 OneTouch Ultrasmart

Aside from being a glucometer, OneTouch Ultrasmart incorporates an electronic logbook. It is more than just a glucometer with the electronic book. Individuals living with DM can use the pieces of information recorded to track progress in their use of insulin to manage the condition. With this combined feature, OneTouch Ultrasmart becomes the very first glucose monitoring device to successfully combine glucometer function with a logbook, hence making blood glucose results easily understood. The device can also be used to track individual general health, exercise, medication, and diet to better know their effect on diabetes. The display screen is easy to use and understand, with clear-cut buttons. An individual living with diabetes can input factors that could affect their results, such as diet, exercise, medication, and other varying health conditions.

8.2.5 TrueTrack

TrueTrack works perfectly well with capillary whole blood and is not recommended for venous blood. The device displays its results in plasma values, and these values are accurate and precise. The device does not work with the strips from other blood glucometer devices because it employs a closed system configuration that allows only TrueTrack test strips and TrueTrack control to be used. TrueTrack cannot be used to diagnose diabetes in an infant or newborn. It is recommended that quality control is done on the device before its first use; this ensures that accurate and precise results are calculated. The device provides two types of quality control test. One is to let you know that the device is working perfectly well and the other is to ensure that the technique used is good. The device performs an automated self-test each time a test strip is inserted.

8.2.6 Ascensia Contour USB

This is the oldest glucometer that provides an attachment straight to a computer, thereby making it possible for users to gain access to data and also share with a healthcare provider for advice. This is a significant improvement when it comes to the management of DM. The device can stockpile about 2,000 test results. It employs a plug-and-play approach that makes getting to and surveying the glucose patterns less demanding than at any previous time. Contour USB is equipped with knowledge about patterns and trends in the patient's blood glucose level, which makes it possible to "Plugin, know more, take action." With a smaller, elegant profile conveying ground-breaking innovation, similarity, and administration programming, the Ascensia Contour USB is a cutting-edge glucometer.

Contour USB incorporates various features to empower individuals with diabetes to be able to properly deal with their blood glucose levels. These functions incorporate pre- and postmeal alerts and reminders to isolate before-a-meal and after-meal readings. The Contour USB comes fitted with built-in diabetes data management software. Simply connect to the Contour USB to a computer USB port to begin utilizing Glucofacts Deluxe software, no compelling reason to download programming or utilize links to associate.

8.2.7   Omnitest 3

The meter is perfect for individuals who wish to possess a blood glucose display screen that is basic, fast, and simple to utilize. The Omnitest 3 passes the 2013 ISO blood glucose meter accuracy standard. Omnitest 3 requires insignificant blood and is one of the quickest blood glucose monitoring devices. Omnitest 3 conveys result with no coding, requires a minor blood test size of 0.3 microliters and takes just 3 seconds to show the result. The glucometer has an easy-to-use navigation and an extensive liquid crystal display (LCD) show an elastic grasp for easy handling. The device has a memory capacity of 500 test results with different markers to distinguish between results (premeal, postmeal, after taking medication and control tests). There are likewise five adaptable alarms that can help with keeping up a relentless treatment administration. Different highlights of the meter include auto-on control with strip addition, auto-off control with strip discharge, five alerts that can be set, rubber handle, pre- and post-meal alerts, and control marking function for better glucose analysis.

8.2.8   iHealth Align

iHealth Align is a portable glucometer that works exclusively with iHealth test strips, which are sold separately. It is about the size of a quarter and fit easily into a pocket. It is attached directly to a smartphone or tablet for fast and accurate reading whenever and wherever. The measuring method in use is Amperometric technology using glucose oxidase. The package comes with the meter, lancing device, lancets, four colored cases, and a clear cap.

8.3   Materials and methods

8.3.1   A brief history

In 1982, J.P. Brans developed the PROMETHEE I (partial ranking) and PROMETHEE II (complete ranking) and later presented it at a conference organized by R. Nadeau and M. Landry at the Université Laval, Québec, Canada (L'Ingéniérie de la Décision. Elaboration d'instrumentsd'Aide à la Décision). That same year, G. Davignon employed this methodology for several applications in healthcare. Subsequently, PROMETHEE III (ranking based on intervals) and PROMETHEE IV (continuous case) were developed by J.P. Brans and B. Mareschal. By 1988, they both proposed a visual interactive module GAIA to enable a graphical supporting the PROMETHEE methodology. Between 1992 and 1994, J.P. Brans and B. Mareschal further extended the methodology by introducing PROMETHEE V (MCDA including segmentation constraints) and PROMETHEE VI (representation of the human brain) [35].

8.3.2 Fuzzy logic

Obtaining crisp data that accurately defines real-life situations is a very challenging feat. Additional to this challenge is the description of imprecise data or information that is not completely true or false. Boolean logic has a system of extremities, a situation is either true (1) or false (0), no room for in-betweens or uncertainties is allowed. In fuzzy logic, however, a machine can treat situations with a degree of uncertainty attached. For instance, Boolean logic in treating the temperature of a room will either state that the room is hot or cold, but at what point does the temperature cross over from being cold to being hot? Fuzzy logic, however, provides an alternative of very cold, cold, warm, hot, very hot, and so on to solve the problem associated with uncertainty.

Fuzzy logic is preferred and has an advantage over other methods, such as predictable logic, Bayesian control, probability theory, classical theory, and so many such systems because fuzzy logic provides a system of computing with words, meaning words are used to represent numbers in computing and reasoning [36]. Instead of the standard "true or false" logic (1 or 0), fuzzy logic is a theoretical method built on a "degree of fact" basis. Dr. Lotfi Zadeh from the University of California at Berkeley in the 1960s first proposed the concept of fuzzy logic. Dr. Zadeh focused on the issue of natural language machine comprehension. It may help to understand fuzzy logic, as the way reasoning works and binary or Boolean logic is a special case. Language in nature (as most other things in existence and even in the universe) is not easily translated into absolute terms of 0 and 1.

Fuzzy logic includes 0 and 1 as extreme cases of truth (or "state of matter" or "fact") but also includes the various states of truth between them so that, for example, the result of a comparison between two things might not be "tall" or "short" but ".38 tall." Fuzzy logic seems closer to how our brains work. We aggregate data and form several partial truths that we further aggregate into higher truths that, in turn, when certain thresholds are exceeded, cause further results such as motor reaction. Neural networks, expert systems, and other artificial intelligence applications use a similar process. Fuzzy logic is essential to the development of human-like AI capabilities, sometimes referred to as general artificial intelligence: the representation of generalized human cognitive capabilities in software so that, faced with an unfamiliar task, the AI system can find a solution.

8.3.3   Multicriteria decision-making

Multicriteria decision-making (MCDM), also referred to as multiple-criteria decision analysis (MCDA), is a research area that analyzes various available choices in a situation or research area that spans daily life, social sciences, engineering, medicine, and many other areas. [37] defined the term as solving a problem with multiple conflicting objectives. MCDM is one of the most popular decision-making tools utilized in various fields [38]. MCDM analyses the alternatives and attempts to compare these alternatives based on the selected criteria, against every other available option in an attempt to assist the decision-maker in selecting an option with the minimal compromise and maximum advantages. The criteria used in the analyses of these criteria can be either qualitative or quantitative.

Division of MCDM can be made into two categories, based on the method used to determine the weight of each alternative [39]:

1. **Compensatory decision-making**: This involves evaluating the criteria, including the weak points and strong points, and allowing the strong points of each criterion to make up for the weak points, thereby putting all the criteria of the criteria into consideration. An example of compensatory decision-making tool is the analytical hierarchy process (AHP) a technique mostly used when the environment for the analysis is complex; it is used in the comparison of criteria that are difficult to quantify.
2. **Outranking decision-making**: This method compares the criteria to determine which criteria rank higher than the others based on the comparisons [40]. A popular example of an outranking decision-making method is elimination and choice expressing reality (ELECTRE) a method that is used to choose, rank, and sort out alternatives to solve a problem.

8.3.4   Preference Ranking Organization Method for Enrichment Evaluations (PROMETHEE)

PROMETHEE is a multicriteria decision-making tool that allows a user to analyze and rank available alternatives based on the available criteria. PROMETHEE is preferred over other multicriteria decision methods for reasons such as:

- PROMETHEE can be used to handle qualitative and quantitative criteria simultaneously.
- PROMETHEE deals with fuzzy relations, vagueness, and uncertainties.
- PROMETHEE is easy to handle and provides the user with maximum control over the weights of the criteria.

PROMETHEE requires only a couple of information from the decision-maker, i.e. information regarding the weights of the selected criteria and the preference function to be used in comparing the alternatives [41].

For the definition of various criteria, different preferential functions (Pj) are available in PROMETHEE. The preference function determines the difference between the evaluations concerning particular criteria with two alternatives, and a preference degree from 0 to 1. The preference functions can be used for practical use at the discretion of the decision-maker (the normal function, V-shape function, level function, u-shape function, linear function, and Gaussian function). A detailed description of the preference functions used and how to make a decision on which function best suits a scenario was discussed by J.P. Brans et al. [42]. Generally, type III (v-shape) and type V (linear) preference functions are mostly used for data with quantitative measures, while type I (usual shape) and type IV (level) preference functions are mostly used for qualitative data.

The significance of the criteria to be defined is as follows:

- q indicates a threshold of indifference.
- p is a threshold that indicates strict preference.
- σ is an intermediate point between q and p.

8.3.5 The steps of the PROMETHEE method

The creators of the technique [42] have discussed the complete steps of the PROMETHEE method; this method has not been altered in any way for this research.

1. Define a specific preference function for each criterion.
2. Determine the weight of each criterion. Normalization of weights or equality of weights can be decided at the discretion of the decision-maker.
3. For every alternative, determine the outranking relation.
4. Determine the positive and negative outranking flows.

The positive outranking flow is an expression of how a particular alternative is better than the other alternatives. The higher the positive outranking value of a particular alternative, the better the alternative. The negative outranking flow is an expression of how a particular alternative is bested by other alternatives. The lower the negative outranking value, the better the alternative. The negative outranking flow is an expression of how a particular alternative is bested by other alternatives. The lower the negative outranking value, the better the alternative.

1. Define the partial preorder on the alternatives.
2. Determine the net outranking flow for each alternative.

8.3.6 Application of fuzzy PROMETHEE

To determine the weight of each criterion, the Yager index was used to defuzzify the triangular fuzzy numbers. The use of the Yager index was preferred over other methods because it puts into consideration all the points and is not hugely affected by extreme values or weights. This paper utilizes fuzzy preference ranking organization method for enrichment evaluation (PROMETHEE) method. This strategy is proposed to analyze options, while the criteria are not numerical. PROMETHEE has been developed to provide a complete ranking of a finite set of alternatives from the best to the worst. The ranking is calculated using a pairwise comparison of alternatives for each criteria, utilizing the preference function, and the data are then aggregated using criteria weighting to provide a net outranking flow and hence a complete ranking of alternatives. Therefore, in the fuzzy PROMETHEE method, we can compare the fuzzy value.

Instructions from manuals of the glucose monitoring systems were also studied for comparison of devices. The PROMETHEE method requires just two sorts of data: the data on the weights of the criteria considered and the decision maker's preference function when looking at the options as far as each different criterion is concerned. In the PROMETHEE method, distinct preference functions are accessible, with a specific end goal to characterize diverse criteria. The preference function signifies the distinction between the assessments gotten with two options with respect to a particular criterion, inside a preference degree running from 0 to 1. There are six distinct sorts of preference function that can be utilized to actualize the PROMETHEE technique: usual function, U-shaped function, V-shaped function, level function, linear function, and Gaussian function. In this study, Gaussian function was selected because the differences between the alternatives were calculated from the standard deviation of the data, while others give an arbitrary different matrix.

Table 8.1 shows the data obtained for each alternative after an extensive literature review. To effectively compare the selected glucometers, we assigned a weight for each criterion after careful consultation with an expert endocrinologist and other health-care providers. Based on these consultations, the cost of the device and turnaround time was assigned with weight 0.92, sample volume and blood source were assigned the weight 0.75, while the result range and the enzyme used were assigned with weight 0.25, as shown in Table 8.2.

8.4 Results

The complete ranking of glucometers as indicated in Table 8.3 shows that iHealth Align emerges as the most preferred glucometer based on the selected criteria and weight. Accu-Chek Aviva emerged as the most inferior of all the glucometer selected. Fig. 8.1 shows each alternative's positive and negative sides.

Fig. 8.1 shows the action profile of the strong and weak points for iHealth Align, having a high positive ranking for cost of glucometer but low ranking for turnaround time, enzyme used, and result range. Fig. 8.2 shows a very strong point for the cost of glucometer for Ascensia Contour USB and a slightly strong point for turnaround time and result range. However, the enzyme used is on a negative overall rating. Fig. 8.3 displays the action profile for Freestyle Lite in

TABLE 8.1 The criteria for glucometer devices and their corresponding values.

Alternatives	Cost ($)	Sample volume (uL)	Blood source	Turn-around time (s)	Enzyme	Result range
Freestyle Lite	19.00	0.3	Discomforting	5.0	Average	Narrow
Accu-ChekAviva	92.50	0.6	Mild	5.0	Average	Narrow
OneTouch Verio IQ	73.38	0.4	Mild	5.0	Good	Narrow
OneTouch Ultrasmart	60.00	1.0	Mild	5.0	Very good	Wide
TrueTrack	36.70	1.0	Mild	10.0	Very good	Wide
Ascensia Contour USB	19.90	0.6	Mild	5.0	Good	Wide
Omnitest 3	32.27	0.3	Mild	3.0	Very good	Narrow
iHealth Align	19.99	0.7	Mild	5.0	Very good	Narrow

TABLE 8.2 Linguistic fuzzy scale.

Linguistic scale for evaluation	Triangular fuzzy scale	Priority ratings of criteria
Very high (VH)	0.75, 1, 1	Turn around, cost
Important (H)	0.5, 0.75, 1	Sample volume, blood source
Medium (M)	0.25, 0.50, 0.75	
Low (L)	0, 0.25, 0.5	Enzyme, result range.
Very low (VL)	0, 0, 0.25	

the management of DM. It shows a very low positive ranking of sample volume, a moderately low positive ranking for turnaround time and a relatively high positive ranking on the cost of glucometer. The ranking of the enzyme used indicates a low negative ranking. Fig. 8.4 shows the net-flow of 0.1022 for Omnitest 3. This is backed by the fact that the sample volume has a very low positive ranking, and the cost of glucometer and the enzyme used is just slightly higher. However, the turnaround time of Omnitest 3 is very high.

Fig. 8.5 shows the action profile for OneTouch Ultrasmart with very low positive ranking for blood source and result range, but a high negative ranking

TABLE 8.3 Complete ranking for glucometer in the management of diabetes.

Ranking	Glucometer	Positive outflow ranking	Negative outflow ranking	Net flow
1	iHealth Align	0.2137	0.0108	0.2030
2	Ascensia Contour USB	0.2128	0.0106	0.2022
3	Freestyle Lite	0.2129	0.0267	0.1862
4	Omnitest 3	0.2130	0.1108	0.1022
5	OneTouch Ultrasmart	0.1066	0.1915	−0.0849
6	OneTouch Verio IQ	0.0654	0.2288	−0.1634
7	TrueTrack	0.1179	0.3185	−0.2006
8	Accu-Chek Aviva	0.0271	0.2718	−0.2447

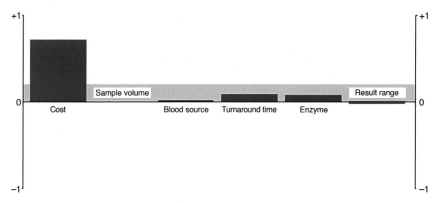

FIGURE 8.1   Action profile for iHealth Align.

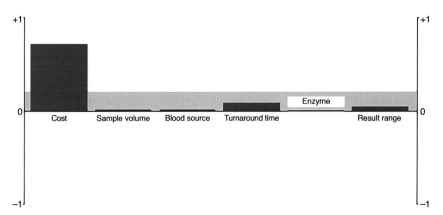

FIGURE 8.2   Action profile for Ascensia Contour USB.

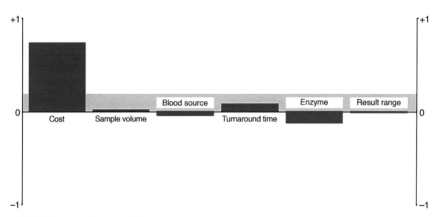

FIGURE 8.3   Action profile for Freestyle Lite.

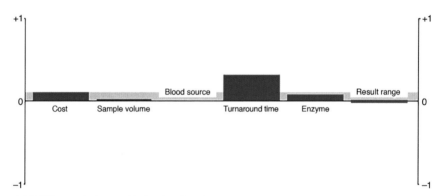

FIGURE 8.4   Action profile for Omnitest 3.

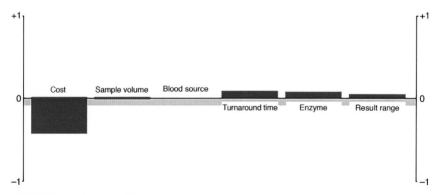

FIGURE 8.5   Action profile for OneTouch Ultrasmart.

for cost of glucometer. The very low negative rankings account for the negative net-flow ranking of OneTouch Ultrasmart in the management of DM. Fig. 8.6 shows the action profile for OneTouch Verio IQ, which indicates a very high negative ranking for cost of glucometer. The enzyme and result range is also on a negative ranking. However, turnaround time ranked positively but not very high. These rankings indicate why the net-flow of OneTouch Ultrasmart is on –0.1634. Fig. 8.7 is an action profile for Accu-Chek Aviva in the management of DM. It shows a very low positive ranking for turnaround time, a low positive ranking for enzyme, and result range with a lower positive ranking for the blood source. Fig. 8.8 highlights the net-flow of –0.2447 for TrueTrack. This is backed by the fact that the sample volume and blood source has a very low positive ranking; the result range is also low on the negative ranking. The turnaround time of TrueTrack is, however, very high.

Fig. 8.9 shows the network ranking view of glucometers in the management of diabetes with negative and positive outranking values.

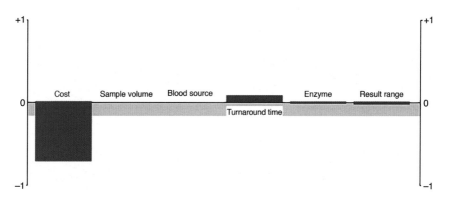

FIGURE 8.6   Action profile for OneTouch Verio IQ.

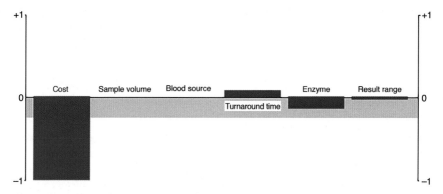

FIGURE 8.7   Action profile for Accu-Chek Aviva.

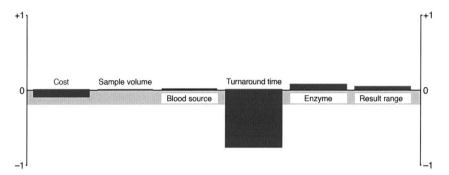

FIGURE 8.8 Action profile for TrueTrack.

This network view can be used to clearly outline how the treatment alternatives are ranked and the order in which they can be undertaken, from the most favorable, to the least favorable. The analysis of these results shows that iHealth Align outclasses other glucometers in the management of DM with a net flow ranking of 0.2030. This is due largely to the fact that iHealth Align has a relatively low sample volume and result range compared to other glucometers in the treatment of DM. Ascensia Contour USB, Freestyle Lite, and Omnitest 3 came second, third, and fourth with a net-flow ranking of 0.2022, 0.1862, and 0.1022, respectively. The negative net-flow ranking of –0.0849 gained by OneTouch Ultrasmart places it above OneTouch Verio IQ, which has a net-flow ranking of –0.134. TrueTrackAccuChek Aviva and TrueTrack are ranked the lowest, with a net-flow ranking of –0.2006 and –0.2447, respectively.

Fuzzy PROMETHEE is an effective method to employ in decision-making situations. It gives the user complete control over the criteria and their importance, fuzzy PROMETHEE weighs these criteria against each other to determine the combination of criteria that make an option better than other available options. Changing the weights of any of the criteria in the analysis will likely result in a different ranking of glucometers. The weights used in this analysis is a generalized weight based on the expert opinion of most likely and commonly seen scenarios. However, the weights can be changed based on the desires, discretion and need of the patient living with diabetes to arrive at a different ranking that will best suit the patient.

8.5 Conclusions

Early studies indicated that glucometers were associated with better ease of use and decreased turnaround time for diabetic patients. However, this study indicates better cost management of DM using POCT (glucometer) as well as a reduced long-term complication of diabetes. Commercially available glucometers varied widely. Nonetheless, the data given will be useful in informing the choice of glucometer for DM patients and healthcare providers. The solution of

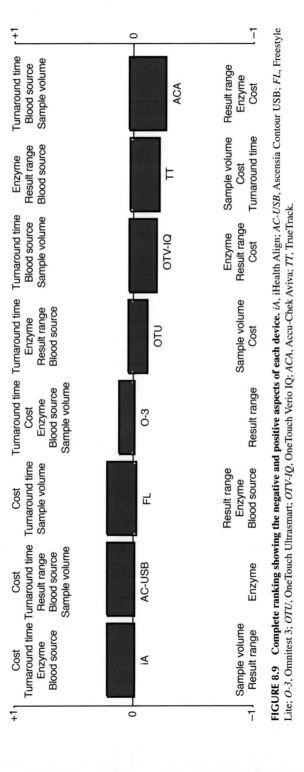

FIGURE 8.9 **Complete ranking showing the negative and positive aspects of each device.** *iA*, iHealth Align; *AC-USB*, Ascensia Contour USB; *FL*, Freestyle Lite; *O-3*, Omnitest 3; *OTU*, OneTouch Ultrasmart; *OTV-IQ*, OneTouch Verio IQ; *ACA*, Accu-Chek Aviva; *TT*, TrueTrack.

a multicriteria problem depends not only on the basic data included in the evaluation table but also on the decision maker. There is no absolute best solution! The best compromise solution also depends on the individual preferences of each decision maker. Consequently, additional information representing these preferences is required to provide the decision maker with the most useful decision aid. An alternative is better than another if it is at least as good as the other on all criteria. If an alternative is better on a criterion and the other one is better on other criteria, it is impossible to decide which one is the best without additional information. Both alternatives are therefore incomparable!

References

[1] S. Peter, An analytical study on early diagnosis and classification of diabetes mellitus, Bonfring Int. J. Data Min. 4 (2) (2014) 07–11 doi: 10.9756/bijdm.10310.

[2] Report of the Expert Committee on the Diagnosis and Classification of Diabetes Mellitus (2003). Diabetes Care 26 (Suppl. 1) (2003) S5–S20, doi: 10.2337/diacare.26.2007.s5.

[3] Diagnosis and classification of diabetes mellitus. Diabetes Care 27(Suppl. 1) (2003) S5–S10. doi:10.2337/diacare.27.2007.s5.

[4] H. Baynest, Classification, pathophysiology, diagnosis and management of diabetes mellitus, J. Diabetes Metab. 06 (05) (2015) doi:10.4172/2155-6156.1000541.

[5] I. Conget, Diagnóstico, clasificación y patogenia de la diabetes mellitus, Revista Española De Cardiología 55 (5) (2002) 528–535 doi:10.1016/s0300-8932(02)76646-3.

[6] R. Goldenberg, Z. Punthakee, Definition, classification, and diagnosis of diabetes, prediabetes, and metabolic syndrome, Can. J. Diabetes 37 (2013) S8–S11. doi:10.1016/j.jcjd.2013.01.011.

[7] Z. Punthakee, R. Goldenberg, P. Katz, Definition, classification and diagnosis of diabetes, prediabetes and metabolic syndrome, Can. J. Diabetes 42 (2018) S10–S15 doi:10.1016/j.jcjd.2017.10.003.

[8] C. Mertoglu, M. Gunay, Neutrophil-lymphocyte ratio and platelet-lymphocyte ratio as useful predictive markers of prediabetes and diabetes mellitus, Diabetes Metab. Syndr. Res. Rev. 11 (2017) S127–S131, doi: 10.1016/j.dsx.2016.12.021.

[9] P. Röder, B. Wu, Y. Liu, W. Han, Pancreatic regulation of glucose homeostasis, Exp. Mol. Med. 48 (3) (2016) e219-e219. DOI: 10.1038/emm.2016.6.

[10] D. Wherrett, D. Daneman, Prevention of type 1 diabetes, Endocrin. Metab. Clin. 38 (4) (2009) 777–790 doi:10.1016/j.ecl.2009.08.006.

[11] C. Quianzon, I. Cheikh, History of current non-insulin medications for diabetes mellitus, J. Commun. Hosp. 2 (3) (2012) 19081 doi:10.3402/jchimp.v2i3.19081.

[12] L. Nedosugova, Sulfonylureas and cardiovascular complications of type 2 diabetes mellitus, Diabetes Mellitus 16 (2) (2013) 26–35 doi:10.14341/2072-0351-3753.

[13] O. Maslova, Y. Suntsov, Epidemiology of diabetes mellitus and microvascular complications, Diabetes Mellitus 14 (3) (2011) 6–11 doi:10.14341/2072-0351-6216.

[14] M. Nair, Diabetes mellitus, part 1: physiology and complications, Brit. J. Nursing 16 (3) (2007) 184–188 doi:10.12968/bjon.2007.16.3.22974.

[15] A. MirghaniDirar, J. Doupis, Gestational diabetes from A to Z, World J. Diabetes 8 (12) (2017) 489–511 doi:10.4239/wjd.v8.i12.489.

[16] S. Soleimanpour, D. Stoffers, The pancreatic β cell and type 1 diabetes: innocent bystander or active participant?, Trends Endocrin. Met. 24 (7) (2013) 324–331 doi:10.1016/j.tem.2013.03.005.

[17] M. Haupt-Jorgensen, L. Holm, K. Josefsen, K. Buschard, Possible prevention of diabetes with a gluten-free diet, Nutrients 10 (11) (2018) 1746 doi:10.3390/nu10111746.

[18] K. Nsiah, V. Shang, K. Boateng, F. Mensah, Prevalence of metabolic syndrome in type 2 diabetes mellitus patients, Int. J. Appl. Basic Med. Res. 5 (2) (2015) 133 doi:10.4103/2229-516x.157170.

[19] R. Prasad, L. Groop, Genetics of type 2 diabetes—pitfalls and possibilities, Genes 6 (1) (2015) 87–123 doi:10.3390/genes6010087.

[20] V. Lyssenko, L. Groop, R. Prasad, Genetics of type 2 diabetes: it matters from which parent we inherit the risk, Rev. Diabetic Stud. 12 (3–4) (2015) 233–242 doi:10.1900/rds.2015.12.233.

[21] R. Prasad, L. Groop, Precision medicine in type 2 diabetes, J. Intern. Med. 285 (1) (2018) 40–48 doi:10.1111/joim.12859.

[22] N. Forouhi, N. Wareham, Epidemiology of diabetes, Medicine 42 (12) (2014) 698–702 doi:10.1016/j.mpmed.2014.09.007.

[23] L. Lupo, C. Palumbo, F. Lupo, G. Lobreglio, Correlation between meningoencephalitis etiology and magnetic resonance imaging: our experience, ClinicaChimica Acta 493 (2019) S557. doi:10.1016/j.cca.2019.03.1171.

[24] Y. Wu, Y. Ding, Y. Tanaka, W. Zhang, Risk factors contributing to type 2 diabetes and recent advances in the treatment and prevention, Int. J. Med. Sci. 11 (11) (2014) 1185–1200 doi:10.7150/ijms.10001.

[25] A. Olokoba, O. Obateru, L. Olokoba, Type 2 diabetes mellitus: a review of current trends, Oman Med. J. 27 (4) (2012) 269–273 doi:10.5001/omj.2012.68.

[26] V. Cerf, Growing the ACM family, Comm. ACM 56 (2) (2013) 7 doi:10.1145/2408776.2408778.

[27] R. Rajendran, G. Rayman, Point-of-care blood glucose testing for diabetes care in hospitalized patients, J. Diabetes Sci. Tech. 8 (6) (2014) 1081–1090 doi:10.1177/1932296814538940.

[28] M. Sayan, F. Sarigul Yildirim, T. Sanlidag, B. Uzun, D. Uzun Ozsahin, I. Ozsahin, Capacity evaluation of diagnostic tests for COVID-19 using multicriteria decision-making techniques, Comp. Math. Method M. 2020 (2020) 1–8 doi:10.1155/2020/1560250.

[29] I. Ozsahin, S. Abebe, G. Mok, A multi-criteria decision-making approach for schizophrenia treatment techniques, Arch. Psychiat. Psychother 22 (2) (2020) 52–61 doi:10.12740/app/111624.

[30] I. Ozsahin, D. Uzun Ozsahin, M. Maisaini, G.S.P. Mok, 'Fuzzy PROMETHEE analysis of leukaemia treatment techniques. World Cancer Res. J. 6 (2019) e1315.

[31] MT Mubarak, I Ozsahin, DU Ozsahin "Evaluation of Sterilization Methods for Medical Devices", Advances in Science and Engineering Technology International Conferences (ASET) 2019, IEEE Xplore, 2019.

[32] M. Maisaini, B. Uzun, I. Ozsahin, D. Uzun, Evaluating lung cancer treatment techniques using fuzzy PROMETHEE approach. International Conference on Theory and Applications of Fuzzy Systems and Soft Computing—ICAFS, 2018.

[33] D. Uzun, B. Uzun, M. Sani, A. Helwan, C. Nwekwo, F. Veysel, et al. Evaluating cancer treatment alternatives using fuzzy PROMETHEE method, Int. J. Adv. Comp. Sci. 8 (10) (2017) doi:10.14569/ijacsa.2017.081024.

[34] D. Ozsahin, B. Uzun, M. Musa, N. Şentürk, F. Nurçin, I. Ozsahin, Evaluating nuclear medicine imaging devices using fuzzy PROMETHEE method, Proc. Comp. Sci. 120 (2017) 699–705.

[35] H. Tang, Multiple-attribute decision making based on attribute preference, J. Software 7 (3.) (2012) doi:10.4304/jsw.7.3.644-650.

[36] L. Zadeh, Fuzzy logic = computing with words, IEEE Trans. Fuzzy Syst. 4 (2) (1996) 103–111.

[37] S. Zionts, MCDM—if not a roman numeral, then what?, Interfaces 9 (4) (1979) 94–101.

[38] A. Mardani, A. Jusoh, K. MD Nor, Z. Khalifah, N. Zakwan, A. Valipour, Multiple criteria decision-making techniques and their applications—a review of the literature from 2000 to 2014, Econ. Res.--EkonomskaIstraživanja 28 (1) (2015) 516–571.

[39] M. Majumder, Impact of urbanization on water shortage in face of climatic aberrations: Multi Criteria Decision Making, Springer (2015) 35–47.

[40] W. Yang, J. Wang, X. Wang, An outranking method for multi-criteria decision making with duplex linguistic information, Fuzzy Sets Syst. 198 (2012) 20–33.

[41] C. Macharis, J. Springael, K. De Brucker, A. Verbeke, PROMETHEE and AHP: The design of operational synergies in multicriteria analysis, Eur. J. Oper. Res. 153 (2) (2004) 307–317.

[42] J. Brans, P. Vincke, B. Mareschal, How to select and how to rank projects: The PROMETHEE method, Eur. J. Oper. Res. 24 (2) (1986) 228–238.

Further reading

[1] T. Amaral, A. Costa, Improving decision-making and management of hospital resources: An application of the PROMETHEE II method in an Emergency Department, Oper. Res. Health Care 3 (1) (2014) 1–6.

[2] T. Dai, J. Fang, W. Yu, G. Xie, Enzyme functionalized AuNPs and glucometer-based protein detection, IOP Conf. Ser.–Mat. Sci. 275 (2017) 012010 doi:10.1088/1757-899x/275/1/012010.

[3] F. Hu, V. Malik, Sugar-sweetened beverages and risk of obesity and type 2 diabetes: epidemiologic evidence, Physiol. Behav. 100 (1) (2010) 47–54 doi:10.1016/j.physbeh.2010.01.036.

[4] L. Ibragimova, Y. Filippov, A. Mayorov, Insulin pump therapy in type 1 diabetes mellitus: education effectiveness and quality of life, Diabetes Mellitus 15 (1) (2012) 35–40 doi:10.14341/2072-0351-5977.

[5] Y. Khalimov, A. Rudakova, A cost-effectiveness analysis of intensive therapy of type 2 diabetes mellitus (results of Steno-2 study), Diabetes Mellitus 14 (2) (2011) 116–120 doi:10.14341/2072-0351-5647.

[6] A. Shanian, O. Savadogo, TOPSIS multiple-criteria decision support analysis for material selection of metallic bipolar plates for polymer electrolyte fuel cell, JJ. Power Sources 159 (2) (2006) 1095–1104 doi:10.1016/j.jpowsour.2005.12.092.

[7] S. Silas, E. Rajsingh, Performance analysis on algorithms for the selection of desired healthcare services, Perspect. Sci. 8 (2016) 107–109.

[8] D. Wilson, B. Buckingham, Prevention of type 1a diabetes mellitus, Pediatr. Diabetes 2 (1) (2001) 17–24 doi:10.1046/j.1399-543x.2001.00000.x-i3.

[9] D. Ozsahin, I. Ozsahin, A fuzzy PROMETHEE approach for breast cancer treatment techniques, Int. J. Med. Res. Health Sci. 7 (5) (2018) 29–32.

[10] M. Yazdani, A. Payam, A comparative study on the material selection of microelectromechanical systems electrostatic actuators using Ashby, VIKOR and TOPSIS, Mater. Des. (1980–2015) 65 (2015) 328–334 doi:10.1016/j.matdes.2014.09.004.

Chapter 9

Comparison of MRI devices in dentistry

Gürkan Ünsal[a,b] and Dilber Uzun Ozsahin[a,c,d]

[a]*DESAM Institute, Near East University, Turkish Republic of Northern Cyprus, Nicosia, Turkey;*
[b]*Department of Dentomaxillofacial Radiology, Near East University, Turkish Republic of Northern Cyprus, Nicosia, Turkey;* [c]*Department of Biomedical Engineering, Near East University, Turkish Republic of Northern Cyprus, Nicosia, Turkey;* [d]*Medical Diagnostic Imaging Department, College of Health Sciences, University of Sharjah, Sharjah, United Arab Emirates*

9.1 Introduction

Magnetic resonance imaging (MRI) was developed for clinical use around the 1980s following the studies by Paul Lauterbur and Peter Mansfield [1]. Both scientists were awarded the Nobel Prize in Physiology/Medicine in 2003. The basic principle of MRI is as follows: The patient is placed inside a large magnet that will affect the nucleus of the atoms in the body, especially hydrogen, and align them with the active magnetic field. Then, a radio frequency pulse is directed into the patient to resonate some hydrogen nuclei. When the radio-frequency is cut off, the accumulated energy is released from the body and detected by the coils. According to the distribution pattern of hydrogens, a detailed image of the body is reconstructed [1].

MRI has a high-contrast resolution of soft tissues which makes it advantageous to other imaging modalities. Disadvantages of this imaging technique are high installation cost, long scanning times, and possible patient injuries due to ferromagnetic metals interacting with the magnetic field. Because of this injury potential, patients with ferromagnetic objects such as cardiac pacemakers cannot have MRI scans. Metal objects that are used in dentistry will not cause harm to the patients since they will not move with the magnetic field; however, these objects distort the images. Titanium dental implants are not ferromagnetic; thus, they will only lower the quality of the image without any harm to the patient. Lastly, claustrophobic patients may not want to take MRI scans if it is in a closed-MRI unit [1–3].

The strength of the magnetic field is defined by Tesla (T). Four main types of magnets are used in MRI units including permanent magnets, resistive magnets, superconducting magnets, and hybrid magnets. Superconducting magnets are

Applications of Multi-Criteria Decision-Making Theories in Healthcare and Biomedical Engineering.
http://dx.doi.org/10.1016/B978-0-12-824086-1.00009-8

the majority of the magnets nowadays in modern MRI unit and the magnetic fields can reach up to 18 T. An externally applied magnetic field affects the specific magnetic nuclei, such as hydrogen (^{1}H), carbon (^{13}C), fluorine (^{19}F), sodium (^{23}Na), oxygen (^{17}O), nitrogen (^{15}N), and phosphor (^{31}P). These atoms are called MRI active atoms [1,4,5].

9.1.1   Main criteria

Since there are lots of imaging criteria for an MRI scan, it is crucial to know the features of each MRI unit. The main criteria are:

- Magnet type
- Magnetic field strength
- Configuration
- Bore diameter
- Clinical approach (whole body or organ dedicated)
- Field of view (FOV)
- Imaging modes (sequences)
- Cooling system
- Fringe field
- Power requirements
- Cost

9.1.1.1   Magnet types

There are four main types of MRI magnets nowadays: permanent, superconductive, resistive, and hybrid magnets [1,4,6].

9.1.1.1.1   Permanent MRI magnets

A permanently magnetized iron bar magnet that has been twisted into a C-shape is used in MRI units. The two poles of this C-shaped bar are parallel and close to each other. Unless the room temperature is changed the magnetic field is uniform enough for MRI scans. Low power consumption, lower operating costs, and cheaper initial purchase prices are the advantages of these magnets. However; the magnetic field strength is relatively weak (0.064 T–0.4 T) and the units are relatively heavy (up to 80 tons) which makes it harder to replace these units. Weaker magnetic field strength is impractical for a chemical shift, spectroscopy, and functional brain imaging. Metals like neodymium can also replace the iron in magnets in order to reduce the weight; however, this will increase the cost of the MRI units significantly [6–8].

9.1.1.1.2   Resistive (air core) MRI magnets

Large electromagnets, which are similar to magnets in junkyards, are used in this MRI units. This magnet type requires a large and constant flow of current for both magnetizing and imaging. The price of resistive MRI magnets is relatively low but the operating costs, due to large power requirements of the coils and cooling system, are high. Solenoid-shaped, cylindrical-shaped, standard copper conductors are the main difference in resistive (air core) MRI magnets. They operate at room temperature. Electrical resistances of the coils require cooling systems and this magnet type produces a lot of heat; thus, a water cooling system is used with these magnets. The weight of these magnets is lighter than the permanent magnets. These magnets are useful for claustrophobic patients. Similar with permanent MRI magnets, resistive MRI magnets have weak magnetic field strength and they are frequently used for open-bore MRI and extremity imaging applications [7,8].

9.1.1.1.3   Hybrid MRI magnets

Hybrid MRI magnets are an alternative magnet type between permanent and resistive magnet systems. Hybrid MRI magnets are iron-cored electromagnets in which the magnetic energy of the resistive magnet is gathered in the space between the soft iron poles. Hybrid MRI units can reach up to 0.4 T and their weight is 10–15 tonnes [1,9,10].

9.1.1.1.4   Superconductive MRI magnets

Superconductive MRI magnets have solenoid-shaped alloys of Nb-Ti or Nb-Sn surrounded by Cu coils. These alloys have zero resistance to electrical current if the temperature is about 10 Kelvin. In order to keep the temperature about 10 Kelvins a liquid helium cooling system is integrated around the wires. Since this cooling system reduces the electrical resistance no external energy is required to maintain the current flow [8,11,12].

Even larger currents can be achieved with this system, which means that larger magnetic fields are possible.

This magnet type has high magnetic field strength, higher homogeneity of the field, higher SNR, faster scanning, and lower power consumption. Since this magnet type has advanced technology, the technical complexity is relatively high. Capital costs and the cryogen costs are also high. For example, a 1.5 T MRI unit with a superconductive MRI magnet costs about $1.5 million for the start-up. There is also a cost for cryogens but newer systems have a "cold head" refrigeration system that condenses cryogens. Other costs are site preparation, radiofrequency shielding, possible magnetic shielding, uninterruptible power supply (UPS), vibration mitigation, and floor reinforcements. There are some issues with these magnets, which are currently discussed in the conferences and studies. The most discussed issues with these magnets are the "quenches" and the constant magnetic field. Superconductive magnets, which have a magnetic field strength of greater than 1.5 T, are frequently used for MR spectroscopy and functional brain imaging [8,11,12].

9.1.1.2   Magnetic field strength

Field strength is the magnitude of a vector-valued field. Electromagnetic field results in both magnetic field strength and electric field strength. In radio frequency communications, the strength of the signal excites a receiver and induces a voltage at a specific polarization and frequency in order to provide an input signal to a receiver. Field strength meters are common for applications such as wi-fi and broadcasting [1].

The Earth's magnetic field strength is 25–30 Gauss (G) (μT) at the equator and 65–70 Gauss (G) (μT) at the poles, which is very weak compared to the magnetic field strength of the MRI units. MR units with 0.2 T to 3.0 T are frequently used commercially, while advanced research centres perform human imaging in almost 12.0 T. For imaging devices 3.0 T is considered as a high field strength; however, this "high" definition is only for the imaging devices since there are laboratory spectrometers that have around 23 T strength of magnetic field [6,13,14].

One of the most important criteria in MRI is the signal-to-noise ratio (SNR). The signal is the impulse from the patient, which is received by the coils during the MRI examination and the noise is the criteria that is caused due to the vibration in response to this magnetic field by the same coils. Having a stronger magnetic field will increase the signals that are read and transmitted by the coils which will lead to higher quality images with less obstruction [1].

Although 1.5 T is still the most common examination strength and has enough SNR to monitor and diagnose pathologies, 3.0 T can provide better image quality in less time for more detailed examination. 7.0 T magnets are not common commercially although they can be useful in the near future due to their increased T1 dispersion and high SNR features [15–17].

9.1.1.3   Bore size

MRI units traditionally had 60 cm bore size, although its possible to see bore sizes up to 70 cm within the previous decade. Those wider MRI units are known as "wide-bore MRIs" [18].

Claustrophobia, one of the most common phobias, is a situational fear which is triggered in tight or crowded spaces. Claustrophobic patients may have a hard time before and during the MRI examination due to the MRI bore diameters. Also, some patients are unable to fit inside some MRI bores. In order to scan the claustrophobic patients and patients who cannot fit inside the bores, some companies have different MRI units that are known as open-bore MRIs [1].

Since the magnetic field will be smaller in narrow-bore MRI units, stronger signals will be acquired, resulting in higher quality images. Wide-bore MRIs, on the other hand, will offer greater patient comfort with a trade off in the image quality. Still, wide-bore MRI units are superior to open-bore MRI units in terms of image quality. Closed-bore units, both traditional "narrow-bore MRI" units, and "wide-bore MRI" units can have magnetic field strengths of 1.5 T and 3.0 T. However, open MRI units have a relatively weaker magnetic field strength of around 0.3 T to 0.7 T [6, 19, 20].

Finally, it should not be forgotten that the scanning times of wide-bore MRI units are almost twice as fast as open MRI units scanning times, which means that the patient has to spend less time in the MRI unit [19].

9.1.1.4   Configuration (clinical approach)

There are two clinical approaches for MRI units: as whole-body MRI systems and as dedicated extremity MRI systems. Whole-body MRI systems are conventional closed MRI systems, whereas dedicated extremity MRI systems isolate only the relevant extremities in an MRI unit without scanning the whole body. Whole-body MRI units mostly have 1.5 T and 3 T magnetic field strength and these units have high capital and high operating costs. Also, whole-body MRI systems are not as accessible as dedicated extremity MRI units, which pose a problem of long wait times. Since the dedicated extremity MRI systems with low and intermediate magnetic field strengths have been introduced, an alternative system is now available to patients, offering greater patient comfort. Moreover, dedicated extremity units require smaller rooms to install, avoid claustrophobia, and reduce the possibilities of a biohazard. Specific to some pathologies and conditions it was shown that whole-body MRI systems with higher magnetic field strength (1.5 T–3 T) and dedicated extremity MRI systems with lower magnetic field strength (0.2 T–1 T) have similar specificity, sensitivity, and diagnostic accuracy. Since this is not applicable for all medical conditions; lower signalto-noise ratio, field inhomogeneities, and restricted field of view criteria are shortcomings of dedicated extremity systems that reduce diagnostic accuracy.

9.1.1.5   Field of view (FOV)

The field of view (FOV) is the extent of the visible volume that is captured by the MRI film. FOV can be specified as mm or cm depending on the manufacturer, denoting the dimensions of the view frustum: width, height and depth. FOV is divided by picture elements (pixels) or volume elements (voxels). As the pixel and voxel sizes vary according to the technology in the imaging unit FOV also varies and every single MRI device has their unique FOV sizes [1,6,21].

9.1.1.6   Imaging modes (sequences)

MRI imaging modes (sequences) are settings of pulsed-field gradients and pulse sequences, that result in a specific image appearance. Sometimes two or more modes can be combined to have a specialized MRI sequence such as spectroscopy.

Some well-known MRI imaging modes are [6,14,22]:

- Spin echo: T1 weighted, T2 weighted, proton density weighted (PD)
- Gradient echo (GRE): Steady-state free precession (SSFP), effective T2-star (T2*)
- Inversion Recovery: Short tau inversion recovery (STIR), fluid-attenuated inversion recovery (FLAIR), double inversion recovery (DIR)
- Diffusion weighted: conventional (DWI), apparent diffusion coefficient (ADC), diffusion tensor (DTI)

- Perfusion weighted: dynamic susceptibility contrast (DSC), dynamic contrast enhanced (DCE), arterial spin labeling (ASL)
- Functional MRI (fMRI): blood-oxygen-level dependent imaging (BOLD)
- Magnetic resonance angiography (MRA): time-of-flight (TOF), phase-contrast magnetic resonance imaging (PC-MRA)
- Susceptibility-weighted (SWI)

9.1.1.7 Fringe field

The peripheral field outside of the MRI unit's magnet core is known as the fringe field. This value of this criterion depends on the design of the magnet and the MRI room. Superconducting magnets have the largest fringe fields. A fringe field may extend beyond the limit of the room in which the MRI unit is installed. The strength of the magnetic fringe field is inversely related to the third power of the distance from the core of the magnet. These criteria are important since it can interact with electronic devices, such as computers and pacemakers. Pacemakers can be affected by magnetic fields exceeding 5 G and computers can get affected by magnetic fields exceeding 10 G. Fringe fields of 5 G and below are considered to be safe fringe field exposures and are inconsequential to magnetic resonance imaging safety [6,23,24].

9.1.1.8 Cost

MRI units have a wide price range, starting from $30,000 and go as high as $550,000. Dedicated extremity MRI units are generally cheaper than the whole-body MRI units, and some units don't even require additional magnetic shielding. This makes dedicated extremity MRI units a more convenient choice compared to the whole-body MRI units for smaller hospitals and clinics. While they're more expensive, whole-body MRI systems come with higher magnetic field strenght and gradients. Magnetic field strenght, gradient strength, manufacturing year, cooling system, channels, and slew rate (peak gradient strength/ rise time) determine the price tag of an MRI unit. Newer units tend to be more expensive as they're equipped with a helium cooling systems and have higher maintenance costs [25–27].

Additional factors for MRI unit costs are as follows [25]:

- Gradient strength
- Slew rate
- Coil type
- Bore diameter

Permanent magnet or helium-cooled magnet

- Installation
- Warranty
- Staff training

9.1.1.9 Synchronization strategy

Magnetic resonance imaging of moving organs requires specific data acquisition strategies due to the differences in each organ's flow constraints and motion. Additionally, each MRI unit/brand follows a different synchronization strategy in order to avoid artefacts of those moving organs. Since there is not any moving organ such as the heart in maxillofacial region, this synchronization does not have a significant effect on the maxillofacial MRI [28].

9.1.1.10 Magnet weight and size

MRI units have various magnet strengths and bore weights and sizes. Magnet weight and sizes do not have a significant contribution to the imaging itself; however, a different shielding and environment should be prepared for different size and weight. An overall low magnetic field MRI unit is around 5 metric tonnes; whereas, a medium/high magnetic field MRI unit is around 8 metric tonnes. Permanent low magnetic field unit can be around 30 metric tonnes which will cause various challenges for the practitioner in order to load and shield the MRI unit.

9.1.2 MRI applications in dentistry

MRI has an increasing demand in dentistry due to its superiority in soft tissue imaging. Temporomandibular joint evaluation is the most common application for MRI, in addition, almost all departments in dentistry have initial studies with MRI, such as orthodontics and prosthodontics [1,29,30].

9.1.2.1 Temporomandibular joint (TMJ)

Most MRI applications in dentistry aim to demonstrate the soft-tissue components of TMJ. Magnetic resonance imaging is superior to conventional 2D imaging and CBCT since it can demonstrate both masticatory muscles and TMJ disc. Localizing the position of the disc during the opening and closing of the jaw is essential to diagnose and treat the pathology, and MRI provides soft tissue visualization with great contrast and spatial resolution on coronal and sagittal MR slices [1,31].

Various studies were conducted to determine the optimal parameters for TMJ evaluation. Field of view, slice thickness, and slice gap were found to be the greater indicators. Van Rensberg and Nostje suggested slice thickness of 5.0–6.0 mm and a slice gap of 1.6–2.0 mm, whereas, Brooks et al. preferred a slice thickness of 3.0 mm and a slice gap of 0.5 mm for the optimal values. FOV values were determined as 24–28 cm to 10 cm for TMJ studies [1,31].

9.1.2.2 Orthodontics

The traditional approach for growth data collection during orthodontic treatments uses conventional 2D imaging and CBCT. Contemporary techniques utilize MRI to avoid ionizing radiation exposure while also providing superior imaging results compared to the 2D techniques such as lateral cephalogram for oropharynx, hypopharynx, and tongue volume assessments. A major challenge with MRI evaluation during orthodontics is archwires since they cause greater metal artefacts than brackets and orthodontic bands [31].

9.1.2.3 Prosthodontics/implantology

MRI can be also used to evaluate prosthetic ear models in maxillofacial prosthodontics. Similar results were found between laser scanning-CT and MRI images; however, MRI's image acquisition does not involve any ionizing radiation, which is a major advantage [32].

9.1.2.4 Malignancies

Malignant lesions in the oral cavity can arise in both hard and soft tissues. Conventional 2D dental radiography techniques are unable to demonstrate those pathologies which arise in soft tissues so MRI evaluation is crucial in order to detect early soft tissue malignancies. Perineural invasions of malignant neoplasia, extension of carcinoma penetrations, and lymph nodes can be interpreted in MRI images [8].

9.1.2.5 Salivary gland

CBCT and 2D conventional dental radiographs are unable to show salivary glands; thus, MRI, US, or Helical-CT should be used in order to evaluate the pathologies in them. Several studies were done with MRI about salivary gland stones (sialolithiasis), salivary gland infections, and malignancies. Evaluation of minor salivary glands are often not possible due to their small size but parotid gland, submandibular gland, and sublingual gland evaluation are achievable with MRI [8].

9.1.2.6 Osteomyelitis

Chronic suppurative osteomyelitis in jaws develops following an odontogenic infection, trauma, fracture, or irradiation to the mandible. With the conventional 2D imaging and CBCT, only the changes in the bone can be evaluated; however, MRI can display edematous changes in the bone marrow and surrounding tissues in addition to the bone area. This leads to earlier diagnosis in osteomyelitis cases, which increases the success of osteomyelitis treatment [8,33].

9.1.2.7 Vascular pathologies

Vascular pathologies such as arteriovenous malformation and cavernous haemangiomas can be life-threatening during maxillofacial surgeries since they can cause major bleeding complications. Conventional 2D imaging and CBCT are unable to show vascular structures and pathologies while MRI is able to display vascular structures due to its higher soft-tissue contrast [8,33].

9.2   Materials and methods

The PROMETHEE approach is a multicriteria selection-making technique, which is based completely on the mutual contrast of each desired pair with regards to every selected criterion. This method is one of the most efficient techniques in notion and application compared to other methods.

The advantages of PROMETHEE technique are:

- PROMETHEE is an outranking method.
- It has been successfully carried out to solve real-life planning problems.
- PROMETHEE I and PROMETHEE II supply partial and total ranking of the selections, respectively, while nonetheless offering simplicity.

The PROMETHEE method requires only two kinds of information: the information on the weights of the standards regarded and the decision-makers choice feature when evaluating the contributions of the options in terms of every separate criterion. In the PROMETHEE method, specific wish functions are on hand in order to outline distinctive criteria. The preference characteristic denotes the difference between the reviews acquired with two preferences two with regards to unique criteria, inside a desire diploma ranging from 0 to 1.

There has been little research principally based on the approach of fuzzy PROMETHEE. In most instances, it is difficult to accumulate crisp information and make a most suitable decision. Using fuzzy sets offers the selection maker the capability to outline the problems underneath the vague scenario, which is more realistic.

PROMETHEE was selected for the ranking process over MCDM techniques since it has more advantageous ease of application and efficiency. PROMETHEE application needs two data as weights of criteria and decision maker's choice of the criteria when comparing the different types of MRI units for each criterion. Each criterion were analyzed with Gaussian preference function on PROMETHEE decision lab software.

The MRI unit criteria that were selected for this fuzzy PROMETHEE study are:

- Bore size
- FOV
- Imaging modes
- Synchronization
- Configuration
- Cost
- Fringe field
- Field strength (T)

- Size
- Magnet weight

After finding the exact values of each criteria from the relevant manufacturer's website or manual, those values were calculated with decision lab software and complete rankings were obtained from the data.

Eighteen novel MRI units were found with exact values for all selected criteria (Table 9.1). Cost, configuration, synchronization, imaging modes, FOV, bore size, field strength, 5 Gauss fringe fields were compared in 18 novel MRI units with PROMETHEE Decision Lab program and Phi values were recorded.

9.3 Results and discussion

Table 9.2 demonstrates the ranking of MRI units according to criteria which are mentioned above (Table 9.2).

It is seen that higher field strength does not always make an MRI unit superior since the top two MRI units were open-bore MRI units with only 0.7 T. However, when open MRI units are compared to each other it is seen that open MRI units with higher field strength are ranked better. Also, it is seen that having an open bore does not make an MRI unit superior solely since three out of the top six MRI units had short-bore configuration. MRI units with low FOV values were ranked as 14th, 17th, and 18th which suggests that low FOV values can significantly decrease the general ranking of an MRI unit.

The cost of two devices was significantly higher than the rest of the 16 units and those units were ranked as 3rd and 5th, which means that higher cost is not what makes an MRI unit superior.

Narrow-bore size was also a negative feature since those three devices were ranked as 14th, 16th and 17th.

In general, thanks to fuzzy PROMOTHEE algorithms, it is fair to state that the overall ranking of an MRI unit depends on the correlation of multiple criteria which cannot be oversimplified with few criteria.

More criteria and more devices should be involved in future studies in order to determine the optimal unit for MRI scans.

Fuzzy PROMETHEE can be used to help the physicians to choose the optimal MRI devices for them. Different organs may require different MRI features; however, this paper focuses on general necessities. Further studies can be planned for each imaging technique and also for each organ.

9.4 Conclusion

Fuzzy PROMETHEE is useful to determine the better combination of criteria for an ideal MRI unit with giving the user the authority to control criteria and their importance. Although the ranking may change for each procedure and for each organ that will be imagined, the results of fuzzy PROMETHEE achieves reliable results that can aid the physicians and hospital material administrators

TABLE 9.1 MRI units and values for each criteria.

Manufacturer	Model	Bore size	FOV	Imaging modes	Synchronization	Configuration	Cost	Fringe field	Field strength (T)	Size	Weight
Hitachi	Altaire	Moderate	High	Moderate	Very good	Vertical field, open MRI	Medium	Moderate	0.7	Large	Very high
GE Healthcare	Signa Open Speed	Wide	Very high	Good	Very good	Open MRI	Low	High	0.7	Large	Very low
GE Healthcare	Signa HDx	Moderate	Very high	Good	Moderate	Short-bore compact	High	High	3.0	Large	Low
GE Healthcare	Signa Ovation	Moderate	High	Very good	Very good	Open MRI	Low	Low	0.35	Large	Moderate
Philips	Intera	Moderate	Very high	Very good	Good	Short-bore compact	High	High	3.0	Medium	Very low
Philips	Intera	Moderate	Very high	Very good	Good	Short-bore compact	Low	Moderate	1.5	Medium	Very low
GE Healthcare	Signa Profile	Wide	High	Very good	Very good	Open MRI	Low	Low	0.2	Medium	Low
GE Healthcare	Signa	Moderate	High	Good	Moderate	Cylindrical—high homogeneity	High	Moderate	3.0	Large	Low
Philips	Infinion	Moderate	Very high	Good	Moderate	Ultra-short-bore	Low	High	1.5	Medium	Very low
Siemens	Magnetom Harmony	Moderate	Very high	Good	Moderate	Compact	Low	Moderate	1.0	Medium	Very low

(Continued)

TABLE 9.1 MRI units and values for each criteria. (*Cont.*)

Manufacturer	Model	Bore size	FOV	Imaging modes	Synchronization	Configuration	Cost	Fringe field	Field strength (T)	Size	Weight
GE Healthcare	signa infinity TwinSpeed w/excite	Moderate	Very high	Good	Moderate	Short bore	Medium	Moderate	1.5	Medium	Very low
Siemens	Magnetom Symphony	Moderate	Very high	Good	Moderate	Compact	Medium	Moderate	1.5	Medium	Very low
GE Healthcare	Signa Infinity	Moderate	Very high	Good	Moderate	Short bore	Low	Moderate	1.0	Medium	Very low
Philips	Panorama	Narrow	Very low	Good	Good	Open MRI/C-arm	Low	Low	0.6	Large	Very high
Hitachi	AIRIS II	Moderate	High	Moderate	Very good	Vertical field,open MRI	Low	Low	0.3	Small	Low
Siemens	Magnetom C	Narrow	High	Good	Good	C-shaped open MRI	Medium	Low	0.35	Medium	Low
Philips	Panorama	Narrow	Very low	Good	Good	Open MRI/C-Arm	Low	Moderate	0.23	Medium	Low
Toshiba	Excelart AG w/Pianissimo	Wide	Very low	Moderate	Moderate	Cylindrical wide short bore	Medium	Moderate	1.5	Medium	Very low

TABLE 9.2 Ranking of the compared MRI devices.

Rank	Alternative	Phi+	Phi-	Phi
1	Altaire	0.0726	0.0238	0.0488
2	Signa Open Speed	0.0481	0.017	0.0311
3	Signa HDx 3.0 T	0.053	0.0272	0.0259
4	Signa Ovation	0.0476	0.0229	0.0247
5	Intera 3.0 T	0,0492	0.0276	0,0216
6	Intera 1.5 T	0.0309	0.0176	0.0133
7	Signa Profile	0.039	0.0272	0.0119
8	Signa 3.0 T	0.0413	0.0314	0.0099
9	Infinion 1.5 T	0.0299	0.0237	0.0061
11	Magnetom Harmony	0.0251	0.0252	-0.0001
11	Signa infinity 1.5 TwinSpeed w/excite	0.0227	0.0266	-0.0039
12	Magnetom Symphony	0.0227	0.0266	-0.0039
13	Signa Infinity 1.0 T	0.0209	0.0266	-0.0057
14	Panorama 0.6 T	0.0612	0.0719	-0.0107
15	AIRIS II	0.0262	0.0443	-0.0181
16	Magnetom C	0.0139	0.0397	-0.0258
17	Panorama	0.0136	0.0748	-0.0612
18	Excelart AG w/Pianissimo	0.0126	0.0806	-0.068

during the MRI unit selection process. Fuzzy PROMETHEE may also provide alternative solutions for decision-making problems in other imaging modalities and medical equipment. Last but not least, Fuzzy PROMETHEE can be easily used with more criteria and MRI units for ranking, which will surely take a longer time for a human being manually.

References

[1] K. Orhan, I. Rozylo-Kalinowska, Imaging of the Temporomandibular Joint, Springer, Cham, (2019).

[2] K. Orhan, H. Nishiyama, S. Tadashi, S. Murakami, S. Furukawa, Comparison of altered signal intensity, position, and morphology of the TMJ disc in MR images corrected for variations in surface coil sensitivity, Oral Surg. Oral Med. Oral Pathol. Oral Radiol. Endod. 101 (4) (2006) 515–522.

[3] K. Orhan, H. Nishiyama, S. Tadashi, M. Shumei, S. Furukawa, MR of 2270 TMJs: prevalence of radiographic presence of otomastoiditis in temporomandibular joint disorders, Eur. J. Radiol. 55 (1) (2005) 102–107.

[4] G. Wang, H. Xie, S. Hou, W. Chen, Q. Zhao, S. Li, Development of the 1.2 T~1. 5 T perma-nent magnetic resonance imaging device and its application for mouse imaging, Biomed. Res. Int. 2015 (2015) 858694.

[5] S. Kathiravan, J. Kanakaraj, A review on potential issues and challenges in MR imaging, Sci. World J. 2013 (2013) 783715.

[6] S.C. Bushong, G. Clarke, Magnetic Resonance Imaging, Physical and Biological Principles, 4th ed., Mosby, (2015).

[7] C. Westbrook, C.K. Roth, J. Talbot, MRI in Practice, 4th ed., Wiley, West Sussex, (2011).

[8] I. Ozcan, Dis̨ Hekimliḡinde Radyolojinin Esasları, Konvansiyonelden—Dijitale, stanbul Medikal Yayıncılık, Istanbul, (2017).

[9] R. Fahrig, K. Butts, J.A. Rowlands, R. Saunders, J. Stanton, G.M. Stevens, et al. A truly hy-brid interventional MR/X-ray system: feasibility demonstration, J. Magn. Reson. Imag. 13 (2) (2001) 294–300.

[10] V. Sherwood, J. Civale, I. Rivens, D.J. Collins, M.O. Leach, G.R. teer Haar, Development of a hybrid magnetic resonance and ultrasound imaging system, Biomed. Res. Int. (2014).

[11] J. Minervini, M. Parizh, M. Schippers, Recent advances in superconducting magnets for MRI and hadron radiotherapy: an introduction to 'Focus on superconducting magnets for hadron therapy and MRI', Supercond. Sci. Tech. (2018) 31.

[12] S. Pittard, P. Feenan, W. Vennart, Superconducting magnets for magnetic resonance imaging, Appl. Supercond. 1 (1993) 1827–1840.

[13] C.C. Finlay, S. Maus, C.D. Beggan, T.N. Bondar, A. Chambodut, T.A. Chernova, et al. Inter-national geomagnetic reference field: the eleventh generation, Geophys. J. Int. 183 (3) (2010) 1216–1230.

[14] A.L. Horowitz, MRI Physics for Physicians, Springer Science & Business Media, (1989).

[15] A. van der Kolk, J. Hendrikse, J.J.M. Zwanenburg, F. Visser, P.R. Luijten, Clinical applica-tions of 7T MRI in the brain, Eur. J. Radiol. 82 (5) (2013) 708–718.

[16] S.L. Paek, Y.S. Chung, S.H. Paek, J.H. Hwang, C.H. Sohn, S.H. Choi, et al. Early experi-ence of pre- and post-contrast 7.0T MRI in brain tumors, J. Korean Med. Sci. 28 (9) (2013) 1362–1372.

[17] S.W. Song, Y.D. Son, Z.H. Cho, S.H. Paek, Experience with 7.0 T MRI in patients with supra-tentorial meningiomas, J. Korean Neurosurg. Soc. 59 (4) (2016) 405–409.

[18] K. Ahn, I.S. Kim, B. Kim, Benefit of Wide-Bore Magnet In Reducing Patient's Motion: Com-parison with Narrow-Bore Magnet. Radiological Society of North America 2010 Scientific Assembly and Annual Meeting 2010.

[19] D. Hailey, Open magnetic resonance imaging (MRI) scanners, Issues Emerg. Health Technol. (92) (2006) 1–4.

[20] W.T. Sobol, Recent advances in MRI technology: implications for image quality and patient safety, Saudi J. Ophthalmol. 26 (4) (2012) 393–399.

[21] K. Orhan, H. Avsever, S. Aksoy, U. Seki, P. Bozkurt, Temporomandibular joint MR images: incidental head and neck findings and pathologies, Cranio. 37 (2) (2019) 121–128.

[22] W. Mangrum, K. Christianson, S. Duncan, Duke Review of MRI Principles: Case Review Series, Mosby, (2012).

[23] J.G. Kok, B.W. Raaymakers, J.J. Lagendijk, J. Overweg, C.H. de Graaff, K.J. Brown, Installa-tion of the 1.5 T MRI accelerator next to clinical accelerators: impact of the fringe field, Phys. Med. Biol. 54 (18) (2009) N409–N415.

[24] J.T. Bushberg, J.A. Seibert, E.M. Leidholdt, J.M. Boone, The Essential Physics of Medical Imaging, Lippincott Williams Wilkins, Philadelphia, 2002.

[25] How much does an MRI machine cost? (2019), https://lbnmedical.com/how-much-does-an-mri-machine-cost/.

[26] D.W. Young, What does an MRI scan cost?, Healthc. Financ. Manage. 69 (11) (2015).

[27] R.W. Westermann, C. Schick, C.M. Graves, K.R. Duchman, S.L. Weinstein, What does a shoulder MRI cost the consumer?, Clin. Orthop. Relat. Res. 475 (3) (2017) 580–584.

[28] T. Frauenrath, T. Niendorf, M. Kob, Acoustic method for synchronization of magnetic resonance imaging (MRI), Acta Acustica United with Acustica 94 (1) (2008) 148–155.

[29] L.K. Niraj, B. Patthi, A. Singla, R. Gupta, I. Ali, K. Dhama, et al. MRI in dentistry—a future towards radiation-free imaging—systematic review, J. Clin. Diagn. Res. 10 (10) (2016) ZE14–ZE19.

[30] H. Demirturk Kocasarac, H. Geha, L.R. Gaalaas, D.R. Nixdorf, MRI for dental applications, Dent. Clin. North Am. 62 (3) (2018) 467–480.

[31] R.P. Langlais, L.J. van Rensburg, J. Guidry, W.S. Moore, D.A. Miles, C.J. Nortje, Magnetic resonance imaging in dentistry, Dent. Clin. North Am. 44 (2) (2000) 411–426.

[32] T.J. Coward, B.J. Scott, R.M. Watson, R. Richards, A comparison of prosthetic ear models created from data captured by computerized tomography, magnetic resonance imaging, and laser scanning, Int. J. Prosthodont. 20 (3) (2007) 275–285.

[33] S.C. White, M.J. Pharoah, Oral Radiology: Principles and Interpretation, 7th ed., Mosby, (2013).

Chapter 10

Application of fuzzy PROMETHEE on hearing aid

Dilber Uzun Ozsahin[a,b,c], Rukayat Salawu[b], Berna Uzun[a,d] and Ilker Ozsahin[a,b,e]

[a]DESAM Institute, Near East University, Turkish Republic of Northern Cyprus, Nicosia, Turkey; [b]Department of Biomedical Engineering, Near East University, Turkish Republic of Northern Cyprus, Nicosia, Turkey; [c]Medical Diagnostic Imaging Department, College of Health Sciences, University of Sharjah, Sharjah, United Arab Emirates; [d]Department of Mathematics, Near East University, Turkish Republic of Northern Cyprus, Nicosia, Turkey; [e]Brain Health Imaging Institute, Department of Radiology, Weill Cornell Medicine, New York, NY, United States

10.1 Introduction

Hearing loss is the inability to hear properly [1]. It can be the partial or total inability to hear at all. This impairment affects about 16% of Americans and consequently affects a number of older people. People suffering from hearing loss also tend to encounter social, emotional, and psychological problems, which can affect the well being of the patient. The loss of hearing can be detrimental to the proper functioning of a person in terms of social, emotional, and psychological association with people. Dementia and low cognitive performance can occur as a result of hearing loss [2]. Hearing loss can be conductive, which might occur as a result of the ears' inability to conduct sound waves via the outer ear, eardrum, and middle ear, or can be sensorineural, which causes stems from the sensory portion of the ear, e.g. the vestibular cochlea nerve and the cochlea [3].

Both can be treated and managed with the use of hearing aids. For effective communication, hearing aids were introduced to aid hearing for people who have hearing loss problems. Hearing aids represent a form of help for hearing loss sufferers, it does not cure age related or noise induced hearing losses. Hearing aids collect sound and amplify them by improving the clarity and send sounds to the ear. There are different types of hearing aids that are tailormade for the specific levels of hearing loss that exist. Once hearing loss is diagnosed and it is noted that amplification would be suitable, hearing aid dispensers or audiologist atake impressions of the patient's ear. Impressions used are usually composed of silicone inserted in the patient's ear canal and the dried-up impressions

Applications of Multi-Criteria Decision-Making Theories in Healthcare and Biomedical Engineering.
http://dx.doi.org/10.1016/B978-0-12-824086-1.00010-4

are taken to the manufacturers for a custom-made hearing aid. Hearing aids are divided into two sets according to the principle of how sound is transmitted to the cochlea, which is either air conduction (AC) or bone conduction (BC) [4]. The hearing aids work in such a way that the remaining hair cells still present in the ear detect large vibrations and convert them into neutral signals and transmit them to the hearing part of the brain. The extent of hearing loss determines the type of hearing-aid amplification that would be provided. When the inner ear is too damaged, large vibrations are not converted into neutral signals, because such a hearing aid would not be effective [5].

In the study by Dawes et al. [2] to measure and model cognitive performance alongside hearing impairment, it was concluded that hearing aid use can be correlated with better cognition, improvement in depression, and decrease in social isolation. The quality of life of a person is improved with effective and consistent utilization of a properly fitted hearing aid and in a cost-effective way. Communication is a very important part of our lives, hence a fair hypothesis can be drawn, and performance of the hearing aid, measured under several criteria can boost cognitive performance and positively reduce the occurrences of social isolation and dementia. Some hearing aids do not enhance spatial location, which could make it difficult for users in complex auditory situations. Other studies conducted to show reasons for low utilization of hearing aids examined the major attributes of a good hearing aid such as performance in quiet places, comfort, its feedback quality, battery replacement frequency, price, and performance in noisy areas. The study showed that the test respondents were more willing to purchase hearing aids that perform better in noisy areas. A good hearing aid should have characteristics such as low cost and high durability, good battery life, wireless connectivity, and comfort. Hearing aid styles include behind-the-ear (BTE), inside-the-ear (ITE), in-the-canal (ITC), completely-in-canal (CIC), receiver-in-canal (RIC), and invisible-in-canal (IIC). Hearing aids also vary depending on the type of electronics used and analogue or digital processing. In this chapter, the fuzzy preference ranking organization method for enrichment evaluations (PROMETHEE), a multi-criteria decision-making technique, is used to evaluate and rank the hearing aid styles based on their criteria.

10.2 Materials and methods

10.2.1 Hearing aids

Hearing aids are provided based on the level of hearing loss, lifestyle of a user (causal, active, etc.), and medical history. This chapter focuses on obtaining the best hearing aid option for a patient with an active lifestyle. Hearing aids are composed of several small components:

I. Microphones

Microphones are introduced to convert sound waves into electrical signals [3].

II. Receiver

A receiver converts electrical signals to sound. The microphone and receiver combined is called a transducer [3].

III. Amplifier and its battery

It is used to magnify the strength of the electrical signal by concentrating on the high-to-weak frequency sounds than the low-to-intense frequency sounds. The battery is used to provide power for the amplifier [3].

The hearing aids style can be customized or sold as a standard product. ITC, ITE, and CIC are forms of custom styles while RIC and BTE are standard styles. The details of these and other types of hearing aid are discussed further on.

There are six different hearing loss degrees based on the range of the decibels, as seen in Table 10.1.

Furthermore, there are four commonly used battery sizes available for the hearing aids: 10 (5.8 mm wide by 3.6 mm high), 312 (7.9 mm wide by 3.6 mm high), 13 (7.9 mm wide by 5.4 mm high), and 675 (11.6 mm wide by 5.4 mm high).

TABLE 10.1 Hearing loss chart.

Hearing loss levels	Degrees of hearing loss described in decibels	In terms of verbal communication, this would generally suggest:	Sounds you could be missing
Minimal	11–25 dB	Few difficulties	Water dripping
Mild	26–40 dB	Difficulty hearing faint or distant speech	A ticking clock
Moderate	41 to 55 dB	Cannot hear faint speech, difficulty at conversational speech	Vacuum cleaner
Moderately severe	56–70 dB	Cannot hear faint speech, difficulty at conversational speech	Dog barking
Severe	71–90 dB	Cannot hear conversational speech, difficulty with loud speech	Baby crying
Profound	91 dB and over	Cannot hear loud speech, difficulty hearing loud sounds	Airplanes

Source: https://global.widex.com/en/hearing-loss/types-of-hearing-loss/degrees-and-shapes-hearing-loss.

10.2.2   In-the-ear (ITE)

ITE is one of the largest in-ear hearing aids. There are various sizes of these type of hearing aid that are used for moderate hearing loss. This type of hearing aid fills the major part of the outer ear and this makes it easier to insert and remove from the ear. It is suitable for people suffering from mild and severe hearing loss. ITE aids allow the use of large size batteries and directional microphones, improving its use in noisy areas. New ITE aids have a magnetic coil called tele-coil that enables a consumer to receive sounds through the circuitry of the hearing aid instead of its microphone [6]. This feature allows the user to hear sounds in places with special sound systems, such as auditoriums. The latest variations of ITE cover the lower portion of the concha (the depression in the external ear) up to the crus-helix (a part of the inner ear). The low-profile ITE does not extend outward from the ear canal enough to fill the concha. Some types of ITE only fill the upper part of the concha and connect to the ear canal [3].

10.2.3   In-the-canal (ITC)

The ITC is a form of ITEs that accommodates the part of the cavum concha parallel to the ear canal. It is small compared to the ITC and is more aesthetic for people who do not like their earpiece to be noticed. The ITC enables the use of a 312 battery size but does not have space for a directional microphone.

10.2.4   Invisible-in-canal (IIC)

This is the smallest aid placed deep in the ear canal, making it invisible. It is beneficial to patients because it decreases the feeling of having a device being 'plugged up' in the ear. The small size of IICs makes it impossible to use a directional microphone.

10.2.5   Completely-in-canal (CIC)

This is another customized form of hearing aid of a very small size that fits in the ear cana. None of the CICs need to protrude into the concha; they are placed at the entrance of the ear canal. It has a handle on the end to enable ease of removal. These are appropriate for people who can handle smaller objects and do not have the directional microphones found in ITE aids. These take a 312 or a 10 battery size and are suitable for patients who have concerns about cosmetic appeal. A type of CIC aid is the peritympanic CIC, which has the medical end extending a few mm of the eardrum [3].

10.2.6   Behind-the-ear (BTE)

The BTE is a standard form of hearing aid that includes a mini-BTE and receiver in the canal (RIC). They are two-piece hearing aids that usually require customization of the earpiece; the receiver, the electronics, and microphone of the BTE are mounted in the BTE case. It carries sound through a tube to an ear-mold, which retains the open end of the tube within the ear canal [3]. These can be used for mild to serious cases of hearing loss. An impression of the patient's ear has to be made before the ear-mold is made. The BTE is suitable for severe to profound hearing loss.

10.2.7   Receiver-in-canal (RIC)

This is a type of BTE that has its receiver within the ear canal and an electrical cable that runs from the electronics to the ear canal. There are several styles: RIC, RITC, and the canal receiver technology (CRT). The RIC is slightly smaller than the BTE and is recommended for moderately severe to severe cases of hearing loss. It does not require an impression. RIC's are the best for high-frequency hearing loss and are quite comfortable. They can accommodate a battery size of 312.

10.3   Fuzzy PROMETHEE

The PROMETHEE was first proposed by Brans in 1984 [1]. The method was used to evaluate a couple of alternatives using certain selected criteria. This system enabled the easiest use of the multicriteria decision-making method in the most efficient way from conception to how it is applied. Fuzzy PROMETHEE created a friendly outranking method and has been used successfully in real-life problems. Only two sets of information are required for this method: the preference function while comparing the effects of the alternatives with regards to each separate criteria and the weight (significance) of the criteria selected. Fuzzy methods have been applied in the decision-making process in manufacturing [7], in the management of drought in the monsoon region of Asia, [8] in cyber physical system [9], material selection problems [10], biomedical devices selections [11], and recently in medicine [11] and [12]. Fuzzy PROMETHEE method allows the decision maker using fuzzy input data when some data are difficult to obtain in real-life scenarios. This would enable easy decision-making by providing flexibility while comparing alternatives in uncertain conditions.

The criteria of the hearing aid selected for this study are the level of hearing loss experienced by the patient, cost of the device, comfort, frequency range, battery life, battery size, and durability. These criteria were derived from expert knowledge, several medical sites, and hearing aid manufacturers. The next step taken in the study was to consult experts to determine the priority rankings of each criteria. Table 10.2 shows the order of importance of each criteria, in terms of very high, high, medium, low, and very low. The Yager index [13] was then applied to defuzzify the triangular fuzzy numbers to evaluate the weight of each of the criteria.

TABLE 10.2 Linguistic scale and importance.

Linguistic scale of evaluation	Triangular fuzzy scale	Priority ratings of criteria
Very high (VH)	(0.75,1,1)	Level of hearing loss
High (H)	(0.50,0.75,1)	Price, battery life, comfort
Medium (M)	(0.25,0.50,0.75)	Durability, frequency range
Low (L)	(0,0.25,0.50)	
Very low (L)	(0,0,0.25)	Battery size

TABLE 10.3 Application of fuzzy PPROMETHEE to different hearing aids.

Criteria	Price ($)	Durability (years)	Battery life (hrs)	Average frequency range (Hz)	Battery size	Comfort	Level of hearing loss
Preferences							
Min/Max	Min	Max	Max	Max	Min	Max	Max
Importance weights	VH	VH	VH	VH	VH	VH	VH
Evaluations							
CIC	940	4	9	4750	10	No	Mild
RIC	1190	4	7	4850	312	Yes	Moderate
ITC	940	4	9	4850	312	Yes	Moderate
BTE	1140	7	11	3850	10	Yes	Severe
ITE	1140	6	15	4150	13	No	Moderate
IIC	1045	4	6	3850	312	Yes	Mild

After the collection of data for hearing aid types, the Gaussian preference function was applied for each criteria. To obtain results the Visual PROMETHEE decision lab was applied. The results are shown in Table 10.3.

10.4   Results and discussion

The results obtained from the analysis showed that ITC performed best with a net flow of 0.2405 followed by the BTE, ITE, CIC, RIC, and the IIC (Table 10.4) based on the importance weights and the preference functions used for each criteria.

The ITC is excellent for a patient with moderate to mild hearing loss because of its low price, high frequency ranges, and comfort. Following this is the BTE at a net flow of 0.1472, which can be used when the patient's comfort is important and the hearing loss level is severe. And IIC is the least effective hearing aid because of its high-average frequency range, battery size, battery life, price, and low durability, and also because it is only useful for the patient with a mild level of hearing loss. ITE is the best alternative with the highest battery life. The CIC also has the lowest price but compared to other types of hearing aids, it is only applicable for mild hearing loss. And BTE is only one alternative for patients with a severe hearing loss level.

The strong features (above the 0-threshold) and the weak features of the hearing aids (below the 0-threshold) are shown in Fig. 10.1.

In order to show how the ranking would change when the importance of each criteria was selected to be equal to depict varying changes for different levels of patient hearing loss. The result is shown in Table 10.5.

For validating the result, the equal importance weights have been used for all the criteria. Based on the results obtained, the BTE and ITC stand out as the best choice for a hearing aid. The ranking result changed only between the first and second alternatives. The other alternative ranks have not changed with equal importance weights.

TABLE 10.4 Ranking of hearing aids.

Rank	Alternatives	Positive (Phi +)	Negative (Phi–)	Net (Phi)
1	ITC	0.3466	0.1061	0.2405
2	BTE	0.3680	0.2208	0.1472
3	ITE	0.3500	0.2316	0.1184
4	CIC	0.2455	0.2794	–0.0339
5	RIC	0.1864	0.3141	–0.1277
6	IIC	0.1097	0.4542	–0.3445

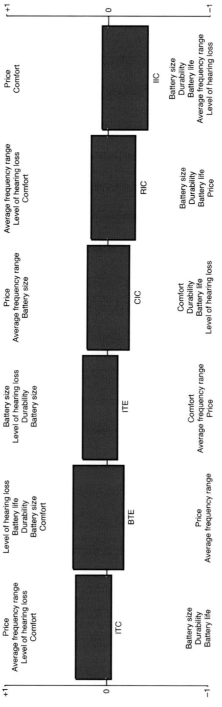

FIGURE 10.1   Evaluation criteria for the hearing aids on positive and negative sides.

TABLE 10.5 The new ranking for equal importance weights of the criteria.

Rank	Alternatives	Positive (Phi +)	Negative (Phi–)	Net (Phi)
1	BTE	0.3676	0.2168	0.1508
2	ITC	0.3057	0.1616	0.1441
3	ITE	0.3736	0.2302	0.1434
4	CIC	0.3139	0.2249	0.0890
5	RIC	0.1761	0.3300	–0.1540
6	IIC	0.0888	0.4621	–0.3733

10.5 Conclusions

In this chapter, the best possible decision in the choice of hearing aids is achieved by using the fuzzy PROMETHEE method, which is a multi-criteria decision-making technique. The criteria used were turned into fuzzy input data and PROMETHEE was used to obtain the results. This study shows that the proposed method is effective in providing alternative solutions in decision-making problems in healthcare that would most benefit the patient as the criteria and their importance level can be varied according to specific patients.

References

[1] V.C. Scanlon, T. Sanders, The senses. in: L.B. Houck (Ed.), Essentials of Anatomy and Physiology, 7th ed. Philadelphia: F.A. Davis Company, 2015, p. 243.

[2] P. Dawes, K.J. Cruickshanks, M.E. Fischer, B.E. Klein, R. Klein, D.M. Nondahl, Hearing-aid use and long-term health outcomes: hearing handicap, mental health, social engagement, cognitive function, physical health, and mortality, Int. J. Audiol. 54 (11) (2015) 838–844 doi: 10.3109/14992027.2015.1059503.

[3] H. Dillon, Hearing aids, 2nd ed. National Acoustic Laboratories of Australia, Sydney, New South Wales: Boomerang Press, 2012.

[4] A. Hagr, BAHA: bone-anchored hearing aid, Int. J. Health Sci. 1 (2) (2007) 265–276.

[5] NIDCD, Hearing aids (2020), https://www.nidcd.nih.gov/health/hearing-aids. Accessed 8/08/20.

[6] NIDCD fact sheet; hearing and balance; hearing Aids. U.S. Department of Health and Human Services, National Institute of Health, NIH Pub. No. 99-4340 (September 2013, reprinted July 2015).

[7] A. Coroiu, Fuzzy methods in decision-making process—a particular approach in manufacturing systems, IOP – Mater. Sci. Engineer. 95 (012154) (2015) 1–3 doi:10.1088/1757-899x/95/1/012154.

[8] Y. Hou, Z. Niu, F. Zheng, N. Wang, J. Wang, Z. Li, et al. Drought fluctuations based on dendrochronology since 1786 for the Lenglongling Mountains at the northwestern fringe of the East Asian summer monsoon region, J. Arid Land 8 (4) (2016) 492–505 doi:10.1007/s40333-016-0009-8.

[9] G. Zhao, A. Chen, G. Lu, W. Liu, Data fusion algorithm based on fuzzy sets and D-S theory of evidence. Tsinghua Sci. Tech. 25 (1) (2020), 12–19.

[10] I. Ozsahin, T. Sharif, D. Ozsahin, B. Uzun, Evaluation of solid-state detectors in medical imaging with fuzzy PROMETHEE, J. Instrument. 14 (01) (2019) 1019–11019.

[11] D. Uzun Ozsahin, B. Uzun, M. Sani, I. Ozsahin, Evaluating X-ray based medical imaging devices with fuzzy preference ranking organization method for enrichment evaluations, Int. J. Adv. Comp. Sci. Appl. 9 (3) (2018) 7–10.

[12] I. Ozsahin, O.D. Uzun, M. Maisaini, Fuzzy PROMETHEE analysis of leukemia treatment techniques, World Cancer Res. J. (2019) 20196–21315.

[13] R.R. Yager, A procedure for ordering fuzzy subsets of the unit interval, Inf. Sci. 24 (1) (1981) 143–161.

Further reading

[1] J.P. Brans, P. Vincle, A preference ranking organization method, Manage. Sci. 31 (6) (1985) 647–656.

[2] Degrees of hearing loss. https://global.widex.com/en/hearing-loss/types-of-hearing-loss/degrees-and-shapes-hearing-loss.

[3] J.J. Eggermont, Implantable hearing aids. In: Hearing Loss. St. Louis: Elsevier (2017)/

[4] FDA.gov. FDA allows marketing of first self-fitting hearing aid controlled by the user, https://www.fda.gov/NewsEvents/Newsroom/PressAnnouncements/ucm622692.htm. Accessed 8/01/19.

[5] J. Hoffman, T.E. Foust, Audiology 101: An introduction to audiology for nonaudiologists, in A Resource Guide for Early Hearing Detection & Intervention (Ch. 5), NCHAM, Utah State University, 2018, pp. 5-1–5-16.

[6] J.L. Northern, Strategies of adult hearing aid selection, Audio. Res. 1 (1) (2011) e20 doi:10.4081/audiores.2011.e20.

[7] D. Ozsahin, N. Isa, B. Uzun, I. Ozsahin, Effective analysis of image reconstruction algorithms in nuclear medicine using fuzzy PROMETHEE. Advances in Science and Engineering Technology International Conferences (ASET) (2018).

[8] D. Ozsahin, B. Uzun, M. Musa, N. Şentürk, F. Nurçin, I. Ozsahin, I., Evaluating nuclear medicine imaging devices using fuzzy PROMETHEE method. Procedia Comp. Sci. 120 (2017) 699–705.

[9] D. Ozsahin, I. Ozsahin, A fuzzy PROMETHEE approach for breast cancer treatment techniques, Int. J. Med. Res. Health Sci. 7 (5) (2018) 29–32.

[10] D. Uzun Ozsahin, B. Uzun, M. Sani, A. Helwan, C. Nwekwo, F. Veysel, N. Sentürka, I. Ozsahin, Evaluating cancer treatment alternatives using fuzzy PROMETHEE method, Int. J. Adv. Comp. Sci. Appl. 8 (10) (2018) 177–182.

[11] K. Yuen, T. Ting, Textbook selection using fuzzy PROMETHEE II method, Int. J. Future Comp. Comm. 1 (1) (2012).

Chapter 11

A comparative study of X-ray based medical imaging devices

Mubarak Taiwo Mustapha[a,b], Berna Uzun[a,c], Dilber Uzun Ozsahin[a,b,d] and Ilker Ozsahin[a,b,e]

[a]DESAM Institute, Near East University, Turkish Republic of Northern Cyprus, Nicosia, Turkey; [b]Department of Biomedical Engineering, Near East University, Turkish Republic of Northern Cyprus, Nicosia, Turkey; [c]Department of Mathematics, Near East University, Turkish Republic of Northern Cyprus, Nicosia, Turkey; [d]Medical Diagnostic Imaging Department, College of Health Sciences, University of Sharjah, Sharjah, United Arab Emirates; [e]Brain Health Imaging Institute, Department of Radiology, Weill Cornell Medicine, New York, NY, United States

11.1 Introduction

The inside of the human body can be visualized without necessarily making a surgical incision. This is useful in the diagnosis and treatment of medical diseases. A term generally referred to as "medical imaging techniques" (MITs) refers to a group of noninvasive techniques, that are capable of mirroring internal organs, tissues, and bones of humans and animals with the sole purpose of revealing their state (healthy or diseased) as shown in Fig. 11.1 [1]. MITs are learning tools used to study human behaviour and neurobiology. It is made up of the source of energy (sensor) which is capable of penetrating the human body. After this, the energy is attenuated at different levels, generating signals [2]. The special detectors as shown in Fig. 11.1 recognize the signals that are consistent with the energy source, thereby generating an image. Most imaging techniques utilize the technologies of magnetic resonance imaging (MRI), ultrasound (sound wave), radiography, endoscopy, thermography, etc., and they have proven to be useful in the field of pathology. However, there are limitations and risks. A medical imaging technique utilizes both ionizing and nonionizing radiation to generate images and as a result poses a threat to healthy cells [3]. Ionizing radiation is a form of energy released after the disintegration of atoms (radioactivity). Ionizing radiation becomes harmful when doses of radiation exceed the accepted level.

X-ray is a type of radiation such as light or radio waves. These rays are capable of penetrating most objects including the human body. When used for medical purpose, an X-ray machine can be targeted at a part of the body to produce a medical image. The absorption of various parts of the body is dependent

Applications of Multi-Criteria Decision-Making Theories in Healthcare and Biomedical Engineering.
http://dx.doi.org/10.1016/B978-0-12-824086-1.00011-6

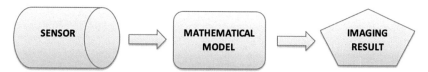

FIGURE 11.1 **Basic principles of medical imaging system.**

on the absorbability of the radiations. Dense bone has a much higher absorbing capability than soft tissues like muscle, fat, and internal organs. This means that muscle, fat, and internal organs will allow easy passage of the radiation, thereby allowing X-rays to pass through them. Because of these, bones refract white on the X-ray, soft tissue looks grey and air appears black. The digital images produced by X-ray are electronically stored and can be retrieved when needed for diagnosis and disease management. To capture a breast image using a digital mammogram, the X-ray is directed toward the side and above the compressed breast.

Imaging devices such as conventional X-ray machine, angiography, computed tomography, fluoroscopy, and mammography utilize high-energy electromagnetic radiation (X-radiation) to produce medical images of value [3]. Although these techniques are similar in their principle (the use of X-radiation), they differ in the type of medical examination in which they are employed. Deciding on which technique to use or buy can be challenging to hospital management and specialist. Therefore, using a multicriteria decision-making method is necessary. This will promote making accurate and precise decisions.

11.1.1 Medical applications of X-ray radiography

1. X-ray radiography is used in many types of examinations, such as chiropractic and dental.
2. Fluoroscopy radiographs used for showing the movement of organs, such as the stomach, intestine, and colon, in the body also can be used for studying the blood vessels of the heart and the brain [4,5].
3. Pathological changes in the lungs, the structure of the stomach and intestines and the extent of a fracture can be determined using projectional radiographs.
4. The human breast tissue can be diagnosed and screen using mammography.
5. The content and density of the bone mineral can be measured using bone densitometry.
6. The inside of the joint can be viewed using arthrography.
7. The uterus and fallopian tubes can be examined using hysterosalpingogram.

11.1.2 A brief history

The origin of medical imaging was marked by the discovery of X-rays in 1895 by a German physicist named Wilhem Conrad Röntgen (Fig. 11.2 [6]). Röntgen

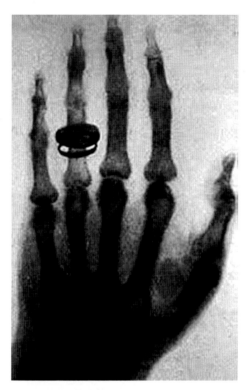

FIGURE 11.2 First X-ray photograph [9].

was at the time studying Lenard and Crookes tubes. He referred to his discovery as "a new kind of ray." He later communicated his findings to the Würzburg's Physical-Medical Society journal in 1895 and later referred to his discovery as "X" since it was an unknown type of radiation [7]. This marked the beginning of the X-ray. Before then X-rays were considered to be energetic electron beams radiating from an experimental cathode tube. William Morgan is considered to have been the first scientist to unknowingly produce X-rays. This was evident in his scientific publication, which was presented to the Royal Society of London in 1785. William described in the paper that when an electric current is passed through a partially evacuated glass tube, a glow occurs [8].

Röntgen was experimenting with cathode rays from the Crookes tube that he had wrapped in black cardboard so as not to interfere with the visible light from the tube, using a fluorescent screen dyed with barium platinocyanide. He noticed a faint green glow coming from the screen, which stood about 1 meter away. Röntgen realized that some invisible rays coming from the tube were passing through the cardboard to make the screen shine. He found that they could pass through books and papers on his desk as well. Röntgen systematically pursued his research into these mysterious rays. He published his paper 2 months after his initial discovery [10].

The image produced when the hand of Röntgen's wife was subjected to an X-ray affirmed the medical importance of X-rays. This was the first X-ray image of a part of the human body. Seeing the image of her hand, Röntgen's wife said, I have seen my death" [11].

John Hall-Edwards was the first person to clinically demonstrate the efficacy of X-rays. In 1896, he radiographed the hand of his partner, which had been stuck with a needle, and further utilized the X-ray in a surgical procedure. [12]. At the beginning of 1896, many weeks after Röntgen's discovery, Ivan Romanovich Tarkhanov irradiated frogs and insects with X-rays, suggesting that the rays "not only capture, but also affect the living structure" [12]. Later on that year, Gilman and Edwin exposed the previously fractured wrist of a patient to X-rays and collected the result [13]. The United States of America (USA) recorded its first production of X-rays using a discharge tube designed by Pulyui. Frank Austin experimented on the discharge tube present in the physics laboratory at Dartmouth College and realized that Pulyui tube is the only discharge tube capable of producing X-rays.

With all the adulations for X-rays come its detrimental effects. There were incidents of hair loss and burns recorded in 1895. An example of such an incident was the one noted by two Vanderbilt University Professors, John Daniel and William Lofland Dudley. They both discovered hair loss as a result of exposure to X-rays. The 20th-century X-ray is made of the Ruhmkorff coil attached to a cold cathode Crookes X-ray tube with a spark gap attached to the high voltage side parallel to the tube [12]. The spark gap made it possible to determine the polarity of the sparks and to measure the voltage by the length of the sparks, thus determining the "hardness" of the vacuum of the tube, and to provide a load if the X-ray tube was disconnected. To detect the hardness of the tube, the spark gap was initially opened to the widest possible setting. When the coil is in operation, the operator reduces the gap until the sparks began to appear [14].

The first vacuum tube was invented by John Ambrose Fleming in 1904. This vacuum tube, also called the thermionic diode, allows the passage of electrical current using a hot cathode. Because of the efficiency of this principle, the unreliable cold cathode initially used for X-ray tubes was replaced with heated-cathode X-ray tubes (Coolidge tubes) by 1920. In 1906, Charles Barkla discovered the possibility of X-rays being dispersed by gasses with each element having a specific X-ray spectrum. Because of this discovery, Charles Barkla won the 1917 Nobel Prize in Physics [10]. The discovery that X-rays could be diffracted by crystals was made by Max von Laue, Paul Knipping, and Walter Friedrich in 1912. This discovery and previous ones done by them gave birth to X-ray crystallography. Henry Moseley conducted crystallography trials with X-rays made of various metals in 1913. He proposed Moseley's law comparing X-ray frequencies to the atomic metal number. [10].

William D. Coolidge invented the Coolidge X-ray tube the same year. This further caused the continuous emissions of X-ray. The continuous X-ray emissions were further driven by this. This design is based on modern X-ray tubes, often with rotating targets which require significantly higher heat dissipation than static targets, thereby permitting higher X-ray power for use in high power applications such as rotary CT scanners [15]. Major John Hall-Edwards was a pioneer of the use of X-rays in Birmingham, England, for medical purposes. In 1908, due to a spread of X-ray dermatitis on his arm, his left arm had to be amputated [16]. Marie Curie designed a mobile X-ray unit using a car battery that provided quick radiological tests during World War 1. First line surgeons could operate faster and more accurately with the use of her machine [17]. X-ray machines were developed between the 1920s and the 1950s to help with fitting footwear and were sold in shops [17]. Concerns about the effect of frequent or poorly controlled exposures to radiation were expressed in the 1950s, leading to the eventual end of that decade of practice [18].

11.2   Medical imaging devices

11.2.1   X-ray radiography

Radiography is a diagnostic technique that uses ionizing electromagnetic radiation to view objects. X-ray is high-energy electromagnetic radiation capable of penetrating solids and ionizing gas; it has a wavelength between 0.01 and 10 manometers. X-rays pass through the body, get absorbed or attenuated at varying levels, depending on the density and atomic number of the different tissues, creating a profile [2,19–21]. The X-ray profile is recorded on the detector as shown in Fig. 11.3. When the electrical current is heated, electrons are emitted by filament wire. The revolving metal anode attracts electrons providing alternating current to the filament wire. The area of the anode from which the X-ray is emitted is referred to as the focal point. The photon energy used varies from 17 to 150 keV; the option for a specific application or tissue examined being a trade-off between an appropriate dose of radiation and the feasible image contrast. Figs. 11.4 and 11.5 show X-ray images of the head and knee.

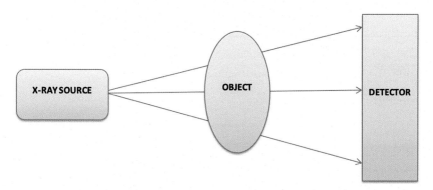

FIGURE 11.3   X-ray imaging principle.

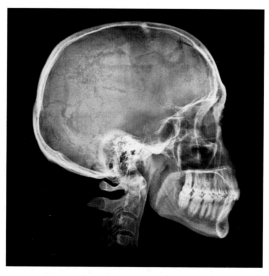

FIGURE 11.4   An X-ray image of the human head [22].

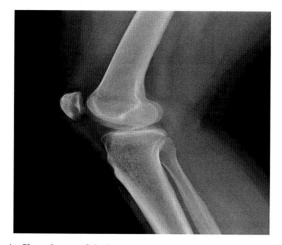

FIGURE 11.5   An X-ray image of the human knee [23].

Benefits of X-rays include:

1. It is a quick, painless, and noninvasive medical imaging technique.
2. X-rays support both medical and surgical treatment planning.
3. It provides a visual guide to physicians when inserting Guide catheters or stents into the body to either treat tumors or remove blood clots.

Harmful effects of X-rays include:

1. There is a high chance of developing cancer if exposed to ionizing radiation for a long time.
2. High level of exposure to radiation can cause cataracts, skin reddening, and hair loss.

11.2.2 Angiography

The medical imaging technique, capable of visualizing the internal organs of the body and particularly the inside of arteries, veins, and the heart chambers, is called angiography or arteriography. The entrance into the blood vessel is most commonly achieved via the femoral artery, depending on the option of angiogram [24]. A type of contrast agent is used to visualize the blood on X-rays using a guidewire and a catheter system. Images are usually taken using a technique called Digital Subtraction Angiography (DSA) for all structures, except the heart. In this case, images are usually taken at a rate of two to three frames per second, which helps the interventional radiologist to measure blood flow to an artery or tube [25]. It "subtracts" bones and other organs to see only vessels filled with the contrasting agent. Cardiac images, not using a subtraction technique, are taken at a rate of 15–30 frames per second [25]. Even though DSA demands the patient to stay motionless, it cannot be applied to the heart. These two techniques allow the interventional radiologist or cardiologist to see stenosis (blockages or narrowings) inside a vessel that may inhibit blood flow and cause pain.

The visualization of blood on coronary arteries is one of the most frequent angiograms (Fig. 11.6). The X-ray contrast agent to the area to be visualized is administered with a catheter. The catheter is inserted into the brachial artery and

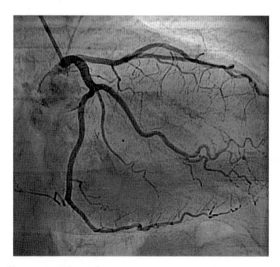

FIGURE 11.6   Coronary angiography.

the tip is transmitted to the main coronary artery through the arterial network. X-ray images of the transient distribution of contrast radiation in the blood flowing into the coronary arteries enable the visualization of openings in the artery. There is no clear indication of the existence or absence of atherosclerosis or atheroma in the walls of the arteries. Stenosis of the coronary artery or blood vessel restriction can be visualized by coronary angiography. By comparing the lumen width in small sections of the blood vessel with wider parts of the neighboring vessel, it is possible to assess the degrees of stenosis [26]. Angiography is also performed in patients with leg claudication or cramps if a vessel needs to be identified. This is done routinely via the femoral artery, but could also be done via the brachial or axillary (arm) artery. Any stenosis found may be treated with balloon angioplasty, stenting, or atherectomy [27–29].

Consequently, angiography presents some complications. A sudden shock can cause some discomfort in the area of surgery following an angiogram, but generally, heart attack and strokes are not caused when surgery is bypassed. When blood flows to a part of the heart is obstructed by a clot, a heart attack occurs. Without oxygenated blood, the heart muscle begins to die. A stroke is a brain attack which reduces oxygen and essential blood supply to the brain. A stroke occurs if a brain-feeding vessel blocks or bursts. Cerebral angiographical complications such as stroke, allergy to aesthetic, embolism, or obstruction are uncommon. Additional minor complications such as bleeding or bruising at the contrast injection site are delayed but rare [30].

11.2.3   Computed tomography

A computed tomography (CT) refers to a computerized X-ray imaging process, where a narrow X-ray beam is directed at the patient and rotated quickly around the body, which creates signals that the machine interprets to produce cross-sectional pictures or "slices" of the body. Such sections are classified as tomographic images, which provide information that is more accurate than traditional X-rays. Once the computer of the machine has computed a variety of successive slices, a three-dimensional image of the patient can be formed that allows the recognition and position of basic structures and possible tumors or anomalies. Unlike traditional X-rays, which utilize a fixed X-ray tube, the CT scanner uses a motorized X-ray source that oscillates around the circular opening of a dough-nut-shaped device called a gantry [31]. During a CT scan, the patient is lying on a bed that moves slowly through the gantry while the X-ray tube rotates around the patient, shooting through the body narrow beams of X-rays. Instead of the film, CT scanners use various digital radiograph detectors which are located directly opposite the X-ray source. The detectors capture the X-rays while they leave the body and then forward the data to the computer [32].

The X-ray source uses a high-tech mathematical technique to construct a 2D patient's image every time it rotates entirely. Depending on the CT machine used, the thickness of the tissue depicted in each image varies between 1 and

10 millimeters [33]. When a full slice is made, the image is processed and the motorized bed is slowly transferred to the doorway. To produce a new image, the scanning process of the X-rays is then repeated. The cycle continues until you obtain the necessary number of slices. Picture slices can be seen or placed individually by a computer to get the patient's 3D image showing skeleton, organs, and tissue, as well as any other abnormalities that the doctor attempts to identify. The advantages of this technique include the ability to rotate a 3D image in space or sequencing slices, thus making it easier to find the exact located locations of the problem.

The bone and other dense internal organs can be easily seen in an X-ray image while soft tissues such as organs avoid X-rays and appear faint. Therefore, intravenous (IV) contrast agents that are highly visible in radiographic or CT scans were developed and can be safe for use in patients. Contrast agents contain substances that are more noticeable on an X-ray image. For instance, an iodine-based contrast agent is injected intravenously to make the illumination of blood vessel possible. The purpose of this type of examination is to check for an obstruction in the blood vessel and the heart. A digestive system such as the esophagus, stomach, and GI tract can be checked using imaging contrast agents, such as barium-based compounds. CT scans may diagnose conditions that threaten life including cancer, blood clots, or haemorrhage. In the end, the early diagnosis of these conditions can save lives [34,35]. The CT scan does not pose a risk to a pregnant woman's fetus unless the scanned part of the body is the pelvis or abdomen [36]. In general, when imagery of the abdomen and pelvis is needed, physicians opt for nonray examinations, such as MRI or ultrasound. However, if none of them can provide the requisite answers or if there is an emergency or other time limit, CT might be a suitable alternative to imaging (Figs. 11.7 and 11.8).

In some patients, an allergic reaction or temporal renal failure may be caused by contrast agents. In patients with abnormal renal function, IV contrast agents should never be given, as they can lead to additional reductions in renal function, which are often irreversible. Children are more susceptible to ionization and therefore more likely to develop cancer than adults [34,35].

11.2.4 Fluoroscopy

Real-time images of an object in the body can be obtained using fluoroscopy. With fluoroscopy, the internal structure of the human body, such as the heart and how it functions, can be observed. Its effectiveness in diagnosis and therapy cannot be overemphasized. A fluoroscope set-up comprises an X-ray source and a fluorescent screen, between which a patient is placed. There is a huge similarity between fluoroscopy, radiography, and CT because they all utilize the same principle of X-rays in the production of images. However, the notable difference between radiography and X-ray is that the former produces still images while the latter generates motion images of the internal organ. When a patient is sub-

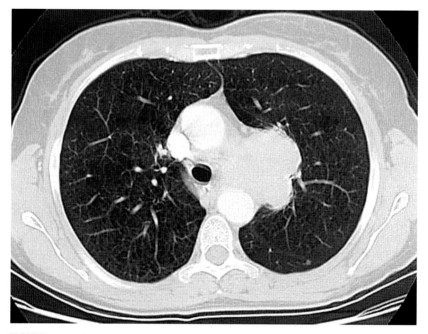

FIGURE 11.7   CT image of the chest [37].

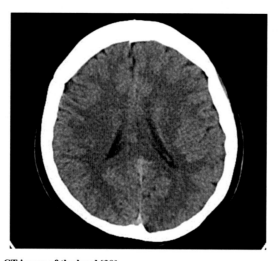

FIGURE 11.8   CT image of the head [38].

jected to an X-ray, the radiation passing through the patient creates shadows of the various tissues it comes across as a result of attenuation. This shadow is reflected on the screen, which a physician can examine. Fig. 11.9 shows the fluoroscopy image of the chest. Fluoroscopy could be detrimental and may increase the risk of cancer to the patient. The radiation exposure to the patient depends

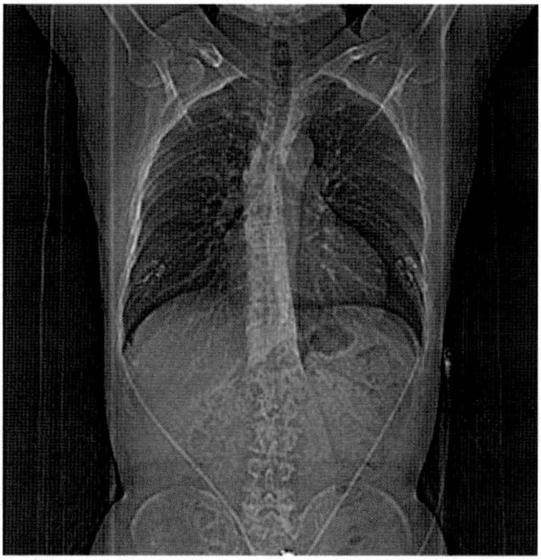

FIGURE 11.9 **Fluoroscopy image of the chest** [40].

significantly on the patient's size and duration of the operation, with average skin dose levels of 20–50 mGy/min [39]. Deterministic radiation effects, ranging from mild erythema, equivalent to sunburn, to more serious burns, have also been observed due to the long duration of procedures, in addition to the risk of cancer and other stochastic radiation effects. While it is possible to produce deterministic radiation effects, radiation burns are not typical of the standard fluoroscopic procedure.

11.2.5 Mammography

The human breast can be checked both for malignant and benign tumors by using a mammogram. Mammography uses the oldest and most well-known medical imaging technique (X-ray). X-ray is a noninvasive technique that requires ionizing radiation to generate images inside the body. This radiation thereby aids in early detection of malignant or benign breast cancer in woman. Breast tomosynthesis, computer-aided detection, and automated mammography are the three most recent developments. During mammography, the breast is placed in the mammography unit by a skilled radiologist. The breast is then placed on a platform and compressed with a clear plastic paddle. Compression of the breast is important to:

- Spread the thickness of the breast to allow visualization of all parts.
- Enable a lower dose of X-rays to be uniformly distributed along the breast tissue.
- Hold the breast still to avoid any blurring of the image.
- Reduce the dispersion of X-rays to increase image sharpness.

While mammography is the best screening instrument for breast cancer today, all breast cancers are not detected. The false-positive result indicates an abnormal mammogram with no true cancer. The mammographic screening by itself is often not enough to determine whether a benign or malignant cancer is present. If abnormalities occur, your radiologist may recommend further diagnostic studies. It is very important to emphasize that mammography cannot show all breast cancers. It can be complicated to interpret mammograms, given that each woman has different breast characteristics. Often, if patients undergo breast surgery, the quality of an image can be affected. Because certain breast cancers are hard to picture, the image of previous research can be compared to a more recent mammography of a patient. A mammographic image of the breast can be seen in Fig. 11.10.

Benefits of mammography are:

- It decreases the risk of death from breast cancer.
- It increases the ability of a physician to identify small tumors.
- It helps to identify small irregular growths of tissue restricted to breast milk ducts, known as ductal carcinomas in situ (DCIS).
- After the X-ray examination, no radiation remains in the patient's body.
- Typically, an X-ray is not detrimental to the patient.

Risks of mammography are:

- There is a little risk of cancer.
- There is variation in the dose of radiation.
- Showing a false-positive result.
- Women should always tell their doctor or technologist about X-rays if there is a chance that they are pregnant.

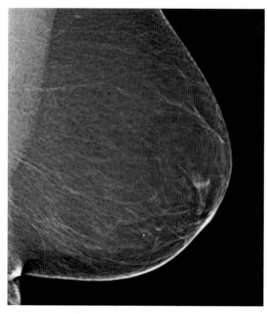

FIGURE 11.10   Mammography image of the breast [41].

11.3 Methodology

11.3.1 TOPSIS

Hwang and Yoon developed the Technique for Order Preference by Similarity to Ideal Solution (TOPSIS) to enable the effective evaluation of alternatives using similarity with the ideal solution. TOPSIS is an effective and widely used numerical method of multicriteria decision making. Its application is broad and uses a simple mathematical model. It is also a suitable practical method because it relies on computer usage. Application of TOPSIS as a decision-making tool has been in use for over three decades [42,43]. Several scientific publications detailing its application, usage, and effectiveness have also been recorded [44,45]. According to the TOPSIS technique, the most preferred alternative will be the one nearest to the positive-ideal solution and farthest from the negative-ideal solution.

The positive-ideal solution maximizes the benefits criteria and minimizes the cost criteria. The negative-ideal solution greatly increases the cost criteria and minimizes the benefit criteria. To summarize, the positive-ideal solution consists of all of the best values of the criteria, while the negative-ideal solution consists of all the worst values of the criteria. The fuzzy number was used to define the linguistic data for this analysis (Table 11.1).

The decision matrix of X-rays as shown in Table 11.2 shows the values of alternatives with their criteria.

After the dataset has been normalized, defuzzification of the linguistic fuzzy data of the dataset of the medical imaging devices was calculated with Yager index. The normalized weighted values of the dataset are shown in Table 11.3.

Furthermore, positive- and negative-ideal solutions of the data used for the analysis of the medical imaging devices has been calculated as shown in Table 11.4 and Table 11.5, respectively.

TABLE 11.1 The fuzzy scale of the linguistic data used for this analysis.

Linguistic scale for evaluation	Triangular fuzzy scale
Very high (VH)	(0.75, 1, 1)
Important (H)	(0.50, 0.75, 1)
Medium (M)	(0.25, 0.50, 0.75)
Low (L)	(0, 0.25, 0.50)
Very low (VL)	(0, 0, 0.25)

TABLE 11.2 Decision matrix of the X-ray.

Alternatives/ criteria	Cost of device (k$)	Scan time (min)	Specificity (%)	Sensitivity (%)	Radiation dose (mSv)
Aim	Min	Min	Max	Max	Min
Important weights of each criteria	H	M	VH	VH	VH
Fluoroscopy	(10, 50, 120)	(30,40,45)	(81,85, 90)	(65, 70, 75)	M
CT	(155, 182.5, 210)	(15, 20, 25)	(78, 80, 87)	(85, 90, 95)	VH
Mammography	(50, 80, 105)	(8, 10,15)	(69, 91, 97)	(79, 82, 95)	H
X-ray	(99, 113, 125)	(5, 10,15)	(63, 70, 75)	(90, 93,95)	L
Angiography	(140,170,200)	(58, 60, 62)	(94, 95, 96)	(94, 95, 96)	L

TABLE 11.3 Normalized weighted values of X-ray-based medical imaging devices.

Alternatives/ criteria	Cost of device	Scan time	Specificity	Sensitivity	Radiation dose
Fluoroscopy	0.0165	0.0348	0.0457	0.0371	0.0344
CT	0.0570	0.0177	0.0431	0.0478	0.0757
Mammography	0.0239	0.0097	0.0469	0.0451	0.0046
X-ray	0.0353	0.0086	0.0381	0.0509	0.0046
Angiography	0.0533	0.0524	0.0511	0.0510	0.1124

TABLE 11.4 Positive-ideal solution of medical imaging devices.

Cost of device	Scan time	Specificity	Sensitivity	Radiation dose
0.0165	0.0086	0.0511	0.0510	0.0046

TABLE 11.5 Negative-ideal solution of medical imaging devices.

Cost of device	Scan time	Specificity	Sensitivity	Radiation dose
0.0570	0.0524	0.0381	0.0371	0.1124

11.4   Results

The distance between the alternatives and both the positive (d_i^+) and negative (d_i^-) ideal solution has been calculated and is shown in Table 11.6.

The net ranking of the medical imaging devices was obtained based on their relative closeness to the positive-ideal solution (Ri), as shown in Table 11.7.

The result shows that the most preferred alternative among the medical imaging devices analysed is mammography with a Ri score 0.9204, X-ray is the second-most preferred alternative with an Ri score of 0.8386. Fluoroscopy, CT, and angiography were the third, fourth, and fifth most preferred alternatives with Ri scores of 0.6797, 0.3850, and 0.1373 respectively.

TABLE 11.6 The distance of the X-ray-based medical imaging devices from the positive-ideal solution and the negative-ideal solution.

Medical imaging devices	(d_i^+)	(d_i^-)
Mammography	0.0424	0.0900
X-ray	0.0828	0.0519
Fluoroscopy	0.0105	0.1212
CT	0.0229	0.1192
Angiography	0.1221	0.0194

TABLE 11.7 Ranking result of the X-ray-based medical imaging devices based on the relative closeness to the positive ideal solution.

Medical imaging devices	Score (Ri)	Ranking
Mammography	0.9204	1
X-ray	0.8386	2
Fluoroscopy	0.6797	3
CT	0.3850	4
Angiography	0.1373	5

11.5   Conclusions

After conducting a comparative analysis among various X-ray-based medical imaging devices and taking into account the cost of the devices, the time of scanning, the specificity, the sensitivity, and dose of radiation, mammography came out on top as the most-preferred X-ray-based medical device. A different but similar outcome may be recorded if the weight of parameters is changed. The result obtained from this study is similar to that conducted using the preference ranking organization method for enrichment evaluations (PROMETHEE) method with mammography also rising to the top of the list. Decision-making tools should be used as a guide and to provide alternative solutions to the decision maker. This is because every decision maker may consider different criteria and weighting that will affect the outcome of the final ranking. It can also be useful to patients. The analysis can indeed be modified by applying more criteria to the alternatives. Also, when compared with fuzzy PROMETHE, TOPSIS proves to be an effective and reliable decision-making tool for all. Application of TOPSIS can be utilized in other medical imaging fields.

References

[1] I. Kurniawan, Integrating big data with medical imaging, Int. J. Engin. Adv. Tech. 8 (6S3) (2019) 721–724, doi: 10.35940/ijeat.f1133.0986s319.

[2] H. Chen, M. Rogalski, J. Anker, Advances in functional X-ray imaging techniques and contrast agents, Phys. Chem. Chem. Phys. 14 (39) (2012) 13469, doi: 10.1039/c2cp41858d.

[3] C. Washington, Principles and practice of radiation therapy, St. Louis: Mosby, 2020.

[4] M. Marziani, A. Taibi, G. Di Domenico, M. Gambaccini, Optimization of radiography applications using X-ray beams emitted by compact accelerators. Part I. Monte Carlo study of the hard X-ray spectrum, Med. Phys. 36 (10) (2009) 4683–4701, doi: 10.1118/1.3223357.

[5] J. Nightingale, Spotlight on the 'humble' chest X-ray, Radiography 24 (1) (2018) 1–2, doi: 10.1016/j.radi.2017.12.007.

[6] X. Riaud, First Dental Radiograph (1896), J. Dent. Health Oral. Disord. Ther. 9 (1) (2018), doi: 10.15406/jdhodt.2018.09.00325.

[7] A. Stanton, Wilhelm Conrad Röntgen on a new kind of rays: translation of a paper read before the Würzburg Physical and Medical Society, 53 (1369) (1896): 274–276.

[8] A. Filler, The history, development and impact of computed imaging in neurological diagnosis and neurosurgery: CT, MRI, and DTI. Nature Proceedings (2009). doi:10.1038/npre.2009.3267.1.

[9] B. Kevles, C. Kelsey, Naked to the bone: Medical imaging in the twentieth century, Phys. Today 50 (8) (1997) 56–156.

[10] J. Scatliff, P. Morris, From Röntgen to magnetic resonance imaging, N.C. Med. J. 75 (2) (2014) 111–113, doi: 10.18043/ncm.75.2.111.

[11] R. Peters, The pendulum in the 21st century—relic or trendsetter, Sci. Educ. 13 (4/5) (2004) 279–295, doi: 10.1023/b:sced.0000041838.62582.ce.

[12] J. Hendry, M. Akahoshi, L. Wang, S. Lipshultz, F. Stewart, K. Trott, Radiation-induced cardiovascular injury, Radiat. Environ. Bioph. 47 (2) (2008) 189–193, doi: 10.1007/s00411-007-0155-7.

[13] P.K. Spiegel, The first clinical X-ray made in America—100 years, Am. J. Roentgenol. 164 (1) (1995) 241–243.

[14] K. Schall, , Electro-Medical Instruments and Their ManagementBemrose & Sons Ltd. Printers, 1905, pp. 96–107.

[15] A.P. James, B.V. Dasarathy, Medical image fusion: a survey of state of the art, Inform. Fusion 19 (2014) 4–19.

[16] K.J. Parker, M.M. Doyley, D.J. Rubens, Imaging the elastic properties of tissue: the 20-year perspective, Phys. Med. Biol. 56 (2) (2011) 513.

[17] K. Matthews, P. Brennan, Optimisation of X-ray examinations: general principles and an Irish perspective, Radiography 15 (3) (2009) 262–268, doi: 10.1016/j.radi.2008.07.002.

[18] B. Stevens, An analysis of the structure and brevity of preliminary clinical evaluations describing traumatic abnormalities on extremity X-ray images, Radiography (2020)doi: 10.1016/j.radi.2020.02.010.

[19] J. De La Vega, U. Häfeli, Utilization of nanoparticles as X-ray contrast agents for diagnostic imaging applications, Contrast Media Mol. I. 10 (2) (2014) 81–95, doi: 10.1002/cmmi.1613.

[20] H. Chen, D. Longfield, V. Varahagiri, K. Nguyen, A. Patrick, H. Qian, et al. Optical imaging in tissue with X-ray excited luminescent sensors, The Analyst 136 (17) (2011) 3438, doi: 10.1039/c0an00931h.

[21] H. Chen, A. Patrick, Z. Yang, D. VanDerveer, J. Anker, High-resolution chemical imaging through tissue with an X-ray scintillator sensor, Analyt. Chem. 83 (13) (2011) 5045–5049, doi: 10.1021/ac200054v.

[22] Human skull X-ray image. (2020). https://www.freepik.com/premium-photo/human-skull-x-ray-image_6368117.htm. Accessed 24 September 2020.

[23] B. Muzio. Normal knees X-rays. Radiopaedia.org. (2020). https://radiopaedia.org/cases/normal-knees-X-rays. Accessed 12 November 2020.

[24] S. Chen, J. Carroll, Coronary angiography, Prac. Sign. I. Proc. Clin. Card. (2010) 157–185, doi: 10.1007/978-1-84882-515-4_13.

[25] M. Weininger, J. Barraza, C. Kemper, J. Kalafut, P. Costello, U. Schoepf, Cardiothoracic CT angiography: current contrast medium delivery strategies, Am. J. Roentgenol. 196 (3) (2011) W260–W272, doi: 10.2214/ajr.10.5814.

[26] Masters, B.R. Harrisons's Principles of Internal Medicine, 18th Edition, two volumes and DVD. Eds: Dan L. Longo, Anthony S. Fauci, Dennis L. Kasper, Stephen L. Hauser, J. Larry Jameson and Joseph Loscalzo, ISBN-13: 9780071748896 McGraw Hill. Graefe's Arch. Clin. Exp. Ophthalmol. 250 (2012), 1407–1408, doi:10.1007/s00417-012-1940-9.

[27] S. Ross, D. Spendlove, S. Bolliger, A. Christe, L. Oesterhelweg, S. Grabherr, et al. Postmortem whole-body CT angiography: evaluation of two contrast media solutions, Am. J. Roentgenol. 190 (5) (2008) 1380–1389, doi: 10.2214/ajr.07.3082.

[28] S. Grabherr, V. Djonov, A. Friess, M. Thali, G. Ranner, P. Vock, R. Dirnhofer, Postmortem angiography after vascular perfusion with diesel oil and a lipophilic contrast agent, Am. J. Roentgenol. 187 (5) (2006) W515–W523, doi: 10.2214/ajr.05.1394.

[29] S. Grabherr, V. Djonov, K. Yen, M. Thali, R. Dirnhofer, Postmortem angiography: review of former and current methods, Am. J. Roentgenol. 188 (3) (2007) 832–838, doi: 10.2214/ajr.06.0787.

[30] S. Grabherr, E. Gygax, B. Sollberger, S. Ross, L. Oesterhelweg, S. Bolliger, et al. Two-step postmortem angiography with a modified heart–lung machine: preliminary results, Am. J. Roentgenol. 190 (2) (2008) 345–351, doi: 10.2214/ajr.07.2261.

[31] D. Ginat, R. Gupta, Advances in computed tomography imaging technology, Annu. Rev. Biomed. Eng. 16 (1) (2014) 431–453, doi: 10.1146/annurev-bioeng-121813-113601.

[32] A. Bhide, S. Datar, K. Stebbins, Magnetic resonance imaging: case histories of significant medical advances, SSRN Electr. J. (2019)doi: 10.2139/ssrn.3427247.

[33] G. Michael, X-ray computed tomography, Phys. Educ. 36 (6) (2001) 442–451, doi: 10.1088/0031-9120/36/6/301.

[34] L. Tanoue, Computed tomography—an increasing source of radiation exposure, Yearb. Pulmon.Dis. 2009 (2009) 154–155, doi: 10.1016/s8756-3452(08)79173-4.

[35] D. Brenner, E. Hall, Computed tomography: an increasing source of radiation exposure, New Eng. J. Med. 357 (22) (2007) 2277–2284, doi: 10.1056/nejmra072149.

[36] A. Lembcke, T. Wiese, J. Schnorr, S. Wagner, J. Mews, T. Kroencke, et al. Image quality of noninvasive coronary angiography using multislice spiral computed tomography and electron-beam computed tomography, Invest. Radiol. 39 (6) (2004) 357–364, doi: 10.1097/01. rli.0000123316.10765.6c.

[37] Mychox.net. CXR and CT scans. (2020). http://www.mychox.net/cf/imaging.php. Accessed 24 September 2020.

[38] Radtechonduty.com. 2020. Normal head scan—CT scan. (2020.) http://www.radtechonduty. com/2016/09/normal-head-scan-ct-scan.html. Accessed 24 September 2020.

[39] N. Stevens, S. Steiner, I. Smith, R. MacKay, Monitoring radiation use in cardiac fluoroscopy imaging procedures, Med. Physics 38 (1) (2010) 317–326, doi: 10.1118/1.3524224.

[40] Ksradiology.com. General radiology and fluoroscopy: Kent & Sussex Radiology Group. (2020). https://www.ksradiology.com/services/X-ray.html. Accessed 24 September 2020.

[41] W. Palmer, Tomosynthesis better long-term than digital mammography for breast cancer screening. Diagn. Imaging (2020). https://www.diagnosticimaging.com/view/tomosynthesis-better-long-term-digital-mammography-breast-cancer-screening. Accessed 24 September 2020.

[42] C.L. Hwang, K. Yoon, Multiple Attribute Decision Making: Methods and Applications, Springer-Verlag, Berlin/Heidelberg/New York, 1981.

[43] G. Jahanshahloo, F. Lotfi, M. Izadikhah, Extension of the TOPSIS method for decision-making problems with fuzzy data, Appl. Math. Comput. 181 (2) (2006) 1544–1551, doi: 10.1016/j. amc.2006.02.057.

[44] K. Huang, J. Huang, G. Tzeng, New hybrid multiple attribute decision-making model for improving competence sets: enhancing a company's core competitiveness, Sustainability 8 (2) (2016) 175, doi: 10.3390/su8020175.

[45] L.P. Yoon, C. Hwang, Multiple Attribute Decision Making: An Introduction, SAGE Publications, California, 1995.

Chapter 12

Evaluation and simulation of dental instrument sterilization techniques with fuzzy PROMETHEE

Dilber Uzun Ozsahin[a,b,c], Ilker Ozsahin[a,b,d], Kudakwashe Nyakuwanikwa[b],
Tapiwa W. Simbanegavi[b] and Berna Uzun[a,e]

[a]DESAM Institute, Near East University, Turkish Republic of Northern Cyprus, Nicosia, Turkey;
[b]Department of Biomedical Engineering, Near East University, Turkish Republic of Northern
Cyprus, Nicosia, Turkey; [c]Medical Diagnostic Imaging Department, College of Health Sciences,
University of Sharjah, Sharjah, United Arab Emirates; [d]Brain Health Imaging Institute,
Department of Radiology, Weill Cornell Medicine, New York, NY, United States; [e]Department of
Mathematics, Near East University, Turkish Republic of Northern Cyprus, Nicosia, Turkey

12.1 Introduction

Sterilization in medicine is defined as the process of making an instrument free of any microbes. Thus, the sterilization of dental instruments focuses only on disinfecting instruments used by dental practitioners. Sterilization is different from disinfection and sanitization in that it eliminates all forms of life. Dental instruments are the tools that are used by dental practitioners to examine, manipulate, treat, extract, and remove teeth, together with the surrounding tissue in some cases. In general dentistry practice, dental instruments are grouped into three basic groups. General instruments are used in a variety of procedures, which include explorers, scalars, and dental mirrors. Extraction instruments include forceps, elevators, and Wilsons. Last are reconstruction instruments used in the reconstruction of teeth, which include carvers, amalgam carriers, and pluggers [1]. In terms of sterilization and disinfection, dental instruments are classified into three groups with respect to the risk of infection transmission: Critical instruments, which are those used to penetrate tissue and bone like scalpels; semicritical instruments, which are in contact with the oral tissue without any penetration, like dental mouth mirrors; and noncritical instruments, which only come into contact with intact skin like the external components of X-ray beams. According to [2], noncritical instruments do not

Applications of Multi-Criteria Decision-Making Theories in Healthcare and Biomedical Engineering.
http://dx.doi.org/10.1016/B978-0-12-824086-1.00012-8

require sterilization but rather can be wiped down with a surface disinfectant After use on a patient, a process of cleaning, disinfecting, and sterilizing the instruments is mandatory before they are used for another patient. Modern dental practices are very busy and face numerous challenges in maintaining productive capacity while also ensuring patient safety [3]. However, advancements in dental processing equipment have allowed dental practices to ensure efficiency in operation, safety of patients, and also save money after sterilization. In this study, we use the fuzzy preference ranking organization method for enrichment evaluation (PROMETHEE) to evaluate the sterilization techniques for dental instruments.

12.2 Materials and methods

12.2.1 Moist heat

Moist heat, also known as autoclaving, is a process in which a cloud of steam at high pressure is used to eliminate infectious viruses, bacteria, fungi, and spores (spores are more resilient, but can be killed if subjected to a harsh environment for long periods of time). Based on temperature, moist heat sterilization is divided into three parts. Temperatures below 100°C are called pasteurization (flash and holder methods); temperature at 100°C, which is the boiling point; and the use of steam under pressure. The most effective method of sterilizing dental instruments is by using steam under pressure [4]. The instrument used to pressurize and heat the steam is called an autoclave, which is a jacketed rectangular chamber invented by Charles Chamberland in 1884 from a precursor device called a steam digester created in 1679 by Denis Papin [5]. In autoclaving, two processes of gravity displacement (most common) and prevacuum sterilization (also called type B sterilization) are available. The only difference between these two processes is the method in which air is ejected from the sterilization chamber. In gravity displacement, the gravitational force is crucial in ejecting the air through escape vents, whereas in prevacuum sterilization a pulse vacuum is used to expel air out of the chamber [3]. In moist heat sterilization, an average temperature of 120°C (250°C) is used for 15 minutes. However, this temperature and time are not mandatory and can depend on the dental instruments to be sterilized. An example is when a temperature of 134°C–138°C is used for roughly 3 minutes, which is enough to kill any microbial life. The purpose of the high pressure of 200 kpa is to raise the temperature in the cylinder to the required 120°C. The temperature applied is also dependent on the amount of water to be heated and used as steam. In this instance, the temperature is inversely proportional to the amount of water present [6]. Since most microorganisms are fundamentally made of protein, the procedure is effective as it subjects the microorganisms in the dental instruments to high temperature and pressure, which disorient their protein structures (denaturing), thus killing them [7]. When compared to other sterilization techniques, such as chemical decontamination sterilization, moist heat is considered the best option to sterilize dental materials that are not heat sensitive and are permeable by steam [8]. In the sterilization of dental instruments, instruments that are not made of stainless steel contain acids, bases, sulfates, and organic solvents, and it is recommended that they are sterilized via an autoclave as they will be ruined by steam or could represent a risk to the autoclave device [7]. It is of utmost importance that the steam sterilization is monitored to prevent over- or underexposure of the instruments. A printout is used to monitor a steam sterilizer by measuring the temperature, the time at the specific temperature, and the pressure. Chemical and biological indicators are used to measure these conditions. Chemical indicator probes are placed at the potentially coolest and least accessible parts of the chamber. In the use of biological indicators, an envelope with spores of *Geobacillus stearothermophilus* is placed inside the chamber during a cycle of sterilization. After the cycle, the bacteria is inoculated into tryptone soya broth and incubated at 56°C for 5 days. No growth of the bacteria ensures that proper sterilization is being done. This specific bacterium is used because of its tolerance to harsh conditions [9]. Some advantages of using moist heat sterilization include non-toxicity to the environment, rapid cycle times and its ability to penetrate device lumens and medical packaging. However, it may leave the instruments wet, making them susceptible to rusting. In poverty-stricken countries that lack the resources to sterilize their dental equipment, recent innovative approaches have been implemented, such as the use of solar-powered autoclaves and waste converters that can carry out the same task as an original autoclave but without the high pressure [7].

12.2.2 Dry heat

Dry heat sterilization is when high temperatures are used to kill microorganisms. Dry heat accomplishes the destruction by oxidizing molecules [6]. This can be done through incineration (combustion of organic substances), flaming, hot air or heating by infrared rays in a vacuum (usually for operating theatre instruments) [3]. Compared to moist heat, dry heat requires longer periods of time (1.5–3 hours) and much higher temperatures. It is usually used to sterilize dental equipment that is impenetrable or damaged by moist heat, such as any petroleum products or sharp objects. The long period of time of an hour serves the purpose of killing the most resistant of spores. The most popular form of dry heat sterilization is a hot air oven. The dry heat is produced by conduction where heat is absorbed by the outer surface then gradually absorbed by the inner layers until it reaches the center. After the heat reaches the center, the whole oven will be hot and thus the sterilization temperature is reached [6]. The tools required to provide dry heat include a hot air oven, conveyor oven, conducted heat, and dry heat in the midst of a vacuum. The hot air oven is principally an oven that can hold a large number of instruments. Thermocouples are used in the oven to prevent temperature variations (which should not reach 5°C) during sterilization and also to test the time taken by some dental objects to reach the sterilization temperature [10]. There are two types of dry heat sterilization, namely static-hot-air oven and forced-hot-air oven (mechanical convection). The static hot-air type uses coils at the bottom of the oven; thus, heat starts at the bottom and rises to the top through convection. This is the slowest type compared to the forced air type [11]. The forced-hot-air type uses a blower that circulates heat throughout the oven, thus maintaining the sterilization temperature in the oven at a constant rate. This is the most frequently used type of sterilizer for reconstruction dental instruments because of the quick transfer of energy. Often, the sterilization temperature is proportional to the time, with 170°C (340°F) for 30 minutes, 160°C (320°F) for 60 minutes, and 150°C (300°F) for 150 minutes or longer, depending on the volume of the dental instruments in the chamber [12]. Due to the excessive temperatures used in dry heat, *Bacillus atrophaeus* spores are used to monitor the efficiency of the sterilization process. These spores are used over *Geobacillus stearothermophilus* because they are tolerant to heat [6]. The advantages of using dry heat include its nontoxicity, lack of harm to the environment, low operating costs, noncorrosiveness due to its compatibility with metal and sharp dental instruments, and its ability to thoroughly penetrate materials. However, this sterilization technique is relatively time consuming, unsuitable for dental instruments made of rubber or plastics, and may also damage instruments made of metal due to the elevated temperatures.

12.2.3 Chemical agents

This is the use of a proprietary chemical that contains alcohol, formaldehyde, or different inert ingredients other than water to kill micro-organisms in dental instruments. Another name for chemical agents cold sterile solutions [3]. It should be noted that in dental sterilization, most chemical agents are used in combination with other agents or other sterilization techniques to achieve optimal efficiency. The main reason for the use of chemical agents is to accommodate dental equipment that is thermo-sensitive and thus cannot withstand elevated temperatures [13]. These chemical agents include quaternary ammonium compounds, phenolics, peracetic acid, hydrogen peroxide, ortho-phthalaldehyde (OPA), Iodophors, glutaraldehyde, formaldehyde, chlorine, and chlorine compounds and alcohols. Alcohols are the most effective sterilizers but have not yet been approved by the Food and Drug Administration to function as the main ingredient in any sterilizer. The mode of action for alcohols is basic in that it causes denaturation of proteins in the unwanted microorganisms. The main alcohols used are isopropyl alcohol and ethyl alcohol. The second most common agent is chlorine. Sodium hypochlorite is the most prevalent liquid chlorine and is usually known as household bleach in most countries. The specific mode of action is not known but it is presumed to be through the oxidation of some enzymes such as sulfhydryl enzymes [14]. Another widely used chemical agent is peracetic acid. One of the first chemical agents to be used as documented in 1988, peracetic acid is supplied at 35% together with an anticorrosive agent in a container that has a single opening. It is provided in a single dose prior to initialising the cycle and is diluted to 0.2% with pure water. At a temperature of approximately 50°C, it is pumped into the chamber containing the dental instruments for 12 minutes. Peracetic acid's mode of action is also controversial, but it is thought to disrupt the permeability of the cell wall [14]. Normally, the dental instruments are immersed in the solution for an average of 8–10 hours and then rinsed with pure water to wash off the sterilizer [15]. The advantages of using these various chemical agents include the very fast turnaround time for the dental instruments, that the procedure is verifiable after it is complete, that corrosion-sensitive instruments such as steel can be sterilized without the fear of them rusting, and also that the instruments come out without any moisture. However, chemical agents face limitations in that heavy clothed instruments may not be thoroughly sterilized due to the inability of some agents to penetrate interior parts, instruments affected by elevated temperatures may not withstand some of the above mentioned agents and also, the odors left on the dental instruments may be unpleasant and will need some time to aerate.

12.2.4 Gases

This is the use of gaseous compounds to sterilize dental equipment. It should be noted that this sterilization technique is rarely used and is only used when the main sterilization techniques of moist heat or dry heat are inapplicable. The most common gases used to sterilize dental equipment today include oxides of nitrogen, chlorine oxide, ozone and ethylene oxide (ETO). According to Switzer [16], the most common is ethylene oxide (ETO). Ethylene oxide is a flammable colourless gas. Its use rose due to the unavailability of alternative sterilization methods for dental instruments that were heat and moisture sensitive. Four parameters, which include temperature (37–63°C), concentration (450–1200 mg/L), relative humidity (40%–80%) and exposure time (1–6 hours), influence the sterilization efficiency of ETO [14]. In certain situations, an increase in the concentration and/or temperature is beneficial in sterilization as it will decrease the exposure time required. The mode of action of ETO is believed to be alkylation (substitution of a hydrogen atom with an alkyl group) of proteins, ribonucleic acid, and deoxyribonucleic acid, thus disrupting metabolism and the division of cells. An ETO sterilization cycle consists of five phases, which include preconditioning and humidification, gas introduction, exposure, evacuation, and lastly aeration [14]. Although ETO is the most common gaseous sterilization technique, its lengthy cycles, operation costs, and hazard potential are a major drawback with respect to its use in the dental field [17]. Sterilization through ozone is very uncommon in dentistry, but it is worth considering as an option. Ozone is a strong oxidizing agent made by shooting a jet of oxygen through a high-voltage magnetic field [16]. A company named Genlantis has recently developed a sterilizing device named Ozilla ozone sterilizer that uses ozone as its sterilizer [18]. The device is quite advantageous because it is relatively safe and efficient, does not use any liquids, harmful UV rays, harsh chemicals, or heat, and does not damage any surfaces or leave any chemical residues behind. To use the device, the operator places the instruments in the ozilla nest, sets the run time and removal time and then presses the start button. However, the device is very costly to purchase, use and maintain [18]. Another gas that may be used is nitrogen dioxide, which is very effective at ambient temperature. Similar to the other gases, nitrogen dioxide is introduced into a chamber containing the dental instruments. Although it produces some residue, the residue is not toxic or carcinogenic [16].

12.2.5 Radiation

Radiation of dental instruments is the use of an ionizing material, primarily X-ray, gamma, or electrons, to eliminate microorganisms including spores, viruses, bacteria, and fungi. The instruments to be sterilized are bombarded with high-energy electromagnetic radiation or electrons. This bombarding causes the creation of free radicals, molecular ions, and secondary electrons in and around the instruments' surfaces. These radiation products then react with the surrounding microorganisms and alter the chemical bonding in them [19]. Radiation is used by first sealing the instruments in an airtight bag after it has been used by the dental practitioner. The bag is then placed in a field of radiation that has the ability to penetrate the bag. After radiation, the clean instruments are kept in the bag to be opened again for use in the medical facility [20]. Gamma radiation is the most widely used form of radiation in dentistry due to its deep penetration ability [3]. Gamma rays are produced by the disintegration of Cobalt-60 (^{60}Co), which is neither too weak nor too strong for sterilization purposes. The energy produced in this gamma radiation type is enough to harm the microorganisms on the instruments, but not enough to cause the instruments to become radioactive [21]. The most beneficial aspect of using gamma radiation over other methods is that it is able to sterilize instruments that have plastic components. However, large or bulky metal instruments will require added controls to ensure effective sterilization, and not all plastics are compatible with gamma, as some become stained or brittle after processing; the reaction is thus dose-dependent [22]. The greatest disadvantage of using gamma is that it is a very expensive method of sterilizing dental instruments. Another method of radiation sterilization is UV radiation, which uses wavelengths that range from 328 to 210 nm. Although this method is not common, its mode of action is by the destruction of nuclei acids through the induction of thymine dimers [3]. In electron beam radiation, high-energy electrons capable of ionization are generated by electron beam accelerators. In most cases, electron energies of ~10

MeV are used, but this value can be changed to optimize depth. Gamma rays and electron beam radiation differ in sample penetration depth, exposure time required for effective sterilization, and product compatibility. In X-ray radiation, high-energy electrons from the accelerator interact with high-atomic-number nuclei, such as atoms of tungsten or tantalum. This procedure is known as bremsstrahlung. Electron energies of 5–7 MeV are commercially used and these can penetrate more than both gamma and electron beams, but excessive use may cause degradation of the instruments. For instruments that require more penetration, X-rays are preferred because they have the highest dose uniformity ratio (DUR), which is the ratio between the maximum and minimum dose required for sterilization [19].

12.3 Fuzzy logic

Fuzzy logic refers to a computation approach based on "degrees of truth" rather than the basic true or false (Boolean logic of 1s and 0s) that is used by computers [23]. Lotfi A. Zadeh published the concept of evaluation in 1965 [24]. To be clear, fuzzy logic includes 0 and 1 as extreme cases of truth, but also includes a number of cases of the truth such that the comparison cannot be hot or cold but a certain numerical temperature, for example. Due to the lack of precise data in real-world situations, statistical methods of computation are most useful when trying to model processes that have incomplete or inaccurate data. Nonstatistical methods such as the fuzzy set theory or fuzzy neural networks are used when dealing with complex systems that have indistinct or vague data [25]. Fuzzy multicriteria decision-making techniques have been constantly developed, starting with fuzzy sets (which were the first to be developed) through to modern complex fuzzy sets. For example, a neuro-fuzzy approach was first proposed to assist in problem-solving in the business environment [25]. A new tool for indistinct data processing known as neutrosophic sets has also emerged and been found to be useful for decision-making processes. Additionally, rough set theory has been proposed and has proved to be an effective method for dealing with information systems that demonstrate inconsistency. Thus, fuzzy-rough models have the ability to evaluate inconsistent and vague data [25]. According to Edmundas Kazimieras Zavadskas [25], aggregation operator theory and fuzzy set theory have led to the formation of a number of decision-making theories and information aggregation methods under the fuzzy aggregation operator. Discussions regarding the relationship and combination of fuzzy and probabilistic representations of unpredictability in multiple-attribute engineering and management problems have been ongoing for a number of years and it is expected that they will continue in the future [25]. Due to the fuzziness of real world data, hybrid multicriteria decision-making models continue to emerge as an alternative method for information modelling. In the scientific field, it can be observed that fuzzy or hybrid decision-making techniques are extensively applied for transportation, logistics, and supplier selection problems that require

TABLE 12.1 Linguistic fuzzy scale.

Linguistic scale for evaluation	Triangular fuzzy scale
Very high (VH)	(0.75, 1, 1)
Important (H)	(0.50, 0.75, 1)
Medium (M)	(0.25, 0.50, 0.75)
Low (L)	(0, 0.25, 0.50)
Very low (VL)	(0, 0, 0.25)

the effective management of information when evaluating alternative solutions and making decisions about the best or most favourible choices [25]. Another relatively frequent application of MCDM techniques is for the assessment of service quality in different industries and various types of economic activities [25]. Zadeh stated that rather than looking at fuzzy logic as a single theory, one should regard the "fuzzification" (process of converting a crisp value into a fuzzy value) of data as methodology to generalize any theory from a discrete to a continous form (fuzzy). The process of fuzzification of input and/or output leads to the development of fuzzy sets. Triangular or trapezoidal shaped curves and tables are mainly used to view the fuzzy sets because they represent the embedded controllers more clearly (Table 12.1).

Each fuzzy set spans a region of values that are graphed against a membership. Any particular input is measured against this fuzzy set to obtain a degree of membership. [26]. The process of obtaining a single number or value from a fuzzy set is called defuzzification. This process is performed to convert the fuzzy results into crisp output. This can be done manually or through the use of an algorithm that picks the best crisp value in the fuzzy set. In this chapter, since the conditions in comparison are indistinct (fuzzy), all the comparison parameters underwent separate fuzzy set procedures using the linguistic fuzzy scale and the linguistic fuzzy inputs were obtained.

In this chapter, the fuzzy PROMETHEE method of evaluation was used to compare the sterilization techniques. PROMETHEE, meaning preference ranking organization method for enrichment evaluation method, was conceived by Professor Jean-Pierre Brans in 1982 at the ULB and VUB universities of Brussels [27]. Given the lack of robust assumptions on the decision maker's preferences, the PROMETHEE can be effectively integrated with participatory methods in order to get enough information to understand whether one alternative is at least as good as another [28]. Further use of fuzzy PROMETHEE is detailed by [29], where the evaluation of various cancer treatment techniques was done.

In order to evaluate the dental instrument sterilization techniques, a triangular fuzzy scale was used to identify how crucial was each criterion following

TABLE 12.2 Visual PROMETHEE application for dental instrument sterilization alternatives.

Sterilization technique	Cost of machinery	Time taken to sterilize	Ease of use of technique	Accessibility of sterilization technique	Benefits	Side effects
Wet/steam sterilization	H	VL	VH	VH	H	H
Dry heat sterilization	VH	H	M	VH	M	M
Gases	M	VH	VL	H	VH	H
Chemical agents	VL	VL	M	H	L	M
Radiation (gamma rays)	M	0	M	VH	H	H

TABLE 12.3 Visual PROMETHEE results for dental sterilization alternative.

Complete ranking	Alternative	Positive outranking flow	Negative outranking flow	Net flow
1.	Radiation (gamma rays)	0.0994	0.0234	0.0760
2.	Gases	0.1052	0.0690	0.0362
3.	Wet/steam sterilization	0.0668	0.0790	−0.0122
4.	Chemical agents	0.0726	0.1016	−0.0290
5.	Dry heat sterilization	0.0263	0.0973	−0.0710

[30]. See Table 12.2 The Yager index was then used to defuzzify the linguistic fuzzy inputs in order to apply the PROMETHEE technique.

12.4 Results and discussion

The visual PROMETHEE was then applied to the results and the outputs are shown here.

As seen from Table 12.3, with its better properties such as time of sterilization and cost of machinery, radiation (gamma rays) is the best sterilization alternative, followed by the use of gaseous compounds, which is the second-best alternative. Moreover, the positive and negative properties of the dental instrument sterilization alternatives are displayed in Fig. 12.1.

12.5 Conclusion

In this study, we displayed the best method for the sterilization of dental instruments by using fuzzy PROMETHEE (a decision-making theory). Fuzzy PROMETHEE is a highly effective tool in the study of fuzzy systems. From this tool, the results acquired in this study give valuable information regarding the dental instrument sterilization alternatives. This study can be extended according to the dental institution's situation to obtain the most suitable results. Furthermore, this study shows that the method used is helpful in multicriteria evaluation in healthcare studies.

Acknowledgments

The authors would like to thank Dr. Gurkan Unsal for his support.

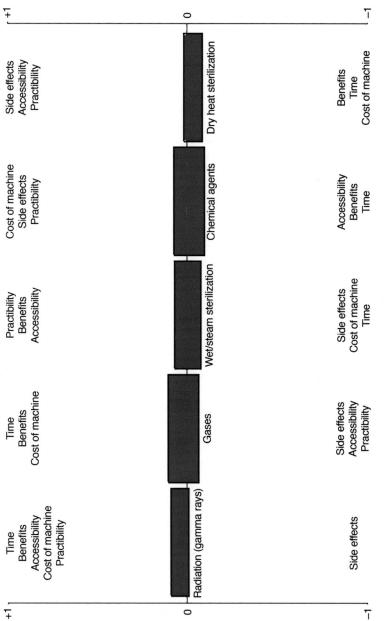

FIGURE 12.1 PROMETHEE evaluation results (visual PROMETHEE).

References

[1] D. Adaire, Classification of dental instruments. Dentistry (2006), https://faculty.atu.edu/cbrucker/Engl2053/Samples/DGA03.htm. Accessed 3/10/19.

[2] R. Olive, Guidelines for infection control by Australian Dental Association. In: D.S. Liberali, Guidelines for Infection Control, third ed. (pp. 16–17). Sydney: Australian Dental Association, 2015.

[3] R.D. Lakshya, Sterilization protocols in dentisty, Journal of Pharmaceutical Sciences and Research 8 (6) (2016) 558–564.

[4] R.D. Malarvizhi, Moist heat sterilization—a review. Slideshare (2017), https://www.slideshare.net/iq1086/moist-heat-sterilization-a-review. Accessed 28.10.19.

[5] D. Washmuth, Nursing hygiene training/science courses. Study.com (2012), https://study.com/academy/lesson/what-is-the-moist-heat-sterilization-method.html. Accessed 25.10.19.

[6] T. Acharya, Dry-heat sterilization: principle, advantages, and disadvantages. Microbeonline (2013), https://microbeonline.com/dry-heat-sterilization-principle-advantages-disadvantages/. Accessed 30.10.19.

[7] A. Peshin, Scienceabc. Scienceabc.com (2017), https://www.scienceabc.com/innovation/what-is-an-autoclave-and-how-does-it-work.html. Accessed 27.10/19.

[8] D. Prince, Prince sterilization services. Princesterilization.com (2018), https://princesterilization.com/difference-between-moist-heat-sterilization-dry-heat-sterilization/. Accessed 28.10.19.

[9] T. Acharya, Microbe online. Microbeonline.com (2013), https://microbeonline.com/moist-heat-sterilization-definition-principle-advantages-disadvantages/. Accessed 28.10.19.

[10] E.M. Darmady, Sterilization by dry heat. Portsmouth and Isle of Wight Area Pathological Service (1951), 38–44.

[11] A. Unfried, Dry heat sterilization: definition, process, and validation. Study.com (2015), https://study.com/academy/lesson/dry-heat-sterilization-definition-process-validation.html. Accessed 31.10.19.

[12] Editorial team, Dry heat sterilization. Laboratoryinfo (2019), https://laboratoryinfo.com/dry-heat-sterilization/. Accessed 1.11.19.

[13] B.R. Enrica Laneve, Sterilization in dentistry: a review of the literature, Int. J. Dentist. (2018) 9.

[14] W.A. Rutala (2016), Guideline for disinfection and sterilization in healthcare facilities. Centers for Disease Control and Prevention, https://www.cdc.gov/infectioncontrol/guidelines/disinfection/disinfection-methods/chemical.html. Accessed 6.11.19.

[15] A.K. Condrin, (2014). Disinfection and sterilization in dentistry. TDA PERKS program (2014), https://tdaperks.com/disinfectionsterilization/. Accessed 2.11.19.

[16] L. Switzer, Gaseous sterilization. Mesalabs.com (2017), https://biologicalindicators.mesalabs.com/2017/01/20/gaseous-sterilization/. Accessed 10.11.19.

[17] A.K. Condrin, OSHA Review Inc., Perks program, from TDAPerks.com (2014), https://tdaperks.com/disinfectionsterilization/. Accessed 10.08.18.

[18] Genlantis.team, Sterilization systems. Genlantis.com: http://www.genlantis.com/ozone-sterilization.html. Accessed 11.11.19.

[19] I. Goronzy, Radiation sterilization. California: Coursework for PH241, Stanford University (2018).

[20] J.P. Hageman, HPS specialists in radiation protection. Hps.org (2004), https://hps.org/publicinformation/ate/q4004.html. Accessed 8.10.04.

[21] M. Finkiel, Sterilization by gamma irradiation. Tuttnauer.com, RTuttnauer: https://tuttnauer.com/blog/sterilization-by-gamma-irradiation. Accessed 4.12.19.

[22] T. Rennison, Leave nothing to chance: sterilizing medical devices. Medicaldevice-developments.com (2013), http://www.medicaldevice-developments.com/features/featureleave-nothing-to-chance-sterilising-medical-devices-different-techniques-pros-cons/. Accessed 4.12.19.

[23] M. Rouse, Techtarget. Techtarget.com (2016), https://searchenterpriseai.techtarget.com/definition/fuzzy-logic. Accessed 21.05.20.

[24] M. Mares, Computations over Fuzzy Quantities, CRC Press, Boca Raton, (1994).

[25] E.K. Zavadskas, Multiple-criteria decision-making (MCDM) techniques for business, Processes Information Management10 (4), doi:10.3390/info10010004: Information.

[26] P. Zhang, Advanced Industrial Control Technology, Applied Science Publishers, (2010) 257-305.

[27] B. Mareschal, PROMETHEE Methods. Promethee-gaia.net (2011), http://www.promethee-gaia.net/promethee.html. Accessed 2019.

[28] C.D. Marta Bottero, Multicriteria evaluation of urban regeneration processes: an application of PROMETHEE method in Northern Italy, Adv. Oper. Res. (2018) 1–3.

[29] K.S.T. Nyakuwanikwa, Evaluation and simulation of colon cancer, IEEE (2018) 4–6.

[30] D. Uzun Ozsahin, B. Uzun, M. Sani Musa, N. Şentürk, F. Nurçin, I. Ozsahin, Evaluating nuclear medicine imaging devices using fuzzy PROMETHEE method, Proc. Comp. Sci. (2017) 699–705.

Further reading

[1] Afful-Dadzie et al. (2016). Using fuzzy PROMETHEE to select countries for developmental aid. SpringerLink.

[2] H. Alexander, K.T.B. Morrison, R.H. Vonderheide, Trends in cancer. Cell.com (2018), https://www.cell.com/trends/cancer/fulltext/S2405-8033(18)30090-6. Accessed 20.7.18.

[3] A. Stunt, Pancreatic cancer action. Pancreaticcanceraction.org (2015), https://pancreaticcanceraction.org/about-pancreatic-cancer/treatment/chemotherapy/about-chemotherapy/. Accessed 1.47.18.

[4] American Cancer Society Staff, American Cancer Society (2016), Cancer.org: https://www.cancer.org/cancer/pancreatic-cancer/treating/medicine-pnets.html. Accessed 17.7.18.

[5] B. Roy, The outranking approach and the foundation of ELECTRE methods, Theor. Decis. (1991) 155–183.

[6] B. Mareschal et al., PROMETHEE Methods (2005). In: Multiple Criteria Decision Analysis: State of the Art Surveys, ResearchGate, Brussels, pp. 163–86.

[7] Burkle, Burkle. Buerkle.de: https://www.buerkle.de/. Accessed 18.04.20.

[8] Cancer Research UK Staff, Cancer Research UK (2018). Cancerresearchuk.org, https://www.cancerresearchuk.org/health-professional/cancer-statistics/statistics-by-cancer-type/pancreatic-cancer/incidence#heading-One. Accessed 1.07.18.

[9] P.C. Chakraborty, A comparative analysis of VIKOR method and its variants, Dec. Sci. Lett. (2016) 469–486.

[10] D. Citrin, B. Gershenhorn, C.K. Brown, Cancer Treatment Centers of America (2018), Cancercenter.com: https://www.cancercenter.com/treatments/hormone-therapy/. Accessed 6.07.18.

[11] E. O'Reilly, Onclice. Onclive.com: https://www.onclive.com/conference-coverage/2018-world-gi/dr-oreilly-on-immunotherapy-in-pancreatic-cancer. Accessed 17.07.18.

[12] E. Jaffee, S. Kimmel, Cancer Research Institute. Cancerresearch.org (2015), https://www.cancerresearch.org/immunotherapy/cancer-types/pancreatic-cancer. Accessed 7.05.18.

[13] FAVPGNG. Favpng.com (May 10, 2020), https://www.favpng.com/. Accessed 10.05.20.

[14] D. Gordon-Dseagu, Devesa, PubMed.gov. Nih.gov (2018), https://www.ncbi.nlm.nih.gov/pubmed/29149259. Accessed 24.06.18.

[15] H.W. Harris, K. Kirkwood, UCSF Department of Surgery. Ucsf.edu (2014), https://general.surgery.ucsf.edu/conditions--procedures/pancreatic-cancer.aspx. Accessed 4.07.18.

[16] C.L. Hwang, K. Yoon, Multiple Attribute Decision Making: Methods and Applications), Springer-Verlag, New York, 1981, pp. 4–12.

[17] IAEA, International Atomic Energy Agency (April 17, 2020). IAEA.org, https://www.iaea.org/. Accessed 17.04.20.

[18] IndiaMartI, Indiamart.com, https://www.indiamart.com/. Accessed 18.04.20.

[19] J. Abbruzzeser, M. Buchler, R. Hruban, Pancreatica.org (2016), http://pancreatica.org/pancreatic-cancer/pancreatic-cancer-causes-and-risk-factors/. Accessed 5.07.18.

[20] S.J.T. Jansen, Chapter 5. The multi-attribute utility method, in: S. Jansen, H. Coolen, R. Goetgeluk (Eds.), Meas. Anal. Hous, Prefer. Choice, 2011, pp. 101–125.

[21] Johns Hopkins Surgeons. John Hopkins University, JHU.edu (2018), http://pathology.jhu.edu/pc/TreatmentSurgery.php?area=tr. Accessed 15.07.18.

[22] P.a. Konidari, A multi-criteria evaluation method for climate change mitigation policy, Energ. Policy 35 (12) (2007) 6235–6257.

[23] L. Abdullah, et al. Application of PROMETHEE method for green supplier selection: a comparative result based on preference functions, J. Ind. Engineering Int. (2019) 271–285.

[24] W.C. Lazim Abdullah, Application of PROMETHEE method for green supplier selection, J. Ind. Engineering Int. (2019) 271–285.

[25] M. Behzadian et al., PROMETHEE: A Comprehensive Literature Review on Methodologies and Applications. Elsevier, 2010, pp. 198–215.

[26] P.T. Mark Velasquez, An analysis of multi-criteria decision making methods, Int. J. Oper. Res. 10 (2) (2013) 56–66.

[27] Mayo Clinic Staff, Mayoclinic.org (2018), https://www.mayoclinic.org/diseases-conditions/pancreatic-cancer/symptoms-causes/syc-20355421.

[28] F.W. Nugent, Medicine.net.com (2018), https://www.medicinenet.com/pancreatic_cancer/article.htm#pancreatic_cancer_facts. Accessed 9.06.18.

[29] Medico Apps, Medicoapps.org (2020), https://medicoapps.org/. Accessed 10.05.20.

[30] M. Yazdani, F.R. Graeml, VIKOR and Its Applications: A State-of-the-Art Survey. Elsevier, 2014.

[31] S. Murat, H. Kazan, S.S. Coskun, An application for measuring performance quality of schools by using the PROMETHEE multi-criteria decision-making method, Procedia 195 (3) (July 2015) 729–738.

[32] R.R. Nurmalini, Study approach of simple additive weighting for decision support system, Indonesia (2016) 1–7.

[33] O. Sadr-Azodi, P. Konings, N. Brusselaers, US National Library of Medicine, NIH.gov (2017), https://www.ncbi.nlm.nih.gov/pmc/articles/PMC5721980/. Accessed 13.07.18.

[34] Pancreatic Cancer Action Network Staff, Pancan.org (2016), https://www.pancan.org/facing-pancreatic-cancer/treatment/treatment-types/radiation-therapy/. Accessed 8.07.18.

[35] J.W. Payne, Measuring constructed preferences: towards a building code, J. Risk Uncertain. 19 (1999) 243–270.

[36] M. Rouse, SearchEnterpriseAI, https://searchenterpriseai.techtarget.com/. Accessed 17.04.20.

[37] P.V. Roy, Multicriteria Decision Aid, John Wiley and sons, (1989) 57-76.

[38] S. Radhika, et al. VIKOR Method for multi-criteria decision making in academic staff selection, STM J. (2013) 30–31.

[39] Sayadi, et al. Extension of VIKOR method for decision making problem with interval numbers, Elsevier (2009) 2257–2262.

[40] S. Birgün, Supplier selection process using ELECTRE method. Conference: Intelligent Systems and Knowledge Engineering (ISKE), 1–8.

[41] S. Birgün, E. Cihan, Supplier selection process using ELECTRE method. Conference: Intelligent Systems and Knowledge Engineering (ISKE), 1–8.

[42] Safe and Simple Quality Sterilization, SSQLLP.com, https://www.ssqllp.com/. Accessed 18.04.20.

[43] STERIS,steris-ast.com, https://www.steris-ast.com/. Accessed 18.04.20.

[44] S.A. Suganya, Multi-criteria decision making using ELECTRE, Sci. Res. (2016).

[45] American Cancer Society medical and editorial content team, American Cancer Society, http://cancer.org. Accessed 5.07.18

[46] D.U. Uzun Ozsahin, Evaluating X-ray-based medical imaging devices with fuzzy preference ranking organization method for enrichment evaluations, Int. J. Adv. Comp. Sci. Appl. 9 (3) (2017).

[47] Geovanna Villacreses, Gabriel Gaona, Javier Martínez-Gómez, Diego Juan Jijón, Wind farms suitability location using geographical information system (GIS), based on multi-criteria decision making (MCDM) methods: The case of continental Ecuador, Renewable Energy 109 (2017) 275–286.

[48] VPTRad, VPT Rad. VTPrad.com: http://www.vptrad.com/. Accessed 17.04.20.

[49] William Blahd, Webmd.com, https://www.webmd.com/g00/cancer/pancreatic-cancer/whipple-procedure?i10c.encReferrer=aHR0cHM6Ly93d3cuZ29vZ2xlLmNvVrLw%3D%3D&i10c.ua=1&i10c.dv=14. Accessed 17.07.18.

[50] XLSTAT. xlstat.com, https://www.xlstat.com/. Accessed 24.04.20.

[51] Z. Pavic´, Notes on TOPSIS method, Int. J. Res. Engin. Sci. (2013).

Chapter 13

Application of fuzzy TOPSIS in the sterilization of medical devices

Mubarak Taiwo Mustapha[a,b], **Dilber Uzun Ozsahin**[a,b,c], **Berna Uzun**[a,d] **and Ilker Ozsahin**[a,b,e]

[a]*DESAM Institute, Near East University, Turkish Republic of Northern Cyprus, Nicosia, Turkey;* [b]*Department of Biomedical Engineering, Near East University, Turkish Republic of Northern Cyprus, Nicosia, Turkey;* [c]*Medical Diagnostic Imaging Department, College of Health Sciences, University of Sharjah, Sharjah, United Arab Emirates;* [d]*Department of Mathematics, Near East University, Turkish Republic of Northern Cyprus, Nicosia, Turkey;* [e]*Brain Health Imaging Institute, Department of Radiology, Weill Cornell Medicine, New York, NY, United States*

13.1 Introduction

The medical sterilization area has become increasingly complicated due to the need to prevent exposure of patients to diseases caused by bacteria on instruments and devices used during their treatment. There are cases of people contracting infections while on a visit to the hospital. These people were free of infection before going to the hospital but contracted diseases while in the hospital. It is usually as a result of the patient being in contact with a surface with harmful microbes on it. This type of infection is referred to as a nosocomial infection. Nosocomial infection can be largely avoided and controlled with the use of various sterilization methods. Failure to properly sterilize medical devices leads to significant costs associated with nosocomial infections, morbidity, and mortality issues [1]. Medical devices are widely used on patients in the hospital. These devices are produced from metallic and nonmetallic material (wood, ceramics, glass, plastic, etc.) [2]. Since some of these devices are reusable, sterilizing them becomes vital for the safety of the patient [2]. Sterilization is a process that involves total destruction, killing, or inactivation of any micro-organism or its spores that could cause any form of disease and infection on human. Sterilization is different from disinfection, which is a method used to reduce instead of kill all forms of biological life. Survivability of microbes on the surface of most material makes the entry of harmful micro-organism possible. This can be fatal if it gets into the body. Effective sterilization of medical devices does not alter

Applications of Multi-Criteria Decision-Making Theories in Healthcare and Biomedical Engineering.
http://dx.doi.org/10.1016/B978-0-12-824086-1.00013-X

the physical or chemical properties of medical devices. This can only happen if the medical device to be sterilized is left in the sterilizer for a much longer time (as in the case of flaming a wire loop) [3].

Medical equipment sterilization is achievable by using physical, chemical, or radiation method of sterilization [4]. In the medical industry, ethylene oxide (EtO) and gamma sterilization methods play a significant role in the sterilization of medical devices [5]. However, steam autoclave remains the oldest form of sterilization [6]. Other methods that are under development are low-temperature peracetic gas plasma, chlorine dioxide, low-temperature hydrogen peroxide gas plasma, hydrogen peroxide vapour-phase, high-intensity visible light and ozone.

Earle Spaulding classification method classifies medical devices into critical, semi-critical, and noncritical devices. This will aid for a better implementation of such devices based on the degree of infection risk. Critical medical devices such as scalpel blade, implants, transfer forceps, etc., are in direct contact with the circulatory system or human tissues. Semi-critical devices such as vaginal ultrasound probe, cystoscopies, respiratory equipment, etc., have contact with the mucosa layer while noncritical devices come in contact only with the skin.

The chapter aims to analyze and evaluate the most commonly used sterilization method based on popular criteria such as cost, volume capacity, cycle time, temperature, and penetration power. The evaluation will be carried out using a multicriteria decision-making method, fuzzy technique for order of preference by similarity to ideal solution (TOPSIS) with the goal of outranking each sterilization techniques.

13.2   History

Demons, monsters, and evil spirits were presumed to be the cause of infections in ancient times and driving the infection away was most often done through witchcraft or shamanic healing. In 3000 BC the Egyptians preserved corpses of royalty and important people using antiseptics (pitch/tar/resins/aromatics). The Egyptians also exploited the use of chemicals, such as common salt and niter, for their antiseptic value in dehydrating tissues. This went on for a long time, as thousands of mummies dating back to 3000 BC have been excavated. Moses (circa 1450 BC) in the books of Numbers, Leviticus, and Deuteronomy prescribed a method of purification using fire. The use of fire was also recommended for purification of infected premises. This directive by Moses serves as the basis for subsequent purification methods. In 550 BC, soldiers from the Greek army already understood the implication of germ entry into the body and thus preferred to fight naked because they feared that a worn cloth could allow the entry of germs into the body if they were stabbed or cut. They believed that a knife, sword, or spear could cause serious infection and possibly death because of the introduction of infection. In this same era, sulphur and fumes from burning chemicals were used as disinfectants [7].

Between 460 and 377 BC, Hippocrates invalidated the notion that infection was caused by an evil spirit, demons, or sins. He recommended the use of boiled water on a wound to remove harmful microbes. The most brilliant physician after Hippocrates was Galen (AD 130–200). Galen was of Greek descent and he treated Roman gladiators' wounds with boiled instruments. Galen and Hippocrates were well-known authorities in the field of medicine in their era. Between AD 900 and 1500, there was neither advancement nor breakthrough in the field of sterilization as all of Europe was ravaged with plague, filth, and pestilence. Efforts were made to disinfect ravaged hospital with fumes of vinegar and sulphur, cleansing solutions, arsenic, aeration, and antimony. The pressure cooker was invented by Denis Papin (a French physicist) in 1680. The principle of operation involves creating a pot and lid so that the air inside the pot cannot escape. The air inside the pot is trapped as the pot is heated. The trapped air generates high pressure as a result of its inability to escape. This is the same with the water in the pot as it increases in temperature. A medical device when penetrated with this extremely hot steam can be sterilized as the heat kills numerous harmful micro-organisms [7].

The first pressure steam sterilizer or autoclave that primarily functioned to kill heat-sensitive micro-organisms was developed by Charles Chamberland, Louis Pasteur's pupil and collaborator in 1876. Later that year, Jon Tyndall discovered that some bacteria can resist heat and as a result be harmful to man. He then develops a method for intermittent heating. In 1881, a notable achievement was made by Robert Koch and his associates when they proved the disinfecting properties of hot air and steam. They developed the first steam sterilizer with no pressure flowing and by the end of 1881, boiling as a method of sterilization was established. Gowns, linens, dressings, and all other things used for surgical operation were first boiled. The year 1886 ushered in the use of mercury chloride as a sterilizer. It was introduced by a German physician named Ernst von Bergmann. He recommended that mercury chloride should be used to scrub anything that came in contact with a wound. From 1885 to 1900, German scientists made a great improvement to the principle guiding steam sterilization. The improvement made by the Germans and the development of a modern temperature-controlled sterilizer by the Americans provoked a widespread adaptation of these principles to sterilizing equipment by the beginning of the 20th century. As a result, the development of high heat-resistance medical devices became popularized. Sword-like amputations were replaced with more sterile procedures.

The early type of hot air sterilizer used at the turn of the century in bacteriological laboratories was of German design; it had a dual wall and attempted to circulate gas-heated hot air through gravity convection [7].

J.J. Perkins's principle and procedures for sterilization of healthcare sciences were published in 1956. In his book, a set of methodology and standards for reusable medical device processing and sterilization were made. Glutaraldehyde, the first chemical solution approved by the Environmental Protection Agency (EPA) as a sterilant for heat-sensitive instruments, was introduced in 1963. In 1989, the Food and Drug Administration (FDA) of the United States approved for sale an ozone sterilizer for healthcare applications. Starting in

1989, an endoscopic low-temperature peracetic acid system for sterilization entered the US marketplace [7].

13.3 Attribute of a standard sterilization method

1. A sterilization method or agent must be effective against bacteria, viruses, fungi, mycobacterium, and spores.
2. It must have the ability to quickly achieve sterilization.
3. It must have the ability to penetrate common medical-device packaging materials and penetrate the interior of device lumens.
4. After repeated cycling, it should create only a minor alteration in the appearance or function of both the device and the material from which it is produced.
5. It must pose no harmful risk to human health or the environment.
6. It must be effective for complex or tiny installations
7. It must be physically, chemically, and biologically capable of monitoring the device to be sterilized.
8. It must be of a reasonable installation and operation cost.

13.4 Methods of sterilization

The methods of sterilization are classified into physical, chemical, or radiation methods [8]. The techniques used are physical, chemical, or radiation. Nevertheless, various medical devices are composed of chemical compounds requiring specific sterilization methods so as not to alter the physical and chemical compositions of these instruments. Fig. 13.1 shows the classification tree of sterilization methods.

Selecting the best form of sterilization is one of the most critical factors in designing a medical device. Using an ineffective or improper sterilization procedure will bar the medical device from having its marketing approval from regulatory bodies such as the FDA. Improper sterilization will lead to infectious disease transmission resulting in patient illness and even death. The year 2015 saw an infection outbreak caused by antibiotic-resistant bacteria associated with the reprocessing of duodenoscopes, which is a medical device inserted via the mouth for examination. As at that time, it was discovered that the

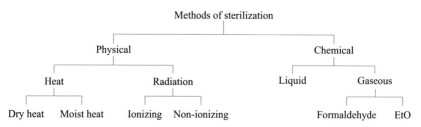

FIGURE 13.1   Method of sterilization.

duodenoscopes had a manufacturer defect that influences the effective sterilization of the device after each use. As a result of this defect, about 400 patients got infected and died. This brought about lawsuits against the duodenoscopes manufacturer, which resulted in eventual revoking of the manufacturing license and recalls mandated by the FDA. Evidence suggests that the manufacturer of the device had prior knowledge of these flaws but refused to disclose this to the FDA or hospitals where these devices were used. Although devices were subjected to high-level disinfectant, FDA was forced to set a new standard recommended for hospitals to find a more potent and robust method of sterilization, which will effectively eliminate harmful microbes. It is believed that if the sterilization method adopted by hospitals has been potent enough, the outbreak could have been averted.

There exist several sterilization methods that can be effectively used to achieve utmost sterilization. The most commonly used sterilization method for medical devices include:

- Steam sterilization.
- Dry sterilization.
- Chemical sterilization (ethylene oxide).
- Radiation.

Not all sterilization method is effective for medical devices [9]. A medical device's sterilization techniques is determined by the type of material from which it was produced, its chemical components, its classification, and intended use. There is a clear distinction between sterilization, disinfectant, and cleaning. Proper removal of physical particles, debris, or dirt from a medical device to be sterilized is very important. Tissue or blood accumulations on medical devices also lessen the potency of a sterilization method. Therefore, neglecting to clean a medical device will ultimately diminish the capability of the sterilization method. Disposable medical supplies are also sterilized by manufacturers before packaging and onward supply to the hospital. This is even more important for reusable medical devices such as clamps, forceps, duodenoscopes, or any other endoscopic devices. Storage and packaging of medical devices should be properly handled. Medical devices that are required to be sterilized prior to usage require less stringent guidelines when transporting while those that do not require presterilization require very careful handing because the sterility potential could be diminished by exposure to temperature, airborne particles, and humidity.

13.4.1 EtO sterilizer

Ethylene oxide is a combustible and volatile gas. Its fundamental components are:

- Gas concentration (450–1200 mg/L)
- Temperature (37°C–63°C)

- Relative humidity (40%–80%)
- Exposure time (1–6 hours)

All these components influence the sterilization capability of the EtO as an effective sterilization technique. However, a discrepancy in these components can limit EtO as a potent sterilizer. Increased temperature and gas concentration can limit sterilization capability of EtO. Among all gas sterilization methods, ethylene remains the most popular. Fig. 13.2 shows the various component of the EtO sterilizer [10].

Ethylene was first introduced in the year 1950. This method of sterilization utilizes a colorless gas that is poisonous to the nucleic components of spores and microbes. It is capable of sterilizing medical devices that cannot withstand temperature above 60°C (heat-sensitive devices). Examples of such devices are endoscopes, surgical staples/staplers, etc. Ethylene's obvious advantages make it one of the commonly used methods for sterilization of medical device. It is extraordinarily effective against virucidal, bactericidal, and sporicidal agents. Nevertheless, ethylene is often concerned with possible hazards to patients, staff, and the environment, as well as hazards associated with the handling of flammable gases [11]. Ethylene has permitted and greatly contributed to the development and evolution of fragile, complicated, and advanced medical devices that would otherwise not be possible because ethylene is the only suitable sterilization process for sensitive materials [12]. Ethylene sterilization has become much more relevant as the demand for medical devices has expanded and a transition has been made to the delivery of medical devices in personalized packages to save costs in health management.

The variety of the products, models, material types, and packaging setups developed resulted in the rapid growth of ethylene sterilization and made this method the most widely used sterilization method for medical devices, with

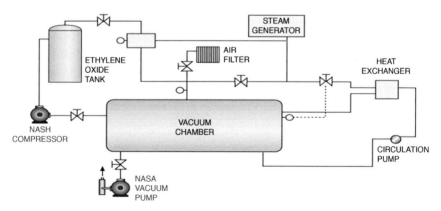

FIGURE 13.2   ETO sterilization.

a consistent growth trend [9,13]. The high reactivity of ethylene in combination with its high diffusivity, expressed by the high energy of its exergonic combustion reaction, is of great importance for the inactivation of microorganisms. Ethylene is a specific alkylating agent that does not need metabolic activation. Its microbiological inactivation properties are known to be the product of its active alkylation reaction with organisms' cellular constituents, such as nucleic acid and functional proteins, including enzymes, leading to consequent denaturation. Through binding to the sulfhydryl and hydroxyl, amino, and carboxyl groups, the introduction of alkyl groups to proteins, DNA, and RNA in microorganisms inhibit normal cellular metabolism and reproductive capacity, which renders affected microbes nonviable [2]. Such organic moieties are not present in almost all of the composition of medical devices; thus, contact with ethylene will not trigger significant structural changes to them.

Considering the mechanism of action described above for ethylene sterilization, ethylene toxicity can be easily understood as a chemical agent and possible associated employee concerns, patient problems, and public health safety. Ethylene has been shown to have the potential for alkylation and mutagenicity properties [14]. Nowadays, ethylene can be safely used, with a limited personal risk of chemical hazardous exposure, using approved practices and compliance with current regulations governing occupational safety and health administration of ethylene. Amidst the discussions about the potential risk of ethylene, it is being used more frequently, especially due to investments in equipment that have dramatically improved the process efficiency and enable worker exposure concerns to be met.

13.4.2   Steam sterilization (autoclave)

Steam sterilization is used to sterilize objects that are capable of withstanding extreme heat (250°F–285°F (121°C–140°C) and pressures of about (16–35 pounds per square inch) [15]. It is among the most accurate methods of sterilization [16]. Its many advantages include microbicidal, sporicidal, nontoxic, cheap cost, relatively easy to use, and safe to use. Moist heat kills microorganisms by irreversible coagulation and denaturation of enzymes and structural proteins. In support of this, it has been found that the presence of moisture significantly affects the temperature of protein coagulation and the temperature at which microorganisms are destroyed. This process of sterilization rapidly destroys resistant strains spores, however, there are limitations. Steam autoclave as shown in Fig. 13.3 is not recommended for heat and moist sensitive medical devices [17]. It has a harmful effect on medical devices that are made from constituents that can corrode. The basic principle of steam sterilization (Autoclave) involves exposure of a clean medical device into an enclosed medium of required heat (steam), temperature and pressure. Autoclave utilizes four criteria, namely steam, temperature, pressure, and time. Autoclave uses saturated steam

FIGURE 13.3 Autoclave.

and entrained water. The required pressure serves to attain high temperature, which is capable of quickly killing microorganisms. The minimum required standard for the exposure of a wrapped medical device is 30 minutes at 121°C or 4 minutes at 132°C in a prevacuum sterilizer. However, sterilization varies from one medical device to another [16]. A good understanding of the principles of steam sterilization is necessary to assure sterility and promote patient safety [15]. Therefore, sterilization is achieved by maintaining a certain temperature with a certain amount of pressure to achieve the death of microorganisms for a certain time. To generate high temperature, high pressure and less time are required [18].

Gravity displacement and high-speed prevacuum sterilizers are the two major types of autoclaves. The sterilizer works by introducing steam to both the top and sides of the chamber. Gravity displacement autoclave is mostly used in the laboratory to process media, medical waste, water, pharmaceutical products, and nonporous devices. The penetration time for this type of sterilizer is prolonged as a result of incomplete air elimination. This point is illustrated by the decontamination of 10 lbs. of microbiological waste, which takes at least 45 minutes at 121°C because the air remaining in the waste load significantly reduces steam permeation and heating efficiency [18].

High-speed prevacuum sterilizers are similar to gravity displacement sterilizers except that they are fitted with a vacuum pump (or ejector) to ensure that the air is removed from the sterilizing chamber and loaded before the steam is allowed. The main benefit of utilizing a vacuum pump is that the steam penetration into porous loads is almost instantaneous. The Bowie-Dick test is used to detect air in the chamber and inadequate air removal and consists of folded 100% cotton surgical towels that are clean and conditioned.

Steam sterilization is a steam pulsing processing design, which eliminates air quickly by constantly rotating a steam pulse and a pressure pulse above atmospheric pressure. Air is quickly removed from the load as it is with the prevacuum sterilizer, but air leakage does not affect this process because the steam in the sterilizing chamber is always above atmospheric pressure. Typical sterilization temperatures and times are between 132°C and 135°C with an exposure time of 3–4 minutes for porous loads and instruments [19]. As with other sterilization devices, the steam cycle is controlled by mechanical, chemical, and biological detectors. Steam sterilizers are usually monitored utilizing a printout or graphically by measuring temperature, temperature time, and pressure. Usually, chemical indicators are added to the exterior and inserted into the pack to track temperature or time and temperature. The efficacy of steam sterilization is controlled by a biological indicator containing Geobacillus stearothermophilus spores. Portable (tabletop) steam sterilizers are used in outpatient, dental, and rural clinics. These sterilizers are designed for small instruments, such as hypodermic syringes and needles and dental instruments. The ability of the sterilizer to reach physical criteria necessary to achieve sterilization should be monitored by mechanical, chemical, and biological indicators.

13.4.3   Dry heat sterilization

Dry heat sterilization, one of the most effective and preferred methods of sterilization, uses hot air blown to remove or deactivate all types of life. Dry heat was one of the very first sterilization methods with extremely reliable performance and can be adjusted to match a wide variety of different sterilization requirements. It uses hot air that is either free from or has very little water vapour, and moisture plays a minimal or no role in the sterilization process. This form of sterilization process destroys micro-organisms by oxidation or simply by burning them to death. As with steam sterilization, dry heat sterilization has a direct relationship between temperature and time [20]. The reason for this is that dry heat is less efficient at penetrating to kill microorganisms than moist steam heat (some microorganisms can withstand high heat in a dry environment). Typically, it takes a very long cycle time (10–11 hours) and a very high temperature (80°C) [20]. Usually, dry heat sterilization is not a suitable choice for an active medical facility. Its drawbacks include a longer time, hence a slower process, than steam and it is specific only for certain materials. The advantages of this method are

FIGURE 13.4   Dry-heat sterilizer.

less difficulty, no pressure needed, no vessels, no outer jacket needed, no pit, lighter weight, and with fewer requirements than for steam sterilization [20].

The hot air oven shown in Fig. 13.4 [21] does not damage any of the items that are being sterilized and is nontoxic to the environment. However, it is time-consuming and needs extremely high temperatures. There are coils on the bottom of the oven to heat the oven. It takes a long time to reach the temperature since the hot air has to rise by convection. This also means that the temperature cannot be constant in the oven. The forced air of a hot air furnace is a better choice than static air. It uses a motorized blower to spread the heat throughout the oven. Forced air is also more effective at spreading hot air evenly in the oven and does not take as long to heat up as static air.

13.4.3.1   How does dry-heat sterilization work?

Dry air is blown onto the surface to be sterilized, transferring energy by conduction (forced air). The oven may use heat coils instead of fans (static air), however, the forced air form is preferred because it delivers heat load to the object with greater homogeneity. Usually, the temperature will be at 160°C (320°F) for 2 hours, 170°C (340°F) for 1 hour and 190°C (375°F) for 6–12 minutes [22]. These are standard cycle times and may be set differently, depending on the particular application. Depending on the type of oven and the blower unit used, the periods of sterilization differ. For example, some ovens deploy high-speed blowers with numerous and powerful fans, delivering massive quantities of hot air to the target. Take into account that the cycle times of these are half what is mentioned above for standard air circulation capacity. The heat passed on to the target induces protein denaturation in all bacterial spores, fungi, viruses, prions, and generally all types of biological agents. Denaturation is the deconstruction of nucleic acids, and all living cells are dying from energy deprivation, whereas viruses are permanently deactivated due to significant damage to their RNA or DNA encoding. It is important to remove any moisture from the air that is blown within the oven chamber, as this moisture can interfere with the process of protein denaturation. All in all, moist heat sterilization is a particular procedure used for a specific collection of applications and sterilization purposes.

13.4.4 Formaldehyde

Formaldehyde sterilization is another low-temperature process for sterilizing heat sensitive products. Formaldehyde is an organic chemical compound that is a by-product of many species' metabolism and widely found in air, rainwater, food, agricultural goods, and textiles. Formaldehyde is a potentially dangerous substance, which can be poisonous, allergenic, and carcinogenic. This is regarded to be much more harmful than EtO and therefore less commonly used for sterilization. It has recently been observed that the survivors of Hurricane Katrina have been harmed by formaldehyde inhalation in trailers provided by the Federal Emergency Management Agency (FEMA). The recent fire in a medical waste facility has caused serious health issues, probably due to the asphyxiation of formaldehyde. Formaldehyde is colorless, but has a foul smell. At concentrations above 0.1 ppm, formaldehyde, which irritates the eyes and mucous membranes, results in watery eyes and causes serious damage. Inhaling formaldehyde at this concentration may cause difficulty breathing, headaches, and a burning sensation in the throat.

Where steam or high-temperature sterilization is not feasible, formaldehyde sterilization is used. Low-temperature steam formaldehyde can be used for the following equipment:

- Rigid or flexible endoscopes.
- All thermal sensitive instruments for advanced eye surgery, for example, cryo-instruments.
- Plastic materials: syringes, coils, or tubes.

Formaldehyde is soluble in water and its inactivation power is greatly enhanced by the presence of moisture. This is most commonly used as a disinfectant but sometimes used as a sterilizing agent. This is classified as low-temperature steam and formaldehyde (LTSF).

The sterilization cycle may consist of the following stages: the initial vacuum removes air from the chamber and the load, followed by a steam discharge into the chamber with a vacuum pump running out of the chamber and heating the load, followed by a series of formaldehyde gas pulses mixed with steam. Formaldehyde gas is generated by liquid formaldehyde, which passes through a heated evaporator. Formaldehyde is removed from the sterilizer and flushed by repeated alternative evacuation and flushing with steam and air. In conclusion, efficient sterilization using formaldehyde is accomplished with a high concentration of gas, a temperature between 60°C and 80°C, and humidity of between 75% and 100% [23].

Compared to the ethylene oxide sterilization process, formaldehyde has the advantage that it does not penetrate plastic materials. Formaldehyde is eroded by steam at the end of the sterilization process. Because formaldehyde can be detected even at very low concentrations. It is very simple to tell the scent that the formaldehyde is extracted from the load. Another method of sterilization destroys microorganisms and their spores through the use of liquid or gaseous chemical compounds. Chemical sterilizers such as EtO or formaldehyde vary. To achieve effective sterilization, surgical equipment must be submerged into a quantity of chemical fluid sufficient to kill all the living species [24]. This is an effective method, but chemical sterilant could react to medical equipment, release toxic residues, and cause potential harm to the operator. Formaldehyde has been used as a liquid chemical sterilizer for a long time.

In countries like the United Kingdom, Germany, Sweden, Denmark, and Norway, LSTF sterilization is accepted but not common. On the contrary, formaldehyde is prohibited as a sterilizing agent in many other countries. The FDA has not cleared LTSF for use in healthcare establishments in the United States.

13.4.4.1 Advantages of formaldehyde steam sterilization

- A very reactive molecule, with a small difference in efficacy between spores and cells.
- When compared with EtO, it has a quicker cycle time.
- When compared with EtO, the cost per cycle is lower.
- Most devices are readily available for immediate use after sterilization.
- Acts as a mutagenic agent, reacting with carbonyl, thiol, and hydroxyl groups.

13.4.4.2 Disadvantages of formaldehyde gas sterilization

- The vapor of formaldehyde is highly irritating.
- Formaldehyde has a poor penetrating capacity in contrast with EtO.
- Formaldehyde acts at a higher temperature in contrast with EtO.
- Sterilized goods can still contain formaldehyde residues if the rinsing process is not completely successful. This can be harmful.
- Relative humidity of about 75% is required to succeed as gas must dissolve in the humidity film around the bacteria.
- Not approved by the FDA.

13.4.5 Radiation (gamma) sterilization

Radiation sterilization has been around since 1950 (Fairand, 2008) [25]. Radiation sterilization is centered on ionizing radiation (gamma, X-ray or electron radiation) to disable microorganisms such as bacteria, fungi, viruses and spores. Due to various advantages over chemical sterilization methods, this model is extremely attractive in medical and health-related fields [22]. For example, radiation sterilization is readily applied during preparation of tissue allografts, pharmaceutical packaging, and the manufacture of medical devices [22].

About 40%–50% of disposable medical devices and materials are sterilized using radiation [23]. For instance, syringes, sutures, adhesive plaster, face masks, gloves, gowns, dressings, and other single-use medical supplies are all produced using gamma radiation [22,23,25]. Radiation sterilization is particularly common for such items since it can be applied to a fully packed, sealed object, thus limiting the potential for contaminations by removing post-sterilization packaging steps. The compatibility with radiation of medical device components and packaging materials must be taken into account. Although many materials are not affected by radiation levels during sterilization, the physical properties of polymers are altered when irradiated.

Radiation sterilization guidelines for medical goods are laid down by the International Organization for Standardization (ISO) [26,27]. The sterilization of medical devices utilizing radiation leaves no sign of radioactivity behind, so the irradiation of medical devices using gamma or electron beam (E-beam) radiation is a safe type of sterilization. Like sterilization of ethylene oxide, radiation can penetrate the packaging of the drug. But this is a less time-consuming process. Dense materials can also be irradiated very effectively. This sterilization procedure is perfectly suited for single-use devices, such as syringes, catheters and needle. When used to sterilize reusable devices, processors that need to conduct quarterly dose audits to guarantee that radiation exposure levels are sufficient to destroy any microorganisms on the device. This sterilization process causes little variation in temperature, making it perfect for use on heat-sensitive plastics and other materials. Auto-injectors such as EpiPen, prefilled syringes and other disposable medical devices can be sterilized by this process. Nevertheless, care must be taken when using this device, as it can cause cosmetic and functional issues, such as discoloration and harmful effect on the various materials used in the tool.

Radiation sterilization is accomplished by either ionizing or nonionizing radiation. Gamma-ray irradiation is a form of ionizing radiation with characteristics of short wavelength, high power intensity used to kill both microorganisms and their spores during the sterilization phase. Gamma rays cause disruption and kill subatomic particles associated with the genetic formation of microorganisms that cause direct or indirect damage to the genetic material, deoxyribonucleic acid (DNA) and ribonucleic acid (RNA) respectively, resulting in cell death and eventual organism death. This method is a good choice for

FIGURE 13.5   **Radiation sterilization.**

sterilizing equipment, which cannot withstand extreme heat-steam autoclaves or dry heat. This method of sterilization is usually associated with greater risk and is not always realistic in practice (not approved by the Food and Drug Administration [FDA]). Its drawbacks are that it can cause unintended changes to irradiated products and cause damage to sterilized material, which is harmful to humans and very costly. The advantages are that it has high permeability (Gryczka, Migdał, Bułka, 2018) [26], sterilization is suitable for all forms of products, such as dry, moist, and even frozen objects, and is considered effective and can be precisely controlled. Additional drawbacks include the possibility of exposure to radiation that may be hazardous to staff, which can lead to adverse changes in the medicinal product, such as color, solubility, and texture. This will potentially destroy the substance it is intended to sterilize; it is costly and the average radiation dose used is 25 kGy [28]. It comprises a gamma electron beam irradiator, product handling, process control and monitoring, room protection, and protection of the total building.

Three types of radiation commonly used for tissue sterilization are gamma radiation, e-beam, and X-rays. Fig. 13.5 shows an ultraviolet sterilization box that can be used for the sterilization of the N95 mask [29].

13.4.5.1   Advantages and disadvantages

Radiation-based sterilization approaches provide several advantages over conventional chemical or heat-based sterilization:

- As a result of the penetration depth of ionizing radiation, medical devices should be stored in their final, tightly sealed packaging. This will reduce any chance of contamination following sterilization.
- The temperature rise during treatment is negligible. Consequently, radiation sterilization does not rely on heat and is effective at both normal temperatures and subzero temperatures.
- No residue on the sterilized product is left by radiation.

- Radiation sterilization is flexible and can sterilize a wide variety, density, thickness and size of numerous medical devices. Also, sterilization can be performed at any temperature and pressure.
- Radio-sterilization type such as e-beam can be completed within seconds to minutes.
- Radiation treatment often produces a high sterility assurance level (SAL) of 10–6 or better, ensuring that fewer than one in a million microorganisms survive the sterilization process.
- It is easy to use.

However, there are some drawbacks to radiation sterilization techniques:

- Instrumentation: high capital costs and often requires specialized facilities. Gamma radiation requires a nuclear reactor; electron beam accelerators produce the e-beam/X-ray radiation.
- Degradation of the product: radiation methods are not compatible with all materials and can result in material and/or product degradation. Gamma radiation is sensitive to popular plastics, such as polyvinyl chloride (PVC) and acetate (PVA). The main chain splits (breaking of the long chains) and the chemical cross-linking of packaging polymers can also be supplied through high energies in the radiation from e-beam.
- Radioactive material: radiation sterilization involves the handling and removal of radioactive material as gamma radiation is used as a means of ionization. Remember that gamma-ray radiation does not contain radioactivity in the treatment sample itself at widely used radiation levels.

13.5 Methodology

This study utilizes a multicriteria decision analysis method called the Technique for Order of Preference by Similarity to Ideal Solution (TOPSIS). This technique was first developed by Ching-Lai Hwang and Yoon in 1981 [30] and further modified by Yoon in 1987 [31], and [32]. TOPSIS is based on the assumption that the alternative chosen should have the smallest geometric distance from the positive ideal solution [33] and the longest geometric distance from the negative ideal solution [33]. TOPSIS presumes that the criteria are monotonically increasing or decreasing.

In this study, we applied the fuzzy-based TOPSIS method to analyze the medical devices (MD) sterilization methods. The triangular fuzzy scale has been used for defining the linguistic data of the criteria of the penetration power and the importance weights of the criteria as seen in Table 13.1.

Decision matrix of the medical devices sterilization methods obtained as shown in Table 13.2.

After defuzzification of the linguistic fuzzy data of the criteria of the penetration power and the importance degree of each criteria using Yager index, normalized weighted values of the dataset has been calculated as in Table 13.3.

TABLE 13.1 Selected fuzzy scale for the linguistic data.

Linguistic scale for evaluation	Triangular fuzzy scale
Very high (VH)	(0.75, 1, 1)
Important (H)	(0.50, 0.75, 1)
Medium (M)	(0.25, 0.50, 0.75)
Low (L)	(0, 0.25, 0.50)
Very low (VL)	(0, 0, 0.25)

TABLE 13.2 Decision matrix of the MD sterilization methods.

Alternatives/criteria	Cost ($)	Volume capacity (uL)	Cycle time (hrs)	Temperature (°C)	Penetration power
Max/min	Min	Max	Min	Min	Max
Linguistic scale of importance	VH	L	M	H	VH
EtO	175,000	10	14	50	M
Gamma rays	63,000	3	36	27	VH
Steam autoclave	7,500	275	0.25	135	H
Dry heat	3,000	107	2	160	L
Formaldehyde	25,000	130	3	70	L

TABLE 13.3 Normalized weighted scores of the MD sterilization methods.

Alternatives/criteria	Cost ($)	Volume capacity (uL)	Cycle time (hrs)	Temperature (°C)	Penetration power
Max/min	Min	Max	Min	Min	Max
Linguistic scale of importance	VH	L	M	H	VH
EtO	175,000	10	14	50	M
Gamma rays	63,000	3	36	27	VH
Steam autoclave	7,500	275	0.25	135	H
Dry heat	3,000	107	2	160	L
Formaldehyde	25,000	130	3	70	L

TABLE 13.4 Positive ideal solution of the medical devices sterilization methods.

Cost	Volume capacity	Cycle time	Temperature	Penetration power
0.0044	0.0638	0.0010	0.0266	0.1897

TABLE 13.5 Negative ideal solution of the medical devices sterilization methods.

Cost	Volume capacity	Cycle time	Temperature	Penetration power
0.2566	0.0007	0.1389	0.1576	0.0516

However, positive and negative ideal solution of the dataset has been obtained as in Tables 13.4 and 13.5, respectively.

13.6   Results

Table 13.6 shows the distance obtained between MD sterilization methods and positive ideal solution (d_i^+) and the distance obtained between MD sterilization methods and negative ideal solution (d_i^-).

Complete ranking of the MD sterilization methods has been obtained based on the relative closeness to positive ideal solution (Ri) as seen in Table 13.7.

TABLE 13.6 The distance of the alternatives from the positive ideal solution and the negative ideal solution. d_i^+ is the distance from the positive ideal solution and d_i^- is the distance from the negative ideal solution.

MD sterilization methods	d_i^-	d_i^+
EtO	0.1470	0.2797
Gamma rays	0.2515	0.1754
Steam autoclave	0.3075	0.1122
Dry heat	0.2853	0.1945
Formaldehyde	0.2708	0.1522

TABLE 13.7 A complete ranking of the MD sterilization methods corresponding to relative closeness to the positive ideal solution.

MD sterilization methods	Score (Ri)	Ranking
Steam autoclave	0.7327	1
Formaldehyde	0.6401	2
Dry heat	0.5947	3
Gamma rays	0.5891	4
EtO	0.3445	5

The best alternative for the MD sterilization method is steam autoclave second with 0.7327 Ri, formaldehyde is second with 6401 Ri, third dry heat with 0.5947 Ri, and fourth gamma rays with 0.5891 Ri. We should also consider that dry heat and gamma rays methods have Ri that is very close, therefore there are not many differences between them. Based on the selected criteria, the least effective alternative is EtO with 0.3445 Ri.

13.7 Conclusions

One form of sterilization may have an advantage over another and yet have an additional disadvantage, and vice versa. Each sterilization method is therefore efficiently effective for specific hospital materials. Also, many other factors influence the decision of the sterilization methods, like the costs involved, the time required for the cycle, the sterility involved, the temperature, and so on. It is important to note that the steam autoclave method of sterilization remains a better method of sterilization of medical devices. Steam autoclave does not pose a risk of irradiation to the user, has the lowest cycle time and high penetration capacity to enable sterility at its peak. Conversely, the EtO method of sterilization may be lethal, carcinogenic, and highly flammable. Toxic contaminants in tubes and surgical instruments may also be present. EtO also requires a special space, protection, and ventilation system that needs a high degree of annual maintenance, services, and consumables.

References

[1] J. Solon, S. Killeen, Decontamination and sterilization, Surgery (Oxford) 33 (11) (2015) 572–578 doi:10.1016/j.mpsur.2015.08.006.

[2] J. Yoo, Review of disinfection and sterilization—back to the basics, Infect. Chemother. 50 (2) (2018) 101 doi: 10.3947/ic.2018.50.2.101.

[3] K. Yates, J. Olson, A. Au, T. Gentle, Alternative sterilization method for heat-sensitive products with safe residual component, J. Med. Devices 6 (1) (2012) doi: 10.1115/1.4026784.

[4] M. Barnett, M. Rios, Preventing hospital-acquired infections from reprocessed multiple-use medical devices, J. Clin. Engineer. 34 (3) (2009) 139–141 doi:10.1097/jce.0b013e3181aae614.

[5] W. Rutala, D. Weber, Guideline for disinfection and sterilization of prion-contaminated medical instruments, Infect. Cont. Hosp. Ep. 31 (2) (2010) 107–117 doi:10.1086/650197.

[6] B.P. Fairand, J.R. Gillis, G.A. Mosley, S Mowitt, Industrial Sterilization for Medical Devices, Association for the Advancement of Medical Instrumentation, Washington, DC, (2003).

[7] B. Skellie, A brief history of sterilization. BRNSKLL.com, https://brnskll.com/shares/a-brief-history-of-sterilization/. Accessed 6.03.20.

[8] WHO Pharmacopoeia Library, https://apps.who.int/phint/en/p/docf/. Accessed 3.06.20

[9] P. Strain, B. Young, Methods to reduce sterilization process time, Med. Design Technol. (2004) 17–18.

[10] G. Denver, Steam sterilization/Liquid ring applications. GardnerDenver.com, https://www.gardnerdenver.com/en-fr/knowledge-hub/articles/sterilization. Accessed 14.07.20.

[11] G.A. Mosley, J.R. Gillis, J.E. Whitbourne, Calculating equivalent time for use in determining the lethality of EtO sterilization processes, Med. Device Diagn. Ind. (2002).

[12] J. Swenberg, A. Ham, H. Koc, E. Morinello, A. Ranasinghe, N. Tretyakova, et al. DNA adducts: effects of low exposure to ethylene oxide, vinyl chloride, and butadiene, Mut. Res.–Rev. Gen. 464 (1) (2000) 77–86 doi:10.1016/s1383-5718(99)00168-0.

[13] P. Strain, W.T. Young, Ethylene-oxide sterilization aids speed to market—process developments reduce process times, Med. Device Technol. 15 (2004) 18–19.

[14] G. Tilton, M. Kauffman, Sterilization: a review of the brain, Manag. Infect. Cont. (2004) 66–71.

[15] M. Dion, W. Parker, Steam sterilization principles, Pharm. 33 (6) (2013).

[16] P. Nania, Immediate use steam sterilization: it's all about the process, AORN J. 98 (1) (2013) 32–38 doi:10.1016/j.aorn.2013.05.003.

[17] Autoclave sterilization principle and working PDF PPT. Pinterest, https://tr.pinterest.com/pin/734438651710129847/?amp_client_id=CLIENT_ID(_)&mweb_unauth_id={{default.session}}&simplified=true. Accessed 14.07.20.

[18] N. Chobin, K. Swanson, Putting patient safety first: the sterile processing department and healthcare technology management, Biomed. Instrum. Techn. 46 (sp12) (2012) 27–31 doi:10.2345/0899-8205-12.1.27.

[19] J. Van Doornmalen Gomez Hoyos, A. Paunovic, K. Kopinga, Steam sterilization does not require saturated steam, J. Hosp. Infect. 97 (4) (2017) 331–332 https://doi.org/10.1016/j.jhin.2017.07.011.

[20] A. Tankeshwar, Dry-heat sterilization: principle, advantages and disadvantages, https://microbeonline.com/dry-heat-sterilization-principle-advantages-disadvantages. Accessed 3.06.20.

[21] FOF—saturated steam sterilizer- Fedegari - innovative solutions for clean and sterile processes, https://fedegari.com/en/prodotto/fof-saturated-steam-sterilizer/. Accessed 14.07.20.

[22] M. Silindir, A.Y. Özer, Sterilization methods and the comparison of e-beam sterilization with gamma radiation sterilization, FABAD J. Pharm. Sci. 34 (2009) 43.

[23] G. Mosley, Using high-temperature formaldehyde sterilization as a model for studying gaseous sterilization, Biomed. Instrumen. Techn. 42 (3) (2008) 236–243. doi:10.2345/0899-8205(2008)42.

[24] C. Bi, Y. Jia, PNS55—Cost-benefit analysis of three types of low-temperature sterilization system: ethylene oxide versus formaldehyde versus peroxide plasma in endoscope sterilization, Value Health 22 (2019) S295 doi:10.1016/j.jval.2019.04.1415.

[25] B.P. Fairand, Radiation Sterilization for Health Care Products: X-Ray, Gamma, and Electron Beam, CRC Press, Boca Raton, (2001).

[26] U. Gryczka, H. Kameya, K. Kimura, S. Todoriki, W. Migdał, S. Bułka, Efficacy of low-energy electron beam on microbial decontamination of spices, Radiat. Phys. Chem. 170 (2020) 108662 doi:10.1016/j.radphyschem.2019.108662.

[27] R. Singh, D. Singh, A. Singh, Radiation sterilization of tissue allografts: a review, World J. Radiol. 8 (4) (2016) 355 doi:10.4329/wjr.v8.i4.355.

[28] N. Bhana, A. Zanwar, V. Trivedi, D. Jain, A review: steam sterilization—a method of sterilization, J. Biol. Sci. Opin. 1 (2) (2013) 138–141 doi:10.7897/2321-6328.01222.

[29] NukeBox—an ultraviolet sterilization box. Hackerfarm, https://hackerfarm.jp/2020/03/nukebox/. Accessed 14.07.20.

[30] C.L. Hwang, K. Yoon, Multiple Attribute Decision Making: Methods and Applications, Springer- Verlag, New York, (1981).

[31] K. Yoon, Reconciliation among discrete compromise situations, J. Operat. Res. Soc. 38 (3) (1987) 277–286 doi:10.1057/jors.1987.44.

[32] C.L. Hwang, Y.J. Lai, T.Y. Liu, A new approach for multiple objective decisions making, Comput. Operat. Res. 20 (8) (1993) 889–899 doi:10.1016/0305-0548(93)90109-v.

[33] N. Chobin, The Basics of Sterile Processing, 4th ed., Sterile Processing University, LLC, Lebanon, NJ, (2012).

Further reading

[1] A. Assari, T. Mahesh, E. Assari, Role of public participation in the sustainability of historical city: usage of TOPSIS method, Ind. J. Sci. Technol. 5 (3) (2012) 2289–2294.

[2] M. Jayabalan, Sterilization and reprocessing of materials and medical devices—reusability, J. Biomater. Applic. 10 (1) (1995) 97–112 doi:10.1177/088532829501000105.

[3] G. Nordgren, A new principle for formaldehyde sterilization of surgical instruments, Acta Path. Micro. Sc. 18 (4) (2009) 503–516 doi:10.1111/j.1699-0463.1941.tb04525.

[4] H. Parker, R. Johnson, Effectiveness of ethylene oxide for sterilization of dental handpieces, J. Dentist. 23 (2) (1995) 113–115 doi:10.1016/0300-5712(95)98977-b.

[5] W. Rutala, D. Weber, Infection control: the role of disinfection and sterilization, J. Hosp. Infect. 43 (1999) S43–S55 doi:10.1016/s0195-6701(99)90065-8.

Chapter 14

Evaluation of the effectiveness of adult HIV antiretroviral treatment regimens using TOPSIS

Nazife Sultanoglu[a,b], Berna Uzun[a,c], Murat Sayan[a,d] and Tamer Sanlidag[a]

[a]*DESAM Institute, Near East University, Turkish Republic of Northern Cyprus, Nicosia, Turkey;* [b]*Faculty of Medicine, Department of Medical Microbiology and Clinical Microbiology, Near East University, Turkish Republic of Northern Cyprus, Nicosia, Turkey;* [c]*Department of Mathematics, Near East University, Turkish Republic of Northern Cyprus, Nicosia, Turkey;* [d]*Faculty of Medicine, Clinical Laboratory, PCR Unit Kocaeli University, Kocaeli, Turkey*

14.1 Introduction

The current chapter presents an overview of human immunodeficiency virus (HIV) and reviews the adult HIV-1 infection treatment evaluation by using multicriteria decision-making techniques. HIV belongs to the *Lentivirus* genus within the *Retroviridae* family, which is capable of infecting humans. Infections with *Lentiviruses* classically lead to a chronic disease with a long period of clinical latency and persistent viral infections [1]. Molecular phylogenetic data and epidemiologic analyses have revealed that HIV was first introduced into the human population between 1920 and 1940; and has remained a global health problem since then. By the end of 2018, it was reported that, 37.9 million people were living with HIV around the world. By virtue of the genetic differences in the viral antigens, HIV is classified into two major types, namely HIV type 1 (HIV-1) and HIV type 2 (HIV-2) [2,3]. HIV-1 is further subdivided into four distinct groups: group M (major) that includes nine subtypes denoted with letters of A, B, C, D, F, G, H, J, and K; group O (outlier), which does not have recognized subtypes; group N (nonoutlier and nonmajor); and the most recently identified group referred to as P [4]. HIV-1 groups; N, O, and P indicate restricted patterns of spread of the disease and are mainly seen in Cameroon and its neighbouring countries [5]. On the other hand, HIV-1 group M is the most predominant circulating form of HIV, accounting for approximately 90% of the global HIV pandemic [6,7]. Within Group M, each subtype is associated with specific geographical regions [8]. Subtype C accounts for nearly 50% of HIV

Applications of Multi-Criteria Decision-Making Theories in Healthcare and Biomedical Engineering.
http://dx.doi.org/10.1016/B978-0-12-824086-1.00014-1

217

infections, and is mainly seen in South Africa and India, subtype B is predominant in Europe, North America, Latin America, and Australia, while subtype D is seen in Central Africa, F is seen in Brazil, G is seen in Russia, H is seen in Africa and Taiwan, J is seen in Zaire, and K is seen in Cameroon [7,9]. On the other hand, HIV-2 infections are rare, less infectious when compared to HIV-1, and are largely restricted to Western and Central Africa [1,6].

HIV is transmitted through the body fluids of a HIV-infected person, such as blood, semen, breast milk, preseminal, rectal, and vaginal fluids. Transmission of HIV happens when these fluids come into contact with damaged tissue or mucous membrane or when directly injected into the bloodstream, such as injection through a needle or syringe [10]. There are several important factors that play a critical role in establishing the transmission of HIV. These are the biological properties of the virus, concentration of the virus within the exposed body fluids mentioned earlier, and the susceptibility of the host in terms of cellular and immunological levels [11]. Once within the human body, HIV has tropism to immune cells including monocytes, macrophages, dendritic cells, and especially to $CD4^+$ T cells. This means that they preferably attack and destroy $CD4^+$ T cells, leading to destruction of the CD4 T^+ cell count in the body [12].

There are three stages of the HIV infection. These are acute, chronic, and the final advanced stage, which is referred to as acquired immune deficiency syndrome (AIDS). In the acute stage of the infection, there are usually no or flulike symptoms and the virus replicates very rapidly accompanying changes in the immune system. At this stage of the infection, the HIV levels in the blood are very high. In the second, chronic stage also known as the clinical latency stage, HIV continues to multiply at low levels and at this stage, infected individuals may not indicate any HIV-related symptoms. The outcome of the infection and the disease progression varies greatly between individuals, but progression is often very slow to the extent that without treatment, it may take 10 years or more for the chronic HIV infection to develop into AIDS [13,14]. Untreated HIV infections lead to a gradual decline in the number of $CD4^+$ T cells, eventually culminating in AIDS. The normal $CD4^+$ T cell count is in the range of 500–1,500 cells per mm^3, but when this falls below 200 cells per mm^3, the HIV-infected individual is diagnosed with AIDS [13,15]. The low level of $CD4^+$ T cell count renders the bodies of AIDS diagnosed individuals more vulnerable to opportunistic infections such as *Mycobacterium tuberculosis, Pneumocystis jirovecii*, cytomegalovirus infections and candidiasis [14,16], and other HIV-associated cancers such as non-Hodgkin's lymphoma and Kaposi's sarcoma [17].

When untreated, the median survival time for HIV-infected individuals is 8 to 10 years. However, with the initiation of antiretroviral therapy (ART) in 1996, the life spans of HIV infected individuals have been extended significantly [18,19]. HIV antiretroviral drugs are grouped into seven classes. Each class targets the specific step of the HIV replication cycle. These seven classes are nucleoside reverse transcriptase inhibitors (NRTIs) (i.e., abacavir, zidovudine), nonnucleoside reverse transcriptase inhibitors (NNRTIs) (i.e., efavirenz, nevirapine), integrase strand transfer inhibitors (INSTIs) (i.e., dolutegravir, raltegravir), protease inhibitors (PIs), fusion inhibitors (i.e., enfuvirtide), CCR5 antagonists (i.e., maraviroc), and postattachment inhibitors (i.e., ibalizumab). ART is the combination of three antiretroviral drugs, including drugs from a minimum of two classes. The combination of HIV medicines is also referred to as an HIV regimen. There are more than 30 HIV antiretroviral drugs approved by the U.S. Food and Drug Administration (FDA) for combination in HIV regimens to treat HIV infections [20–22]. ART is initiated immediately after the diagnosis of HIV regardless of the CD4$^+$ T cell count in order to prevent disease progression and improve clinical outcomes [23].

Unfortunately, the effectiveness of ART may be reduced as a result of the emergence of drug resistance. This is due to the fact that, HIV has a very high replication rate with 10^{10} rounds of replication per day as well as a very rapid mutation rate, which enables HIV to gain resistance to administered ART. The genome of HIV is approximately 10,000 nucleotides in length and it is predicted that 1–10 mutations may occur in each replication cycle. Error-prone HIV reverse transcription is responsible for the rapid mutation rate with an estimated one mutation for every 1000–10,000 nucleotide synthesis. Thus, involving three drugs from at least two classes ensures that even if the HIV in the infected individual acquires resistance to one of the applied drugs, the others can still function by reducing the replication of the virus. A combination of anti-HIV drugs is used to control the viral load more efficiently and to help prevent the development of drug resistance by attacking multiple different sites of the viral replication cycle [24,25].

Exposure to ART may lead to the development of resistance by HIV, or drug-naive HIV infected individuals may even be infected with strains of the virus that are resistant. Thus, drug resistance and patient-specific clinical presentations such as the CD4$^+$ T cell count, and presence of other diseases including heart or kidney problems are important for the health practitioners in order to treat their patient with the correct ART regimen. Most of the ART regimens are oral medicines and strict adherence to regimes is important for management of the infection. HIV positive individuals receiving ART are usually kept under continuous surveillance to monitor any resistance development and other adverse effects. In such cases, the health practitioners evaluate the laboratory findings, clinical presentation and change the ART regimens accordingly [26,27]. In addition to the development of drug resistance, other factors such as tolerability, anticipation of potential new drug interactions, pregnancy or drug toxicities may be reasons for switching ART regimen [27]. Currently, there is no cure for HIV infection. Once the HIV infection is established, the virus remains within the body and the treatment is life-long. HIV is a chronic and manageable disease [19]. Therefore, the correct combination of HIV drug regimens for patient specific conditions and daily administration of the ART is critical for the HIV positive individuals to control the infection and maintain their lives. With the correct ART regimen selected in a patient-specific manner and properly daily administration of the ART, it is possible to reduce the viral load of HIV infected individuals to undetectable levels. Undetectable viral load means that even with the available technology, the level of the HIV in the blood is too low to be detected. HIV-infected individuals with undetectable viral load effectively means that HIV transmission to others is prevented, which provides both individual and public health benefits [20,27].

Many different HIV clinical guidelines are available for health practitioners to follow. However, prescribing the most effective HIV regimens in a patient-specific manner still remains a complicated task. HIV treatment guidelines are available on various platforms including the World Health Organization, Centers for Disease Control and Prevention, and the Ministries of Health in many countries [28–32]. Many guidelines classify the ART regimens for naive HIV positive individuals as: recommended, alternative, and other regimens [33].

The HIV treatment guidelines should be updated periodically with the development of new anti-HIV agents. The availability of many guidelines published by different platforms may confuse health practitioners since there is not a single standardized guideline that they should follow. Also, the prescription of HIV regimens should be individualized in a patient-specific manner to achieve successful management of the disease with minimum side effects and toxicity. As a consequence, there are numerous alternatives (HIV regimens) and many criteria (determined by the decision maker) that need to be compared in the evaluation of HIV treatment assignment. This process is highly complex and cannot be performed manually by the decision maker. In this case, the health practitioners should compare the HIV regimens based on each criterion. In order to resolve this issue, we propose that the technique for order preference by similarity to ideal solution (TOPSIS), one of the multicriteria decision-making methods, be used in the evaluation of HIV regimen effectiveness with the criteria including cost, plasma turnover, drug–drug interaction, and side effects, which could not be evaluated manually. TOPSIS evaluates the alternatives through the similarity to an ideal solution. When the alternative is closest to the positive-ideal solution and has the greatest distance from the negative-ideal solution, the best alternative is determined. The positive-ideal solution maximizes the benefit of criteria with minimum disadvantages, whereas the negative-ideal solution maximizes the disadvantages of the criteria and minimizes the benefit [34]. TOPSIS was the choice of multicriteria analysis in this study since it is rapid, rational, simple, and offers good computational efficiency. However, we applied to fuzzy logic in order to define the linguistic data of the HIV regimens. In this way, the time between HIV diagnosis and ART initiation can be reduced in a reliable manner.

14.2   Methods and materials

In the TOPSIS method, ratings and rates are well presented via numerical data. When there is more than one decision-maker, the complexity arises. However, in this analysis the opinions of two experts in the related field with same goals were agreed. Thus, the single decision-maker algorithm of TOPSIS was combined with fuzzy logic adapted to evaluate selected HIV-1 regimens with related criteria, which is described systematically in the following:

Step 1. Development of the decision matrix and determination of the weights (*W* of the criteria)

Step 2. Normalized decision matrix calculation (n_{ij})

Step 3. Weighted normalized decision matrix calculation ($w_j n_{ij}$)

Step 4. Determination of the positive ideal solution (A⁺) and negative ideal solution (A⁻)

Step 5. Calculating the distance between the alternatives and the positive ideal and the distance between the alternatives and the negative ideal solutions

Step 6. Calculation of the relative closeness to the positive ideal solution for alternatives (R_i)

Step 7. Preference order ranking or the selection of the alternative closest to 1

Alternatives are ranked in descending order in terms of the value of R_i. Ranking is determined by the relative closeness to the positive ideal solution for each alternative.

As the name implies, the positive solution is the best possible outcome (solution) with regard to each criterion. The aim of the criteria is at maximum with the combination of the maximum value of the alternatives. On the other hand, the negative ideal solution is the worst outcome among all the criteria with the minimized aim of the criteria and minimum value. The best option among the alternatives in TOPSIS is the positive ideal solution. However, in real-life problems where the environment is fuzzy, none of the options have the best possible outcome (maximum value) in terms of each criterion. In such real-world situations, the TOPSIS model is a good choice for multicriteria analysis as it provides the best alternative, which is the closest to the positive ideal solution and the one with the greatest distance from the negative ideal solution given simultaneously in terms of the Euclidian distance. By the TOPSIS method, alternatives are ranked according to the relative closeness to the positive ideal solution and the greatest distance from the negative ideal solution with descending net ranking results. In this study, the alternatives to be analyzed are selected adult HIV-1 regimens, which are indicated in Table 14.1.

Also, the experts in the related field chose the importance weights of the parameters with a linguistic fuzzy scale, as seen in Table 14.2.

The weights of the parameters were firstly converted into single values via the Yager index and were then normalized for the use of the TOPSIS analysis. Subsequently, after collecting the parameters (Table 14.1.) of the adult antiretroviral treatment regimens, the Yager index was also used convert the linguistic fuzzy data (such as side effect) into single values to obtain the decision matrix of the adult HIV-1 ART regimen alternatives. Afterwards, the decision matrix of the adult HIV-1 ART treatment regimens was normalized and the normalized weighted matrix was calculated (Table 14.3.).

TABLE 14.1 Selected antiretroviral drugs for the adult HIV-1 treatment.

Recommended antiretroviral combinations

Integrase inhibitor-based regimens:
BIC + TAF/FTC (bictegravir + tenofovir alafenamide/emtricitabine)
DTG + ABC/3TC (dolutegravir + abacavir/lamivudine)
DTG + TAF/FTC (dolutegravir + tenofovir alafenamide/emtricitabine)
EVG/c + TDF/FTC (elvitegravir/cobicistat + tenofovir disoproxil fumarate/emtricitabine)
EVG/c + TAF/FTC (elvitegravir/cobicistat + tenofovir alafenamide/emtricitabine)
RAL + TAF/FTC (raltegravir + tenofovir alafenamide/emtricitabine)
Protease inhibitors-based regimens:
DRV/r + TDF/FTC (darunavir/ritonavir + tenofovir disoproxil fumarate/emtricitabine)
DRV/c + TAF/FTC (darunavir/cobicistat + tenofovir alafenamide/emtricitabine)
Non-nucleoside reverse transcriptase inhibitor-based regimens:
RPV/TDF/FTC (rilpivirine/tenofovir disoproxil fumarate/emtricitabine)
RPV/TAF/FTC (rilpivirine/tenofovir alafenamide/emtricitabine)

Alternative antiretroviral combinations

Integrase inhibitor-based regimens:
RAL + ABC/3TC (raltegravir + abacavir/lamivudine)
Protease inhibitor-based regimens:
ATV/r + TAF/FTC (atazanavir/ritonavir + tenofovir alafenamide/emtricitabine)
ATV/r + ABC/3TC (atazanavir/ritonavir + abacavir/lamivudine)
DRV/r + ABC/3TC (darunavir/ritonavir + abacavir/lamivudine)
Non-nucleoside reverse transcriptase inhibitor-based regimens:
EFV + TDF/FTC (efavirenz + tenofovir disoproxil fumarate/emtricitabine)
Other antiretroviral combinations:
RAL + DRV/r (raltegravir + darunavir/ritonavir)
LPV + DRV/r (lopinavir + darunavir/ritonavir)

TABLE 14.2 Triangular fuzzy scale and the selected importance weights of the parameters.

Linguistic scale for evaluation	Triangular fuzzy scale	Criteria (parameter)
Very high (VH)	(0.75, 1, 1)	Side effects, plasma turnover, drug-drug interaction, false prescription, compliance, previous treatment, pregnancy, opportunistic infection, immunologic recovery, virologic recovery
Important (H)	(0.50, 0.75, 1)	Number of tablets, dose frequency, genetic barrier, time of suppression, age, working condition, sero-discordant couple status, cancer, glomerular filtration rate of the kidneys (GFR), CD4+ T cell count, coinfection, comorbidity, mental disorder
Medium (M)	(0.25, 0.50, 0.75)	Limitation, inefficient drug combination, genetic testing, bone density, member of key population, transmitted drug resistance mutation (TDRM), viral load
Low (L)	(0, 0.25, 0.50)	Cost, size of tablet, supplement, drug absorption, HIV genotype/subtype
Very low (VL)	(0, 0, 0.25)	Not determined

TABLE 14.3 Weighted normalized matrix of the recommended adult HIV-1 medicine alternatives.

Alternative	Disadvantage	Number of tablet	Dose frequency	Side effect	Immunologic recovery	Virologic recovery	TDRM	Viral load	HIV genotype-subtype
Max/Min	Min	Min	Min	Min	Max	Max	Min	Min	Min
BIC + TAF/FTC	0.0028	0.0032	0.0000	0.0117	0.0128	0.0121	0.0027	0.0000	0.0000
DTG + ABC/3TC	0.0024	0.0032	0.0000	0.0078	0.0128	0.0121	0.0027	0.0000	0.0000
DTG + TAF/FTC	0.0028	0.0064	0.0000	0.0117	0.0128	0.0121	0.0027	0.0000	0.0000
EVG/c + TDF/FTC	0.0028	0.0032	0.0000	0.0078	0.0128	0.0121	0.0054	0.0000	0.0000
EVG/c + TAF/FTC	0.0025	0.0032	0.0000	0.0039	0.0128	0.0121	0.0054	0.0000	0.0000
RAL + TAF/FTC	0.0027	0.0097	0.0103	0.0078	0.0128	0.0121	0.0054	0.0000	0.0000
DRV/r + TDF/FTC	0.0028	0.0097	0.0103	0.0117	0.0085	0.0081	0.0027	0.0000	0.0000
DRV/c + TAF/FTC	0.0030	0.0097	0.0103	0.0117	0.0085	0.0081	0.0027	0.0000	0.0000
RPV/TDF/FTC	0.0025	0.0032	0.0000	0.0078	0.0043	0.0040	0.0081	0.0146	0.0060
RPV/TAF/FTC	0.0023	0.0032	0.0000	0.0039	0.0043	0.0040	0.0081	0.0146	0.0060
RAL + ABC/3TC	0.0018	0.0097	0.0103	0.0078	0.0128	0.0121	0.0054	0.0000	0.0000
ATV/r + TAF/FTC	0.0028	0.0097	0.0103	0.0117	0.0085	0.0081	0.0054	0.0000	0.0000
ATV/r + ABC/3TC	0.0019	0.0097	0.0103	0.0117	0.0085	0.0081	0.0054	0.0000	0.0000
DRV/r + ABC/3TC	0.0019	0.0097	0.0103	0.0117	0.0085	0.0081	0.0027	0.0000	0.0000
EFV + TDF/FTC	0.0023	0.0032	0.0000	0.0117	0.0043	0.0040	0.0081	0.0000	0.0060
RAL + DRV/r	0.0026	0.0097	0.0103	0.0117	0.0085	0.0121	0.0027	0.0000	0.0000
LPV + DRV/r	0.0022	0.0097	0.0103	0.0117	0.0085	0.0121	0.0027	0.0000	0.0000

Transmitted drug resistance mutation (TDRM).

Positive ideal solution set of the adult HIV-1 antiretroviral regimens has been obtained as:

(0.0018, 0.0032, 0.0000, 0.0039, 0.0093, 0.0139, 0.0091, 0.0092, 0.0000, 0.0000, 0.0044, 0.0000, 0.0000, 0.0137, 0.0106, 0.0036, 0.0000, 0.0000, 0.0000, 0.0000, 0.0000, 0.0000, 0.0000, 0.0092, 0.0060, 0.0025, 0.0000, 0.0000, 0.0000, 0.0000, 0.0000, 0.0128, 0.0121, 0.0027, 0.0000, 0.0000)

Negative ideal solution set of the adult HIV-1 antiretroviral regimens has been obtained as:

(0.0030, 0.0097, 0.0103, 0.0117, 0.0031, 0.0046, 0.0030, 0.0000, 0.0084, 0.0031, 0.0133, 0.0146, 0.0137, 0.0046, 0.0035, 0.0108, 0.0031, 0.0156, 0.0109, 0.0114, 0.0155, 0.0109, 0.0103, 0.0031, 0.0000, 0.0025, 0.0126, 0.0146, 0.0093, 0.0109, 0.0073, 0.0043, 0.0040, 0.0081, 0.0146, 0.0060)

For each of the adult HIV-1 regimen alternatives, the relative closeness to the positive solution denoted as d_i^+ and the distance to the negative solution denoted as d_i^- are shown in Table 14.4. In addition to this, the sum of the positive and negative solutions is represented as $d_i^- + d_i^+$.

TABLE 14.4 The distance of the alternatives from the positive ideal solution and the negative ideal solution.

Alternative HIV-1 regimen	d_i^-	d_i^+	$d_i^- + d_i^+$
BIC + TAF/FTC	0.052112822	0.023934661	0.076047484
DTG + ABC/3TC	0.047900523	0.031037963	0.078938487
DTG + TAF/FTC	0.052369553	0.02234721	0.074716764
EVG/c + TDF/FTC	0.044690346	0.034412401	0.079102747
EVG/c + TAF/FTC	0.046882282	0.03183537	0.078717652
RAL + TAF/FTC	0.044732238	0.033746114	0.078478352
DRV/r + TDF/FTC	0.042364702	0.037251857	0.079616559
DRV/c + TAF/FTC	0.038558892	0.041183268	0.07974216
RPV/TDF/FTC	0.043014887	0.036406106	0.079420993
RPV/TAF/FTC	0.043446452	0.036310568	0.07975702
RAL + ABC/3TC	0.043594208	0.035210803	0.078805011
ATV/r + TAF/FTC	0.033637566	0.044431917	0.078069483
ATV/r + ABC/3TC	0.030983693	0.046324123	0.077307815
DRV/r + ABC/3TC	0.037364606	0.041961055	0.079325661
EFV + TDF/FTC	0.043645409	0.035927199	0.079572608
RAL + DRV/r	0.044348427	0.034978909	0.079327336
LPV + DRV/r	0.043462895	0.036072369	0.079535264

14.3 Results

The highest score represented as Ri is the closest to the positive ideal solution. Thus, for this reason, the highest Ri is the best solution among the analyzed alternatives within the system. Ri values between the alternatives that are very close to each other (when there is a not strict difference) means that they are not considered to be superior to each other. Their uses within the system may have be considered to have the same advantages. Table 14.5 indicates the analysed alternatives—adult HIV-1 ART regimens by TOPSIS in descending order of the Ri scores. With the highest Ri scores of: 0.7009, 0.6853, and 0.6068, DTG + TAF/FTC, BIC + TAF/FTC, and DTG + ABC/3TC were the best three adult HIV-1 ART regimens compared to the others selected, respectively. On the other hand, with the lowest Ri scores of 0.4710, 0.4308 and 0.4008, DRV/r + ABC/3TC, ATV/r + TAF/FTC, and ATV/r + ABC/3TC were the worst three regimens among the others compared, respectively.

TABLE 14.5 Relative closeness to the positive ideal solution for each alternative and complete ranking of the alternatives.

Alternatives adult HIV-1 regimen	Score (Ri)	Ranking
DTG + TAF/FTC	0.7009	1
BIC + TAF/FTC	0.6853	2
DTG + ABC/3TC	0.6068	3
EVG/c + TAF/FTC	0.5956	4
RAL + TAF/FTC	0.5700	5
EVG/c + TDF/FTC	0.5650	6
RAL + DRV/r	0.5591	7
RAL + ABC/3TC	0.5532	8
EFV + TDF/FTC	0.5485	9
LPV + DRV/r	0.5465	10
RPV/TAF/FTC	0.5447	11
RPV/TDF/FTC	0.5416	12
DRV/r + TDF/FTC	0.5321	13
DRV/c + TAF/FTC	0.4835	14
DRV/r + ABC/3TC	0.4710	15
ATV/r + TAF/FTC	0.4309	16
ATV/r + ABC/3TC	0.4008	17

14.4 Discussion and conclusion

In this study, 17 frequently used adult HIV-1 regimens were compared using the multicriteria decision-making method: fuzzy TOPSIS. This decision-making tool is an effective method that enables the selection of the most advantaged alternatives among different ART regimens. These selected regimens and their associated criteria with weights were determined by experts in the field, based on the given fuzzy scale. According to the fuzzy TOPSIS analysis, the best regimens with the highest Ri scores were all from the integrase-base ART regimens: DTG + TAF/FTC, BIC + TAF/FTC, and DTG + ABC/3TC. However, the worst three regimens with the lowest Ri scores were from the older regimens with high adverse effects, suggesting that the fuzzy-based TOPSIS method can be used successfully in the evaluation of these regimens.

The 17 selected adult HIV regimens were also evaluated by another multicriteria decision-making method: the Fuzzy PROMETHEE method. According to the fuzzy PROMETHEE results, the best three adult HIV-1 regimens were the same and there were only slight changes in terms of the ranking of the worst [35]. This also implies that the previously obtained results from Fuzzy PROMETHEE were also validated with the fuzzy TOPSIS method. These methods should be applied during the process of updating the guidelines to provide the most effective way of comparing and giving feedback on each available regimen.

References

[1] E. Fanales-Belasio, M. Raimondo, B. Suligoi, S. Buttò, HIV virology and pathogenetic mechanisms of infection: a brief overview. Ann. 1st Super Sanità 47 (4) (2011) 363–72.

[2] German Advisory Committee Blood (Arbeitskreis Blut), Subgroup, Assessment of pathogens transmissible by blood: S 'assessment of PT by B. Human immunodeficiency virus (HIV). Transfus. Med. Hemother. 43 (3) (May 2016) 203–22, http://www.ncbi.nlm.nih.gov/pubmed/27403093. Accessed 22.12.18.

[3] WHO, Data and statistics. World Health Organization, https://www.who.int/hiv/data/en/. Accessed 19.05.20.

[4] T. Mourez, F. Simon, J.C. Plantiera, Non-M variants of human immunodeficiency virus type, Clin. Microbiol. Rev. 26 (3) (2013 Jul) 448–461.

[5] D.M. Junqueira, S.E. de Matos Almeida, HIV-1 subtype B: traces of a pandemic, in: Virology, vol. 495, Academic Press, 2016, pp. 173–84.

[6] N. Bbosa, P. Kaleebu, D. Ssemwanga, HIV subtype diversity worldwide, Curr. Opin. HIV/AIDS. 14 (3) (2019) 153–160.

[7] A. Ndjoyi-Mbiguino, S. Zoa-Assoumou, G. Mourembou, M.M. Ennaji, Human immunodeficiency virus: a brief review, in: Emerging and Reemerging Viral Pathogens, vol. 1: Fundamental and Basic Virology Aspects of Human, Animal, and Plant Pathogens, Elsevier, 2019, pp. 183–200.

[8] HIV database. HIV sequence database: nomenclature overview, https://www.hiv.lanl.gov/content/sequence/HelpDocs/subtypes-more.html. Accessed 19.05.20.

[9] F. Cassis-Ghavami, M. Curlin, R. Geise, A. Duerr. Human immunodeficiency virus, in: Vaccines for Biodefense and Emerging and Neglected Diseases, Elsevier, 2009, pp. 441–68.

[10] AIDS info. The basics of HIV prevention. understanding HIV/AIDS, https://aidsinfo.nih.gov/ understanding-hiv-aids/fact-sheets/20/48/the-basics-of-hiv-prevention. Accessed 19.05.20.

[11] J.A. Levy, HIV pathogenesis: 25years of progress and persistent challenges, AIDS 23 (2) (2009) 147–160 http://content.wkhealth.com/linkback/openurl?sid=WKPTLP:landingpage& an=00002030-200901140-00001.

[12] G. Maartens, C. Celum, S.R. Lewin, HIV infection: epidemiology, pathogenesis, treatment, and prevention, Lancet 384 (9939) (2014) 258–271 http://dx.doi.org/10.1016/S0140-6736(14)60164-1.

[13] AIDSinfo. The stages of HIV Infection. understanding HIV/AIDS, https://aidsinfo.nih.gov/ understanding-hiv-aids/fact-sheets/19/46/the-stages-of-hiv-infection. Accessed 19.05.20.

[14] H.M. Naif, Pathogenesis of HIV infection, Infect. Dis. Rep. 5 (Suppl.1) (2013) 26–30.

[15] U.S. Department of Veterans Affairs. CD4 count (or T-cell test): HIV/AIDS, https://www.hiv. va.gov/HIV/patient/diagnosis/labs-CD4-count.asp. Accessed 15.04.19.

[16] Z. Grossman, M. Meier-Schellersheim, W.E. Paul, L.J. Picker, Pathogenesis of HIV infection: what the virus spares is as important as what it destroys, Nat. Med. 12 (3) (2006) 289–295.

[17] R. Yarchoan, T.S. Uldrick, HIV-associated cancers and related diseases, N. Engl. J. Med. 378 (11) (2018) 1029–1041.

[18] C.A. Sabin, Do people with HIV infection have a normal life expectancy in the era of combination antiretroviral therapy?, BMC Med. 11 (1) (2013) 1 BMC Medicine.

[19] M. Sankaranantham, HIV: Is a cure possible?, Ind. J. Sex Transm. Dis. AIDS. 40 (1) (2019) 1.

[20] AIDS info, HIV treatment: the basics: understanding HIV/AIDS. AIDS info, https://aidsinfo.nih.gov/understanding-hiv-aids/fact-sheets/21/51/hiv-treatment--the-basics. Accessed 19.05.20.

[21] AIDS info, Drug class: definition. AIDS info, https://aidsinfo.nih.gov/understanding-hiv-aids/ glossary/1561/drug-class/. Accessed 19.05.20.

[22] AIDS info, What to start: choosing an HIV regimen. Understanding HIV/AIDS, https://aidsinfo.nih.gov/understanding-hiv-aids/fact-sheets/21/53/what-to-start--choosing-an-hiv-regimen. Accessed 19.05.20.

[23] M.S. Saag, C.A. Benson, R.T. Gandhi, J.F. Hoy, R.J. Landovitz, M.J. Mugavero et al., Antiretroviral Drugs for Treatment and Prevention of HIV Infection in Adults: 2018 Recommendations of the International Antiviral Society–USA Panel. JAMA, http://www.ncbi.nlm.nih.gov/ pubmed/30043070. Accessed 24.07.18.

[24] E.J. Arts, D.J. Hazuda, HIV-1 antiretroviral drug therapy, Cold Spring Harb. Perspect. Med. 2 (4) (2012).

[25] T.K. Chen, G.M. Aldrovandi. Review of HIV antiretroviral drug resistance, in: Pediatric Infectious Disease Journal, vol. 2, Lippincott, Williams, and Wilkins, 2008, pp. 749–52.

[26] M.M. Zdanowicz, The pharmacology of HIV drug resistance, Am. J. Pharm. Educ. 70 (5) (2006).

[27] H.F. Günthard, M.S. Saag, C.A. Benson, C. Del Rio, J.J. Eron, J.E. Gallant, et al. Antiretroviral drugs for treatment and prevention of HIV infection in adults, JAMA–J. Am. Med. Assoc. 316 (2) (2016 Jul 12) 191–210.

[28] Ministry of Health Malaysia. Medical Development Division Ministry of Health Malaysia Guidelines for the Management of Adult HIV Infection with Antiretroviral Therapy, https:// www.moh.gov.my/moh/resources/autodownload images/589d71c4dd799.pdf. Accessed 19.05.20.

[29] WHO, Clinical guidelines: antiretroviral therapy 4.1: Preparing people living with HIV for Art. World Health Organization, 2002.

[30] WHO, WHO guidelines on HIV/AIDS. World Health Organization, https://www.who.int/publications/guidelines/hiv_aids/en/. Accessed 19.05.20.

[31] CDC. Guidelines and recommendations: HIV/AIDS. https://www.cdc.gov/hiv/guidelines/index.html. Accessed 19.05.20.

[32] Health FMO, Nigeria, National guidelines for HIV and AIDS treatment and care in adolescents and adults. Federal Ministry of HealthAbuja-Nigeria, https://www.who.int/hiv/amds/Nigeria_adult_2007.pdf. Accessed 19.0520.

[33] AIDS info, Guidelines for the use of antiretroviral agents in adults and adolescents living with HIV. National Institutes of Health, http://www.aidsinfo.nih.gov/ContentFiles/. Accessed 19.05.20.

[34] S. Erpolat Tasabat, D. Morais, A novel multicriteria decision-making method based on distance, similarity, and correlation: DSC TOPSIS, Math Probl. Eng. (2019) 2019.

[35] M. Sayan, D. Uzun Ozsahin, T. Sanlidag, N. Sultanoglu, F. Sarigul Yildirim, B. Uzun, Efficacy evaluation of antiretroviral drug combinations for HIV-1 treatment by using the fuzzy PROMETHEE, in: 10th International Conference on Theory and Application of Soft Computing, Computing with Words and Perceptions–ICSCCW-2019, http://link.springer.com/10.1007/978-3-030-35249-3_23. Accessed 19.05.20.

Chapter 15

Evaluating the effectiveness of recommended HIV adult postexposure prophylaxis drug regimens by using fuzzy PROMETHEE

Berna Uzun[a,b], Nazife Sultanoglu[a,c], Tamer Sanlidag[a] and Murat Sayan[a,d]

[a]DESAM Institute, Near East University, Turkish Republic of Northern Cyprus, Nicosia, Turkey;
[b]Department of Mathematics, Near East University, Turkish Republic of Northern Cyprus,
Nicosia, Turkey; [c]Faculty of Medicine, Department of Medical Microbiology and Clinical
Microbiology, Near East University, Turkish Republic of Northern Cyprus, Nicosia, Turkey;
[d]Faculty of Medicine, Clinical Laboratory, PCR Unit Kocaeli University, Kocaeli, Turkey

15.1 Introduction

HIV infection and treatment were described in detail in Chapter 14. As discussed in Chapter 14, HIV infection is a chronic disease that is manageable with antiretroviral therapy (ART). Apart from managing the HIV infection, ART agents also have their uses before or after potential exposure to HIV infection, called pre- and post-exposure prophylaxis (PrEP and PEP), respectively. Both application aims to reduce the risk of acquisition of the HIV infection. PEP is the short term (28 days) use of ART agents after a possible occupational or nonoccupational exposure [1–3]. Occupational exposure to HIV infection includes needle-stick injuries that can occur among healthcare workers, whereas nonoccupational exposure to HIV infection can include having an unprotected sex [4,5].

It is critical that a PEP regimen is started within 72 hours after the potential exposure to HIV, with the best effects observed within the golden period of less than 2 hours [2]. It has been declared that little or no effect has been observed in preventing HIV infection if the PEP regimen is administered more than 72 hours after HIV exposure [6,7]. However, when PEP is administered in a timely manner, it is able to prevent the establishment of chronic HIV infections via inhibiting the replication of the initial inoculum of the virus [2]. Since it is very important to start the PEP regimen soon after the potential exposure

Applications of Multi-Criteria Decision-Making Theories in Healthcare and Biomedical Engineering.
http://dx.doi.org/10.1016/B978-0-12-824086-1.00015-3

to HIV, it leaves very limited time for health practitioners to determine which combination of HIV ART agents is more appropriate for their patients.

The differences in the international and national guidelines, such as the categorization of recommended adult PEP ART regimens depending on whether the HIV transmission route is occupational or nonoccupational, make the available guidelines complicated [4,8–11]. In addition, the patients' specific conditions (presence of other diseases such as kidney problems) render the health practitioners' decisions in terms of the selection of the most potent PEP regimen even more difficult, considering potential interactions with other drugs, minimal side effects, and the associated toxicity. To overcome this issue, we propose the use of fuzzy PROMETHEE (preference ranking organization method for enrichment evaluations), a multicriteria decision-making method that can be utilized to evaluate the most effective adult PEP ART regimen among the 22 different recommended adult PEP ART regimens.

The fuzzy PROMETHEE method is a decision support system that can be applied to evaluate and rank a discrete set of alternatives within a system. This process involves the decision makers providing qualitative and quantitative data for each alternative with respect to each criterion and the linked relative importance (weight) of the criteria. In the fuzzy logic applications, linguistic terms are used such as "very high" and "important," which are linked with fuzzy numbers (the fuzzy logical system). Fuzzy numbers can be any integer value between 0 and 1. In some cases, a number of decision makers are involved in determining the criteria and their weights in order to obtain more discrete results. This system allows results to be obtained through outranking each alternative by ordering them from best to worst. In this way, the decision makers will be able to select the best alternative within the system based on their criteria and weights [12,13].

Technique for order preference by similarity to ideal solution (TOPSIS), fuzzy ELECTRE (elimination et choix traduisant la realité) and analytical hierarchy process (AHP) are also commonly used multicriteria decision-making methods that can be used in addition to PROMETHEE to obtain net outranking results. As opposed to other methods, PROMETHEE gives more options to the decision maker to define the preference function for each criterion, while other methods use only one preference function for all criteria. This makes the PROMETHEE method more sensitive in ranking the alternatives. Moreover, the PROMETHEE method is the latest improved multicriteria decision-making method that provides more balanced outranking results. The PROMETHEE method gives the outranking results using only quantitative data for alternatives, while fuzzy PROMETHEE—the combination of PROMETHEE method with fuzzy logic— allows the decision maker to use and analyze alternatives with quantitative and qualitative data simultaneously, which is more suitable for real-world problems. Therefore, the fuzzy PROMETHEE method was used rather than other available methods to obtain outranking results for the adult PEP ART regimens [13,14].

The demonstrated Fuzzy PROMETHEE model was adapted and used as a method for comparing the effectiveness of selected adult PEP ART regimens based on the following criteria: side effects, practicability, size of tablet, number of tablets, drug-drug interaction, pregnancy, genetic barrier, glomerular filtration rate of the kidneys (GFR), and being a member of a key population. Their associated weights were determined by clinical infectious disease experts. The results were obtained through the ranking system of the method in a rapid and reliable fashion, and were ranked according to their effectiveness with regard to the selected criteria and their weights. In this way, we were able to rank the selected 22 PEP ART regimens from best to worst in terms of their use.

15.2   Materials and methods

PROMETHEE is a multicriteria decision-making method that permits a mutual comparison between alternatives in a system. This method can be easily adapted into real-life decision-making problems. Partial and complete ranking of the alternatives can be obtained via PROMETHEE I and PROMETHEE II, respectively. By evaluating the differences of the outranking between the alternatives, the PROMETHEE method is able to rank the alternatives in a system from best to worst. In order to facilitate this evaluation, two types of information are needed. These are the weights (relative importance) of the criteria and the preference function associated with each criterion paired with the alternatives. However, the PROMETHEE method is unable to process linguistic fuzzy data in the actual decision-making environment. Thus, the fuzzy PROMETHEE method was used, which is an adaptation of the PROMETHEE method that uses a fuzzy scale with fuzzy numbers. The triangular fuzzy numbers can be any real number between 0 and 1 that is considered to be fuzzy. The magnitude of the triangular fuzzy numbers $\tilde{F} = (N, a, b)$ was determined by the Yager index in relation to the center of the triangle with the formula $YI = (3N - a + b)/3$. The alternatives within the system, which in this case were the adult PEP ART regimens with their categorized classes, and were chosen from the related guidelines and with regard to infectious disease experts' opinions (listed in Table 15.1) [4,10,15,16].

The different adult postexposure prophylaxis (PEP) antiretroviral therapy (ART) regimens categorized by their class bases, namely: integrase inhibitor, protease inhibitor, and non-nucleoside reverse transcriptase inhibitor, are listed accordingly. Guidelines and field experts' opinions were used to determine the selected PEP ART regimens for adults.

The criteria associated with each alternative regimen were side effects, practicability (the need to take the drug during or after the consumption of food), size of tablet, number of tablets, drug-drug interaction (possible drug interaction with ART agents when an HIV-treated individual is being treated for another disease such as a cardiac problem), pregnancy, genetic barrier (drug resistance that can arise due to mutation of the virus), GFR and being a member of a key population (prisoners, intravenous drug users, sex workers and lesbian, gay, bisexual, and transgender individuals are considered to be disadvantaged). Key population is a concept used in the literature. The concept implies that this population is vulnerable, meaning that it is more susceptible to HIV transmission. Therefore, when we consider PEP procedures and the frequency of usage

TABLE 15.1 List of recommended adult post-exposure prophylaxis antiretroviral therapy regimens.

Integrase inhibitor-based regimens

DTG + TDF/FTC (dolutegravir + tenofovir disoproxil fumarate/emtricitabine)

EVG/c + TDF (elvitegravir/cobicistat + tenofovir disoproxil fumarate)

RAL + TDF/FTC (raltegravir + tenofovir disoproxil fumarate/emtricitabine)

RAL + TDF + 3TC (raltegravir + tenofovir disoproxil fumarate + lamivudine)

RAL + ZDV + FTC (raltegravir + zidovudine + emtricitabine)

RAL + ZDV + 3TC (raltegravir + zidovudine + lamivudine)

Protease inhibitor-based regimens

DRV/r + TDF/FTC (darunavir/ritonavir + tenofovir disoproxil fumarate/emtricitabine)

DRV/r + TDF + 3TC (darunavir/ritonavir + tenofovir disoproxil fumarate + lamivudine)

DRV/r + ZDV + FTC (darunavir/ritonavir + zidovudine + emtricitabine)

DRV/r + ZDV + 3TC (darunavir/ritonavir + zidovudine + lamivudine)

ATV/r + TDF/FTC (atazanavir/ritonavir + tenofovir disoproxil fumarate/emtricitabine)

ATV/r + TDF + 3TC (atazanavir/ritonavir + tenofovir disoproxil fumarate + lamivudine)

ATV/r + ZDV + FTC (atazanavir/ritonavir + zidovudine + emtricitabine)

ATV/r + ZDV + 3TC (atazanavir/ritonavir + zidovudine + lamivudine)

LPV/r + TDF/FTC (lopinavir/ritonavir + tenofovir disoproxil fumarate/emtricitabine)

LPV/r + TDF + 3TC (lopinavir/ritonavir + tenofovir disoproxil fumarate + lamivudine)

LPV/r + ZDV + FTC (lopinavir/ritonavir + zidovudine + emtricitabine)

LPV/r + ZDV + 3TC (lopinavir/ritonavir + zidovudine + lamivudine)

Non-nucleoside reverse transcriptase inhibitor-based regimens

RPV + TDF/FTC (rilpivirine + tenofovir disoproxil fumarate/emtricitabine)

RPV + TDF + 3TC (rilpivirine + tenofovir disoproxil fumarate + lamivudine)

RPV + ZDV + FTC (rilpivirine + zidovudine + emtricitabine)

RPV + ZDV + 3TC (rilpivirine + zidovudine + lamivudine)

of the PEP, the key population should have access to the drug continuously. Also, the risk of HIV exposure being continuous and high makes the risk assessment useless and disadvantageous in terms of PEP use [17,18].

Each above-mentioned criterion also possesses a numerical value (fuzzy number) determining the importance of the criterion (weight) with a corresponding linguistic term ("very high," "high," "medium," and "low"). The linguistic terms were linked with fuzzy values to ease the understanding of the importance of each criterion. Therefore, when stating the fuzzy values of 1, 0.75, 0.50, 0.25, the use of terms such as "very high," "important," and "medium" is preferred for interpreting the results. The weights of the criteria were determined by the decision maker—field experts' opinions. The opinions of two clinical infectious

TABLE 15.2 Linguistic fuzzy scale.

Linguistic evaluation scale	Triangular fuzzy scale	Criteria
Very high (VH)	(0.75, 1,1)	Side effect, drug-drug interaction
Important (H)	(0.50, 0.75, 1)	Drug genetic barrier, glomerular filtration rate of the kidney (GFR)
Medium (M)	(0.25, 0.50, 0.75)	Practicability, member of key population*
Low (L)	(0, 0.25, 0.50)	Size of the tablet

Practicability: the need to take the drug with or after consumption of food. Member of key population: prisoners; intravenous drug users; sex workers; lesbian, gay, bisexual, and transgender people are considered to be disadvantaged.

disease experts with over 20 years of experience who can authorize prescriptions were used. The criteria with their weights and corresponding linguistic terms are presented as a linguistic fuzzy scale in Table 15.2. The clinical efficacy for each selected regimen was compared according to the stated criteria with their corresponding weights, but nothing else.

The linguistic fuzzy scale indicating the linguistic terms "very high," "high," "medium," and "low" with their associated numerical value (weight) for each criterion are listed with regard to field experts' opinions. The represented linguistic fuzzy scale was applied in the fuzzy PROMETHEE method.

The linguistic fuzzy scale is a limitation of the method since it is created by the decision maker and it will only evaluate the criteria that have been added to the linguistic fuzzy scale. This limitation section is an advantage rather than a disadvantage of the system, since it allows the system to evaluate selected ART regimens in a patient-specific manner by only including the relevant criteria with their chosen weights for the related patient. The triangular fuzzy scale could be changed, modified, or added by the decision maker (health practitioner) prior to the evaluation-ranking process. In this study, in order to make a comparison between the fuzzy numbers obtained in the outranking flow calculation by fuzzy PROMETHEE, defuzzification of the results was performed by the Yager index with Gaussian preference function. The Gaussian preference function formula is shown below.

$$P(d) = \begin{cases} 0, & d \leq 0 \\ 1 - e^{\frac{d^2}{2s^2}}, & d > 0 \end{cases} \tag{15.1}$$

Here, d stands for the difference between the alternative adult PEP regimens and their corresponding criteria.

Ranking within the system was performed using the visual PROMETHEE decision lab program. This method defines three outranking flows: net flow, positive flow, and negative flow. Net flow is the difference between the positive and negative outranking flow.

15.3 Results

Ranking of the alternatives allowed the determination of the best and worst PEP ART regimens within the system. The higher the positive—and the lower the negative—outranking flow, the better is the alternative in a system (as a result, the higher the net flow). The ranking results of the 22 adult PEP ART regimens analyzed are demonstrated in Table 15.3. The regimes are listed in descending order in terms of net flow, with the PEP ART regimes therefore ranked from best to worst.

TABLE 15.3 Fuzzy PROMETHEE ranking results of adult post-exposure antiretroviral therapy regimens.

No.	Complete ranking	Adult PEP ART regimen	Net flow	Positive outranking flow	Negative outranking flow
1	1	DTG + TDF/FTC	0.0736	0.0742	0.0006
2	2	EVG/c + TDF	0.0533	0.0610	0.0078
3	3	RAL + TDF/FTC	0.0481	0.0525	0.0045
4	4	RAL + TDF+ 3TC	0.0402	0.0476	0.0074
5	5	RAL + ZDV + FTC	0.0334	0.0445	0.0111
6	5	RAL + ZDV + 3TC	0.0334	0.0445	0.0111
7	7	RPV + TDF/FTC	0.0265	0.0483	0.0218
8	8	RPV + TDF + 3TC	0.0236	0.0387	0.0151
9	9	RPV + ZDV + FTC	0.0090	0.0307	0.0217
10	9	RPV + ZDV + 3TC	0.0090	0.0307	0.0217
11	11	DRV/r + TDF/FTC	−0.0142	0.0152	0.0295
12	12	DRV/r + TDF+ 3TC	−0.0195	0.0130	0.0324
13	13	ATV/r + TDF/FTC	−0.0228	0.0092	0.0320
14	14	DRV/r + ZDV + FTC	−0.0262	0.0099	0.0361
15	14	DRV/r + ZDV + 3TC	−0.0262	0.0099	0.0361
16	16	ATV/r + TDF+ 3TC	−0.0306	0.0043	0.0349
17	16	LPV/r + TDF/FTC	−0.0306	0.0043	0.0349
18	16	LPV/r + TDF + 3TC	−0.0306	0.0043	0.0349
19	19	ATV/r + ZDV + FTC	−0.0374	0.0012	0.0386
20	19	ATV/r + ZDV + 3TC	−0.0374	0.0012	0.0386
21	19	LPV/r + ZDV + FTC	−0.0374	0.0012	0.0386
22	19	LPV/r + ZDV + 3TC	−0.0374	0.0012	0.0386

Table 15.3 presents the fuzzy PROMETHEE ranking results of different adult postexposure prophylaxis (PEP) antiretroviral therapy (ART) regimens. The higher the calculated net flow, the more effective is the regimen. The different adult PEP ART regimens are listed in descending order of effectiveness, from best to worst. Some of the net flows of PEP ART regimens were found to be equal. These are ranked with the same complete ranking number, meaning their effectiveness is equal.

According to our results, the best adult PEP ART regimen was determined to be the integrase inhibitor-based regimen DTG + TDF/FTC, which has the highest net flow among the other compared PEP ART regimens of 0.0736. Following this, the second, third, fourth, and fifth PEP ART regimens were EVG/c + TDF, RAL + TDF/FTC, RAL + TDF/FTC, RAL + TDF+ 3TC, and RAL + ZDV + FTC, respectively, which are all from the integrase inhibitor-based regimen class.

15.4 Discussion

This study analyzed the selected 22 recommended adult PEP ART regimens (Table 15.1] that can be used after potential exposure to HIV-1 infection by using the fuzzy PROMETHEE method [4,9,10,15,16,19–21]. The evaluations of the effectiveness of the selected adult PEP ART regimens were made solely according to the criteria and their corresponding weights determined by the infectious disease experts (presented in Table 15.2). As a result of the evaluation, the integrase inhibitor-based regimen of DTG + TDF/FTC was found to be the most effective PEP regimen for use in adults. Moreover, the results indicated that the top five most effective adult PEP regimens were all from the integrase inhibitor-based regimens. The integrase inhibitors are a new class of antiretroviral agents which have recently been approved for clinical use and are now used in first line regimens for HIV-1 infection treatment. They target the HIV encoded enzyme integrase, inhibiting HIV genome integration into the host cell genome. Consequently, integrase inhibitors are very effective in declining the viral load, exhibit very low drug-drug interactions, have low pill burden and offer convenient dosing frequency [22,23]. However, it should be considered that the DTG + TDF/FTC regimen is not the first-line treatment option for active tuberculosis (TB) patients with HIV. In such cases, efavirenz- (EFV-) based regimens are preferred. Thus, it is also not suitable as an adult PEP ART regimen if the patient is being treated for active TB [24].

On the other hand, older regimens were at the bottom of the ranking results, such as the ATV/r + TDF+ 3TC, LPV/r + TDF/FTC, LPV/r + TDF + 3TC, ATV/r + ZDV + FTC, ATV/r + ZDV + 3TC, LPV/r + ZDV + FTC, and LPV/r + ZDV + 3TC regimens, as illustrated in Table 15.3. This firmly implies that the results obtained were concrete, as older regimens had more negative properties, such as the highest side effects and drug-drug interactions, among others. These were replaced with new generation regimens that possessed more positive prescription attributes. Also, the same group of regimens—the integrase inhibitors—indicated similar net flow rankings, suggesting that the results obtained were consistent.

In this study, during the process of evaluating the effectiveness of the selected adult PEP ART regimens, each regimen was considered and compared based on their general properties obtained from the latest available guidelines. For particular patient situations, a specific fuzzy scale should be prepared by the decision maker according to the condition of the patient. This feature of the system allows patient-specific evaluation of each specified ART regimen.

The fuzzy PROMETHEE method is used successfully in different health sciences fields including in the comparison and evaluation of the effectiveness of: cancer treatment alternatives [25,26], image reconstruction algorithms in nuclear medicine [27], nuclear medicine imaging devices [28], and X-ray based medical imaging devices [29]. This suggests that the application of the Fuzzy PROMETHEE method will be adopted widely in health sciences in the immediate future.

15.5 Conclusion

Furthermore, this study aimed to shed light on HIV infection prevention by evaluating the effectiveness of different adult PEP ART regimens based on their corresponding criteria with associated weights, thus helping to determine the most potent adult PEP ART regimen. The use of fuzzy PROMETHEE can be also adapted to a patient's specific condition, further helping the health practitioners to select patient-specific regimens in a rapid and reliable manner that could not otherwise be achieved manually. In conclusion, fuzzy PROMETHEE can overcome the complications of selecting appropriate PEP ART regimens by using the guidelines and does not require health practitioners to have extensive experience in the field.

References

[1] S. Naswa, Y.S. Marfatia, Pre-exposure prophylaxis of HIV. Indian J. Sex Transm. Dis.: AIDS 32 (1) 1–8,, http://www.ncbi.nlm.nih.gov/pubmed/21799568. Accessed 6.02.19.

[2] M. Shevkani, B. Kavina, P. Kumar, H. Purohit, U. Nihalani, A. Shah, An overview of postexposure prophylaxis for HIV in healthcare personals: Gujarat scenario. Indian J. Sex. Transm. Dis.: AIDS 32 (1) 9–13, http://www.ncbi.nlm.nih.gov/pubmed/21799569. Accessed 6.02.19.

[3] B. Sultan, P. Benn, L. Waters, Current perspectives in HIV postexposure prophylaxis. HIV AIDS (Auckl.) 6 (2014) 147–58. http://www.ncbi.nlm.nih.gov/pubmed/25368534. Accessed 6.02.19.

[4] N. Ford, K.H. Mayer, L. Barlow, F. Bagyinszky, A. Calmy, M. Chakroun, et al., World Health Organization guidelines on postexposure prophylaxis for HIV: recommendations for a public health approach. Clin. Infect. Dis. 60 (3) (Jun. 1, 2015) 161–64,https://academic.oup.com/cid/article/60/suppl_3/S161/374040. Accessed 6.02.19.

[5] K.L. Dominguez, D.K. Smith, T. Vasavi, N. Crepaz, K. Lang, W. Heneine, et al., Updated guidelines for antiretroviral postexposure prophylaxis after sexual, injection drug use, or other nonoccupational exposure to HIV—United States. Centers for Disease Control (2016), https://stacks.cdc.gov/view/cdc/38856. Accessed 6.02.19.

[6] AIDS info, FDA-approved HIV medicines: understanding HIV/AIDS. AIDS info (2019), https://aidsinfo.nih.gov/understanding-hiv-aids/fact-sheets/21/58/fda-approved-hiv-medicines. Accessed 6.02.19.

[7] HIV.gov, Post-exposure prophylaxis. HIV.gov (2019), https://www.hiv.gov/hiv-basics/hiv-prevention/using-hiv-medication-to-reduce-risk/post-exposure-prophylaxis. Accessed 6.02.19.

[8] CDC. Updated guidelines for antiretroviral postexposure prophylaxis after sexual, injection drug use, or other nonoccupational exposure to HIV—United States. Centers for Disease Control (2016), https://stacks.cdc.gov/view/cdc/38856

[9] CDC, Updated U.S. public health service guidelines for the management of occupational exposures to HIV and recommendations for postexposure prophylaxis (2016) pp. 1–91, https://stacks.cdc.gov/view/cdc/38856.

[10] European AIDS Clinical Society. European AIDS Clinical Society Guidelines Version 9.0 [Internet]. 2017 [cited 2019 Apr 16]. Available from: http://www.eacsociety.org

[11] WHO. Guideline on when to start antiretroviral therapy and on pre-exposure prophylaxis for HIV. World Health Organization (2018), https://www.who.int/hiv/pub/guidelines/earlyrelease-arv/en/. Accessed 20.02.19.

[12] L.A. Zadeh, Fuzzy sets. Inf. Control 8 (3) (Jun. 1, 1965) 338–53, https://www.sciencedirect.com/science/article/pii/S001999586590241X. Accessed 9.08.19.

[13] E.A. Adalı, A.T. Işık, N. Kundakcı, An alternative approach based on fuzzy PROMETHEE method for the supplier selection problem, Uncertain Supply Chain Manag. (January 2016) 183–94.

[14] A.K. Digalwar, P.A. Date, Development of fuzzy PROMETHEE algorithm for the evaluation of Indian world-class manufacturing organisations, Int. J. Serv. Oper. Manag. 24 (3) (2016) 308.

[15] L.E. Chapman, E.E. Sullivent, L.A. Grohskopf, E.M. Beltrami, J.F. Perz, K, Kretsinger, et al., Recommendations for postexposure interventions to prevent infection with hepatitis B virus, hepatitis C virus, or human immunodeficiency virus, and tetanus in persons wounded during bombings and other mass-casualty events—United States, 2008. Centers for Disease Control, Morb. Mortal Wkly. report 57 (RR-6) (Aug. 1, 2008) 1-21-4, http://www.ncbi.nlm.nih.gov/pubmed/18668022. Accessed 20.02.19.

[16] M.S. Saag, C.A. Benson, R.T. Gandhi, J.F. Hoy, R.J. Landovitz, MJ. Mugavero, et al. Antiretroviral drugs for treatment and prevention of HIV infection in adults: 2018 recommendations of the International Antiviral Society—USA Panel. JAMA 320 (4) (Jul. 24, 2018) 379, http://www.ncbi.nlm.nih.gov/pubmed/30043070. Accessed 20.02.19.

[17] WHO Collaborating Centre for HIV Strategic Informatio, M27: HIV prevention, diagnosis, treatment and care for key populations and programme evaluation, http://www.whohub-zagreb.org/903. Accessed 9.08.19.

[18] UNAIDS, Terminology guidelines. UNAIDS (2011), https://www.unaids.org/sites/default/files/media_asset/JC2118_terminology-guidelines_en_1.pdf. Accessed 9.08.19.

[19] IAS , No occurrences of neural tube defects among 382 women on dolutegravir at pregnancy conception in Brazil. IAS (2019), http://programme.ias2019.org/Abstract/Abstract/4991. Accessed 9.08.19.

[20] IAS, Addressing the safety signal with dolutegravir use at conception: Additional surveillance data from Botswana, IAS (2019),http://programme.ias2019.org/Abstract/Abstract/5089. Accessed 9.08.19.

[21] WHO, Update of recommendations on first- and second-line retroviral regimens. World Health Organization (2019), http://apps.who.int/bookorders. Accessed 9.08.19.

[22] Z. Hajimahdi, A. Zarghi, Progress in HIV-1 integrase inhibitors: a review of their chemical structure diversity. Iran J. Pharm. Res. (2016), http://www.ncbi.nlm.nih.gov/pubmed/28243261. Accessed 9.08.19.

[23] M. D'Abbraccio, A. Busto, M. De Marco, M. Figoni, A. Maddaloni, N. Abrescia, Efficacy and tolerability of integrase inhibitors in antiretroviral—naive patients. AIDS Rev. (2017), http://www.ncbi.nlm.nih.gov/pubmed/26450805. Accessed 20.02.19.

[24] WHO. Management of tuberculosis and HIV coinfection. World Health Organization (2006), http://www.euro.who.int/__data/assets/pdf_file/0004/78124/E90840_Chapter_4.pdf. Accessed 24.07.19.

[25] D. Uzun, B. Uzun, M. Sani, A. Helwan, C. Nwekwo, F. Veysel, Evaluating cancer treatment alternatives using fuzzy PROMETHEE method, Int. J. Adv. Comput. Sci. Appl. 8 (10) (2017) 177–182.

[26] D.U. Ozsahin, A fuzzy PROMETHEE approach for breast cancer treatment techniques Int. J. Med. Sci. Public Health 7 (May) (2018) 29–32.

[27] D.U. Ozsahin, N.A. Isa, B. Uzun, I. Ozsahin, Effective analysis of image reconstruction algorithms in nuclear medicine using fuzzy PROMETHEE. In: 2018 Advances in Science and Engineering Technology International Conferences (ASET). IEEE.org (2018) 1–5, https://ieeexplore.ieee.org/document/8376892/. Accessed 7.02.19.

[28] D.U. Ozsahin, B. Uzun, M.S. Musa, N. Şentürk, F.V. Nurçin, I. Ozsahin, Evaluating nuclear medicine imaging devices using fuzzy PROMETHEE method. Proc. Comput. Sci. 120 (Jan. 1, 2017) 699-705, https://www.sciencedirect.com/science/article/pii/S1877050917325103. Accessed 7.02.19.

[29] D. Uzun, B. Uzun, M. Sani, I. Ozsahin, Evaluating X-ray-based medical imaging devices with fuzzy preference ranking organization method for enrichment evaluations. Int. J. Adv. Comput. Sci. Appl. 9 (3) (2018), http://thesai.org/Publications/ViewPaper?Volume=9&Issue=3&Code=ijacsa&SerialNo=2. Accessed 7.02.18.

Chapter 16

The use of multicriteria decision-making method—fuzzy VIKOR in antiretroviral treatment decision in pediatric HIV-infected cases

Murat Sayan[a,b], Tamer Sanlidag[a], Nazife Sultanoglu[a,c] and Berna Uzun[a,d]

[a]*DESAM Institute, Near East University, Turkish Republic of Northern Cyprus, Nicosia, Turkey;*
[b]*Faculty of Medicine, Clinical Laboratory, PCR Unit Kocaeli University, Kocaeli, Turkey;*
[c]*Faculty of Medicine, Department of Medical Microbiology and Clinical Microbiology, Near East University, Turkish Republic of Northern Cyprus, Nicosia, Turkey;* [d]*Department of Mathematics, Near East University, Turkish Republic of Northern Cyprus, Nicosia, Turkey*

16.1 Introduction

HIV infection is not only a problem in adults but is also a health problem in infants and children. Among the 37.9 million people living with HIV worldwide in 2018, 1.7 million were children below 15 years of age. In 2018, 160,000 children became newly infected with HIV and 100,000 HIV-related children's deaths occurred [1,2]. It is estimated that approximately 1500 children become infected with HIV each day and up to 90% of these infections occur in Sub-Saharan Africa [3].

The primary route of infant HIV infection is through mother-to-child transmission, also known as vertical transmission, which is the spread of HIV infection from mother to baby during pregnancy, labor, delivery, or breastfeeding [4,5].

Normal birth, in which the baby is in contact with the vaginal canal of HIV-positive mothers, increases the risk of acquiring HIV infection in babies. HIV-positive mothers should be monitored frequently during pregnancy and should be given ART treatment to decrease the viral load of HIV in the blood, thus decreasing the chances of transmission to the baby. Also, rather than normal birth (vaginal delivery), cesarean-section delivery should be the preferred method for delivering the baby to reduce the acquisition of HIV infection through birth canal [6].

Applications of Multi-Criteria Decision-Making Theories in Healthcare and Biomedical Engineering.
http://dx.doi.org/10.1016/B978-0-12-824086-1.00016-5
239

Breastfeeding is another way that the mother can pass the HIV infection to her baby. Although this is a way of transmitting the disease, HIV-positive mothers or their infants receiving ART are recommended by the World Health Organization (WHO) to breastfeed for 22 months. This ensures that the baby benefits from breastfeeding with little risk of becoming infected [7].

In the absence of effective interventions, the rate of vertical transmission including during pregnancy, labor or breastfeeding may vary from 15% to 45%. The majority of transmission occurs in the peripartum stage with up to 65%, whereas 35% occurs during pregnancy, and the transmission rate during breastfeeding varies from 7% to 22%. These variations result from different factors such as the stage of the disease (advanced), presence of other infections, viral load, and the delay or nonuse of ART at the beginning or during pregnancy. However, the use of the correct ART regimens by the HIV positive mother significantly reduces the risk of transmission from mother to baby to below 2% [8]. Also, it is recommended that infants born from HIV positive mothers receive antiretroviral drugs for a short period of time [4,9]. This happens when the mothers are unaware of their HIV status, they are not receiving ART and preventative interventions are not followed. The number of infants becoming infected with HIV from their mothers has decreased significantly due to increased HIV testing, as well as the use of ART by mothers during pregnancy and after birth, and also the application of ART to the baby after birth [10,11].

In adolescence, sexual interests may develop due to physical growth and sexual maturation, often leading to intimate relationships. Also, other risk factors such as adolescent sex workers, childhood sexual abuse, child labor, and child trafficking play a role in adolescents contracting HIV infections [12]. On the other hand, some are infected at an early age or as infants, but are diagnosed later on in their lives.

HIV-1 disease progression in untreated paediatric HIV-1 cases is faster when compared to untreated adults. Most paediatric HIV-1 infections occur in Sub-Saharan Africa. It is reported that in this area, 53% of children die before 2 years and 75% before the age of 3 due to HIV-1 infection [13].

Thus, initiation of ART in pediatric cases of HIV-1 is much more critical than adult infections for managing the disease and prolonging the lives of the HIV-1 infected children. In this study, the fuzzy VlseKriterijumska Optimizacija i Kompromisno Resenje (VIKOR) method, which is one of the multiple-criteria decision-making methods, was used to analyze the most frequently used ART regimens in categorized aged groups: birth to age <14 days, ≥ 14 days to <3 years, ≥ 3 years to <6 years, ≥ 6 years to <12 years, and ≥ 12 years and older [14].

16.2 Methods and materials

The VIKOR method is used for the optimization of multicriteria complex systems. The compromise solution, the foundations of which were laid by Yu (1973) and Zeleny (1982), is to reach an agreement—an alternative solution closest to an ideal solution—upon comparing contradicting criteria associated with each criterion to be evaluated. The VIKOR method was proposed by Trajkovic, Amakumovic, and Opricovic in 1997 [15]. This method enables conciliatory analysis for the decision maker on sorting and selecting contracting alternatives [16].

In the VIKOR method, the best alternative is the closest to the ideal solution and alternatives are ranked based on maximum "group benefits" with minimal individual regrets. In the past decade, VIKOR has become a popular decision support tool for multicriteria decision analysis and enables the selection of the best alternative in real-life problems by the decision maker [17].

16.3   Fuzzy VIKOR application

The VIKOR method deals with the compromise solution and multicriteria optimization, whereas the fuzzy VIKOR method consists of ranking the selected alternatives to be compared with multiconflicting or noncommensurable criteria. The ranking of the alternatives is obtained in the sense that the decision maker wants a solution for a real-life problem, which is closest to the ideal solution.

In this study, using the fuzzy-based VIKOR method, a compromise ranking is established for the evaluation of the selected ART regimens in paediatric HIV-1 cases. Below is the list of frequently used ART regimens determined for the groups of children to be evaluated according to the criteria, and their associated weights selected based on the opinions of experts in the field.

ART regimens for infants from birth to age < 14 days are:
NVP + 3TC/ZDV (nevirapin + lamivudine/zidovudine)
NVP + FTC + ZDV (nevirapin + emtricitabine + zidovudine)
RAL + 3TC/ZDV (raltegravir + lamivudine/zidovudine)
RAL + FTC + ZDV (raltegravir + emtricitabine + zidovudine)

For the children (aged ≥ 14 days to <3 years) are:
RAL + 3TC/ZDV (raltegravir + lamivudine/zidovudine)
RAL + FTC + ZDV (raltegravir + emtricitabine + zidovudine)
RAL + ABC + 3TC (raltegravir + abacavir + lamivudine)
RAL + ABC + FTC (raltegravir + abacavir + emtricitabine)
LPV/r + 3TC/ZDV (lopinavir/r + lamivudine/zidovudine)
LPV/r +ABC/3TC (lopinavir/r + abacavir/lamivudine)
LPV/r +FTC + ZDV (lopinavir/r + emtricitabine + zidovudine)
LPV/r +ABC + FTC (lopinavir/r + abacavir + lamivudine)

ART regimens for children ≥3 years to <6 years old are:
RAL + 3TC/ZDV (raltegravir + lamivudine/zidovudine)
RAL + FTC + ZDV (raltegravir + emtricitabine + zidovudine)

ATV/r + 3TC/ZDV (atazanavir/r + lamivudine/zidovudine)
ATV/r + FTC + ZDV (atazanavir/r + emtricitabine + zidovudine)
ATV/r + ABC/3TC** (atazanavir/r + abacavir/lamivudine)
ATV/r + ABC + FTC** (atazanavir/r + abacavir + emtricitabine)
DRV/r + 3TC/ZDVx2 (darunavir/r + abacavir/lamivudine)
DRV/r + FTC + ZDVx2 (darunavir/r + emtricitabine + zidovudine)
DRV/r + ABC/3TC**x2 (darunavir/r + abacavir/lamivudine)
DRV/r + ABC + FTC**x2 (darunavir/r + abacavir + emtricitabine)
RAL + ABC/3TC**(raltegravir + abacavir/lamivudine)
RAL + ABC + FTC**(raltegravir + abacavir + emtricitabine)

ART regimens for ≥ 6 years to <12 years old:
ATV/r + 3TC/ZDV (atazanavir/r + lamivudine/zidovudine)
ATV/r + FTC + ZDV (atazanavir/r + emtricitabine + zidovudine)
ATV/r + ABC/3TC** (atazanavir/r + abacavir/lamivudine)
ATV/r + ABC + FTC** (atazanavir/r + abacavir + emtricitabine)
DTG + 3TC/ZDV (dolutegravir + lamivudine/zidovudine)
DTG + FTC + ZDV (dolutegravir + emtricitabine + zidovudine)
DTG + ABC/3TC (dolutegravir + abacavir/lamivudine)
DTG + ABC + FTC** (dolutegravir + abacavir + emtricitabine)

ART regimens for children ≥12 years old and older are:
ATV/r + 3TC/ZDV (atazanavir/r + lamivudine/zidovudine)
ATV/r + FTC + ZDV (atazanavir/r + emtricitabine + zidovudine)
ATV/r + ABC/3TC** (atazanavir/r + abacavir/lamivudine)
ATV/r + ABC + FTC** (atazanavir/r + abacavir + emtricitabine)
DRV/r + 3TC/ZDV x1 (dolutegravir + lamivudine/zidovudine)
DRV/r + FTC + ZDVx1 (dolutegravir + emtricitabine + zidovudine
DRV/r + ABC/3TC**x1 (dolutegravir + abacavir/lamivudine)
DRV/r + ABC + FTC**x1 (dolutegravir + abacavir + emtricitabine
DTG*** + 3TC/ZDV (dolutegravir + lamivudine/zidovudine)
DTG*** + FTC + ZDV (dolutegravir + emtricitabine + zidovudine)
DTG*** + ABC/3TC**(dolutegravir + abacavir/lamivudine)
DTG*** + ABC + FTC**(dolutegravir + abacavir + emtricitabine)
EVG****/COBI/TDF/FTC (elvitegravir/cobistat/tenofovir disproxil fumarat/
emtricitabine)
EVG****/COBI/TAF/FTC (elvitegravir/cobistat/tenofovir alafenamid/
emtricitabine)
(** >3 months, ***DTG weighing ≥30 kg, ****EVG weighing ≥35 kg)

For this aim, the data of the available ART regimens in pediatric HIV-1 cases were first collected using a linguistic fuzzy scale (Table 16.1). However, the importance degree of the chosen criteria was defined with a linguistic fuzzy scale. Then, the Yager index was used for converting the fuzzy data into single points for use in the VIKOR technique.

TABLE 16.1 Linguistic fuzzy scale.

Linguistic evaluation scale	Triangular fuzzy scale	Importance ratings of criteria
Very high (VH)	(0.75, 1, 1)	Side effect, drug-drug interaction, false prescription, compliance, previous treatment, opportunistic infection, immunology recovery, virologic recovery
High (H)	(0.50, 0.75, 1)	Number of tablets, dose frequency, plasma turnover, time of suppression, glomerular filtration rate (GFR), CD4 + T-cell counts, coinfection, mental disorder.
Medium (M)	(0.25, 0.50, 0.75)	Genetic barrier, practicability, limitations, genetic testing, bone density, transmitted drug resistance mutation (TDRM), viral load, inefficient drug combination
Low (L)	(0, 0.25, 0.50)	Absorption, size of tablet
Very low (VL)	(0, 0, 0.25)	Supplement

The fuzzy VIKOR method used in the evaluation of categorized ART regimens for the determined age groups was based on the following steps:

Step 1. The expression of the multicriteria decision-making problem is made by the matrix format

Step 2. The construction of the defuzzified decision matrix and the weight vector by the decision maker

Step 3. The evaluation of the fuzzy importance of criteria weight

Step 4. Computation of the normalized decision matrix

Step 5. Computation of S_j, R_j, and Q_j, which represent the maximum group utility for the majority, the minimum individual regret for the opposers, and the ideal solution, also known as the VIKOR index, respectively

Step 6. Ranking of the alternatives in the increasing order

Step 7. The best alternative determination, which is the alternative with the minimum Q_j

The same data consisting of the ART regimens in determined aged groups of groups of: birth to age <14 days, ≥ 14 days to <3 years, ≥ 3 years to <6 years, ≥ 6 years to <12 years and ≥ 12 years and older, and their associated criteria linked to weight were analyzed previously by fuzzy PROMETHEE [18,19].

16.4 Results

By using the fuzzy VIKOR method, net ranking results of the ART regimens for the HIV-1 cases in infants from birth to age <14 days (Table 16.2), children aged ≥14 days to <3 years (Table 16.3), children aged ≥3 years to <6 years (Table 16.4), children aged ≥6 years to <12 years (Table 16.5), and adolescents aged ≥12 years and older (Table 16.6) were obtained. The lower the Q_i within the evaluated alternatives, the better is that alternative (closest to the ideal solution). The best regimen among the other alternative for birth to age <14 days, children aged ≥14 days to <3 and children aged ≥3 years to <6 years was determined to be RAL + 3TC/ZDV with the lowest Q_i 0.000.

TABLE 16.2 Ranking of the antiretroviral regimens for the infants, from birth to age <14 days.

Rank	Alternatives	S_j	R_j	Q_j
1	RAL + 3TC/ZDV	4	1	0.0000
2	RAL + FTC + ZDV	5.25	1	0.1087
3	NVP + 3TC/ZDV	6.75	1	0.2391
4	NVP + FTC + ZDV	9.75	1	0.5000

TABLE 16.3 Net ranking results of the antiretroviral regimens of the children aged ≥14 days to <3 years.

Rank	Alternatives	S_j	R_j	Q_j
1	RAL + 3TC/ZDV	1.5	1	0.0000
2	RAL + FTC + ZDV	2.375	1	0.1194
2	RAL + ABC/3TC**	2.375	1	0.1194
4	RAL + ABC + FTC**	3.25	1	0.2387
5	LPV/r + ABC/3TC**	6.5111	2	0.6836
6	LPV/r + 3TC/ZDV	7.955	1	0.8806
7	LPV/r + FTC + /ZDV	8.33	1	0.9318
8	LPV/r + ABC + FTC**	8.83	1	1.0000

TABLE 16.4 The net ranking results of the antiretroviral regimens of the children aged ≥3 years to <6 years.

Rank	Alternatives	S_j	R_j	Q_j
1	RAL + 3TC/ZDV	2.50	1	0.0000
2	RAL + FTC + ZDV	3.38	1	0.1083
2	RAL + ABC/3TC**	3.38	1	0.1083
4	RAL + FTC + ZDV	3.75	1	0.1547
5	RAL + ABC + FTC**	4.25	1	0.2166
6	DRV/r + 3TC/ZDV x2	6.83	1	0.5359
6	DRV/r + FTC + ZDV x2	6.83	1	0.5359
8	DRV/r + ABC/3TC**x2	7.33	1	0.5978
8	DRV/r + ABC + FTC**x2	7.33	1	0.5978
10	ATV/r + 3TC/ZDV	9.71	1	0.8917
11	ATV/r + FTC + ZDV	10.08	1	0.9381
12	ATV/r + ABC/3TC**	10.21	1	0.9536
13	ATV/r + ABC + FTC**	10.58	1	1.0000

TABLE 16.5 The net ranking results of the antiretroviral regimens of the children aged ≥6 years to <12 years.

Rank	Alternatives	S_j	R_j	Q_j
1	DTG*** + ABC/3TC**	2.75	1	0.0000
2	DTG*** + 3TC/ZDV	4	1	0.1103
3	DTG*** + FTC + ZDV	5.375	1	0.2317
4	DTG*** + ABC + FTC**	5.875	1	0.2758
5	ATV/r + 3TC/ZDV	13.205	1	0.9228
6	ATV/r + FTC + ZDV	13.58	1	0.9559
7	ATV/r + ABC/3TC**	13.705	1	0.9669
8	ATV/r + ABC + FTC**	14.08	1	1.0000

On the other hand, among the selected alternatives for children aged ≥6 years to <12 years, the best regimen was found to be the DTG*** + ABC/3TC**with Q_i being 0.000 and for adolescents aged ≥12 years and older EVG****/COBI/TAF/FTC with Q_i being 0.000.

TABLE 16.6 The net ranking results of the antiretroviral drugs of the adolescents aged ≥12 years and older.

Rank	Alternatives	Sj	Rj	Qj
1	EVG****/COBI/TAF/FTC	4.705	1	0.0000
2	DTG*** + ABC/3TC**	4.75	1	0.0040
3	EVG****/COBI/TDF/FTC	4.955	1	0.0220
4	DTG*** + 3TC/ZDV	6.5	1	0.1578
5	DTG*** + FTC + ZDV	7.875	1	0.2787
5	DTG*** + ABC + FTC**	7.875	1	0.2787
7	DRV/r + 3TC/ZDV x1	11.58	1	0.6044
8	DRV/r + ABC/3TC**x1	11.705	1	0.6154
9	DRV/r + FTC + ZDV x1	12.08	1	0.6484
10	DRV/r + ABC + FTC**x1	12.58	1	0.6923
11	ATV/r + 3TC/ZDV	15.205	1	0.9231
12	ATV/r + FTC + ZDV	15.58	1	0.9560
13	ATV/r + ABC/3TC**	15.705	1	0.9670
14	ATV/r + ABC + FTC**	16.08	1	1.0000

16.5 Conclusion

In this study, the most frequently used ART regimens for child HIV-1 cases selected by experts in the field were compared with their criteria and associated weights using the multiple-criteria decision-making method—fuzzy VIKOR. Five different age groups of children: from birth to age <14 days, children aged ≥14 days to <3 years, children aged ≥3 years to <6 years, children aged ≥6 years to <12 years and adolescents aged ≥12 years and older, with the set of ART regimens mentioned in the materials and method section were evaluated in terms of the most potent regimen with the maximum benefit and minimum regrets. Based on the evaluation made by fuzzy VIKOR, it was determined that among all the alternatives compared for each age group, for children from birth to age <14 days, children aged ≥14 days to <3 and children aged ≥3 years to <6 years, the RAL + 3TC/ZDV regimen was determined as the best regimen with the lowest Q_j 0.000. On the other hand, for children aged ≥6 years to <12 years and adolescents aged ≥12 years and older, the EVG****/COBI/TAF/FTC regimen, with Q_j being 0.000, was the best option among the other alternatives.

The same set of data, children's ART regimens and their criteria linked with associated weights, were also previously studied by another multicriteria decision-making method—fuzzy PROMETHEE. Similar results were obtained in that for children from birth to age <14 days, children aged ≥14 days to <3 years, and children aged ≥3 years to <6 years, RAL + 3TC/ZDV was found to be the best regimen, and for children ≥6 years to <12 years, the DTG*** + ABC/3TC** regimen was determined to be the best option among others. These results were exactly the same as the results of the fuzzy VIKOR analysis. The only exemption was in the adolescents aged ≥12 years and older group where the fuzzy PROMETHEE indicated that DTG*** + ABC/3TC** was the best regiment. This regimen was ranked as the second-best regimen in the same age group when compared using the fuzzy VIKOR method. This firmly implies that multicriteria decision-making methods are reliable and consistent in the evaluation of children's ART regimens.

References

[1] WHO. Summary of the global HIV epidemic. World Health Organization (2018), https://www.who.int/hiv/data/2018_summary-global-hiv-epi.png?ua=1. Accessed 23.05.20.

[2] WHO, Data and statistics. World Health Organization, (2019) https://www.who.int/hiv/data/en/. Accessed 19.05.20.

[3] WHO. Taking stock: HIV in children. World Health Organization (2006), https://www.who.int/hiv/toronto2006/Children2_eng.pdf. Accessed 23.05.20.

[4] WHO. Mother-to-child transmission of HIV. World Health Organization (2020), https://www.who.int/hiv/topics/mtct/about/en/. Accessed 23.05.20.

[5] WHO. Infant feeding for the prevention of mother-to-child transmission of HIV. World Health Orgnaization (2019), https://www.who.int/elena/titles/hiv_infant_feeding/en/. Accessed 23.05.20.

[6] M.L. Newell, Vertical transmission of HIV-1 infection, Trans. R. Soc. Trop. Med. Hyg. 94 (1) (2000) 1–2.

[7] WHO. Breast is always best, even for HIV-positive mothers. World Health Organization (2010), https://www.who.int/bulletin/volumes/88/1/10-030110/en/. Accessed 23.05.20.

[8] M.F.M. Barral, G.R. Oliveira, R.C. De Lobato, R.A. Mendoza-Sassi, A.M.B. Martínez, C.V. Gonçalves, Risk factors of HIV-1 vertical transmission (VT) and the influence of antiretroviral therapy (ART) in pregnancy outcome, Rev. Inst. Med. Trop. Sao Paulo 56 (2) (2014) 133–138.

[9] A.H. Krist, A.M.Y. Crawford-Faucher, Management of newborns exposed to maternal HIV infection, Am. Fam. Physician 65 (10) (2002) 2049–2056.

[10] Stanford Children's Health. AIDS/HIV in children. Stanford Children's Health (2020), https://www.stanfordchildrens.org/en/topic/default?id=aidshiv-in-children-90-P02509. Accessed 28.01.20.

[11] AIDSinfo, Antiretroviral management of newborns with perinatal HIV exposure or HIV infection—management of infants born to women with HIV infection. AIDSinfo 2020, https://aidsinfo.nih.gov/guidelines/html/3/perinatal/187/antiretroviral-management-of-newborns-with-perinatal-hiv-exposure-or-hiv-infection. Accessed 23.05.20.

[12] S. Naswa, Y.S. Marfatia, Adolescent HIV/AIDS: issues and challenges, Indian J. Sex. Transm. Dis. AIDS. 31 (1) (2010) 1.

[13] K. Luzuriaga, L.M. Mofenson, Challenges in the elimination of pediatric HIV-1 infection. E. W. Campion (ed.). N. Engl. J. Med. (Feb. 25, 2016), http://www.nejm.org/doi/10.1056/NEJMra1505256. Accessed 22.11.18.

[14] AIDSinfo, Guidelines for the use of antiretroviral agents in pediatric HIV infection. AIDSinfo (2019), https://aidsinfo.nih.gov/contentfiles/lvguidelines/pediatricguidelines.pdf. Accessed 2.06.20.

[15] A. Sanayei, S. Farid Mousavi, A. Yazdankhah, Group decision making process for supplier selection with VIKOR under fuzzy environment, Expert Syst. Appl. 37 (1) (2010) 24–30.

[16] N. Çetin Demirel, G.N. Yücenur, The cruise port place selection problem with extended VIKOR and ANP methodologies under fuzzy environment. Proc. World Congr. Eng. 2 (2011) 1128–33.

[17] Q.L. Zeng, D.D. Li, Y.Bin. Yang, VIKOR method with enhanced accuracy for multiple criteria decision making in healthcare management, J. Med. Syst. 37 (2) (2013 Apr).

[18] N. Sultanoglu, B. Uzun, F.S. Yildirim, M. Sayan, T. Sanlidag, DiU. Ozsahin, Selection of the most appropriate antiretroviral medication in determined aged groups (≥3 years) of HIV-1 infected children. In: 2019 Advances in Science and Engineering Technology International Conferences (ASET), Institute of Electrical and Electronics Engineers Inc., 2019.

[19] B. Uzun, F.S. Yildirim, M. Sayan, T. Sanlidag, D.U. Ozsahin, The use of Fuzzy PROMETH-EE technique in antiretroviral combination decision in pediatric HIV treatments. In: 2019 Advances in Science and Engineering Technology International Conferences (ASET), IEEE (2019) pp. 1–4, https://ieeexplore.ieee.org/document/8714389/. Accessed 17.05.19.

Chapter 17

Evaluation of oral antiviral treatments for chronic Hepatitis B using fuzzy PROMETHEE

Figen Sarigül[a], Sadettin Hülagü[b] and Dilber Uzun Ozsahin[c,d,e]

[a]Health Science University, Antalya Educational and Research Hospital, Clinical of Infectious Diseases, Antalya, Turkey; [b]Medical Faculty, Department of Gastroenterology, Kocaeli University, Izmit, Kocaeli, Turkey; [c]Department of Biomedical Engineering, Near East University, Turkish Republic of Northern Cyprus, Nicosia, Turkey; [d]DESAM Institute, Near East University, Turkish Republic of Northern Cyprus, Nicosia, Turkey; [e]Medical Diagnostic Imaging Department, College of Health Sciences, University of Sharjah, Sharjah, United Arab Emirates

17.1 Introduction

Hepatitis B virus (HBV) is a small double-stranded DNA virus from the Hepadnaviridae family [1]. General transmission routes include: sexual intercourse, from mother to baby during birth, and the use of blood or products that have not been tested with reliable tests. It can also be transmitted via different kinds of invasive interventions made with instruments that have not been sterilized correctly, through the shared use of syringes, of the shared use of items such as toothbrushes and razors, as well as by applying body jewelry or tattoos using nonsterilized instruments [2].

Groups at risk of HBV infection are:

- Bone marrow and solid organ transplant candidates and recipients, hemodialysis patients
- Healthcare professionals and students
- Those who have to use blood and blood products frequently
- Those who are not vaccinated following contact of hepatitis. B carriers/patients in the family
- Substance abusers
- Children of hepatitis B surface antigen (HBsAg) positive mothers
- Gay/bisexual men
- Those who with multiple sexual partners and who have sexual relations with sex workers
- Prisoners and employees in correctional facilities and prisons,

Applications of Multi-Criteria Decision-Making Theories in Healthcare and Biomedical Engineering.
http://dx.doi.org/10.1016/B978-0-12-824086-1.00017-7

- Manicurists/pedicurists, hairdressers
- Those who are in nursing homes for the mentally disabled
- Those with other chronic liver diseases
- Those who have risky dental treatment and history of interventions
- People with piercings or who are planning to get tattooed
- Those living in orphanages
- First aiders
- Those who come from places where HBV incidence is high

17.2   Epidemiology of hepatitis B

Despite the widespread treatment of chronic hepatitis B (CHB) infection and vaccination against HBV, there are approximately 2 billion people around the world who have encountered HBV, and approximately 400 million CHB patients. An estimated 500,000–700,000 people die annually due to complications related to or associated with HBV infection [3]. The vision of the World Health Organization is to eliminate the threat of viral hepatitis to public health by 2030, the deaths due to viral hepatitis by 65% and the number of new cases by 90%. However, migration and population movements have changed its prevalence and frequency in some low endemic countries in Europe (e.g. Italy, Germany) [4]. The number of HBV-related deaths due to liver cirrhosis and / or liver cancer (HCC) increased by 33% worldwide between 1990 and 2013 [5].

With current treatments, the proliferation of HBV is suppressed with antiviral therapy, which stops the progression of liver damage and decreases the development of HCC [6]. Unfortunately, completely removing the virus from the body is currently not possible with the drugs used today [7]. Various antiviral drugs are used in the treatment of HBV infection. In line with the recommendations of international guidelines, effective antiviral drugs are used in treatment [8–10]. The latest epidemiological data showed that the estimated national hepatitis s antigen (HBsAg) prevalence in the general population in 2016 was 6.1% [11]. The latest epidemiological data showed that the estimated national HBsAg prevalence in the general population in 2016 was 6.1%.

17.3   The natural history of hepatitis B virus infection

The virus replicates in the host and is collected only in hepatocytes [12]. HBV itself does not cause liver cell damage, but the host's antiviral immune response against HBV can damage liver inflammation and hepatocytes while eliminating the virus [13]. The natural course of HBV infection is quite variable. The development of the body's immune system, the severity of the immune response, and virus-related features are factors that determine the course of the infection [13].

In the diagnosis of HBV infection, HBsAg is the most important marker. Besides HBsAg, other HBV serum markers used are antibody to HBsAg (anti-HBs), hepatitis e antigen (HBeAg), antibody to HBeAg (anti-HBe) and anti-HBc.

HBV DNA level is detected by HBV nucleic acid real-time polymerase chain reaction method. Viral replication is shown by serum HBV DNA levels and evaluation of the success of antiviral therapy during treatment is performed by monitoring HBV DNA levels.

Acute hepatitis B (AHB) can occur with different clinical pictures, ranging from asymptomatic infection to fulminant hepatitis and liver failure, after 6 weeks to 6 months of incubation after encountering HBV [14]. In AHB, if the body's immune response is sufficient, the disease will recover, but if it is inadequate, the disease will become chronic [13]. The recovery period is less than six months. If the antibody of HBV does not occur within six months following infection, the person is considered to have a chronic infection [14].

In adults, CHB develops in 5% of those who have had acute hepatitis B, while 95% will recover, which is the opposite in newborns [15]. Cirrhosis or HCC can develop in approximately 25-40% of people with CHB infections [15]. The natural history of CHB infection can be characterized into four phases: (1) immune-tolerant phase, (2) HBeAg- positive immune-active phase, (3) inactive CHB phase, and (4) HBeAg-negative immune reactivation phase [8]. In the immune-tolerant phase, HBV-infected subjects are characterized by high levels of HBV DNA, positive HBeAg, but normal liver enzyme levels and a significant absence of inflammation or fibrosis in the liver. In the HBeAg-positive immune-active phase, patients infected with HBV are characterized by high liver enzyme levels and high HBV DNA levels due to liver damage [9]. The immune-inactive phase is reflected by the seroconversion from HBeAg to antibody to anti-HBe, normal liver enzyme levels, and low or undetectable HBV DNA levels. However, around 10–30% of those patients continue to have elevated liver enzyme and high HBV DNA levels and are therefore are defined as HBeAg-negative CHB patients [9].

In addition to acute and chronic hepatitis, HBV infection is also the etiological factor that causes liver cirrhosis and HCC. The annual incidence of liver cirrhosis is 2–10% when there is no antiviral treatment in CHB patients [16]. The risk of progression from compensated cirrhosis to decompensated cirrhosis is 3–5%, and the 5-year survival rate is only 14–35% in patients with decompensated cirrhosis [17].

Permanent liver inflammation plays an important role in the progression of CHB to cirrhosis and HCC. The innate immune response plays a role in the early stages of HBV infection and induces subsequent adaptive immune responses [18].

17.4 Antiviral drugs against HBV

The main goals of antiviral therapy are to improve the survival and the quality of life for CHB patients [19]. The suppression of HBV replication with antiviral treatment with normalization of liver enzymes results in an improvement in histology, so that the fibrosis is reversed or the HCC decreased [20].

"Functional therapy" is defined as the loss of HBsAg due to the occurrence of anti-HBs [20]. In fact, it is a realistic goal and can be achieved in a proportion of eligible CHB patients.

Indications for starting antiviral therapy are usually based on serum HBV DNA, liver enzyme levels, and severity of liver disease. In order to make the treatment decision, serial testing of liver function tests, HBV DNA and HBV antigens are required in addition to follow-up of patients [8]. Antiviral therapy is not recommended in CHB patients who are under the age of 30 and are in the immune-tolerant phase, defined by continuous normal liver enzymes, high levels of HBV DNA, and no biopsy damage [21]. CHB patients are also not treated in the inactive phase due to the absence of liver damage [8].

There are two types of treatment in CHB: using pegylated interferon (PEG-IFN), which is a subcutaneous injection treatment once a week for 48 weeks, and oral antiviral drugs, which are used for life but can be discontinued under certain conditions.

The advantage of PEG-IFN treatment is that the duration of treatment is short-term, and the treatment success rates are high, while the disadvantage is that the side effects are high and severe. PEG-IFN therapy produces side effects such as muscle aches, fever, nausea, vomiting, hair loss, and weight loss. It is a treatment method with a high success rate if used with close follow-up in selected patients with CHB [22]. Oral antivirals, on the other hand, have advantages such as ease of use and less side effects; however, they must be used for life and the treatment success rates are low [22]. They can be stopped under certain conditions. Anti-HBe seroconversion in positive HBeAg noncirrhosis oral antivirals may be discontinued 12 months after development. In these cases, patients should be closely monitored for the risk of acute exacerbation and still developing HCC. An optimal therapy was designed for individual patients. While physicians are planning therapy, they must take into account many factors including the side effects of the chosen drugs, the patients' characteristics, the treatment costs, the duration of treatment and the drug resistance.

There are six oral nucleos(t)ide analogues (NAs): lamivudine (LAM), adefovir (ADV), telbivudine (LdT), entecavir (ETV), tenofovir disoproxil fumarate (TDF), tenofovir alafenamide (TAF) [15]. They are shown in Table 17.1.

LAM was the first nucleoside analogue approved for the treatment of CHB by the Food and Drug Administration (FDA) in 1998. LAM even shows good antiviral effects in CHB patients with advanced liver disease. Resistance to LAM can be easily improved. It has been reported that LAM resistance can reach up to 80% after 5 years of treatment [23]. ADV was the second antiviral drug approved by the US FDA in 2002 for anti-HBV treatment. However, ADV also has a low genetic barrier and drug resistance can be easily improved, and on the other hand, its disadvantage is nephrotoxicity. [24]. However, long-term ADV has high drug resistance rate of up to 20–29% after 5-year treatment [25]. LdT is another nucleoside analogue for antiviral treatment of CHB. It has a proven reliable profile, is a drug that can be used in pregnancy, and has been used to prevent infectious mother-to-child transmission [25,26]. On the other

TABLE 17.1 The drugs used in chronic hepatitis B treatment.

Drug	Dose	Time
Pegylated interferon alfa-2a	135–180 ug/week	48 weeks
Pegylated interferon alfa-2b	1.5 mg/kg/week	48 weeks
Lamivudin	100 mg	*
Telbuvidin	600 mg	*
Entecavir	0.5-1 mg	*
Tenofovir disoproxil fumarate	245 mg	*
Tenofovir alafenamid	50 mg	*

CHB: chronic hepatitis B
When oral antivirals disappear HBsAg (anti-HBs positive or negative).

hand, long-term LdT treatment leads to high rates of drug resistance (34% after 3-year LdT therapy) [27]. When drug resistant develops in CHB patients, the clinical benefit of the treatment is reduced and hepatitis exacerbations and even liver failure may occur. Therefore, choosing potent and low-resistance antiviral drugs is highly recommended for treatment naive CHB patients.

Both ETV and TDF can strongly inhibit HBV replication and have a high genetic barrier to drug resistance. ETV has been commercially available since 2005 [28] and it has been shown to have a 3-year total resistance rate of 1.7–3.3% [29]. ETV suppresses HBV at least 100 times stronger than LAM or ADV [30]. Patients with LAM-resistance showed a high rate of ETV-resistance (51% vs. 1.2% 5-year treatment naive ETV therapy) [31]. TDF was approved for HBV treatment by the FDA in 2008 and is categorized as a pregnancy category B drug. TDF has high antiviral efficacy for CHB patients with LAM or LdT resistance [32]. TAF is a newly approved drug for the antiviral treatment of CHB. In 2017, TAF was approved for the treatment of CHB in adults [9]. TAF has lower bone and kidney abnormalities than TDF [33]. Numerous case reports of TDF-induced nephrotoxicity have been reported [34–37]. TAF is found at a lower dose in the circulation compared to TDF. Thus, kidney and bone toxicity decrease as there will be less systemic exposure.

Most patients require many years and often lifelong treatment to derive continued benefit. Long durations of treatment are associated with increasing risks of adverse reactions, antiviral drug resistance, costs, and nonadherence to medications. Potent drugs (TDF, TAF, or ETV) should be preferred in patients with high viral load. LAM, ADV and LdT have low barriers against HBV resistance therefore, they are not among the treatment options in international guidelines [8–10]. However, they are still among the CHB treatment options in the national guidelines of low-income countries manifestations, liver transplants, acute hepatitis B or severe CHB exacerbation [38].

The fuzzy-based preference ranking organization method for enrichment evaluations (PROMETHEE) method, which is one of the successful multicriteria decision-making techniques (MCDM), was applied by using the guidelines of the specified HBV treatment drugs in order to decrease the complexity of the selection of the effective HBV treatment. This method is based on evaluating multiple criteria with conflicting aims together and comparing the options to evaluate the most suitable alternative.

17.5 Fuzzy based PROMETHEE application results

The PROMETHEE method was first introduced by Professor Jean-Pierre Brans at a conference in Quebec, Canada in 1982. This method has also been compared to other multicriteria decision-making methods and has been proposed as one of the best because of its diversity in providing different kinds of preference functions to each criteria according to the decision maker's aims [39]. This model has been used extensively in the solutions of decision problems in the fields of medicine, business, education, transportation, and many more [40]. Recently, studies have been carried out using the fuzzy PROMETHEE model to solve multicriteria decision problems involving uncertainty [41–50]. Fuzzy PROMETHEE is a multicriteria decision-making technique that has paved the way for the analysis of vague data or linguistically expressed data. This method helps decision-makers make decisions based on the selection of criteria to evaluate alternatives. This technique is a powerful technique based on the importance of criteria to determine the most appropriate alternative. In a multicriteria problem, the most appropriate decision alternative is determined by modeling according to the information about the preferences and priorities of the decision makers. The information required for PROMETHEE is usually provided by analysts and decision makers. The model consists of a preference function associated with each criteria and weights that define their relative importance. The preference function allows the decision maker to choose whether a criteria is to be desired at the maximum or minimum level. Very important criteria can be ranked higher than less important ones. This order can also be very low, low, medium, high and very high, as shown in Table 17.2.

The criteria specified for the HBV treatment options specified in this study were determined by doctors specializing in infectious diseases. The weights assigned to each criteria were also used from the data observed by specialist doctors in infectious diseases. While the aim is defined as the minimum for the criteria that are expected to take low values, the goal is determined as the maximum for the criteria that are expected to take high values. Criteria that are important to be considered in treatment and their importance levels determined by the experts and the fuzzy scale used for these criteria are shown in Table 17.2.

A triangular fuzzy scale was used to obtain the weights of the criteria determined according to their importance. These data were then converted into numerical data for use in the PROMETHEE method using the Yager index. Then, using these data, the PROMETHEE method was applied, positive outranking flow, nega-

TABLE 17.2 Linguistic fuzzy scale and the selected importance weights of the criteria.

Linguistic scale	Triangular fuzzy scale	Importance weights of criteria
Very high	(0.75, 1, 1)	Compliance, previous treatment, drug resistance
High	(0.50, 0.75, 1)	Age, working condition, pregnancy, GFR, comorbidity, mental disorder, member of key population, HBV genotype
Medium	(0.25, 0.50, 0.75)	False prescription
Low	(0, 0.25, 0.50)	Drug-drug interaction, cancer, absorption, basal HBV DNA load
Very low	(0, 0, 0.25)	Coinfection

tive outranking flow and net ranking flow of alternatives were calculated, and the net order of alternatives was obtained, as seen in Table 17.3. TAF was determined as the best alternative with the highest net flow value of 0.0305, ETV was determined as the second-best HBV treatment drug with a net flow value of 0.0248 and TDF was determined as the third best alternative with a net flow value of 0.0177, while PEG-IFN ranked as the 7th and last alternative with a net flow value of –0.0375.

The strong and weak features of the HBV treatment options are shown in Fig. 17.1. In this figure, the criteria above 0-level express the positive aspects of the specified treatment option, while the criteria below 0-level indicate the

TABLE 17.3 Complete ranking result of the hepatitis B virus treatment alternatives.

Complete ranking	Drug	Net flow	Positive outranking flow	Negative outranking flow
1	Tenofovir alafenamide	0.0305	0.0346	0.0041
2	Entecavir	0.0248	0.0310	0.0061
3	Tenofovir disoproxil fumarate	0.0177	0.0262	0.0085
4	Lamivudine	–0.0054	0.0166	0.0220
5	Telbivudine	–0.0125	0.0119	0.0244
6	Adefovir	–0.0176	0.0093	0.0270
7	Pegylated interferon	–0.0375	0.0232	0.0608

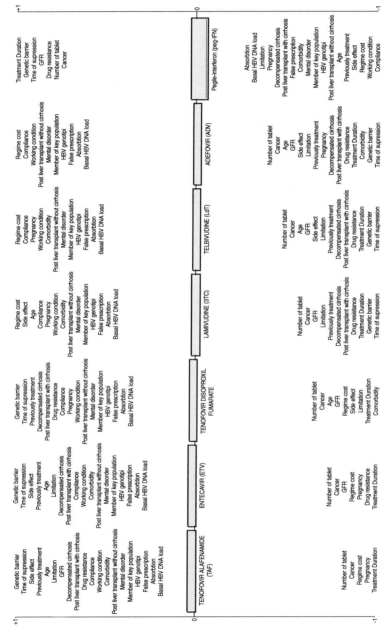

FIGURE 17.1   Fuzzy PROMETHEE evaluation results of chronic hepatitis B treatment options.

negative aspects of the specified treatment. Accordingly, it has been observed that TAF is superior to other treatment options in terms of numerous criteria. However, PEG-IFN was weaker than other treatment options with respect to many of the criteria.

While choosing drugs in the treatment of HBV patients, different criteria are considered important including the doctor, the treatment methods, and the host. Regime cost, side effects, number of tablets, dose frequency, treatment duration, plasma stability, plasma turnover, time of suppression, practicability, intravenous form, oral form, and drug-drug interaction were chosen as the treatment method–related criteria. Age, pregnancy, glomerular filtration rate, decompensated cirrhosis, post–liver transplant without cirrhosis, post–liver transplant with cirrhosis were selected as the host-related criteria. These are symptoms and phases of diseases in HBV patients. False prescription and inefficient drug combination were chosen as the doctor-related criteria. All these factors are important when selecting the treatment methods for HBV patients.

17.6 Conclusions

It was concluded that by using the fuzzy PROMETHEE method to evaluate the effectiveness of HBV regimens in the presence of different factors, TAF, ETV, TDF, LAM, LdT, ADV, and peg-IFN were found to be effective in the treatment of HBV infection, respectively.

The use of fuzzy PROMETHEE in health sciences is increasing rapidly due to its ability to quickly and reliably evaluate rough data in the real environment. This application can be easily adapted or modified by decision makers to enable the determination of the best regimens to be used in a patient-specific manner.

References

[1] C. Shih, C.C. Yang, G. Choijilsuren, C.H. Chang, A.T. Liou, Hepatitis B Virus, Trends Microbiol 26 (4) (2018) 386–387.

[2] S.Z. Wiktor, Viral hepatitis. In: K.K. Holmes, S. Bertozzi, B.R. Bloom, P. Jha, (eds.),Major Infectious Diseases, 3rd ed. Washington (DC): The International Bank for Reconstruction and Development/The World Bank, 2017, Chapter 16.

[3] World Health Organization. Guidelines for the prevention, care, and treatment of persons with chronic hepatitis B infection. World Health Organization, http://www.who.int/hiv/pub/hepatitis/hepatitis-b-guidelines/en/. AccessedMarch 2, 2020.

[4] A. Hampel, P. Solbach, M. Cornberg, R.E. Schmidt, G.M. Behrens, A. Jablonka, Current seroprevalence, vaccination and predictive value of liver enzymes for hepatitis B among refugees in Germany, Bundesgesundheitsblatt 59 (2016) 578–583.

[5] J.D. Stanaway, A.D. Flaxman, M. Naghavi, C. Fitzmaurice, T. Vos, I. Abubakar, et al. The global burden of viral hepatitis from 1990 to 2013: findings from the Global Burden Disease Study, 2013, Lancet 388 (2016) 1081–1088.

[6] D.Q. Huang, S.G. Lim, Hepatitis B: Who to treat? A critical review of international guidelines, Liver Int 40 (Suppl. 1) (2020) 5–14.

[7] M. Buti, L. Roade, M. Riveiro-Barciela, R. Esteban, Optimal management of chronic hepatitis B patients receiving nucleos(t)ide analogues, Liver Int 40 (1) (2020) 15–21.

[8] N.A. Terrault, A.S.F. Lok, B.J. McMahon, K.M. Chang, J.P. Hwang, M.M. Jonas, et al. Update on prevention, diagnosis, and treatment of chronic hepatitis B: AASLD 2018 hepatitis B guidance, Hepatology (Baltimore, MD) 67 (4) (2018) 1560–1599.

[9] European Association for the Study of the LiverClinical practice guidelines on the management of hepatitis B virus infection, J. Hepatol. 67 (2) (2017) 370–398.

[10] S.K. Sarin, M. Kumar, G.K. Lau, Z. Abbas, H.L. Chan, C.J. Chen, D.S. Chen, H.L. Chen, P.J. Chen, R.N. Chien, A.K. Dokmeci, E. Gane, J.L. Hou, W. Jafri, J. Jia, J.H. Kim, C.L. Lai, H.C. Lee, S.G. Lim, C.J. Liu, S. Locarnini, M. Al Mahtab, R. Mohamed, M. Omata, J. Park, T. Piratvisuth, B.C. Sharma, J. Sollano, F.S. Wang, L. Wei, M.F. Yuen, S.S. Zheng, J.H. Kao, Asian-Pacific clinical practice guidelines on the management of hepatitis B: a 2015 update, Hepatol. Int. 10 (2016) 1–98.

[11] Polaris Observatory—CDA Foundation, Global prevalence, treatment, and prevention of hepatitis B virus infection in 2016: a modelling study, Lancet Gastroenterol. Hepatol. 3 (6) (2018) 383–403.

[12] M.L. Chang, Y.F. Liaw, Hepatitis B flares in chronic hepatitis B: pathogenesis, natural course, and management, J Hepatol 61 (6) (2014 Dec) 1407–1417.

[13] J. Wu, M. Han, J. Li, X. Yang, Yang D, Immunopathogenesis of HBV Infection, Adv. Exp. Med. Biol. 1179 (2020) 71–107.

[14] S. Yapali, N. Talaat, A.S. Lok, Management of hepatitis B: our practice and how it relates to the guidelines, Clin. Gastroenterol. Hepatol. 12 (1) (2014) 16–26.

[15] Mysore KR1, Leung DH2 Hepatitis B and C, Clin. Liver Dis. 22 (4) (2018) 703–722.

[16] Y.S. Hsu, R.N. Chien, C.T. Yeh, I.S. Sheen, H.Y. Chiou, C.M. Chu, et al. Long-term outcome after spontaneous HBeAg seroconversion in patients with chronic hepatitis B, Hepatology (Baltimore, MD) 35 (6) (2002) 1522–1527.

[17] G. Fattovich, F. Bortolotti, Donato F, Natural history of chronic hepatitis B: special emphasis on disease progression and prognostic factors, J. Hepatol. 48 (2) (2008) 335–352.

[18] L.G. Guidotti, F.V. Chisari, Noncytolytic control of viral infections by the innate and adaptive immune response, Annu. Rev. Immunol. 19 (2001) 65–91.

[19] G. Grossi, M. Vigano, A. Loglio, P. Lampertico, Hepatitis B virus long-term impact of antiviral therapy nucleot(s)ide analogues (NUCs), Liver Int. 37 (1) (2017) 45–51.

[20] W.K. Seto, A.J. Hui, V.W. Wong, G.L. Wong, K.S. Liu, C.L. Lai, et al. Treatment cessation of entecavir in Asian patients with hepatitis B e antigen negative chronic hepatitis B: a multicenter prospective study, Gut 64 (4) (2015) 667–672.

[21] G.L. Wong, Management of chronic hepatitis B patients in immunotolerant phase: what latest guidelines recommend, Clin. Mol. Hepatol. 24 (2) (2018) 108–113.

[22] F. Sarıgül, U. Üser, M. Sayan, et al. Does pegylated-interferon still have high efficacy treatment properties against chronic hepatitis B?, J. Viral Hepat. 24 (3) (2018) 90–95.

[23] M. Sayan, M. Akhan SC, Meric, Naturally occurring amino–acid substitutions to nucleos(t)ide analogues in treatment naive Turkish patients with chronic hepatitis B, J. Viral Hepat. 17 (2010) 23–27.

[24] Trepo C, A brief history of hepatitis milestones, Liver Int. 34 (1) (2014) 29–37.

[25] G.R. Han, H.X. Jiang, X. Yue, Y. Ding, C.M. Wang, G.J. Wang, et al. Efficacy and safety of telbivudine treatment: an open-label, prospective study in pregnant women for the prevention of perinatal transmission of hepatitis B virus infection, J. Viral Hepat. 22 (9) (2015) 754–762.

[26] P. Marcellin, T.T. Chang, S.G. Lim, W. Sievert, M. Tong, S. Arterburn, et al. Long-term efficacy and safety of adefovir dipivoxil for the treatment of hepatitis B e antigen-positive chronic hepatitis B, Hepatology 48 (3) (2008) 750–758.

[27] W.K. Seto, C.L. Lai, J. Fung, D.K. Wong, J.C. Yuen, I.F. Hung, et al. Significance of HBV DNA levels at 12 weeks of telbivudine treatment and the 3 years treatment outcome, J. Hepatol. 55 (3) (2011) 522–528.

[28] K.H. Kim, N.D. Kim, Seong BL, Discovery and development of anti-HBV agents and their resistance, Molecules 15 (9) (2010) 5878–5908.

[29] O. Yokosuka, K. Takaguchi, S. Fujioka, M. Shindo, K. Chayama, H. Kobashi, et al. Long-term use of entecavir in nucleoside-naive Japanese patients with chronic hepatitis B infection, J. Hepatol. 52 (6) (2010) 791–799.

[30] D.J. Tenney, S.M. Levine, R.E. Rose, A.W. Walsh, S.P. Weinheimer, L. Discotto, et al. Clinical emergence of entecavir-resistant hepatitis B virus requires additional substitutions in virus already resistant to Lamivudine, Antimicrob. Agents Chemother. 48 (9) (2004) 3498–3507.

[31] D.J. Tenney, R.E. Rose, C.J. Baldick, K.A. Pokornowski, B.J. Eggers, J. Fang, et al. Long-term monitoring shows hepatitis B virus resistance to entecavir in nucleoside-naive patients is rare through 5 years of therapy, Hepatology 49 (5) (2009) 1503–1514.

[32] M.F. Yuen, C.L. Lai, Treatment of chronic hepatitis B: evolution over two decades, J. Gastroenterol. Hepatol. 26 (1) (2011) 138–143.

[33] Y.C. Hsu, M.T. Wei, M.H. Nguyen, Tenofovir alafenamide as compared to tenofovir disoproxil fumarate in the management of chronic hepatitis B with recent trends in patient demographics, Exp. Rev. Gastroenterol. Hepatol. 11 (11) (2017) 999–1008.

[34] S. Zheng, L. Liu, J. Lu, X. Zhang, H. Shen, H. Zhang, Y. Xue, L. Lin, Efficacy and safety of tenofovir disoproxil fumarate in Chinese patients with chronic hepatitis B virus infection: a 2-year prospective study, Medicine 98 (42) (2019 Oct) e17590.

[35] B. Matłosz, J.D. Kowalska, E. B kowska, E. Firl g-Burkacka, A. Vassilenko, A. Horban, Discontinuation of tenofovir due to nephrotoxicity: insight into 12 years of clinical practice, Przegl Epidemiol. 73 (2) (2019) 249–255.

[36] Novick TK1, M.J. Choi, A.Z. Rosenberg, B.A. McMahon, D. Fine, M.G. Atta, Tenofovir alafenamide nephrotoxicity in an HIV-positive patient: A case report, Medicine 96 (36) (2017) e8046.

[37] G.L.-H. Wong, W.-K. Seto, V.W.-S. Wong, M.-F. Yuen, H.L.-Y. Chan, Review article: long-term safety of oral anti-viral treatment for chronic hepatitis B aliment, Pharmacol. Ther. 47 (6) (2018) 730–737, doi: 10.1111/apt.14497.

[38] Health Ministry of Turkey. Health implementation guideline (March 25, 2017), p. 30018. www.sgk.gov.tr. Accessed March 2, 2020.

[39] J.P. Brans, P. Vincke, A preference ranking organisation method: The PROMETHEE method for MCDM, Managen Sci. 31 (1985) 647–656.

[40] A. Asemi, M.S. Baba, R. Abdullah, N. Idris, 3rd, Fuzzy multi criteria decision making applications: a review study, Conference, Langkawi, Malaysia, (2014).

[41] D. Ozsahin, K. Nyakuwanikwa, T. Wallace, I. Ozsahin, Evaluation and simulation of colon cancer treatment techniques with Fuzzy PROMETHEE, 2019 Advances in Science and Engineering Technology International Conferences, 2019, pp. 1–6.

[42] M. Sani Musa, D. Uzun Ozsahin, I. Ozsahin, A comparison for liver cancer treatment alternatives, 2019 Advances in, Science and Engineering Technology International Conferences (ASET) (2019) 1–4, doi: 10.1109/ICASET.2019.8714471.

[43] I. Ozsahin, D. Uzun Ozsahin, M. Maisaini, G. Mok, Fuzzy PROMETHEE analysis of leukemia treatment techniques. World Canc. Res. J. (2019), https://www.wcrj.net/article/1315. Accessed July 4, 2019.

[44] I. Ozsahin, D. Uzun Ozsahin, K. Nyakuwanikwa, T. Wallace Simbanegav, Fuzzy PROMETHEE for Ranking Pancreatic Cancer Treatment Techniques, 2019 Advances in Science and

Engineering Technology International Conferences (ASET), Arab Emirates, Dubai, United, (2019), pp. 1–5.

[45] B. Uzun, I. Ozsahin, D. Uzun, Evaluating lung cancer treatment techniques using fuzzy PRO-METHEE approach, 13th International Conference on Theory and Application of Fuzzy Systems and, Soft Computing—ICAFS (2018) 209–215, doi: 10.1007/978-3-030-04164-9_29.

[46] D. Uzun Ozsahin, I. Ozsahin, A fuzzy PROMETHEE approach for breast cancer treatment techniques, Int. J. Health Sci. Res. (2018) 29–32.

[47] D. Uzun, B. Uzun, M. Sani, I. Ozsahin, Evaluating X-ray based medical imaging devices with fuzzy preference ranking organization method for enrichment evaluations, Int. J. Adv. Comp. Sci. Appl. 9 (3) (2018) 10.14569/ijacsa.2018.090302.

[48] D. Ozsahin, N. Isa, B. Uzun, I. Ozsahin, Effective analysis of image reconstruction algorithms in nuclear medicine using fuzzy PROMETHEE, in 2018 Advances in Science and Engineering Technology International Conferences (ASET) (2019), pp. 1–5.

[49] I. Ozsahin, T. Sharif, D. Ozsahin, B. Uzun, Evaluation of solid-state detectors in medical imaging with fuzzy PROMETHEE, J. Instrument. 14 (1) (2019) C01019, doi: 10.1088/1748-0221/14/01/c01019.

[50] M. Taiwo Mubarak, I. Ozsahin, D. Uzun Ozsahin, Evaluation of Sterilization Methods for Medical Devices, 2019 Advances in Science and Engineering Technology International Conferences (ASET), IEEE Xplore, Dubai, United Arab Emirates, (2019), pp. 1–4.

Chapter 18

Evaluation of migraine drugs using MCDM methods

Dilber Uzun Ozsahin[a,b,c], Lafi Hamidat[b], Funsho David Alimi[b], Berna Uzun[a,d] and Ilker Ozsahin[a,b,e]

[a]DESAM Institute, Near East University, Turkish Republic of Northern Cyprus, Nicosia, Turkey; [b]Department of Biomedical Engineering, Near East University, Turkish Republic of Northern Cyprus, Nicosia, Turkey; [c]Medical Diagnostic Imaging Department, College of Health Sciences, University of Sharjah, Sharjah, United Arab Emirates; [d]Department of Mathematics, Near East University, Turkish Republic of Northern Cyprus, Nicosia, Turkey; [e]Brain Health Imaging Institute, Department of Radiology, Weill Cornell Medicine, New York, NY, United States

18.1 Introduction

Some individuals cannot distinguish between headaches and migraines. The term migraine is misused in patients and migraine is used interchangeably for headache in others. Nevertheless, these two conditions are defined and the families derive from the same source. Headache is a common term for headaches of any form whereas migraines are a special type of headache that needs to be uniquely treated. It is important to define both in layman's terms to understand the simple difference between headache and migraines. In the basic description of headache, it is defined as perceived pain on either side of the head or in either part of the brain. Its characteristics may mean that it is located around the brain at a specific position with pain radiating from that particular location [1].

Migraines, on the other hand, can be referred to as headache, with throbbing symptoms or a sensation of discomfort in one section of the head by nature. Tiredness and hearing loss in the patient can be treated. Headache, however, has no warning sign (prodrome) because only common migraines occur and are not identified with associated symptoms like nausea, vomiting, stomach pain, and fatigue. Despite their differences, migraines are a type of headache and are usually from the same family. It is also important to note that other forms of headaches are wave, pain, sinus, migraine, etc.

Migraines are more common than traditional headaches. It is recognized by medical practitioners as a complex neurological disorder which can affect the entire body and cause several symptoms without any indication of headache. Most people only misdiagnose and mistake migraine because of certain health issues. Despite multiple ongoing studies on migraine causes, there is however

Applications of Multi-Criteria Decision-Making Theories in Healthcare and Biomedical Engineering.
http://dx.doi.org/10.1016/B978-0-12-824086-1.00018-9

no consensus on migraine causes. Therefore, there is currently not a very good diagnostic and screening process. For migraine cases, the health practitioner may prescribe medicines or other treatments to treat the disease and its symptoms to minimize the impact and to allow people to carry out their day-to-day activities.

18.2   Definition and characteristics of migraines

Migraines are headaches that affect half the brain. It is, of course, a serious headache that affects the patient, because this headache mentally impacts the patient in such a way that the patient becomes confused, thinking about how possible it is for half of the head to affected with the pain while the other half is not. Migraine headaches can therefore be simply defined as a recurrent type of headache which the pain continuously affects one part of the brain. This may be attributed to nausea and the patient's visual deficiency, an attribute commonly used to describe migraine headaches as classic/unconventional migraine attacks or migraine attacks. Classic and nonclassic migraines were among the earliest terms used to describe migraines until recently when they were replaced by migraines with auras [2].

The human body can be targeted for up to 4-72 hours. Mild to moderate or very intense pain or palpitations or spikes on the pain's side are typical signs of unilateral migraine. According to [3], there may be other effects of other kinds of migraines, including fear of light or phobia. Some characteristics include supporting menstrual relationship, a lowering incidence of breastfeeding [4], an increase of discomfort in all physical exercises (also experienced in men). It is paramount to understand the medicines used in these headaches and try to choose accordingly to benefit the patients.

18.3   Causes and triggers of migraine

No specific cause for migraines is known. Also, there is no consensus on what causes migraines. Nevertheless, it is widely considered to be a consequence of abnormal neural processes that briefly change nerve pulsations, hormones, and blood vessels of the brain. The potential explanations for such irregular neurological events have no obvious causes, though all scientists know irregular neurological causes migraines. Symptoms of migraines may be divided into biochemical, cognitive, physical, nutritional, ambient, and pharmaceutical causes. However, the majority of migraines are related to a trigger factor, but the person can manage it so that the triggers are understood and make them more sensitive. The first approach to prevent the occurrence or recurrence of migraines is to use drugs, while the second solution breaks down the general series of chemical events triggering migraine attacks.

Triptans are more migraine-specific but there are also triptans that are more robust in order to avoid a reoccurrence of migraines. In these circumstances, the two triptans also provide migraine relief in relation to other medications for patients.

18.4   Overview of migraine medications

Because migraines are a serious health issue that can put people's lives and daily activities at risk, patients can receive different medication forms. To treat migraine symptoms, two methods are employed. Patients may be encouraged to take preventive therapy when a person has migraine attacks more than once a week or when the patient has migraines that are not responsive to abortive medications.

18.4.1   Different type of migraine medications

There are two primary forms of treatment for aggression in migraines: first, to prevent the occurrence or recurrence of migraines is to use drugs, and second, to break down the overall series of chemical events triggering migraine attacks. Below is a list of over-the-counter medications for migraine pain relief, including nonsteroidal anti-inflammatory drugs (NSAIDS) and caffeine:

- Ibuprofen (Motrin)
- Naproxen (Naprosyn, Anaprox, Anaprox DS)
- Aspirin
- Acetaminophen (Tylenol)
- A mixture of both these medications.

However, the pain could worsen if patients regularly use these analgesics and NSAIDs. Such drugs are primarily used for therapeutic purposes so that the blood vessel dilatation in the brain is not fixed. Ergotamines and triptans are used for blood-vessel constriction.

Ergot alkaloids are strong drugs that inhibit the blood flow of the brain, including medicines such as Ergotamine Tartrate (Cafergot), D.H.E. 45, and Migranal Nasal Spray. Ergot alkaloids are efficient. Some of these ergots can cause nausea. Patients who cannot tolerate this side effect also use ergotamines in combination with other medications to prevent diarrhea [5-8].

Triptans are known to be more powerful because they not only cause blood-vessel constrictions, but the overall sequence of chemical reactions that contribute to migraines is also disrupted. There are some exceptional triptans for serotonin receptors:

- Axert, which stands for Almotriptan
- Relpax, which stands for Eletriptan
- Frova, which stands for Frovatriptan
- Amerge, which stands for Naratriptan
- Maxalt, Maxalt-MLT which stands for Rizatriptan
- Imitrex, Zecuity, which stands for Sumatriptan
- Zomig, Zomig-ZMT, which stands for Zolmitriptan

Triptans were intended to be more migraine-specific, but some triptans are restarted to avoid the reoccurrence of migraines. Despite this, both triptans are equally effective in providing migraine relief to patients compared to other drugs (ergotamines). Other relief-enhancing drugs such as vasoconstrictor isometheptene mucate, sedative dichloralphenazone, and analgesic acetaminophen (Midrin), antihistamines (diphenhydramine), and nonsedatives (loratadine/Claritin) had been produced.

18.5 Literature review

The PROMETHEE ranking claims to be one of the most common methods for making decisions, created as an explicit method to achieve the ranking of partial or complete combinations of real-world events. Thiago and Ana [9] applied PROMETHEE on resource management using longitudinal information collected at a public hospital in Brazil. It was assumed that PROMETHEE would help decision-makers to choose the right solutions to address the problems caused by overcrowding in hospital emergency departments and that this approach could be applied to other hospital departments [10] [11] used multiple multicriteria assessment approaches to assess the implementation of healthcare facilities. The MCDM methods selected for analysis were ELECTRE, PROMETHEE, and AHP. The findings of their study showed that PROMETHEE is a good MCDM method for use in health provider research, with 95% of users choosing PROMETHEE algorithms to choose healthcare services [10,12-15].

There have been few studies based on the use of multicriteria decision-making applications on healthcare. Analysis and the selection of the solid-state detectors in medical imaging [16], lung cancer treatment techniques [17], evaluation of the breast cancer treatment techniques [18], X-ray based medical imaging devices analysis [19], image reconstruction algorithms in nuclear medicine analysis [20], cancer treatment techniques analysis [11], nuclear medicine imaging devices analysis [21], colon cancer treatment techniques analysis [22], liver cancer treatment techniques analysis [23], pancreatic cancer treatment techniques analysis [24], and sterilization methods for medical devices analysis [25] are among the few studies.

The most widely used techniques for the production of images in nuclear medicine were then compared using the fuzzy PROMETHEE approach. The fuzzy choice rating method for enrichment research is used for the evaluation of X-ray medical imaging systems. They used fluorescent PROMETHEE to evaluate the image quality criteria for certain radiological devices to determine the performance, capacity, and disadvantages of each device. Precision, sensitivity, cost of medications, and radiation dose as well as instrument costs were the criteria used for the analysis. The criteria were identified and assessed based on patient and hospital impacts. The Yager Index was used to display the magnitude of each alternative criteria. In their studies, they chose to use techniques for surgical, radiotherapy, chemotherapy, and hormonal therapy to treat breast cancer by using the overall survival rate of every technique, side effects, cost, and duration of treatment. Based on their criteria, their research findings rated surgery as the most efficient treatment for breast cancer patients with a net flux of 0.5156.

18.6   Materials and methods: TOPSIS

In the classical TOPSIS method, we assume that ratings and weights are well represented by numerical data for any problem to be resolved by a single decision-maker. Complexity arises for more than one decision-maker, as the preferred solution must be agreed upon by stakeholders who often have different objectives. A single TOPSIS decision-maker algorithm will be used for this study.

This study aims to assess migraine medicine using a fluorogenic TOPSIS methodology that includes criteria such as side effects, reaction to medicines and costs, tablet volume, absorption, capacity, dosing time, and half-life. The weight of each criteria was defined as shown in Table 18.1 with a triangular fuzzy scale. In addition, with the Fuzzy scale, side effects and efficacy data were defined.

The migraine drug dataset was collected (see Table 18.2) and fuzzy data (side effect and efficacy and weights of importance) was defuzzified with the Yager index for the use of the TOPSIS technique. Then, the migraine drug data was normalized as seen in Table 18.3 and the weighted normalized drug matrix has been shown in Table 18.4.

Positive and negative ideal solutions of the migraine drugs are shown in Table 18.5 and Table 18.6.

TABLE 18.1 Selected fuzzy scale for the linguistic data.

Linguistic scale for evaluation	Triangular fuzzy scale	
Very high (VH)	(0.75, 1, 1)	Drug-drug interaction, side effect, efficacy
High (H)	(0.50, 0.75, 1)	Dose frequency, number of tablets
Medium (M)	(0.25, 0.50, 0.75)	
Low (L)	(0, 0.25, 0.50)	Cost, absorption, half-life
Very low (VL)	(0, 0, 0.25)	

TABLE 18.2 Dataset of the migraine drugs.

Drugs	Number of tablets	Half-life (h)	Dose frequency	Efficacy	Cost ($)	Absorption (%)	Drug-Drug (D-D) interaction	Side effect
Aspirin	5	5	300-900 mg	M	3.22	75	505	L
Paracetamol	8	1-3	500 mg	M	3.09	70	179	M
Diclofenac	4	12	50 mg	M	6.98	65	551	L
Excedrin Migraine	2	2	377 mg	H	3.37	40	668	M
Flurbiprofen	1	4.7-5.7	150-200 mg	H	21.8	45	449	L
Ibuprofen	48	1.8-2.0	300-400 mg	VH	7.74	62	459	L
Naproxen	6	12-17	750 mg	L	2.24	95	518	L
Almotriptan	9	3-4	12.5 mg	H	174	70	229	M
Naratriptan	2	6	2.5-5mg	H	360	70	196	H
Eletriptan	2	4	40 mg	H	399	50	273	H
Rizatriptan	6	2-3	10-20 mg	H	29.4	70	175	H
Frovatriptan	3	26	7.5 mg	H	513	20-30	204	VH
Sumatriptan	1	2.5	50-300 mg	VH	618	10	655	M
Zolmitriptan	6	2.5-3	2.5-10 mg	VH	112	75	241	H
Ergotamine	3	2	8 mg	VH	96	60	587	VH
Propranolol	5	4	160-320 mg	M	113	85	1087	H
Atenolol	3	6-7	50-200 mg	M	104	50	953	H
Metoprolol	9	3-4	100 mg	M	2	45	1023	H
Nadolol	3	20-40 hours	80 mg	M	6	30	963	M
Timolol	6	2.5-5 hours	10-30 mg	M	2.5	60	1016	M
Pizotifen	1	23 hours	500 µg-1.5 mg	H	2	80	N/A	H
Botulinum Toxin type A	Injection	230-260 min	100 [USP'U]/1	H	397	75	377	H
Metoclopramide	4	5-6 hours	10 mg	M	105	80	695	L
Domperidone	3	7 hours	250-500 mic /kg	M	4.5	15	350	M

TABLE 18.3 Normalized decision matrix of the migraine drugs.

Aim	Min	Max	Min	Max	Min	Max	Min	Min
Drugs/Criteria	Number of tablets	Half-life	Dose frequency	Efficacy	Cost	Absorption	D-D inter-action	Side effect
Aspirin	0.0942	0.0200	0.4754	0.1507	0.0030	0.2455	0.1719	0.0854
Paracetamol	0.1507	0.0080	0.3961	0.1507	0.0028	0.2292	0.0609	0.1708
Diclofenac	0.0753	0.0479	0.0396	0.1507	0.0064	0.2128	0.1876	0.0854
Excedrin Migraine	0.0377	0.0080	0.2987	0.2260	0.0031	0.1310	0.2274	0.1708
Flurbiprofen	0.0188	0.0208	0.1386	0.2260	0.0201	0.1473	0.1528	0.0854
Ibuprofen	0.9041	0.0076	0.2773	0.2773	0.0071	0.2030	0.1562	0.0854
Naproxen	0.1130	0.0579	0.5942	0.0753	0.0021	0.3110	0.1763	0.0854
Almotriptan	0.1695	0.0140	0.0099	0.2260	0.1602	0.2292	0.0780	0.1708
Naratriptan	0.0377	0.0239	0.0030	0.2260	0.3314	0.2292	0.0667	0.2562
Eletriptan	0.0377	0.0160	0.0317	0.2260	0.3674	0.1637	0.0929	0.2562
Rizatriptan	0.1130	0.0100	0.0119	0.2260	0.0271	0.2292	0.0596	0.2562
Frovatriptan	0.0565	0.1038	0.0059	0.2260	0.4723	0.0818	0.0694	0.3143
Sumatriptan	0.0188	0.0100	0.1386	0.2773	0.5690	0.0327	0.2230	0.1708
Zolmitriptan	0.1130	0.0110	0.0050	0.2773	0.1031	0.2455	0.0820	0.2562
Ergotamine	0.0565	0.0080	0.0063	0.2773	0.0884	0.1964	0.1998	0.3143
Propranolol	0.0942	0.0160	0.1901	0.1507	0.1040	0.2783	0.3700	0.2562
Atenolol	0.0565	0.0259	0.0990	0.1507	0.0958	0.1637	0.3244	0.2562

(Continued)

TABLE 18.3 Normalized decision matrix of the migraine drugs. (Cont.)

Aim	Min	Max	Min	Max	Min	Max	Min	Max	Min	Min
Metoprolol	0.1695	0.0140	0.0792	0.1507	0.0018	0.1473	0.3482	0.1708		
Nadolol	0.0565	0.1197	0.0634	0.1507	0.0055	0.0982	0.3278	0.1708		
Timolol	0.1130	0.0150	0.0158	0.1507	0.0023	0.1964	0.3458	0.1708		
Pizotifen	0.0377	0.0918	0.0008	0.2260	0.0018	0.2619	0.0000	0.2562		
Botulinum Toxin type A	0.0000	0.9777	0.0004	0.2260	0.3655	0.2455	0.1283	0.2562		
Metoclo-pramide	0.0753	0.0219	0.0079	0.1507	0.0967	0.2619	0.2366	0.0854		
Domperidone	0.0565	0.0279	0.0003	0.1507	0.0041	0.0491	0.1191	0.1708		

TABLE 18.4 Weighted normalized decision matrix of the migraine drugs.

Drugs/ Criteria	Number of tablets	Half- life	Dose frequency	Efficacy	Cost	Absorption	D-D interaction	Side effect
Aspirin	0.0141	0.0010	0.0712	0.0277	0.0001	0.0123	0.0316	0.0157
Paracetamol	0.0226	0.0004	0.0593	0.0277	0.0001	0.0114	0.0112	0.0314
Diclofenac	0.0113	0.0024	0.0059	0.0277	0.0003	0.0106	0.0344	0.0157
Excedrin Migraine	0.0056	0.0004	0.0447	0.0415	0.0002	0.0065	0.0418	0.0314
Flurbiprofen	0.0028	0.0010	0.0208	0.0415	0.0010	0.0074	0.0281	0.0157
Ibuprofen	0.1353	0.0004	0.0415	0.0509	0.0004	0.0101	0.0287	0.0157
Naproxen	0.0169	0.0029	0.0890	0.0138	0.0001	0.0155	0.0324	0.0157
Almotriptan	0.0254	0.0007	0.0015	0.0415	0.0080	0.0114	0.0143	0.0314
Naratriptan	0.0056	0.0012	0.0004	0.0415	0.0165	0.0114	0.0123	0.0471
Eletriptan	0.0056	0.0008	0.0047	0.0415	0.0183	0.0082	0.0171	0.0471
Rizatriptan	0.0169	0.0005	0.0018	0.0415	0.0014	0.0114	0.0109	0.0471
Frovatriptan	0.0085	0.0052	0.0009	0.0415	0.0236	0.0041	0.0128	0.0577
Sumatriptan	0.0028	0.0005	0.0208	0.0509	0.0284	0.0016	0.0409	0.0314
Zolmitriptan	0.0169	0.0005	0.0007	0.0509	0.0051	0.0123	0.0151	0.0471
Ergotamine	0.0085	0.0004	0.0009	0.0509	0.0044	0.0098	0.0367	0.0577
Propranolol	0.0141	0.0008	0.0285	0.0277	0.0052	0.0139	0.0679	0.0471
Atenolol	0.0085	0.0013	0.0148	0.0277	0.0048	0.0082	0.0596	0.0471

(Continued)

TABLE 18.4 Weighted normalized decision matrix of the migraine drugs. (*Cont.*)

Drugs/ Criteria	Number of tablets	Half- life	Dose frequency	Efficacy	Cost	Absorption	D-D interaction	Side effect
Metoprolol	0.0254	0.0007	0.0119	0.0277	0.0001	0.0074	0.0639	0.0314
Nadolol	0.0085	0.0060	0.0095	0.0277	0.0003	0.0049	0.0602	0.0314
Timolol	0.0169	0.0007	0.0024	0.0277	0.0001	0.0098	0.0635	0.0314
Pizotifen	0.0056	0.0046	0.0001	0.0415	0.0001	0.0131	0.0000	0.0471
Botulinum toxin type A	0.0000	0.0488	0.0001	0.0415	0.0182	0.0123	0.0236	0.0471
Metoclopramide	0.0113	0.0011	0.0012	0.0277	0.0048	0.0131	0.0434	0.0157
Domperidone	0.0085	0.0014	0.0000	0.0277	0.0002	0.0025	0.0219	0.0314

TABLE 18.5 Positive ideal solution for migraine drugs.

Number of tablets	Half-life	Dose frequency	Efficacy	Cost	Absorption	D-D interaction	Side effect
0.0000	0.0488	0.0000	0.0509	0.0001	0.0155	0.0000	0.0157

TABLE 18.6 Negative ideal solution for migraine drugs.

Number of tablets	Half-life	Dose frequency	Efficacy	Cost	Absorption	D-D interaction	Side effect
0.1353	0.0004	0.0890	0.0138	0.0284	0.0016	0.0679	0.0577

18.7 Results and discussion

The distance between alternative migraine drugs and the positive ideal solution and the distance between alternative migraine drugs and the negative ideal solution have been calculated (Table 18.7) in order to obtain the relative closeness to the positive ideal solution of each alternative.

Ranking results of the migraine drugs have been obtained according to their relative closeness to the positive ideal solution (R_i) under the given criteria and the importance weights as shown in Table 18.8.

The preferable alternative is the one with the highest R_i. This study shows that Botulinum toxin Type A is the first alternative between the migraine drugs with an R_i value of 0.8004, and Pizotifen is the second best alternative with an R_i value of 0.7613, if the decision-maker gives less priority to cost, absorption, and half-life of the alternatives. However, Ibuprofen with a 0.3667 value of R_i should be the preferred drug between the migraine drugs.

While this study has successfully accomplished its objectives of comparing alternative migraine drugs under specific conditions, preferred methods of classification, like the TOPSIS technique, are typically not intended for a single diagnosis. They are structured and work to support care practitioners or other appropriate decision-makers in making informed decisions about the delivery of medications or other alternative treatments that may be unique to the patient for better therapy. As the analysis from this research has shown, of the 24 chosen alternatives, the best alternative migraine drug is Botulinum toxin Type A due to its outstanding efficacy characteristics, while the worst in the category is

TABLE 18.7 The distance of the alternatives from the positive ideal solution and the negative ideal solution.

Migraine drugs	d_i^-	d_i^+	$d_i^- + d_i^+$
Aspirin	0.1386	0.0953	0.2339
Paracetamol	0.1364	0.0854	0.2218
Diclofenac	0.1620	0.0638	0.2257
Excedrin Migraine	0.1475	0.0808	0.2283
Flurbiprofen	0.1647	0.0605	0.2252
Ibuprofen	0.0883	0.1524	0.2407
Naproxen	0.1344	0.1128	0.2472
Almotriptan	0.1568	0.0598	0.2166
Naratriptan	0.1699	0.0617	0.2316
Eletriptan	0.1659	0.0641	0.2300
Rizatriptan	0.1630	0.0619	0.2249
Frovatriptan	0.1665	0.0684	0.2349
Sumatriptan	0.1581	0.0754	0.2335
Zolmitriptan	0.1635	0.0621	0.2257
Ergotamine	0.1638	0.0747	0.2385
Propranolol	0.1391	0.0974	0.2365
Atenolol	0.1502	0.0877	0.2379
Metoprolol	0.1406	0.0897	0.2303
Nadolol	0.1555	0.0807	0.2363
Timolol	0.1526	0.0863	0.2389
Pizotifen	0.1765	0.0554	0.2319
Botulinum Toxin type A	0.1778	0.0444	0.2222
Metoclopramide	0.1623	0.0697	0.2320
Domperidone	0.1668	0.0613	0.2280

Ibuprofen, due to its poor efficacy with respect to most of its performed characteristics. Yet again, this finding depends on the generic weight used on the criteria and the general considerations regarded prior to medication administration; however, the weights may be adjusted to obtain a more patient-specific treatment, depending on the patient's wishes and health status.

TABLE 18.8 Ranking results of the migraine drugs using the TOPSIS technique.

Ranking	Migraine drugs	R_i
1	Botulinum toxin type A	0.8004
2	Pizotifen	0.7613
3	Naratriptan	0.7336
4	Flurbiprofen	0.7313
4	Domperidone	0.7313
6	Rizatriptan	0.7248
7	Zolmitriptan	0.7247
8	Almotriptan	0.7239
9	Eletriptan	0.7214
10	Diclofenac	0.7176
11	Frovatriptan	0.7089
12	Metoclopramide	0.6995
13	Ergotamine	0.6869
14	Sumatriptan	0.6772
15	Nadolol	0.6583
16	Excedrin Migraine	0.6461
17	Timolol	0.6387
18	Atenolol	0.6314
19	Paracetamol	0.6150
20	Metoprolol	0.6106
21	Aspirin	0.5925
22	Propranolol	0.5883
23	Naproxen	0.5437
24	Ibuprofen	0.3667

References

[1] R. Ryan, G. Geraud, J. Goldstein, R. Cady, C. Keywood, Clinical efficacy of frovatriptan: placebo-controlled studies, Headache: J. Head Face Pain 42 (2002) 84–92.

[2] Elrington Giles, Migraine: diagnosis and management, J. Neurol. Neurosurg. Psychiat. (2002) [http://jnnp.bmj.com/10.1136/jnnp.72.suppl_2.ii15].

[3] P. Martelletti, T.J. Schwedt, M. Lanteri-Minet, et al. My Migraine Voice survey: a global study of disease burden among individuals with migraine for whom preventive treatments have failed, J. Headache Pain 19 (2018) 115 https://doi.org/10.1186/s10194-018-0946-z.

[4] R. Burch, Epidemiology and treatment of menstrual migraine and migraine during pregnancy and lactation: a narrative review, Headache: J. Head Face Pain 60 (2020) 200–216 doi:10.1111/head.13665.

[5] Joint Formulary Committee, British National Formulary. BNF 67 (2014). London: British Medical Association and the Royal Pharmaceutical Society of Great Britain 2014.

[6] R.D. Howland, M.J. Mycek, R.A. Harvey, P.C. Champe, Lippincott's Illustrated Reviews: Pharmacology, Lippincott Williams & Wilkins, Philadelphia, (2006) (159-171).

[7] C.R. Craig, R.E. Stitzel (Eds.), Modern Pharmacology with Clinical Applications. Lippincott Williams & Wilkins, 2004.

[8] M.A.M. Bomhof, J. Heywood, A.A. Pradalier, H. Enahoro, P. Winter, H. Hassani, Naratriptan Long-term Study Group, Tolerability and efficacy of naratriptan tablets with long-term treatment (6 months), Cephalalgia 18 (1) (1998) 33–37.

[9] T.M. Amaral, A.P.C. Costa, Improving decision-making and management of hospital resources: an application of the PROMETHEE II method in an Emergency Department. Operat. Res. Health Care 3 (1) (March 2014) 1–6.

[10] S. Salaja, E.B. Rajsingh, Performance analysis on algorithms for selection of desired healthcare services, Perspect, Sci. 8 (September 2016) 107–109.

[11] D.U. Ozsahin, B. Uzun, M.S. Musa, A. Helwan, C.N. Wilson, F.V. Nurcin, N. Şentürk, I. Ozsahin, Evaluating cancer treatment alternatives using fuzzy PROMETHEE method. Int. J. Adv. Comp. Sci. Appl. 8 (10) (2017).

[12] H. Weistroffer, C. Smith, S. Narula, Multiple criteria decision support software, in: Multiple Criteria Decision Analysis: State of the Art Surveys, Int. Ser. Oper. Res. Man. 78 (VIII) (2005), 989–1009.

[13] W. Yang, J. Wang, X. Wang, An outranking method for multi-criteria decision making with duplex linguistic information, Fuzzy Sets Sys. 198 (2012) 20–33.

[14] L. Zadeh, Fuzzy logic = computing with words, IEEE Trans. Fuzzy Syst. 4 (2) (1996) 103–111.

[15] S. Zionts, MCDM-if not a roman numeral, then what?, Interf. 9 (4) (1979) 94–101.

[16] I. Ozsahin, D. Uzun Ozsahin, B. Uzun, Evaluation of solid-state detectors in medical imaging with fuzzy PROMETHEE, J. Instrumen. 14 (2019).

[17] M. Maisaini, B. Uzun, I. Ozsahin, D. Uzun, Evaluating Lung Cancer Treatment Techniques Using Fuzzy PROMETHEE Approach, in: R. Aliev, J. Kacprzyk, W. Pedrycz, M. Jamshidi, F. Sadikoglu (Eds.), 13th International Conference on Theory and Application of Fuzzy Systems and Soft Computing, ICAFS-2018. ICAFS 2018. Advances in Intelligent Systems and Computing, 896, Springer, Cham, 2019. doi: 10.1007/978-3-030-04164-9_29.

[18] D.U. Ozsahin, I. Ozsahin, A fuzzy PROMETHEE approach for breast cancer treatment techniques, International Journal of Medical Research & Health Sciences, Int. J. Med. Res. Health Sci. 7 (5) (2018) 29–32.

[19] D.U. Ozsahin, B. Uzun, S.M. Musa, I. Ozsahin, Evaluating X-ray-based medical imaging devices with fuzzy preference ranking organization method for enrichment evaluations. Int. J. Adv. Com. Sci. Appl. 9 (3) (2018), 7–10.

[20] D.U. Ozsahin, N.A. Isa, B. Uzun, I. Ozsahin, Effective analysis of image reconstruction algorithms in nuclear medicine using fuzzy PROMETHEE. 2018, Advances in Science and Engineering Technology International Converences (ASET), IEEE Xplore (2018). doi: 10.1109/ICASET.2018.8376892.

[21] D.U. Ozsahin, B. Uzun, M.S. Musa, N. Şentürk, F.V. Nurçin, I. Ozsahin, Evaluating nuclear medicine imaging devices using fuzzy PROMETHEE method. Proc. Comp. Sci. 120 (2017), 699–705.

[22] D.U. Ozsahin, K. Nyakuwanikwa, T. Wallace, I. Ozsahin, Evaluation and simulation of colon cancer treatment techniques with fuzzy PROMETHEE. IEEE Xplorer (2019). doi:10.1109/ICASET.2019.8714509.

[23] M.S. Musa, D.U. Ozsahin, I. Ozsahin, A comparison for liver cancer treatment alternatives, 2019 Advances in Science and Engineering Technology International Conferences (ASET), IEEE Xplorer (2019).

[24] I. Ozsahin, D.U. Ozsahin, K. Nyakuwanikwa, T.W. Simbanegavi, Fuzzy PROMETHEE for ranking pancreatic cancer treatment techniques. IEEE Xplorer (2019). doi: 10.1109/ICASET.2019.8714554.

[25] M.T. Mubarak, I. Ozsahin, D.U. Ozsahin, Evaluation of sterilization methods for medical devices, 2019 Advances in Science and Engineering Technology International Conferences (ASET), IEEE Xplorer (2019).

Chapter 19

Top cancer treatment destinations: a comparative analysis using fuzzy PROMETHEE

Nuhu Abdulhaq Isa[a], Dilber Uzun Ozsahin[a,b,c] and Ilker Ozsahin[a,b,d]

[a]Department of Biomedical Engineering, Near East University, Turkish Republic of Northern Cyprus, Nicosia, Turkey; [b]DESAM Institute, Near East University, Turkish Republic of Northern Cyprus, Nicosia, Turkey; [c]Medical Diagnostic Imaging Department, College of Health Sciences, University of Sharjah, Sharjah, United Arab Emirates; [d]Brain Health Imaging Institute, Department of Radiology, Weill Cornell Medicine, New York, NY, United States

19.1 Introduction

Cancer is still among the top 10 causes of death in 2018; therefore, it is important to keep the discussion moving in order to increase survival rate. In the US, cancer accounts for one in every four deaths, making it the second leading cause of death. Despite the US being one of the major high-income countries with the highest gross domestic product (GDP) in the world, cancer still remains a huge crisis in regards to prevalence and cost. Studies have indicated that the average cost required for the treatment of cancer with a newer medication in the United States could possibly be above $100,000 annually per patient [1–4]. However, other major high-income countries with high GDP compared to the US have lower costs of cancer drugs. For instance, the average cost of cancer treatment with prominent branded cancer drugs in the United States, United Kingdom, and Australia are $8700, $2600, and $2700, respectively [5]. This shows a huge difference in price bearing in mind that the above-listed Western countries are top global economies with similar GDP. Furthermore, imagine comparing the above countries with more cancer treatment vital criteria, we can see which countries stand out as the preferred destinations for cancer treatment when all criteria are considered.

In several countries, global and local organizations are making great efforts and progress in combating the challenges of cancer [6]. They are achieving this through development of comprehensive control programs that are intended to lower cancer incidence and mortality rate through extensive research on evidence-based strategies for cancer prevention, early cancer screening and

Applications of Multi-Criteria Decision-Making Theories in Healthcare and Biomedical Engineering.
http://dx.doi.org/10.1016/B978-0-12-824086-1.00019-0

diagnosis, and improvements in treatment as well as palliative care, etc. [7]. There are countries that have not only improved cancer treatment for their citizens, they have also welcomed cancer patients from around the world through medical tourism. Some developing countries such as India, Singapore, Turkey, Mexico, and a lot more have seen boosts in medical tourism. These developing countries provide quality cancer treatment at a much lower cost compared to developed Western countries. A country's quality of cancer treatment can be analyzed through the following criteria: number of qualified and specialized medical staff (oncologists, radiographers, nurses, etc.), cancer research centers, cost of treatment, palliative care, survival rate, clinical services, and national cancer control programs. The criteria for medical tourism may further include conditions of accommodation, country safety, shopping opportunities, and general tourism/recreational activities. Both cancer patients from developed and developing countries are visiting medical tourist destinations for lower rate of cancer treatment.

As stated earlier, this study compared six top cancer treatment destinations, including Nigeria, India, the United States, Turkey, Australia, and the United Kingdom. The following criteria were considered for all countries involved under the same conditions: average cost of treatment, 5-year relative survival rate, doctors to patient ratio (DPR) per 100k patients, security, safety and peace, clinical services and research, availability of clinical oncologists, ratio of new cancer incidence to an oncologist, number of cancer centers, and tourism. The methodological approach is by means of fuzzy preference ranking organization method for enrichment evaluations (PROMETHEE), an effective user-friendly multi-criteria decision-making approach. Section 19.1 presents an introduction to the study; section 19.2 provides a review of a comprehensive standard cancer care system by Gospodarowicz et al. [7]; section 19.3 provides information about the materials and methods used in collecting and analyzing data as well as the layout of the study, including general information on fuzzy PROMETHEE; section 19.4 provides a description of selected cancer treatment criteria, their conditions and application of criteria value in a PROMETHEE decision lab; section 19.5 presents the findings and discussions while section 19.6 discusses conclusions drawn from the findings in relation to the standard cancer system by Gospodarowicz et al. [7].

19.2 Standard cancer care

The standard cancer care provides a comprehensive framework for the establishment of a standard cancer care model. It was developed by Gospodarowicz et al. [7] with the aim of enhancing the quality of cancer patients lives at all stages. Standard cancer care system must include the establishment, integration, and implementation of the following components; prevention, screening, diagnosis, treatment, survivorship, palliative, and integrated care. An effective and efficient standard cancer care system must be established, taking into consideration the nation's population, the prevalence and aggressiveness of cancer, and the availability of both financial and human resources, etc. According to [7], standard cancer care system must include a set of specialized and detailed functions required for effectiveness and efficiency. These functions comprise a national cancer control program or population-based cancer plans, a functioning cancer registry in all healthcare facilities, a good healthcare system that includes all level of clinical cancer care, as well as public health functions, etc.

19.2.1   A comprehensive and standard cancer care system

According to [8] and the work of [6], the framework for a cancer care system must include the functions of stewardship, financing (budgeting and allocating resources), service delivery, and resource generation. More important, the leadership or responsible health institution of a given country should establish and implement national cancer plans otherwise known as population-based cancer control plans in order to not only provide screening, diagnosis, and treatment of cancer, but also to create awareness of the prevention of cancer through education and other means of spreading awareness.

Therefore, a well-developed population-based cancer plan should include cancer registration system, general guidelines and standard for practice and operation, compliance and accountability, promoting and implementing research, creating awareness and cancer education, certifying and accrediting service providers, ensuring quality assurance, and evaluating and monitoring system performance [7]. In general, the component of their proposed standard cancer care system is divided into clinical management, clinical services, and core services. However, their proposed framework focused more on clinical services, which includes the cancer center. A center provides all the services required for the prevention, screening, diagnosis, treatment, survivorship, palliative, and integrated care.

19.2.1.1   Clinical management

Clinical management is the first layer in a cancer system that provides patient specific clinical evidence-based assessment and decision making to individuals to determine the likelihood of cancer (screening) or diagnosis of cancer. It is a framework that is intended to assist both the medical practitioner and the patient in making effective decisions [9]. Therefore, this layer based on personalized data provides an individual clinical management plan that is reviewed by a multidisciplinary team that manages the quality of the clinical decision based on evidence bases as well as the resultant outcomes from such decisions. After such assessment, and if an individual is found to have no cancer in his/her body, information such as risk factors will be provided for further prevention measures.

However, if an individual is diagnosed with cancer, the clinical management team will recommend the goals of care, appropriate interventions, and optimal time frames to such individual. These recommendations must be tailored based on the individual's evidence and consensus-based data. These include results from histopathologic/molecular diagnosis (e.g., biopsy) that present the specific type of cancer, the anatomical location and functional activity of the cancer (stage), and the size of cancer. The patient specific clinical recommendations also take into consideration an individual's characteristics such as gender, age, geographical location, risk factors, as well as genetic or family history, etc.

As mentioned earlier, clinical management ensures that cancer patients are provided with defined goals of cancer care, intervention, treatment time frame, as well as prognosis. A defined cancer care goal for a patient involves the cure for cancer and its control. Appropriate psychological intervention is usually needed to reduce stress and anxiety during the course of treating cancer, with the general aim of improving their quality of life as well as alleviating the symptoms and treating side effects. If the guidelines are not adhered to effectively, poor clinical decision may occur in the form of misdiagnosis (false-positive and negative), which could either show absence of cancer, while in actuality there is cancer in the individual's body, and vice versa; hence they either are given cancer treatment inappropriate for their cancer situation (false-positive), or they are receiving insufficient treatments/care that are poorly timed out and less effective due to false-positive misdiagnosis. This has contributed to increased morbidity, disability, premature death, and more costly health services.

Clinical management in a comprehensive cancer care system should include research centers or units where continuous research is observed to develop or improve guidelines for a wide range of cancer scenario. This can be done in collaboration with other professional, well-equipped, and well-funded organizations to achieve the goals of cancer treatment for reduced/controlled symptoms and side effects, increased survival rate, and general quality of life. These guidelines should be made compulsory after verification, in every healthcare institution (locally and nationally) that provides cancer care in the country, hence the role of stewardship. It is important to also note that these guidelines should include indications for the processes in medical imaging, biopsy, and other diagnostic approaches, as well as indications for the roles of nurses and other health professionals.

Prior to administration of cancer treatment to a patient, there are several structural and systematic review of the evidence base data of that patient as well as decided and alternative treatment plan as required by jurisdiction. According to [10], the treatment of cancer for most patients requires multimodality therefore, effective guidelines and standards must be put in place to avoid any kind of interference and complications, and for effective decision making. In fact, a comprehensive and modern clinical management system must integrate the services of multidisciplinary care teams as indicated by [11], multidisciplinary clinics, and multidisciplinary cancer conferences. From evidence-based results, experiences, and the collective professional knowledge of these teams of medical specialists, general guidelines for appropriate diagnostic test, treatment alternatives, and customized plans for individual patients are drawn [11,12].

As the condition of cancer continues to grow and become complex, the development of computer-aided diagnosis CAD has been supporting and assisting medical radiologists to automate processes that may consume a lot of time. Results from CAD systems show promising high sensitivity, specificity, accuracy, precision, and minimal errors. Other fields of artificial intelligence have been growing significantly in decision making where support tools are established independently or incorporated to medical devices/machines with the purpose to guide complex clinical management decisions regarding the treatment of cancer patients.

Of course, a comprehensive clinical management requires vast and readily available resources, which requires funding or financing. According to [13], all clinical guidelines at all levels would require optimal resources to be successfully carried out, however, when such required resources are not available optimally, the guidelines can be adapted to the available resources in such scenarios. Therefore, cost effectiveness is an important aspect to take care of when developing a clinical management guideline. This is in line with the opinion of Chalkidou et al. [14] who said that organizers of guidelines should consider cost effectiveness while recommending or requesting funding. according to Strother et al. [15], a country needs collective efforts, experience, and expertise of clinicians to customize standard guideline to the local context taking in to consideration readily available resources.

19.2.1.2 Clinical services

After clinical management, the second layer of the cancer care system is clinical services. After decisions are made based on evidence-based data, clinical services are there to implement or put these decisions into action, within a time frame and deliver high-quality treatment as much as possible. In other words, they are the service providers. As discussed in clinical management, most cancer patients require multimodality treatment plan such as a combination of services including laboratories and pathology, diagnostic imaging, surgery, systemic treatment/ chemotherapy, and/or radiation, as well as pain management and supportive care.

All health-care institutions that provide clinical services much have a well-equipped set of facilities, devices/machines, materials and human resources (both professional and nonprofessional), and guidelines (policies and procedures) required to guide a uniform process for the administration of diagnostic, treatment, and supportive care. The services provided to one step serve as perquisites for another step; the function of clinical services is to integrate these services for optimal performance—if not the desired goals will not be achieved. For instance, the functions of screening, diagnosis, and treatment of cancer are related to each other and are sequentially prerequisites, which means that the required goal of reducing mortality will not be realized when the quality of screening services do not meet the quality of diagnosis and treatment; moreover, the quality of diagnostic services should meet the quality of treatment services in order to achieve the desired goal of increasing survivorship.

According to the Canadian Partnership Against Cancer [16], clinical services are so important in as much as they are considered the continuum of cancer control despite the lack of use of the services in a unidirectional manner [6]. Clinical services should be easily accessible to patients on time and in full range, this can help in early screening, diagnosis and a high chance of cancer survival and general quality of life. On the other hand, when clinical services cannot be easily accessed, this will lead to cancer growing from one stage to another until it becomes too complicated or risky to the patient or even result in premature death.

Furthermore, quality is required for all clinical process at all levels. In a situation where clinicians observe incorrect or incomplete diagnosis (pathology and radiology results), this could result in either false-positive or false-negative results, which result in complex emotional distress and unnecessary services, in the case of a false-positive result. However, when a patient's incorrect or incomplete diagnosis results in a false-negative, the situation is even worst. This means there is a presence of cancer that was not identified by the clinicians for optimal decision and treatment, and general cancer care. Hence, victims of poor clinical practices may be properly identified only after the cancer has metastasized and has probably become unresponsive to treatment options, leading to unnecessary illness, disability, premature death, and costs to patients, their families, the healthcare system, and society. Therefore, it is important for all clinical services to be on time, accurate, effective, and efficient. Clinical services also require special or general accreditation for the purpose of addressing the clinical services (such as safety for imaging and radiotherapy, external accreditation for laboratory services, and cell therapy), and service-specific credentialing bodies. Fig. 19.1 shows necessary departments needed for a comprehensive clinical service provision.

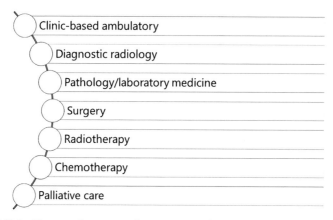

FIGURE 19.1   Necessary departments for a comprehensive clinical service for cancer patients.

19.2.1.2.1 Clinic-based ambulatory care

Clinic-based ambulatory care is offered by official clinical settings and are usually the first place that patients receive basic screening services (e.g., clinical interviews, physical examinations, Pap smears, blood samples, or endoscopies) before further services by specialized medical professionals. Based on the activities, guidelines, and jurisdiction, the clinic-based ambulatory care offices should be equipped with necessary devices such as special examining tables for gynecologic malignancies, chairs, and special endoscopic equipment for assessing head and neck cancers, etc.

19.2.1.2.2 Diagnostic radiology

Diagnostic radiology, also known as biomedical imaging, is the use of medical devices/machines to image a patient's whole or part of the body to determine the presence or absence of tumors. In the event of cancer occurrence, biomedical imaging procedure is not only capable of detecting the cancer, but it can also detect its location and the anatomical (size/location) and functional (stage and spread) data of the cancer. Imaging of the body is not used only for diagnosis; it is also used for treatment procedures, for example, real-time imaging during radiotherapy to target only cancer cells and save neighboring healthy cells. In fact, the general function of cancer imaging also includes, assessment of therapy risks, side effects, complications, check-ups for monitoring the recurrence of cancer, and screening of the general population for cancerous conditions, etc. Biomedical imaging is very important, especially for diagnosis.

The procedure of biopsy usually needs the guidelines of ultrasound imaging to collect epithelial cells from the surface of tumors. If not, there could be increased complication that may lead to misdiagnosis, as is the case with cancer where improper biopsy procedures result in higher levels of PSA (prostate specific antigen) in the blood, which is an indication of high possibility of prostate cancer. The use of ultrasound, computed tomography (CT), and magnetic resonance imaging (MRI) for the purpose of embolization and tumor ablation is another important example. Some of the most popular imaging devices or machines include conventional X-rays, CT, MRI, single photon computed tomography (SPECT), Positron emission tomography (PET), and ultrasound, etc. Several of these imaging innovations exist as multi modalities in order to maximize acquisition of patient data.

There are several specialists involved starting form biomedical/clinical engineers who are needed for procurement of effective imaging devices and managing them, radiologists, to biomedical technicians that services the medical devices to make sure they are at their best working condition at all times. A radiologist and radiologist technologists have dependent function in the radiology unit. The radiologist technologist is responsible for operating the imaging devices, image acquisition, and application of appropriate reconstruction algorithm as well as assisting cancer patients during the whole scan procedure to minimize anxiety, unnecessary models for accurate diagnosis. On the other hand, a radiologist is responsible for interpreting and making sense of the acquired images and translating the results into useful diagnostic information. All of these professions need guidelines within which they can operate individually or collectively to contribute to the general desired quality of cancer care.

Furthermore, safety is an essential consideration in all health institutions, especially in the radiology unit where ionization radiation is the principle governing most medical imaging approaches. There are readily available safety standards, guidelines, and procedures for the effective establishment of radiology units, installation of medical imaging devices, and guidance for how they should be operated, from organizations such as the International Atomic Energy Agency, the International Society of Radiology, and the World Health Organization (WHO). One of the major achievements was the establishment of picture archiving and communication systems (PACS) and other web-based systems to help report and analyze medical imaging data in remote areas.

19.2.1.2.3   Pathology and laboratory medicine

The services of pathology and laboratory medicine are vital for patient-specific analysis to generate evidence-based data needed for treatment plan. Biochemists and other pathologists acquire biological specimens or samples from individual patients for analysis to either confirm the presence and state of cancers using biological indicators (biomarkers) or to engineer biological agents to fight cancer, etc. Other functional services provided by laboratory medicine include pathology, hematology, biochemistry, microbiology, and cytogenetic and molecular testing. There are several specialists involved in the operation of pathology and laboratory medicine. Several specialized and sophisticated medical machines, devices, and instruments are essential for successful operation. These must also be managed by biomedical/clinical bioengineers as well as services by biomedical technicians within prescribed time frames. All of these processes must also be guided by common standards, guidelines, and procedures, and must be accredited, as well.

According to Gralow et al. [17], a basic pathology lab should be able to provide services for specimen fixation, embedding into paraffin, tissue slicing, and staining; modern facilities must include immunohistochemistry, flow cytometry, as well as molecular and cytogenetic testing. The inclusion of web-based systems (telepathology, a branch of telemedicine) is useful for reporting and analyzing data from remote areas of the world where there are fewer resources. This can be achieved through partnership with more comprehensive institutions, usually located in different cities or even in different countries such as the network partnership between Ghana and Norway in the Breast Health Global Initiative.

It is also important to note that various automation processes using the principles of artificial intelligence (e.g., CAD) are helpful for augmentation throughput and rapid reporting among networks.

19.2.1.2.4 Surgery

Surgery is one of the safest and most effective methods of treatment when cancer is detected at a very early stage. It completely removes the tumor from the patient body. It is also used together with other therapy techniques for better results. It is also used to prevent the occurrence of cancer in precancerous body tissues of the patient, such as mastectomy. Other functions include the diagnosis of cancer by biopsy, size and spread of cancer determination, reconstruction or restoration of function or appearance, survival and management of complications, etc. [17,18]. Aside from being safe, another great advantage of surgery is that it is cost effective, as studies show that removal of precancerous body tissues is effective for treatable cancers, including cancer of the breast, cervix, and colon [19].

A surgical theater needs several specialized and sophisticated medical devices and machines for successful surgical procedures. Surgical services include those needed from the moment of decision for surgery, to the time of discharge of the patient from the hospital, with quality as an integrating theme. Therefore, the surgical units must be well equipped with anesthesia devices/services, postanesthetic recovery units, critical care or high dependency units, and frequently inpatient units for long-term recovery. Cancer surgery procedures depend on some factors, such as the type and stage of cancer; therefore, there should be general surgeons as well as specialty surgeons. In the surgical theater, the collective effort, knowledge, experience, and expertise of surgeons, nurses, anesthesiologists, biomedical/clinical engineers, as well as other support staff is required for a successful operation. For example, a biomedical/clinical engineer is needed in case of a flaw in a medical device during the process. All processes in the surgical unit must align with common standards, guidelines, and procedures, such as the Surgical Safety Checklist.

19.2.1.2.5 Radiotherapy

Radiotherapy administers ionizing radiation to cancer cells to disturb the nuclei and eventually kill them. According to Gralow et al. [17] and the International Atomic Energy Agency [20,21], radiotherapy is used for the treatment of cancer and in palliative care. External beam radiotherapy and brachytherapy (use of linear accelerators) are the two main approaches to radiotherapy. The importance of radiotherapy cannot be underestimated; apart from being cost effective, it can be used to treat thousands of cancer patients over a long period of time [22].

Radiation therapists are usually responsible for the operation of radiotherapy machines on cancer patients; however, support from other medical workers may be required. A complete radiotherapy service is provided by a multispecialty team of radiotherapists and radiation oncologists, etc. In establishing a radiotherapy unit, several standards, procedures, and guidelines must be adhered to for the safety of both clinician and patients [23]. This will also lead to the realization of the desired result. Such standards, procedures, and guidelines regarding the use of radiation and radioactive sources on patients may be established and regulated by national or international regulatory bodies. Some of the requirements for radiotherapy units include facilities such as patient rooms, planning, treatment wards for the radiotherapy machines that are insulated with lead or other shielding materials, consoles for clinician safety, and should be aided by a nearby physics laboratory as well as quality-assurance standards.

19.2.1.2.6 Chemotherapy

Systematic therapy is the use of drugs to kill cancer. This can be accomplished through intravenous and oral methods. The basic intention of systematic therapy is to reduce recurrence, improve survival, and help preserve organs. Chemotherapy is the most popular systematic therapy; however, other systematic therapy methods include hormone therapy, vaccine or immunotherapy, and molecular targeted therapy. Although systematic therapy on its own is effective in shrinking or killing cancer cells especially in early stage, in most cases, it is used in combination with other treatment methods like surgery and radiotherapy for the optimal goal of destroying cancer cells [17,24,25]. For example, after surgery to remove cancer, hormone therapy may be used to shrink and eventually kill smaller tumors that could not be removed during surgery. Most hospitals and clinical centers have special ambulatory sections reserved for the administration of systematic therapy; however, the systematic therapy services can be performed in inpatient units since there is no radiation involved. In the case of specially designed ambulatory sections, it should be able to provide intravenous therapy, transfusions, and minor procedures, such as bone-marrow biopsies, thoracentesis, paracentesis, and lumbar puncture, for cancerous and noncancerous conditions.

Systematic therapy units are run by medical oncologists in collaboration with specialized pharmacists, pharmacy technicians, and nurses. Of course, the use of drugs is helpful in the fight against cancer; however, complications associated with several risks may occur, therefore, systematic therapy must be coordinated by a set of guidelines, standards, and procedures that are accredited by national and international governing bodies. There are several challenges to the establishment and operation of systematic therapy units, such as lack of specialized oncologists, and support services, etc.; however, cost is a driving force that a lot of cancer patients are not able to afford.

19.2.1.2.7 Palliative care

Palliative care services are provided to cancer patients in order to generally improve their quality of life by managing the symptoms and side effects of cancer and other life-threatening diseases that may have developed during the process of treatment. Palliative care services are intended not only for the patient, but also to ease the emotional pain of the family and friends of the patients. According to a comprehensive view of palliative care by WHO [26], it is the provision of services that are aimed at preventing, relieving, and managing suffering, to provide early identification and assessment of symptoms, and to address other physical, psychosocial, and spiritual issues. Most important, it should be provided in a timely manner and be done through the utilization of either pharmacologic and nonpharmacologic interventions.

The services provided by the palliative care team range from simple to very sophisticated services, depending on the condition of the patient, which depends on several factors, such as age, stage of cancer, and complications, etc. These services can be provided in a cancer center, general hospital, community clinic, hospice, or at home [27]. According to Zimmermann et al. [28], palliative care services are provided by medical physicians, nurses, and support from other staff in the health sector. Just like any other clinical care services, palliative care must be coordinated by a set of accredited guidelines, standards, and procedures.

Another important point is ethical issues in regards to nurses who take care of these patients. Pain management is an important part of palliative care. There are several approaches for relieving pain, such as the use of reasonably priced opioids and other pain relievers that are helpful to cancer patients. However, it is disappointing to find that most cancer patients in developing countries do not have access to cheap opioids. In fact, reports show that 10% of the poorest cancer patients suffer from the pain of cancer without the use of opioids [6].

19.2.1.3   Core services

In a cancer center, core services include services of administration/management, human resources, information technology and management, physical facilities, pharmacy, infection prevention and control, quality assurance, finance and additional key supports, which operate individually and collectively to see to the success of clinical cancer services. All aspects of cancer core services must be coordinated by rules, standards, guidelines, and procedures, and must be accredited by national or international bodies. When cancer core services are well taken care of, the clinical services will be able to perform effectively, and vice versa [29]. ineffective operation of core services will result in services being poor in quality, there will be inefficient use of available resources, as well as a general impact on the health of the patients.

19.2.1.3.1   Administration and management

Administrative management may be required in each aspect of cancer care, which should be controlled by an apex administration. Administrative management is required because of the complexity of cancer care and the services it requires. This means cancer care services have to be delivered and maintained according to guidelines and standards. The administrative management should be run by a skilled and accountable team. When there is better management in the cancer system, there is clarity in the road to achieving the goals and objectives of the system as well as better clinical outcomes and general quality of health for the patients [30]. There are readily available frameworks for effective administration and management of cancer care system such as the framework presented by WHO (health manager), which contains information on how improvements can be made regarding the management and delivery of healthcare services.

19.2.1.3.2 Human resources

Human resources for a cancer care system include all workers directly or indirectly involved in the provision of cancer care to patients, from the receptionists to appropriately trained and licensed oncologists. The human resources needed for the successful operation of a cancer system consist of a multidisciplinary team of workers who work individually and collectively in their roles to achieve the common goals and objectives of the system. Hence, they are very essential. The leadership of the cancer care system should make it a priority to train, license, recruit, and retain clinicians, administrative and other workers related to cancer care. Workers should also be provided opportunities to continue to develop and improve their knowledge and experience as well as become aware of trending approaches to cancer care and how they can be implemented.

The leaders should recruit the workforce by estimating the number of workers required for each of the centers in the country, identifying the roles and responsibilities of these workers, including the positions required for the cancer care system, improving job satisfaction for workers by establishing effective and efficient compensation and benefit levels, analyzing individual as well as collective performance of the workforce, establishing stewardship teams for management and supervision of workers, and provision of conflict resolution services to the workers. Telemedicine services can also be incorporated as core human resources services to gain easy access to information and assistance from the international clinical workforce.

19.2.1.3.3 Information technology and management

The significance of information technology cannot be underestimated. It is necessary for effective implementation of telemedical services; the management of high volumes of information; informed, safe, efficient, and effective care; and the improvement of access for patients. The concept of information technology implies the establishment of technological systems and their applications. A good example of an information technology system and their applications include computer hardware and software as well as telecommunication that gathers, stores, utilizes, and shares useful information. This means that the operation of information technology is electronic based.

On the other hand, information management enables the organization, linking, analysis, and presentation of information for the purpose of encouraging guided decisions. This means the operation of information management is not only electronic based, it can be printed out or can be stored in a combination of electronic and paper folders. Therefore, the cancer systems require the establishment and implementation of information technology and management in health records, operational systems, such as human resources, pharmacy, supplies, and equipment; financing; and other systems. As mentioned earlier, telemedicine is very crucial for linking a nation's cancer care system to the international community of clinical professionals; it requires the services of information technology, which is also required for cancer-care call centers or helpline (cell phones required for mHealth (mobile health)).

19.2.1.3.4 Physical facilities

The physical facilities house all the services administered by the clinicians and other workers to the patients. Hence it is very essential for effective performance of clinical services in cancer care centers. It includes the buildings that contain the internal areas such as reception or inpatient and outpatient rooms, ambulatory clinic space, etc. it also includes equipment such as furniture; power supply; backup systems; and waste disposal, electrical, mechanical, ventilation, and plumbing systems. According to Debas et al. [31], Hensher et al. [9], and Gralow et al. [17], healthcare services or cancer care systems that possess extensive physical facilities tend to maximize their healthcare resources in a situation where they are centralized in a few facilities. Most important, these facilities need to be operated by workers in a way that is at a sufficient capacity in order to ensure efficiencies of scale [32].

19.2.1.3.5 Pharmacy services

Pharmacy services are very essential in the administration of drugs at all levels of cancer care, ranging from simple painkillers to complex chemotherapy drugs, etc. The pharmacy unit of a cancer center should ensure safety in the administration of effective medicine to patients. According to the [33], some of the functions of pharmacy include managing practice; policies on medication use; optimizing medication therapy; procuring drug products and managing inventory; preparing, packaging, and labeling medications; delivering medications; monitoring medication use; evaluating the effectiveness of the medication-use system; and conducting research. Pharmacists must be appropriately trained about medication useful for cancer care (including complications, side effects, as well as drug toxicities) and they must be licensed by the appropriate national regulatory groups.

19.2.1.3.6 Infection control

Because of the complexity of cancer care, nosocomial infection may occur in the process of treatment. The most susceptible are patients admitted for a long stay in the hospital due to treatment course and effective monitoring of clinical outcomes. Therefore, the services of infection control in cancer centers is very important. The function of infection control must focus on measures for the prevention and control of nosocomial infections and other infections that can be incurred in the process of treatment or diagnosis within the cancer center. Some of the main measures needed for infection control include hand hygiene, disinfecting and sterilizing surfaces and equipment, investigating and monitoring suspected infections, managing outbreaks, providing personal protective equipment, taking appropriate precautions, and vaccinating and educating healthcare providers. To achieve these measures, the infection control unit may use various means of communication to the patients, healthcare workers, and other workers within the center to communicate the implications of infections and personal prevention approaches. According to Raka [34], infection control can introduce prevention bundles, improving compliance with hand hygiene, making prudent use of antimicrobials, translating research results into practice, and upgrading the capabilities of microbiology.

19.2.1.3.7 Quality assurance

Quality should be a theme associated with not only all aspects of cancer centers but the cancer care system as a whole due to the complexity of cancer care and the resulting risks and complication that may occur. No matter how small or big a workers' role is in the cancer system, quality as a theme should be associated with their duties. Therefore, the cancer system is required to have personalized as well as general indicators that are helpful in monitoring and assessing the quality and effectiveness of individual and collective duties. Similarly, there should be indicators for monitoring and assessing the quality, safety, and effective performance of structures, processes, and outcomes [35]. The effective use of information technological systems will be helpful in measurement as well as assessment of baseline performance of each indicator and changes over time can be tracked. Therefore, it is the collective duty of leaders and stewards in the cancer care system to provide regular quality checks, monitoring, and assessment of performance in order to identify key areas that need improvement.

19.2.1.3.8 Finance

Of course, services and resources needed for cancer care systems require funding and financing. Without proper funding, then realization of an effective and efficient cancer care system is just a dream. Competent financial systems should be established to not only monitor revenue and expenses, but to also attract investment and international financial support through practicing revenue generation. The sources of funds should mainly come from a national level however, financial sources can also come from a subnational level (states, local government, communities), insurance companies, nongovernmental organizations, cross-border contracts among countries, as well as international bodies, etc. The availability of financial resources directed to the cancer care system determines the level of services to be rendered and the overall performance of the system. The higher the financial support, the more the services and performance of the system and vice versa.

19.2.1.3.9 Additional key supports

The major requirements of a cancer care system have already been listed; however, the following additional support will be helpful in the operations of a cancer care system: equipment and technology support services, supplies and materials management, supply-chain processes, patient transport, fire safety and radiation protection, occupational health and safety, and security. In some areas where there is high population, robbery, or insecurities, additional support is also needed, such as the employment of security personnel to protect both patients and workers in cancer care centers.

19.3 Materials and methods

The concept of fuzzy logic and PROMETHEE has been employed by very few researchers. It has been shown to effectively compare alternative methods using vital criteria to determine their performances. These criteria can be qualitative or quantitative values that are converted into fuzzy scale and weighted for each criterion to define a linguistic data. The result will provide ranking of the alternatives from the most favorable to the least favorable. Some of the earliest studies that used this methodology include [36–38], and [39]. Recent studies that incorporated the idea of fuzzy logic and PROMETHEE include the studies of [40–52].

All of these studies made effective comparative analysis of the alternatives in various fields depending on the criteria and importance weight of the criteria. There may be difficulties when we try to gather crisp data in a real-life situation in order to achieve optimal decision making. Therefore, when fuzzy logic is used, the decision maker is given the opportunity to define the problem using crisp data based on vague conditions.

19.3.1 Data and technique

The quantitative research methods involve the utilization of the excellent decision making and user friendliness of fuzzy PROMETHEE to compare analyze cancer care in Nigeria to top cancer treatment destinations in developing countries and around the world, including India, United States, Turkey, Australia, and the United Kingdom. Vital criteria such as average cost of treatment, 5-year relative survival rate, doctors-to-patient ratio (DPR), security, safety and peace, clinical services and research, availability of clinical oncologists, ratio of new cancer incidence to an oncologist, number of cancer centers, quality of health systems, population, welcoming countries rank, and tourism opportunities.

TABLE 19.1 Linguistic scale of importance.

Linguistic scale for evaluation	Triangular fuzzy scale	Importance ratings of criteria
Very high (VH)	(0.75, 1, 1)	Survival rate, Annual average cost, 5-year relative survival rate, clinical services and research, availability of clinical oncologists
Important (H)	(0.50, 0.75, 1)	DTP ration/100,000 patients, number of cancer centers
Medium (M)	(0.25, 0.50, 0.75)	Ratio of new cancer incidence to an oncologist
Low (L)	(0, 0.25, 0.50)	Security, safety, and peace
Very low (VL)	(0, 0, 0.25)	Tourism

Afterwards, linguistic fuzzy scale of preference (triangular fuzzy linguistic scale) was analyzed to choose which criteria were more important than others and obtain the importance weight of each criteria value. The triangular fuzzy linguistic scale as shown in Table 19.1. The Yager index was used to defuzzify each criteria value. Lastly, the defuzzified values were applied to PROMETHEE GAIA decision lab software with Gaussian preference function for analysis. In summary, the internet was used as a major source of secondary data, including gray literature, Google books, Google Scholar, journals articles specializing in cancer issues, as well as PROMETHEE applications, publications, reports, standards, procedures, and policies of national and international organizations, such as WHO and NCCP, etc.—all these sources were well referenced in the thesis.

The basic steps of the PROMETHEE method include six steps ([53]; Brans et al. 1986 [90,91])

Step 1. For each criteria j, determine a specific preference function $p_j(d)$.

Step 2. Define the weights of each criteria.

$$w_T = (w_1, w_2, \ldots, w_k) \tag{19.1}$$

The weights of each criteria are decided by the user (decision maker), which is observed according to the preference of the user. For example, if the criteria have equal importance, then the weights of each criteria will be equal and vice versa. Normalization can also be used for the weights:

$$\sum_{i=1}^{k} w_k = 1 \tag{19.2}$$

Step 3. For all the alternatives a_t, $a_{t'} \in A$, define the outranking relation:

$$\pi\pi(a_t, a_{t'}) = \sum_{k=1}^{K} w_k \cdot \left[p_k \left(f_k(a_t) - f_k(a_{t'}) \right) \right], \quad AXA \to [0,1] \qquad (19.3)$$

In this part, the preference index is indicated as π (a,b). The preference index is a measure of magnitude of a user's preference in regards to an alternative a_t, with respect to another alternative $a_{t'}$ while considering all criteria simultaneously.

Step 4. The following formulas is used to obtain the leaving (positive) and entering (negative) outranking flows as follows:

- Leaving (or positive) flow for the alternative a_t :

$$\Phi^+(a_t) = \frac{1}{n-1} \sum_{\substack{t'=1 \\ t' \neq t}}^{n} \pi(a_t, a_{t'}) \qquad (19.4)$$

- Entering (or negative) flow for the alternative a_t :

$$\Phi^-(a_t) = \frac{1}{n-1} \sum_{\substack{t'=1 \\ t' \neq t}}^{n} \pi(a_{t'}, a_t) \qquad (19.5)$$

From the above formulas, n represents the number of alternatives. The comparative analysis for each alternative among the alternatives is -1. Furthermore, A_t is preferred to $a_{t'}$ ($a_t P a_{t'}$) if $\Phi^{net}(a_t) > \Phi^{net}(a_{t'})$, which is the positive outranking flow, signifies the strength of alternative $a_t \in A$, while $\Phi^-(a_t)$, the negative outranking flow, signifies the weakness of alternative $a_t \in A$.

The PROMETHEE I has the ability to give a partial preorder of the alternatives via these outranking flows, while the PROMETHEE II method has the ability to provide the complete preorder based on net flow; however, it doesn't give much information about the preference relations.

Step 5. Determine the partial preorder on the alternatives of A according to the following principle:

In PROMETHEE I, alternative a_t is preferred to alternative $a_{t'}$ ($a_t P a_{t'}$) if it satisfies one of the following conditions:

$$a_t P a_{t'}) \text{ if;}$$

$$\begin{cases} \Phi^+(a_t) > \Phi^+(a_{t'}) \text{ and } \Phi^-(a_t) < \Phi^-(a_{t'}) \\ \Phi^+(a_t) > \Phi^+(a_{t'}) \text{ and } \Phi^-(a_t) = \Phi^-(a_{t'}) \\ \Phi^+(a_t) = \Phi^+(a_{t'}) \text{ and } \Phi^-(a_t) < \Phi^-(a_{t,} a_{t'}) \end{cases} \qquad (19.6)$$

When two alternatives a_t and $a_{t'}$ have the same leaving and entering flows, a_t is in different to $a_{t'}$ ($a_t I a_{t'}$):

($a_t I a_{t'}$) if: $\Phi^+\left(a_t\right) = \Phi^+\left(a_{t'}\right)$ and $\Phi^-\left(a_t\right) = \Phi^-\left(a_{t'}\right)$.

a_t is incomparable to $a_{t'}$ ($a_t R a_{t'}$) if;

$$\begin{cases} \Phi^+\left(a_t\right) > \Phi^+\left(a_{t'}\right) \text{ and } \Phi^-\left(a_t\right) > \Phi^-\left(a_{t'}\right) \\ \Phi^+\left(a_t\right) < \Phi^+\left(a_{t'}\right) \text{ and } \Phi^-\left(a_t\right) < \Phi^-\left(a_{t'}\right) \end{cases} \tag{19.7}$$

Step 6. Determine the net outranking flow for each alternative

$$\Phi^{net}\left(a_t\right) = \Phi^+\left(a_t\right) - \Phi^-\left(a_t\right) \tag{19.8}$$

Via PROMETHEE II, the complete preorder can be obtained by the net flow and defined by:

$$A_t \text{ is preferred to } a_{t'} \ (a_t P a_{t'}) \text{ if } \Phi^{net}\left(a_t\right) > \Phi^{net}\left(a_{t'}\right) \tag{19.9}$$

$$A \text{ is indifferent to } a_{t'} \ (a_t I a_{t'}) \text{ if } \Phi^{net}\left(a_t\right) = \Phi^{net}\left(a_{t'}\right) \tag{19.10}$$

Basically, the better alternative is the one having the higher $\Phi^{net}\left(a_t\right)$ value.

19.4 Selected cancer treatment criteria

The selected cancer treatment criteria include average cost of treatment; 5-year relative survival rate; doctor-to-patient ratio (DPR); security, safety and peace; clinical services and research; availability of clinical oncologists; ratio of new cancer incidence to an oncologist and number of cancer centers. Details of the above-mentioned criteria are briefly discussed below.

19.4.1.1.1 Average cost

Annual average cost for all the selected countries per patient are given as follows: USA $150,000 [54]; India $18,182 [55]; UK average of £40,000, equivalent to $51,240 [56]; Australia $33,400 [57]—similar prices were reported in another journal, at $33,944 [58]; and for Turkey, the estimated cost is greatly uncertain [59]—however, the estimated Turkish government expenditure on cancer care is approximately $2.5 billion, which means an annual average cost of $16,666. Moreover, a study from 2018 shows a fall in cancer cases to 148,000 and an increase in government expenditure to $3 billion. This means the estimated annual average cost is $20,270 [60] for Turkey. Annual average cost for all countries involved should be as low as possible. Lastly, the annual cost of cancer treatment in Nigeria is reported to range from N5 million to N20 million which is equivalent to 13886.4916–55545.9662, depending on the cancer [61]. Therefore, the average cost is calculated to be N6943.24578 for 10 cancer types. However, the estimated annual cost for diagnosis and treatment of cancer in Nigeria was N15222.3720 [62].

19.4.1.1.2   Survival rate

Relative 5-year survival rate is calculated with the United States having 61.2% [63,64]. Australia's 5-year survival rate from 2010 to 2014 was estimated at 69% (68% for males and 69% for females). That was an increase from 49% (1985–89) to 69% (2010–14) [65]. The UK has an estimated average 5-year survival rate of 50.1% for 18 of the most common cancers [66]. India is reported to have a 5-year survival rate of only 30% ([67,68]). In Turkey, there is no specific data about the 5-year survival rate. However, relative 5-year survival rate in the country calculated by the WHO [69] shows that men have 41.6%, while that for women is 67.5%. Therefore, the average 5-year survival rate should be around 54.55%. For Nigeria, the 5-year relative survival rate was 24.4%.

19.4.1.1.3   Doctor-to-patient ratio (DPR)

This implies the number of medical physicians per 1000 or 100,000 population. As was stated, the treatment of cancer involves the collective teamwork of qualified and specialized medical staff (oncologists, radiographers, nurses, etc.). According to a report, in India there are 450,000 follow-up patients annually and 50,000 newly registered patients, with a permanent staff (upper limit) of 150 doctors [70]. For Turkey, the Organization for Economic Co-operation and Development (OECD) in 2014 found that the average number of doctors per 100,000 population was 237 [71]. The USA from 2010 to 2016 saw an increase in ratio from 277 to 295 physicians per 100,000 population [72]. DPR in the UK was 2.8 practicing doctors per 1,000 population, which is below the standard European average of 3.4 and below other major high-GDP countries, such as France, Germany, Spain and Italy [73]. Lastly, Australia had 392 medical practitioners per 100,000 population in 2015, which was an increase from 374 per 100,000 in 2012, 382 per 100,000 in 2013, and 388 per 100,000 in 2014 [74]. For Nigeria, there are 75 doctors to 100,000 patients [75,76].

19.4.1.1.4   Security, safety, and peace

No patient would like to visit a medical tourism destination if it is not safe. According to SafeAround, countries can be ranked according to their safety in the following index from 100, meaning perfectly safe, while 0 means extremely dangerous. The ranking takes into consideration all kinds of threats to humans, including mugging, crime, road-death toll, occurrence of terrorist attacks, wars, etc. The safety index for selected countries is: Australia 86.3, UK 76.5, USA 69.2, India 47.1, Turkey 44.8, and Nigeria 31.9.

19.4.1.1.5   Clinical services and research

Clinical services are the incorporation of general services from facilities, equipment, skilled personnel, and policies and procedures in order to deliver effective diagnosis therapy and supportive care. Cancer patients; access to a full range of clinical services encourages early and effective cancer diagnosis and treatment. A timely and accurate diagnosis is critical, because early detection can make

TABLE 19.2 Selected cancer criteria.

	Nigeria	USA	India	UK	Australia	Turkey
Criteria						
Annual average cost $	15222	150,000	18,182	51,240	33,400	20,270
Relative 5-year survival rate %	24.4%	61.2%	30%	50.1%	69%	54.55%
DTP ration/100k patients	75	295	150	280	392	237
Tourism (millions)	1.889	75.6	14.6	35.8	8.12	37.6
Security, safety, and peace %	31.9	69.2	47.1	76.5	86.3	44.8
Clinical services and research		22.4		17.5	21.5	5.5
Number of oncologists	26	11,700	1,500	476	448	400
Ratio of new cancer case/oncologist	3,923	137	677	689	272	370
Approved cancer centers	9	1,500	27	13	1157	198
Health system	187	37	112	18	32	70
WSC	198	79	20	53	78	25
Roundedpopulation (billion)	0.200	0.327	1.354	0.067	0.025	0.082

the difference between a curable cancer and an untreatable one [7]. Moreover, cancer research is also important because it shows a country's commitment to fighting the cancer either by understanding how it works or finding new drugs and therapy. For this criterion the ratio of citation per published clinical cancer research for the selected countries is given [77] in Table 19.2.

19.4.1.1.6 Availability of clinical oncologists

As was stated earlier, the treatment of cancer is a collective team work of qualified and specialized medical staff (oncologists, radiographers, nurses, etc.). A lack of well-trained clinical oncologists can result in significant cancer health disparities. Data on clinical oncologist workforce for the selected countries is presented in Table 19.2 [78].

19.4.1.1.7 Ratio of new cancer incidence to an oncologist

The ration of new cancer incidence to an oncologist indicates the number of new cancer patients to a s single oncologist. This is an important indicator of the burden of cancer in a country and how the country has mobilized their health-care workers to tackle it. Although cancer care involves a collective effort of a wide range of medical professionals, oncologists are at the forefront of the care process. Therefore, the availability of oncologist per a 10,000 is an important parameter used in this study and is shown in Table 19.2 [78].

19.4.1.1.8   Cancer centers

The number of cancer centers in the following countries is provided, with USA, 49 Comprehensive Cancer Centers, 13 Cancer Centers, and 7 Basic Laboratory Cancer Centers. In total, the country has approximately 1500 cancer centers [79]. Turkey is reported to have 198 cancer centers [80] and India 27 [81]. The number of cancer centers in the UK is 13 [82] and Australia has 1157 cancer centers [83].

19.4.1.1.9   Health systems

Health systems are the systems in which a comprehensive cancer care can be found [84]. That is to say, a good healthcare system may be a worthwhile determinant of the quality cancer care services a country can give. Information about the global ranking of health systems of the selected countries is provided in Table 19.2.

19.4.1.1.10   Population

The population of a country signifies the responsibility of a country in handling patients. A country with a high population may not be the best destination for cancer tourism, since people may struggle for limited medical resources. However, it is not a critical parameter that determines the quality of cancer care of a given geographical location. All information about population for the selected countries is provided in Table 19.2.

19.4.1.1.11   Welcoming countries rank (2018)

Selected countries ranked by how many passports they accept visa-free, with visa on arrival or with electronic travel authorization (eTA). Welcoming country score (WSC) [85].

19.4.1.1.12   Tourism

The criteria for medical tourism may further include condition of accommodation, country safety, shopping opportunities and general tourism/recreational activities. For this criteria, high numbers of visitors signify the popularity of tourism opportunities. The following tourism data, the number of visitors to the selected countries, is presented for 2017.

UK recorded 35.8 million visitors. it was ranked the sixth most visited country in the world due to developed tourism infrastructure accompanied with an interesting history and culture. London receives most of the visitors while the Tower of London is the most visited attraction in the United Kingdom. Other popular places include the Scottish Highlands, Stonehenge, Edinburgh, and York [86].

The USA recorded 75.6 million visitors. The US receives tourists throughout the year in such cities as New York, Los Angeles, and Las Vegas. The most popular attractions include the Grand Canyon, Yellowstone National Park, the Alaskan subarctic wonders, Hawaiian beaches, etc. Other popular places include Manhattan and the Statue of Liberty, the Golden Gate Bridge in San Francisco, and Niagara Falls at the border with Canada [86].

Turkey is always among the top tourist destinations, with 37.6 million visitors. A very beautiful country with very rich historical and multicultural heritage. It also has unique breathtaking attractions and landscape. Istanbul is the most populous and popular city. Night life is epic in the city of Bodrum; Pamukkale's offers visitors perfect relaxation with its thermal spa terraces; Kahramanmaraş is known for its amazing ice creams; and Antalya is famous for beautiful sand beaches, etc. Other popular places include Cappadocia, Ephesus, and Side [86].

India recorded 14.6 million visitors. It has a rich cultural and historical heritage. It has the famous Taj Mahal, which is one of the world's seven wonders. Popular visited places in India include Meherangarh Fort, Khajuraho Temples, Agra Fort, and Amber (Amer) Fort and Palace in Jaipur.

Australia recorded 8.12 million visitors. With coastal cities in Sydney such as Brisbane and Melbourne, Australia is a good place to have a stop. Other popular places include regional Queensland, the Gold Coast, and the Great Barrier Reef (the world's largest reef), Uluru, the Australian outback, the Tasmanian wilderness. The unique Australian wildlife is also another significant point of interest in the country's tourism. [87].

Nigeria, India, Australia, Turkey, United States, and the United Kingdom were considered as alternative cancer treatment destinations. The criteria (criteria) equally applied to these treatment destinations include average cost of treatment; 5-year relative survival rate; doctor-to-patient ratio (DPR) per 100,000; security, safety, and peace; clinical services and research; availability of clinical oncologists; ratio of new cancer incidences to an oncologist; number of cancer centers; quality of health systems; population; welcoming countries rank; and tourism opportunities.

Afterwards, linguistic fuzzy scale of preference (triangular fuzzy linguistic scale) was analyzed to choose which criteria were more important than others and to obtain the importance weight of each criteria value. It is important to note that in the triangular fuzzy linguistic scale shown in Table 19.1 includes the weight each criterion was given in this analysis, based on an expert opinion, arrived at from experience with cancer treatment quality. These weights can also be altered depending on the decision maker. The Yager index was used to defuzzify each criteria value because Yager index considers all the points and is not hugely affected by extreme values or weights. Lastly, the defuzzified values were imputed in the PROMETHEE method with Gaussian preference function for the comparative analysis of five alternative cancer destinations.

The Gaussian preference function was applied to each criterion using visual PROMETHEE decision lab program. Table 19.3 shows the criteria and weights of the criteria, including the values of the criteria used for the analysis. Gaussian preference function has been preferred over the other preference functions due

TABLE 19.3 Visual PROMETHEE application for cancer treatment destination alternatives.

Criteria	AAC	RYS	DPR/P	T	SSP	R	NOF	RON/O	ACC	HS	WSC	RPB
Unit	$	%		million	%							Billion
Preferences												
(min/max)	min	Max	max	max	max	max	max	min	max	min	max	min
Weight	0.5	1.0	0.75	0.25	0.75	0.75	1	0.75	1	1	0.25	0.25
Nigeria	15222	24.4	75	1.889	31.9	N/A	26	3923	9	187	198	0.200
USA	150000	61.0	295	75.600	69.2	22.4	11700	137	1500	37	79	0.327
India	18182	30.0	150	14.600	47.1	N/A	1500	677	27	112	20	1.354
UK	51240	50.1	280	35.800	76.5	17.5	476	689	13	18	53	0.067
Australia	33400	69.0	392	8.120	86.3	21.5	448	272	1157	32	78	0.025
Turkey	20270	54.6	237	37.600	44.8	5.50	400	370	198	70	25	0.082

to the fact that it does not take into account and is not affected by minute and inconsequential deviations in the input values of the criteria [88].

Due to lack of space in Table 19.3, the criteria are represented in abbreviations: annual average cost (AAC); relative 5-year survival (RYS); doctor-to-patient ratio (DPR/P) per 100,000 (DPR); tourism (T); security, safety, and peace (SSP); research (R); number of oncologists (NOF); ratio of new cancer/oncologist (RON/O); approved cancer center (ACC); health system (HS); welcoming country score (WSC); and rounded population billion (RPB) in Table 19.3.

19.5 Findings and discussion

In regards to the criteria being considered for the selected countries as well as the importance scale of importance applied to the criteria, the PROMETHEE method provided the positive, net, and negative outranking flow for each of the selected alternative cancer destination as shown in Table 19.4. The positive outranking flow signify the cumulative performance of a given cancer destination in terms of the conditions provided. The negative outranking flows signify low performance. The net flow is the distance between positive flow and negative flow which provides the full ranking.

From Table 19.4 above, United States has the highest positive outranking flow as well as the lowest negative outranking flow with 0.6272 and 0.2113 respectively. Australia is second with a positive and negative outranking flow of 0.6047and 0.2450 respectively. On the other hand, Turkey comes third with positive and negative outranking flow values of 0.4438 and 0.4025, respectively. The United Kingdom is ranked fourth with positive and negative outranking flow values of 0.3612 and 0.4748, respectively. India is fifth with positive and negative outranking flow values of 0.2997 and 0.5180, respectively. Nigeria comes last with lowest positive outranking flow value of 0.1679 and highest negative outranking flow of 0.6550.

TABLE 19.4 PROMETHEE results showing the completing ranking of the alternative cancer treatment destinations with their positive, net, and negative outranking flows.

Complete ranking	Treatment destinations	Negative outranking flow	Positive outranking flow	Net flow
1	USA	0.2113	0.6272	0.4160
2	Australia	0.2450	0.6047	0.3592
3	Turkey	0.4025	0.4438	0.0414
4	UK	0.4748	0.3612	−0.1116
5	India	0.5180	0.2997	−0.2183
6	Nigeria	0.6550	0.1679	−0.4872

United States was ranked the highest based on several criteria (weighted as very important in the ranking scale) in its positive ranking flow. United States is weak only in terms of her health system, tourism (annual number of visitors), and ease of obtaining visa, that is, WSC. Moreover, Nigeria was ranked the lowest because only few criteria such as ease of obtaining visa, average annual cost, health systems, and in number of approved cancer centers. In general, the criteria for United States, Australia, the United Kingdom, and Turkey are on the positive outranking flow compared to the India and Nigeria. The United Kingdom has her criteria roughly shared between the negative and positive outranking flow. Decision Lab visual PROMETHEE program was used to have the result. This program is user friendly and the decision maker can change the criteria easily and can compare the therapy techniques according to criteria they wish.

19.6 Conclusions

This study was able to provide a comprehensive and effective ranking of cancer care quality after a comparative analysis of Nigeria, Turkey, India, United States, United Kingdom, and Australia. In this study, the standard cancer care system that was established by pervious researchers was reviewed and used as a reference from which the comparative analysis was achieved. These cancer care system criteria include leadership/stewardship, data management and registry operations, health system, cancer center, clinical research, medical workforce, service delivery, quality and safety, resources generation, funding and financing, maintenance, accountability, and awareness/community outreach.

Fuzzy PROMETHEE, a promising a multi-criteria decision-making model which effectively compares alternative criteria was used to compare cancer treatment destinations including the United Kingdom, United States, Australia, India, Nigeria, and Turkey. The study shows that the proposed PROMETHEE method is very effective at giving solutions to decision-making problems in closely related criteria. Our study is in agreement with previous studies of other researchers who have applied fuzzy PROMETHEE in their studies. It simply and clearly showed that fuzzy PROMETHEE provides a ranking of alternative cancer treatment destinations. The result of our comparative analysis is solely dependent on the selected criteria and our weighing of the criteria. This study can be improved with more criteria, and improved weighing.

References

[1] H. Kantarjian, D. Steensma, J.R. Sanjuan, et al. High cancer drug prices in the United States: reasons and proposed solutions, J. Oncol. Pract. 10 (4) (2014) e208–e211.

[2] E. Dolgin, Bringing down the cost of cancer treatment (2018), https://www.nature.com/articles/d41586-018-02483-3.

[3] K.R. Yabroff, T. Gansler, R.C. Wender, K.J. Cullen, O.W. Brawley, Minimizing the burden of cancer in the United States: Goals for a high-performing health care system, CA: A Cancer J. Clin. 69 (2019) 166–183 doi:10.3322/caac.21556.

[4] S. McGrail, Cost of cancer care reaches nearly $150B nationally (2020), https://healthpayer-intelligence.com/news/cost-of-cancer-care-reaches-nearly-150b-nationally.

[5] D.O. Sarnak, D. Squires, S. Bishop, S., Paying for prescription drugs around the world: why is the U.S. an outlier? The Commonwealth Fund, https://www.commonwealthfund.org/publications/issue-briefs/2017/oct/paying-prescription-drugs-around-world-why-us-outlier.

[6] F. Knaul, J. Gralow, R. Atun, A. Bhadelia, Strengthening stewardship and leadership to expand access to cancer care and control, in: Closing the Cancer Divide: An Equity Imperative, Harvard University Press, Boston, MA, 2012, Chapter 10.

[7] M. Gospodarowicz, J. Trypuc, A. D'Cruz, J. Khader, S. Omar, F. Knaul, Cancer services and the comprehensive cancer center, in: H. Gelband, P. Jha, R. Sankaranarayanan, et al. (eds.), Cancer: Disease Control Priorities, 3rd ed., vol. 3, The International Bank for Reconstruction and Development/The World Bank, Washington, DC, 2015, Chapter 11.

[8] WHO, The World Health Report 2000: health systems: improving performance (2000). Geneva, WHO, http://www.who.int/whr/2000/en/whr00_en.pdf?ua=1. Accessed 5.07.19.

[9] M. Hensher, P. Max, A. Sarah, Referral hospitals. In: Disease Control Priorities in Developing Countries (2), 122943. Washington, DC: Oxford University Press and World Bank, 2006.

[10] National Breast and Ovarian Cancer Centre, Multidisciplinary cancer care in Australia: a national audit 2006. National Breast Cancer and Ovarian Centre, Camperdown NSW (2008), http://canceraustralia.gov.au/sites/default/files/publications/mdnawmultidisciplinary-cancer-care-in-aus-full-report_504af02d3b84d.pdf. Accessed 10.07.19.

[11] National Cancer Action Team (National Health Service), The characteristics of an effective multidisciplinary team (MDT) (2010), http://ncat.nhs.uk/sites/default/files/NCATMDTCharacteristics.pdf. Accessed 10.07.19.

[12] Cancer Care Ontario., Multidisciplinary cancer conference tools (2013a), https://www.cancercare.on.ca/toolbox/mcc_tools/. Accessed 10.07.19.

[13] David J. Kerr, Midgley Rachel, Can we treat cancer for a dollar a day? Guidelines for low-income countries, New Engl. J. Med. 363 (9) (2010) 80103.

[14] K. Chalkidou, et al. Evidence-informed frameworks for cost-effective cancer care and prevention in low, middle, and high-income countries, Lancet Oncol. (2014) http://dx.doi.org/10.1016/S1470-2045 (13)70547-3.

[15] R. Strother, et al. AMPATH-oncology: a model for comprehensive cancer care in Sub-Saharan Africa, J. Cancer Policy 1 (3) (2013) e42–48 http://dx.doi.org/10.1016/j.jcpo.2013.06.002.

[16] Canadian Partnership Against Cancer, The cancer journey (2013), http://www.partnership-againstcancer.ca/priorities/cancer-journey/.

[17] J.R. Gralow et al., Core elements for provision of cancer care and control in low- and middle-income countries. In: Closing the Cancer Divide: An Equity Imperative. Global Task Force on Expanded Access to Cancer Care and Control in Developing Countries. Boston, MA: Harvard Global Equity Initiative, 2012.

[18] E.C. Smith, et al. Delay in surgical treatment and survival after breast cancer diagnosis in young women by race/ethnicity, J. Amer. Med. Assoc. Surg. 148 (6) (2013) 516–523.

[19] M.L. Brown et al., Health service interventions for cancer control in developing countries. In: Disease Control Priorities in Developing Countries, 2nd ed., 569–89. Washington, DC: Oxford University Press and World Bank, 2006.

[20] IAEC (International Atomic Energy Agency), A Silent Crisis: Cancer Treatment in Developing Countries. Vienna: IAEC, 2003.

[21] IAEC (International Atomic Energy Agency), AGaRT (The Advisory Group on increasing access to Radiotherapy Technology in low- and middle-income countries) (2010). Brochure. http://cancer.iaea.org/documents/AGaRTBrochure.pdf.

[22] D. Rodin, D. Jaffray, R. Atun, F.M. Knaul, M. Gospodarowicz, The need to expand global access to radiotherapy, Lancet Oncol. 15 (4) (2014) 378–380.

[23] IAEC (International Atomic Energy Agency), Setting up a Radiotherapy Programme: Clinical, Medical Physics, Radiation Protection and Safety Aspects. Vienna: IAEC, 2008.

[24] R.B. Livingston, Combined modality therapy of lung cancer, Clin. Cancer Res. 3 (12 Pt 2) (1997) 2638–2647.

[25] V. Valentini, M.C. Barba, M.A. Gambacorta, The role of multimodality treatment in M0 rectal cancer: evidence and research, Eur. Rev. Med. Pharmacol. Sci. 14 (4) (2010) 334–341.

[26] WHO, Planning cancer control: knowledge into action: WHO guide for effective programmes, module 1. Geneva: WHO (2006), http://www.who.int/cancer/publications/cancer_control_planning/en/index.html. Accessed 5.07.19.

[27] Palliative Care AustraliaA Guide to Palliative Care Service Development: A Population-based Approach, Palliative Care Aus., Canberra, (2005).

[28] C. Zimmermann, S.A. Dori, W. David, R. Gary, Bringing palliative care to a Canadian cancer centre: the palliative care program at Princess Margaret Hospital, Support Care Cancer (14) (2006) 982–987.

[29] C.E. Grimes, G. Kendra, C.M. Bowman, et al. Systematic review of barriers to surgical care in low-income and middle-income countries, World J. Surg. 35 (2011) 941–950.

[30] K. Carter, D. Stephen, L. Dennis, Why hospital management matters, Health Int. (2011) 11.

[31] T.H. Debas, G. Richard, M. Colin, T. Amardeep, T., Surgery, in: Disease Control Priorities in Developing Countries, vol. 2, Oxford University Press and World Bank, Washington, DC, 2006, pp. 1245–59.

[32] A. Mills, R. Fawzia, T. Stephen, Strengthening health systems, in: Disease Control Priorities in Developing Countries, vol. 2, Oxford University Press and World Bank, Washington, DC, pp. 87–102.

[33] American Society of Health-System PharmacistsASHP guidelines: minimum standard for pharmacies in hospitals, Am. J. Health-Sys. Pharm. 70 (2013) 1619–1630.

[34] L. Raka, Prevention and control of hospital-related infections in low- and middle-income countries, Open Infect. Dis. J. 4 (2010) 125–131.

[35] A. Donabedian, Evaluating the quality of medical care, Milbank Mem. Fund Quar. 44 (3) (1966) 166–203.

[36] A. Ozgen, G. Tuzkaya, U.R. Tuzkaya, D. Ozgen, A Multicriteria decision making approach for machine tool selection problem in a fuzzy environment, Int. J. Comp. Intell. Syst. 4 (4) (2000) 431–445.

[37] R.U. Bilsel, G. Buyukozkan, D. Ruan, A fuzzy preference ranking model for a quality evaluation of hospital web sites, Journal of Intelligent SystemsJ. Intell. Syst. 21 (11) (2006) 1181–1197.

[38] W.-C. Chou, W.-T. Lin, C.-Y. Lin, Application of fuzzy theory and PROMETHEE technique to evaluate suitable ecotechnology method: a case study in Shismen reservoir watershed, Taiwan, J. Ecol. Engin. 31 (2007) 269–280.

[39] G. Tuzkaya, B. Gülsün, C. Kahraman, D. Özgen, An integrated fuzzy multi-criteria decision-making methodology for material handling equipment selection problem and an application, Exp. Syst. Appl. 37 (4) (2010) 2853–2863.

[40] D. Uzun Ozsahin, B. Uzun, M. Musa, N. Şentürk, F. Nurçin, I. Ozsahin, Evaluating nuclear medicine imaging devices using fuzzy PROMETHEE method, Proc. Comp. Sci. 120 (2017) 699–705.

[41] D. Uzun Ozsahin, B. Uzun, M. Sani, A. Helwan, C.N. Wilson, F.V. Nurcin, N. Şentürk, I. Ozsahin, I. (2017b). Evaluating cancer treatment techniques using fuzzy PROMETHEE method. Int. J. Adv. Comp. Sci. Appl. 8, 177–85.

[42] D. Uzun Ozsahin, I. Ozsahin, A fuzzy PROMETHEE approach for breast cancer treatment techniques, Int. J. Med. Res. Health Sci. 7 (5) (2018) 29–32.

[43] D. Uzun Ozsahin, N.A. Isa, B. Uzun, I. Ozsahin, Effective analysis of image reconstruction algorithms in nuclear medicine using fuzzy PROMETHEE. 2018 Advances in Science and Engineering Technology International Conferences (ASET), Abu Dhabi, 1–5.

[44] D. Uzun Ozsahin, B. Uzun, M. Sani, I. Ozsahin, Evaluating X-Ray based Medical Imaging Devices with Fuzzy Preference Ranking Organization Method for Enrichment Evaluations, International Journal of Advanced Computer Science and Applications 9 (3.) (2018) http://dx.doi.org/10.14569/IJACSA.2018.090302.

[45] D. Uzun Ozsahin, K. Nyakuwanikwa. T. Wallace, I. Ozsahin, Evaluation and simulation of colon cancer treatment techniques with fuzzy PROMETHEE. IEEE, pp. 1–6.

[46] I. Ozsahin, T. Sharif, D. Uzun Ozsahin, B. Uzun, Evaluation of solid-state detectors in medical imaging with fuzzy PROMETHEE, J. Instrumen. 14 (01) (2019) 1019–11019.

[47] I. Ozsahin, D. Uzun Ozsahin, M. Maisaini, G.S.P. Mok, Fuzzy PROMETHEE analysis of leukemia treatment techniques, World Canc. Res. J. 6 (2019) e1315 2019.

[48] I. Ozsahin, S.T. Abebe, G.S.P. Mok, A multi-criteria decision-making approach for schizophrenia treatment techniques, Arch. Psych. Psychoth. 2 (2020) 52–61.

[49] I. Ozsahin, D. Uzun Ozsahin, K. Nyakuwanikwa, T.W. Simbanegavi, Fuzzy PROMETHEE for ranking pancreatic cancer treatment techniques, Advances in Science and Engineering Technology International Conferences (ASET), Dubai, United Arab Emirates, 2019, pp. 1–5. doi:10.1109/ICASET. 2019.8714554.

[50] M. Taiwo, I. Ozsahin et al. Evaluation of sterilization methods for medical devices. IEEE xplore (2019), pp. 1–4.

[51] M. Sayan et al. Determination of post-exposure prophylaxis regimen in the prevention of potential pediatric HIV-1 infection by the multi-criteria decision making theory. IEEE xplore (2019), pp. 1–5.

[52] N. Sultanoglu, B. Uzun, B. et al. Selection of the most appropriate antiretroviral medication in determined aged groups (≥3 years) of HIV-1 infected children. IEEE xplore (2019), pp. 1–6.

[53] J. Geldermann, T. Spengler, O. Rentz, Fuzzy outranking for environmental assessment. Case study: iron and steel making industry, Fuzzy Sets Syst. 115 (1) (2000) 45–65.

[54] P. Moore, The high cost of cancer treatment (2018), https://www.aarp.org/money/credit-loans-debt/info-2018/the-high-cost-of-cancer-treatment.html.

[55] K. Nair, S. Raj, V. Tiwari, L. Piang, Cost of treatment for cancer: experiences of patients in public hospitals in India, Asian Pac. J. Canc. Prev. 14 (9) (2013) 5049–5054.

[56] NHS, Cancer survival rates "threatened by rising cost" (2019), https://www.nhs.uk/news/cancer/cancer-survival-rates-threatened-by-rising-cost/.

[57] C. Paul, E. Fradgley, D. Roach, H. Baird, Impact of financial costs of cancer on patients—the Australian experience, Cost of Cancer to the Patient 41 (2) (2017) 4–9.

[58] D. Goldsbury, S. Yap, M. Weber, L. Veerman, N. Rankin, E. Banks, et al. Health services costs for cancer care in Australia: estimates from the 45-and-Up Study, PLOS ONE 13 (7) (2018) e0201552 doi:10.1371/journal.pone.0201552.

[59] M. Tatar, I. Sahin, Cancer Expenditures in Turkey, National Cancer Advisory Board of Turkey, Ankara, (2008).

[60] E. Sağlam, Annual cost of cancer treatment in Turkey expected to triple by 2030: cancer, oncology, Turkey, health budget (2018), http://www.hurriyetdailynews.com/annual-cost-of-cancer-treatment-in-turkey-expected-to-triple-by-2030-association-126758.

[61] C. Muanya, Nigeria: high cost of few cancer screening, treatment centres reduces patients' survival chances (2019), https://allafrica.com/stories/201902070071.html.

[62] Nigeria National Cancer Control Plan, The Federal Ministry of Health, Nigeria (2018), https://www.iccp-portal.org/system/files/plans/NCCP_Final%20%5B1%5D.pdf. Accessed 5.07.19.

[63] American Cancer Society, Cancer Facts & Statistics, (2018), https://cancerstatisticscenter.cancer.org/?_ga=2.240618051.1342769329.1543095194-1275756810.1535122790#!/.

[64] R. Max, R. Hannah R. Cancer. OurWorldInData.org (2018), https://ourworldindata.org/cancer.

[65] Australia government, Cancer in Australia statistics (2018), https://canceraustralia.gov.au/affected-cancer/what-cancer/cancer-australia-statistics.

[66] M. Thaxter, UK cancer survival rates still trailing European peers—thoughts from the Centre (2018),. https://blogs.deloitte.co.uk/health/2018/02/uk-cancer-survival-rates-still-trailing-european-peers.html.

[67] S. Varma, Cancer survival rate in India among the lowest in the world. Times of India (2014), https://timesofindia.indiatimes.com/india/Cancer-survival-rate-in-India-among-the-lowest-in-the-world/articleshow/45399391.cms.

[68] G.S. Mudur, Cancer survival rate in India lower: study (2018), https://www.telegraphindia.com/india/cancer-survival-rate-in-india-lower-study/cid/1334362.

[69] World Health Organization, Cancer country profile: Turkey (2014), http://www.who.int/cancer/country-profiles/tur_en.pdf.

[70] S.S. Debarati, Cancer treatment: India vs. abroad. Times of India (2017), https://timesofindia.indiatimes.com/life-style/health-fitness/health-news/cancer-treatment-india-vs-abroad/articleshow/12581132.cms.

[71] Turkiye Odalar ve Borsalar Birligi, Turkey healthcare landscape (2017), https://www.tobb.org.tr/saglik/20171229-tss-genel-bakis-en.pdf.

[72] Wikipedia, Physicians in the United States (2018), https://en.wikipedia.org/wiki/Physicians_in_the_United_States.

[73] L. Donnelly, UK has fewer doctors than almost every EU country (2014), https://www.telegraph.co.uk/news/politics/11271216/UK-has-fewer-doctors-than-almost-every-EU-country.html.

[74] AIHW, Medical practitioners' workforce 2015, How many medical practitioners are there? (2016), https://www.aihw.gov.au/reports/workforce/medical-practitioners-workforce-2015/contents/how-many-medical-practitioners-are-there. Accessed 20.07.19.

[75] The emigration of doctors from Nigeria is not today's problem, it is tomorrow's (2018), https://blogs.lse.ac.uk/africaatlse/2018/10/15/the-emigration-of-doctors-from-nigeria-is-not-todays-problem-it-is-tomorrows/.

[76] Y. Adegoke, Does Nigeria have too many doctors to worry about a 'brain drain'? (2019), https://www.bbc.com/news/world-africa-45473036. Accessed 25.07.19.

[77] R. Neumann, Publication statistics: cancer research—publication analysis 1998–2009, http://www.labtimes.org/labtimes/ranking/2012_01/index.lasso.

[78] A. Mathew, Global survey of clinical oncology workforce, J. Global Oncol. 4 (2018) 1–12.

[79] National Cancer Institute, NCI-designated cancer centers, (2018), https://www.cancer.gov/research/nci-role/cancer-centers.

[80] Daily Sabah, Cancer treatment now free in Turkey's landmark health reform (2018), https://www.dailysabah.com/turkey/2018/07/06/cancer-treatment-now-free-in-turkeys-landmark-health-reform.

[81] India Against Cancer, Most important cancer treatment centers in India: cancer treatment centers (2018), http://cancerindia.org.in/cancer-treatment-centers/.

[82] M. Bradbrook, Cancer Research UK: the key centers for research (2017), https://www.telegraph.co.uk/science/cancer-research-uk/key-research-centres/.

[83] E. Lim, Australian Cancer Resources Directory | CancerIndex E. (2017), http://www.cancer-index.org/clinks61.htm.

[84] Canadian Health Care Information, World Health Organization's ranking of the world's health systems (2018), http://thepatientfactor.com/canadian-health-care-information/world-health-organizations-ranking-of-the-worlds-health-systems/.

[85] Passportindex. (2018). Most Welcoming Countries Rank | The Passport Index 2018. Retrieved from https://www.passportindex.org/byWelcomingRank.php.

[86] K. Cripps, World's 10 most popular tourist destinations (and their future rivals) (2018), https://edition.cnn.com/travel/article/world-most-popular-destinations-2017/index.html. Accessed 1/08/19.

[87] Statista, Number of international visitor arrivals to Australia from 2007 to 2017 (2018), https://www.statista.com/statistics/620187/australia-number-of-international-visitors/.

[88] R. Parreiras, J. Vasconcelos, A multiplicative version of PROMETHEE II applied to multiobjective optimization problems, Eur. J. Oper. Res. 183 (2) (2007) 729–740.

[90] J.P. Brans, P. Vincle, A preference ranking organization method, Manage. Sci. 31 (6) (1985) 647–656.

[91] J.P. Brans, P. Vincle, B. Mareschal, How to select and how to rank projects. the PROMETHEE method, Eur. J. Oper. Res. 24 (1985) 228–238.

Further reading

[1] Association of Community Cancer Center, Cancer centers cancer program guidelines (2012), https://www.accc-cancer.org/docs/Documents/publications/cancer-program-guidelines-2012. Accessed 5.07.19.

[2] L. Fayed, How cancer was first discovered and treated (2019), https://www.verywellhealth.com/the-history-of-cancer-514101. Accessed 20.07.19.

[3] J. Ferlay, H.R. Shin, F. Bray, D. Forman, C. Mathers, D.M. Parkin, Estimates of worldwide burden of cancer in 2008: GLOBOCAN 2008, Int. J. Cancer 127 (2014) 2893–2917.

[4] J. Ferlay, I. Soerjomataram, M. Ervik, R. Dikshit, S. Eser, C. Mathers et al., Globocan 2012: Estimated cancer incidence, mortality and prevalence worldwide in 2012. World Health Organization v1.0. IARC Cancer Base No. 11 (2012), https://publications.iarc.fr/Databases/Iarc-Cancerbases/GLOBOCAN-2012-Estimated-Cancer-Incidence-Mortality-And-Prevalence-Worldwide-In-2012-V1.0-2012. Accessed 8.07.19.

[5] C. Fitzmaurice, C. Allen, R.M. Barber, et al. Global, regional, and national cancer incidence, mortality, years of life lost, years lived with disability, and disability-adjusted life-years for 32 cancer groups, 1990 to 2015: A systematic analysis for the Global Burden of Disease Study, JAMA Oncol. 3 (2017) 524–548.

[6] Globocan, Nigeria cancer facts sheets. The Global Cancer Observatory (2018),. http://gco.iarc.fr/today/data/factsheets/populations/566-nigeria-fact-sheets.pdf. Accessed 7.07.19.

[7] M. Goumas, V. Lygerou, An extension of the PROMETHEE method for decision making in fuzzy environment: ranking of alternative energy exploitation projects, Eur. J. Oper. Res. 123 (2000) 606–613.

[8] L.V. Holm, Danish cancer patients' rehabilitation needs, participation in rehabilitation activities and unmet needs. PhD Thesis, Research Unit of General Practice, Institute of Public Health, Faculty of Health Sciences, University of Southern Denmark, 2013.

[9] Institute of Medicine (IOM)Ensuring quality cancer care, National Academy Press, Washington, DC, (1999).

[10] V. Iwenwanne, With one of the world's highest cancer death rates, what can be done to save more patient lives in Nigeria? (2019), https://www.equaltimes.org/with-one-of-the-world-s-highest#.XT4Zt_ZuLIV. Accessed 7.07.19.

[11] E. Kiral, B. Uzun, Forecasting closing returns of Borsa Istanbul Index with Markov Chain Process of fuzzy states, Pressacademia 4 (1) (2017) 15–24 doi:10.17261/pressacademia.2017.362.

[12] C. Macharis, A. Verbeke, K. De Brucker, The strategic evaluation of new technologies through multicriteria analysis: The Advisors case, Res. Transport. Econ. 8 (2004) 443–462.

[13] Maisaini M., Uzun B., Ozsahin I., Uzun D., Evaluating lung cancer treatment: techniques using fuzzy PROMETHEE approach, in: Advances in Intelligent Systems and Computing, vol. 896, Springer, Cham, Switzerland, 2019, pp. 209–215.

[14] H. Martin, M. Price, S. Adomakoh, Referral hospitals. In: Disease Control Priorities in Developing Countries (2nd ed.), 122943. Washington, DC: Oxford University Press and World Bank, 2006.

[15] B. Matthews, L. Ross, Data collection. In: Research Methods: A Practical Guide for the Social Sciences. London: Pearson Longman, 2010, pp. 180–190).

[16] D.V. Mavalankar, K.V. Ramani, P. Amit, S. Parvathy, Building the infrastructure to reach and care for the poor: trends, obstacles, and strategies to overcome them. Center for Management of Health Services: Indian Institute of Management Ahmedabad.(2005), http://www.iimahd.ernet.in/publications/data/2005-03-01mavalankar.pdf. Accessed 5.07.19.

[17] M.S. Musa, D.U. Ozsahin, I. Ozsahin, I., A comparison for liver cancer treatment alternatives. IEEE (2019) 1–4.

[18] S.R.N. Njaka, A systemic review of incidence of cancer and challenges to its treatment in Nigeria, J. Canc. Sci. Ther. 8 (12) (2016) 286–288 doi:10.4172/1948-5956.1000429.

[19] M. Patlak, E. Balogh, S. Nass, et al. Patient-centered cancer treatment planning: improving the quality of oncology care: workshop summary, Oncologist 16 (12) (2011) 1800–1805.

[20] G.W. Prager, et al. Global cancer control: responding to the growing burden, rising costs and inequalities in access, ESMO Open 3 (2018) e000285 2018 doi:10.1136/ esmoopen-2017-000285.

[21] Safearound, World's safest countries ranked, https://safearound.com/danger-rankings/.

[22] G.M. Saibu, et al. Epidemiology and incidence of common cancer in Nigeria, J. Canc. Biol. Res. 5 (3) (2017) 1105.

[23] B. Stewart, C.P. Wild, World cancer report 2014. Int. Agency Res. Canc. (2016), http://publications.iarc.fr/Non-Series-Publications/World-Cancer-Reports/World-Cancer-Report-2014. Accessed 5.07.19.

[24] S. Stringhini, I. Guessous, The shift from heart disease to cancer as the leading cause of death in high-income countries: a social epidemiology perspective, Ann. Intern. Med. 169 (2018) 877–878 doi:10.7326/M18-2826.

[25] A. Tashakkori, C. Teddlie, Current Developments and Emerging Trends in Integrated Research Methodology, in: A. Tashakkori, C. Teddlie, B.T. Charles (Eds.), Handbook of Mixed Methods in Social and Behavioral Research, Sage, Thousand Oaks, CA, 2003, pp. 31–35.

[26] R.J.S. Thomas, R. Callahan, R. Bartlett, J. Geissler, Delivering affordable cancer care: a value challenge to health systems. Report of the WISH Delivering (2015).

[27] B. Ülengin, F. Ülengin, Ü. Güvenç, A multidimensional approach to urban quality of life: the case of Istanbul, Eur. J. Oper. Res. 130 (2) (2001) 361–374.

[28] B. Uzun, E. Kıral, Application of Markov chains—fuzzy states to gold price, Proc. Comput. Sci. 120 (2017) 365–371 doi:10.1016/j.procs.2017.11.251.

[29] WHO, Cancer country profile: Turkey (2014), http://www.who.int/cancer/country-profiles/tur_en.pdf.

[30] WHO, Latest global cancer data: cancer burden rises to 18.1 million new cases and 9.6 million cancer deaths in 2018 (2018), https://www.who.int/cancer/PRGlobocanFinal.pdf. Accessed 11.07.19.

[31] World population review, 2019 World Population by Country, http://worldpopulationreview. com/. Accessed 12.07.19.

[32] R.R. Yager, Concepts, theory, and techniques: a new methodology for ordinal multi-objective decisions based on fuzzy sets, J. Decis. Sci. Inst. 12 (4) (1981) 589–600.

[33] W. Yang, J.H. Williams, P.F. Hogan, et al. Projected supply of and demand for oncologists and radiation oncologists through 2025: an aging, better-insured population will result in shortage, J. Oncol. Pract. 10 (2014) 39–45.

Index

Printed in the United States
by Baker & Taylor Publisher Services